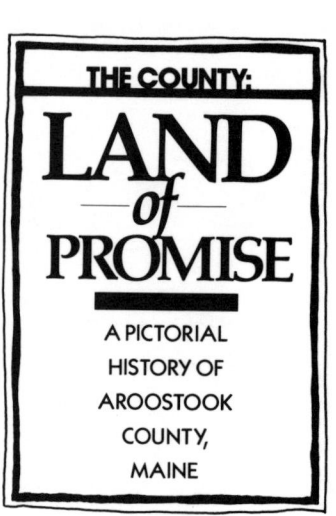

This book is one of a limited edition of 3,000

For the Friends of Aroostook County Historical Center

General Editor
Anna Fields Mcgrath

Contributing Authors
Clifton Boudman
Iris Fields Brewer
Richard Cohen
Shirlee Connors-carlson
Joseph Donald Cyr
Guy F. Dubay
John Graves
Jere W. Green
Richard Hede
Evelyn Kok
David Laing
John Lisnik
Anna Fields Mcgrath
Maureen McGrath Murchison
Andrea Bear Nicholas
Harald Prins
D. A. Savage
Philip Turner
Dena Winslow York

Photographic Reproducers
Diana Higgins
Connie Tucker

Key Bank is pleased to present *The County: Land of Promise, A Pictorial History of Aroostook County, Maine.* Most of us tend to think of Aroostook County as the picture-perfect place. Our unique area of Maine is the picture of beauty, the picture of neighborliness, and the picture of pride.

Key Bank's roots in "The County" began in November 1933. Following the closing of all banks in 1933, a group of businessmen gathered for the purpose of establishing a bank to restore banking services to the area. The First National Bank of Fort Fairfield was formed.

Like Aroostook County, Key Bank has grown and developed over the years. It is our hope that in the years ahead our branch-banking system will continue to provide a connecting link that enriches the quality of life in the communities we serve. With this in mind, Key Bank is proud to sponsor the first pictorial history of Aroostook County.

Join us in saluting the authors of this great book, for they have provided us with many insights and memories of the Aroostook County heritage.

Happy 150th Birthday Aroostook County, and best wishes for another picture-perfect 150 years.

Photograph by Larry Parks

THE COUNTY:
LAND *of* PROMISE

A PICTORIAL HISTORY OF AROOSTOOK COUNTY, MAINE

Anna Fields Mcgrath
General Editor

For the Friends of Aroostook County Historical Center

THE DONNING COMPANY
PUBLISHERS
NORFOLK/VIRGINIA BEACH

Mount Katahdin at sunset, from central Aroostook on the highlands of the Aroostook River, stands like a sentinel at the very edge of the Wildlands that became Aroostook County. For the first adventurers up the Penobscot to the Allagash, Aroostook, Meduxnekeag, and St. John Rivers, and for those adventurers of today who trek into the wilderness, the words of Henry David Thoreau in the 1850s, when he visited the Maine Woods, ring true, "This was primeval, untamed...Nature....This was that Earth of which one has heard, made of Chaos and Old Night...the home, this, of Necessity and Fate" (from The Maine Woods*). Photograph by Clifton Boudman*

Maliseet Indians spear salmon by torchlight at Aroostook Falls, New Brunswick, just across the United States/Canadian border where the Aroostook River enters the St. John River (1836), by Sir Richard R. G. A. Levinge, National Archives of Canada—C-35960

Copyright © 1989 by The Friends of the Aroostook County Historical Center

All rights reserved, including the right to reproduce this work in any form whatsoever without permission in writing from the publisher, except for brief passages in connection with a review. For information write:

    The Donning Company/Publishers
    5659 Virginia Beach Boulevard
    Norfolk, Virginia 23502

Library of Congress Cataloging-in-Publication Data

The County : land of promise : a pictorial history of Aroostook County, Maine / Anna Fields Mcgrath, general editor.
    p.   cm.
    "For the Friends of the Aroostook County Historical Center."
    Bibliography: p.
    ISBN 0-89865-773-3 (lim. ed.)
    1. Aroostook County (Me.)—History—Pictorial works.
2. Aroostook County (Me.)—Description and travel—Views.
I. Mcgrath, Anna Fields, 1932-   . II. Friends of the Aroostook County Historical Center.
F27.A7C68   1989   89-7655
974.1'1—dc20   CIP

Printed in the United States of America

Rainbow, symbol of hope for the future, over the Aroostook River.
Photograph by Clifton Boudman

*Subdued sentinel on the Aroostook plain, the erosion-resistant lava ridge of Quoggy Joe Mountain in Aroostook State Park forms the eastern rim of a great volcanic basin that exploded catastrophically about four hundred million years ago. Echo Lake (foreground) and Arnold Brook Lake (background) occupy a belt of less resistant muddy limestone. The quiet city of Presque Isle lies to the right (east) of Arnold Brook Lake.
Courtesy of Frank Appleby*

CONTENTS

Acknowledgments 6
Introduction 7
Out of Chaos by David Laing 9
Into the Wilderness
   The Spirit in the Land:
   The Native People of Aroostook *by Andrea Bear
   Nicholas, with contributions
   by Harald Prins* 19
   Perceptions: A Cartographic Unfolding
   by Guy F. Dubay 39
   The Acadians: A People Distinct
   by Joseph Donald Cyr 41
   Land of Promise: Introduction
   by Anna Fields Mcgrath with Philip Turner 45
   Heading for the Aroostook
   by Dena Winslow York 49
   A Pocketful of Irish:
   A Settlement in the Woods
   by Shirlee Connors-carlson 59
   Aroostook Becomes a County
   by Jere W. Green 63
"The County" Aroostook County, Maine 74
   Cultivation of the Spirit in the Garden of Maine
   *by Iris Fields Brewer, with contributions
   by Joseph Donald Cyr* 75
   The Garden Blooms 94
   Sunshine and Moonlight: Re-creation
   by Maureen Murchison 95
   Meadows and Other Cultural Centers
   by Clifton Boudman 103
   Springs, Rivers, and Artistic Flows
   *by Anna Fields Mcgrath with contributions by
   Evelyn Kok, Kathy Finnemore, and
   Harald Prins* 109
   North Winds and Humming Strings:
   Music in Aroostook *by Evelyn Kok* 115

Cultivating the Mind: Education in Aroostook
   by Shirlee Connors-carlson 123
Wellsprings and Irrigation Pools:
Libraries, Historical Societies, Museums, and
and Other Educational Support Systems
   by Anna Fields Mcgrath 129
Pathways in the Garden and Other
Communication Routes
   by Shirlee Connors-carlson 139
The Land: In Common and Undivided
   by Guy F. Dubay 145
The Garden of Maine
   by Guy F. Dubay 153
Aroostook: The Military Impact
   by Guy F. Dubay 161
Roots in the Garden:
History of Medicine in Aroostook County
   by Richard Cohen 171
Trellises in the Garden of Maine:
Structure in a Pioneer Land
   *by Anna Fields Mcgrath, with contributions
   by John Lisnik and John Graves* 179
Essences of the Garden:
Neighbors Caring: Fire Fighting
   by D. A. Savage 191
Storms Over Aroostook
   by Anna Fields Mcgrath 194
Det Utlovade Landet:
Maine's Swedish Colony *by Richard Hede* . . . 197
Still the Land of Promise:
The County Looks to the Future
   by Richard Cohen 205
Bibliography 214
About the Authors 216
Index 217
Boxed Texts/introductions by editor/compiler
Anna Fields Mcgrath

*The conical lava summit of Haystack Mountain is a familiar landmark visible from much of Aroostook County. Shallow water mudstone overlying the lava indicates that Haystack was the root of a volcanic island that rose above the broad, tropical ocean that covered the County 440 million years ago. Northern hardwood forest clothes the mountain's lower slopes, giving way to dark, spruce-fir forest near the summit.
Courtesy of Voscar,
the Maine Photographer*

*Mature sugar maples overlook Square Lake.
Photograph by David Laing*

ACKNOWLEDGMENTS

A work of this magnitude could not have been accomplished without the input of numberless individuals providing pictures and information to our team of authors. As compiler and editor, I want to give accolades to the authors for their unselfishness and tolerance as the book evolved. We all want to thank the University of Maine at Presque Isle for use of their facilities in the reproduction of the pictures, and the Friends of the Aroostook County Historical Center at the Library, University of Maine at Presque Isle for their encouragement and support. We also want to thank Laurel Daigle, Fort Kent, for the theme of this work, based on his winning medal design, Land of Promise. To all Aroostook County librarians, historical society members and museum curators, a special thanks from all. The authors would like to acknowledge a special debt to the following: Clifton Boudman, to Marilyn Clark; Iris Brewer, to Carolyn Riggs and Frank Dunn, Betty Blake; Richard Cohen, to Marilyn Dean, Jack Ginty, Wm. Flagg, Sue Butts, Romeo Parent, Gretta Moulton, Dr. William Forbes, and Dr. Stuart Gelder; Shirlee Connors-carlson, to Judy Hager and Roland Burns at the University of Maine at Fort Kent, and James Connors; Guy Dubay, to Robert Sawyer; Jere Green, to Betty Blake, and Voscar; Richard Hede, to the New Sweden and Stockholm Historical Societies; Evelyn Kok, to Jan Kok, Leon Michaud, and Dan Ladner; David Laing, to David Roy; Anna McGrath, to Patricia Tompkins and Timothy McGrath; Maureen Murchison, to Rebecca Hayden-McGrath, Becky Jeanne McGrath, Mark Putnam, and Colleen Ellis, Betty McCoy; Andrea Bear Nicholas, to Dr. Peter Paul, Gary Ennis, the Houlton Band of Maliseets and Aroostook Micmac Council; Dena York, to Levi Knowles, Basil and Larry Fox, and Blanche Beckwith, Vaughn, Christopher, Thomas and Eric Winslow, Carl and Wilma Winslow, Jeff and Willie Winslow, Addie and Alvin Winslow, Bert Winslow, Jackie Moreau, Mr. and Mrs. Alden Bull, Mr. and Mrs. Arden Bull, Mrs. Cluney McPherson, Sr., Maxine Smith, Rod Lamereau, Lena Kenny, Harold Drost, Martha Anderson, Gladys Craig, Mary Hews, Lucy and Frank Allen, Diana Allen, Pauline and Claude Hughes, Mrs. Joe Gagnon, Lois Stimpson, Lester McKee, Bill Clark, Cathy Winslow, and Acil and Essie York.

Hello! Surprised at her winter browsing, a white-tailed deer poses warily among trunks of maple and spruce in a young Aroostook forest.
Courtesy of Timothy Finnemore

Graceful in its Madawaska Lakeshore setting, an open-grown paper birch displays the branching, white-barked stem characteristic of this pioneer species.
Courtesy of Constance Tucker

An eye-catching summer resident of Aroostook County, the fish-eating great blue heron is often seen around wetland habitats.
Courtesy of Timothy Finnemore

INTRODUCTION
by John L. Martin
Speaker of the Maine House of Representatives

It has been well over fifty years since the last writing of a comprehensive history of the land we call home—Aroostook County. Much has happened since then, not only here in the County, but in events around the world that have helped shape and have affected the quality of our lives here in this northern corner of Maine.

Wars have been fought, dynasties have risen and fallen, space has been explored, and generations have been born and have died. Yet, life goes on and certain qualities in our people endure the passage of time and events. We are rooted in French and Irish and Scottish and Yankee and American Indian stock and are in some measure a product of our heritage.

However, there is a special quality that binds all of our diverse backgrounds together and makes us one people. It is a certain breed of independence that arises out of decades of self-reliance; out of the knowledge that the only ones we could count on in times of adversity were ourselves. But for our dependence on one another, there was no one else to whom to turn. We take a degree of pride from living in a land of harsh winters where a person must work hard in order to achieve economic survival and from the fact that many of our families have succeeded for generations in this endeavor.

The sons and daughters of Aroostook have historically been lured to the south by the jobs that modern technology has created in southern Maine and the rest of New England, but they all continue to call the County home, no matter how many years they have lived away.

It is fitting that our story be retold in modern language and that a pictorial record be established to chronicle the rich past upon which we work to build a more promising future. It should be our goal for coming generations, not only to preserve a proud heritage, but to build an Aroostook County where our young people do not have to look south to find opportunity.

Glacial deposits of Aroostook County reveal clues to the waxing and waning of a great ice sheet. Light blue and gray areas indicate a blanket of stony clay laid down by the advancing glacier. Olive green and brown are gravel ridges left at the margins of the glacier during its final retreat. Red streaks in the south are eskers, gravel ridges formed by streams that flowed beneath the melting ice. Orange and pink patches are gravel deposited by meltwater on the glacier margin. Yellow is post-glacial stream deposits, and blue is swamp muck that formed in glacially scarred basins. The pronounced northwest-southwest grain indicates the direction of glacier flow, especially in southern Aroostook.

Seeing a moose is not as elusive a goal as many visitors to the County assume. Maine's largest mammal is quite trusting of human beings, often allowing close approaches to photographers and hunters. Photograph by David Laing

All around this beautiful globe we call Earth, or Gaia, peoples tell creation stories. They all seem to tell the same story, that from Chaos came the sun, the stars, and planets of the universe, Earth, Order, and Beauty.

There are wondrous places on Earth, aglow with creatures and plants unlike the other wondrous places. And Aroostook is a place like no other, where the rivers run north, with mountains and hills occasionally punctuating the vast forests and rolling fertile hills. Where the skies are gorgeous winter or summer, and the total ambiance is a glowing garden.

*St. John River below Grand Falls.
Courtesy of ACHC*

OUT OF CHAOS
by David Laing

The familiar face of the land we know as Aroostook has not always been as it appears today. The County has worn many masks over the unimaginable span of geologic time. Among them are the muddy bottom of an ocean deep, a tropical island paradise replete with coral reefs, an inferno of explosive volcanism, a deltaic plain with backswamps and bayous, a rugged mountain highland, and a featureless expanse of glacial ice. Even the present pastoral landscape of rolling country with mixed evergreen/hardwood forests and agricultural fields will, in time, give way to other masks yet unconceived. In this chapter, I will sweep you back through eons of geologic time and then wind you forward again at a more leisurely pace through a bizarre, rocky newsreel to reveal the strange and distant roots of Aroostook. This will be no prosaic ramble, for beneath Aroostook County's subdued and mutred landscape lies New England's most complete and most readily interpreted record of the complex events that led to the birth and maturity of one of the world's great mountain systems, the Appalachians.

The end of our whirlwind journey through time will bring us back to the more familiar forests and fields of today, where we will have a brief look at the distinctive blend of living things that forms the fabric of the ecology in Aroostook County.

The series of regional maps will serve as guideposts as we trace the evolution of the County and its environs through geologic time. These maps show the changing relative positions of the continents that border the present-day Atlantic Ocean. Until the middle 1960s, the concept of *continental drift* was regarded with profound suspicion by most reputable geologists. In that decade, however, it was proven that the deep ocean floors are constantly spreading away from great cracks, or *rift zones*, such as the one that divides the Atlantic Ocean precisely and symmetrically down its center (see world map on page 11). That key discovery has not only made continental drift a respectable concept, but has given rise to the more sophisticated theory of *plate tectonics* (literally, "plate structures"). The essential features of this theory are shown and explained in the diagram on page 13. In our modern world, we have identified seven major *tectonic plates*, and a number of minor ones makes up Earth's rigid, outer shell (see world map).

Aroostook County has contributed significantly to the immense body of data from which geologists have painstakingly reconstructed the intricate history that lies behind the regional maps shown here. Since Maine State geologist Charles T. Jackson's first reconnaissance in 1837, many prominent geologists have visited the County to study the well-preserved fossils in Aroostook's rocks, and to study the composition of the rocks themselves and the bizarre forms into which they have been twisted and broken by mountain-building forces. The reason for this ongoing geological pilgrimage to northern Maine is that the rocks here have been much less affected by the crushing pressures and searing heat of mountain building than the rocks in central and southern New England, and therefore they are much easier to interpret.

The latest state-of-the-art compilation of geological studies in Aroostook County was published in 1986 by the Maine State Geologic Survey in the form of the Bedrock Geologic Map of Maine. The northern portion of the state geologic map is reproduced in this section. The distribution of the various bedrock units, or *formations*, beneath the soil is shown in different colors, and each has its own symbol, an abbreviation that combines the geologic age of the formation with its name.

Each of the County's bedrock formations was created under a fairly uniform set of geological conditions: one may represent the sand laid down on an ancient beach; another the mud deposited on a deep ocean floor; a third the lava flows of an ancient volcano; and so on. All the formations in the County have been affected by at least one mountain-building event, which has variously folded and broken them, thereby destroying their originally horizontal attitude. Long-continued erosion by rivers and glaciers has stripped many thousands of feet of rock from the surface, thereby truncating all the formations, and removing some of them altogether. The end result of all these happenings is the map pattern we see today.

For those readers who wish to follow the geologic story in greater detail, I have included an annotated list of the most significant of Aroostook's rock formations and of the principal mountain-building events that have affected them. The list is keyed to the geologic map by means of the formation symbols.

And now, with our navigational tools in order, we can embark without further delay on our fantastic, 600 million year long journey.

Our study could begin 4,600 million years ago with the birth of our planet. The oldest known rocks in Aroostook County, however, are only slightly older than 500 million years, so I will begin shortly before then, a mere 600 million years ago (MYA) in the Ediacaran Period, named for a locality in Australia, where fossils of the oldest known many-celled organisms have been found in marine sandstones.

The map of the Ediacarian Period (beginning 700 MYA) shows a topsy-turvy world with a somewhat abbreviated North America cocked on its side and resting squarely astraddle the equator. Toward the southwest lies a "supercontinent," comprising South America, Africa, a portion of western Europe (including southern England and southern Ireland), and the southeastern United States. Arabia, still attached to Africa at the time, lay close to the south pole (SP). An archipelago of several large islands was located northeast of the "African" coast, and among them was a shallowly submerged shelf that would, in time, become the site of Aroostook County. On that shelf, sand and mud of the Grand Pitch Formation (rock unit Cgp) was deposited.

A few hundred kilometers to the northeast of the islands, a double line indicates a spreading rift in the dark lava rock of the ocean floor. The arrow on Africa shows that sea floor spreading along the rift was moving the supercontinent toward the southwest. North America stayed put, which means that the spreading rift itself must also have been moving southwestward. The curved arrow indicates that North America was rotating in a counterclockwise sense.

If you were to reverse the sea floor spreading shown in the Ediacarian map, you would find that the reversed motion would bring the supercontinent up against the shoreline of North America. It appears, in other words, that until Ediacarian time, North America was itself a part of the supercontinent!

The Middle Epoch of the Ordovician Period (about 470 MYA) found northwest Africa located over the south pole. In the map for that time, an arrow pointing northeast indicates that something happened to reverse the supercontinent's direction of drift. A likely possibility is that sea floor spreading had begun on its far side. To accommodate this radical change, a *subduction zone* (barbed line) formed in the sea floor between the supercontinent and North America. Within this zone of convergence, the edge of the North American plate was thrust, somewhat obliquely, beneath the edge of the plate that carried the supercontinent (the left side of the plate tectonics diagram on page 13 shows what is happening here).

At the same time, smaller, local subduction zones formed among the various islands in the archipelago, tending to gather them into a single, larger landmass called *Bronsonia*. This coalescence of the islands about 500 million years ago resulted in what has been called the *Penobscot disturbance*, an event that crumpled the Grand Pitch and a number of other rock formations within a belt that now extends from northern Maine to southern Connecticut. Haystack Mountain, a prominent, conical peak between Ashland and Mapleton, is composed of light colored felsite lava (rock unit Ow) that was erupted above one of these smaller subduction zones, or perhaps above the larger one (see the left side of the plate tectonics diagram). Erosion of the volcanic islands produced units Osb, Om, Odms, Odmp, and SOcm. (See page 6)

This same Mid-Ordovician map shows another new development. Between the Bronsonia archipelago and the supercontinent to the south, a new spreading rift has formed. Although we have no direct evidence for this rift, similar rifts are known to occur today within the overriding plate of a subduction zone, and its presence would help to explain the otherwise mystifying breakneck surge of Bronsonia toward North America.

The catastrophic result of that surge is shown in the Late Ordovician map (450 MYA). Spreading on the new rift swept both the subduction zone and the Bronsonia island complex up against the "east" coast of North America. This so-called *Taconian* mountain-building event was the first of three such collisions that built the Appalachian Mountains. Traces of the suture between the North American mainland and Bronsonia can be found from central Alabama through southeastern New York, central Vermont, eastern Quebec,

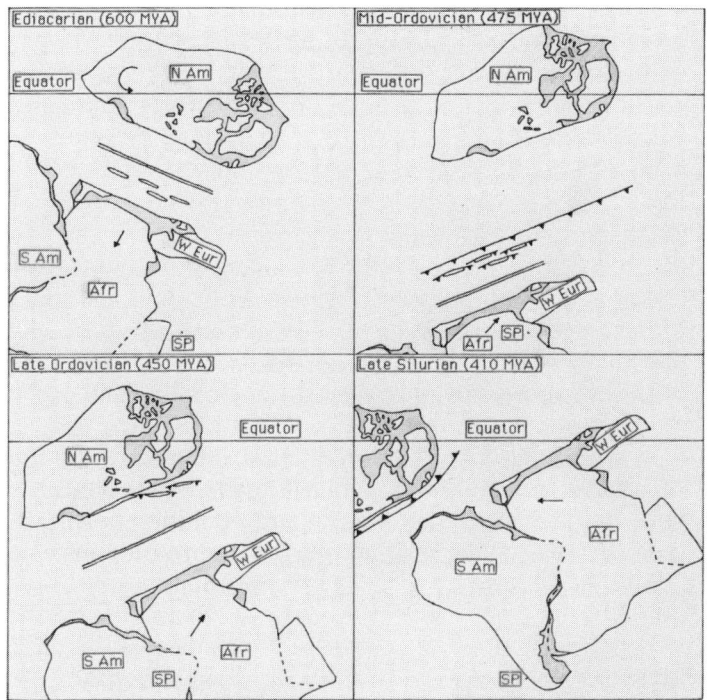
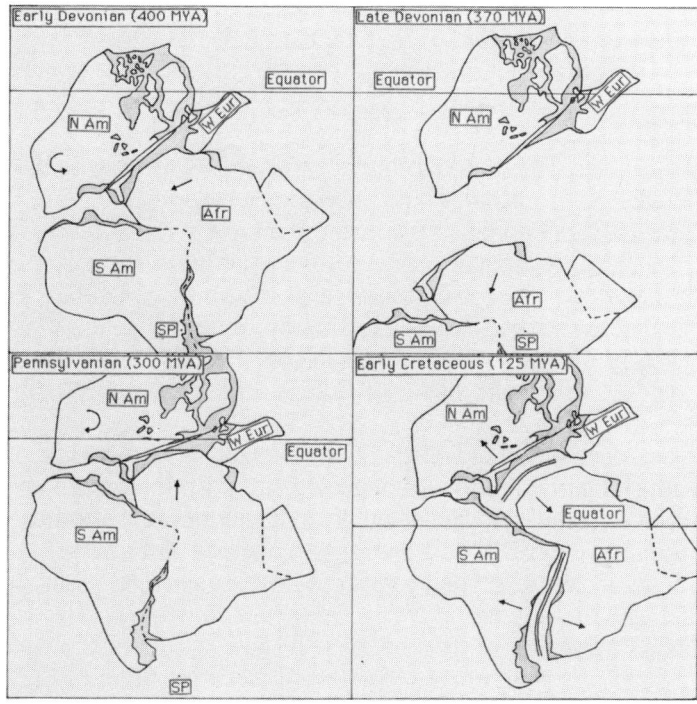

The wandering of continents through time has been the chief architect of Aroostook County's geological underpinnings. The label in the upper left corner of each map gives the time portrayed by the map in millions of years ago (MYA) and the name of the corresponding geologic period. The south pole (SP) is near bottom center of each map. Notice that over time, parts are shuffled and traded among continents (e.g., western Europe and the Florida peninsula). Shaded areas indicate those portions of the continents that are shallowly submerged beneath the sea at the present time. Double lines represent rifts where the sea floor is spreading apart. Barbed lines represent deep sea trenches in which the sea floor on the unbarbed side is sliding underneath the sea floor on the opposite side. Notice that North America remains on the equator until the Early Cretaceous Period, simply rotating slightly while the other continents wander extensively throughout the southern hemisphere, colliding with North America on two separate occasions. (Paleogeographic reconstructions based, in part, on data of R. van der Voo, C. Scotese, and R. Neuman.)

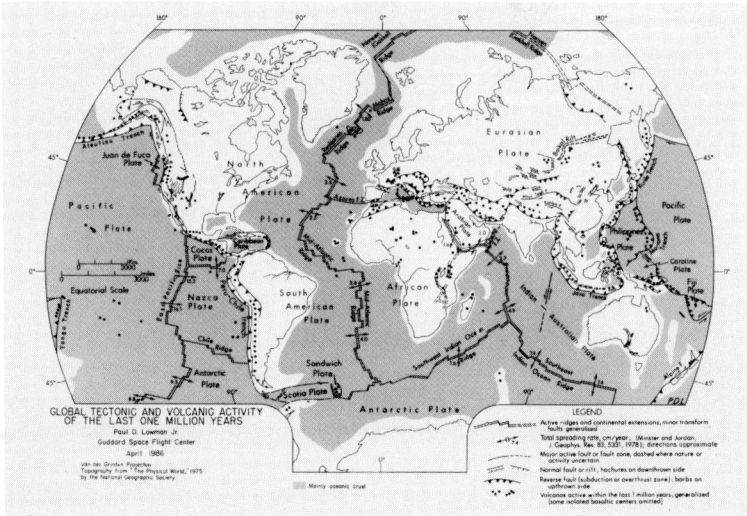

A plate tectonic map of the world reveals that the familiar continents are simply portions of larger plates bordered by spreading rifts (double lines), subduction zones (barbed lines), and transverse fracture zones (solid lines offsetting the rifts). Because continents (unshaded) are lightweight and highstanding, they can not be subducted, hence they have been around for a long time, and are composed of relatively old rocks (up to 4,000 million years). The non-continental portions of the plates are composed of dense, subductable basalt (shaded), hence the sea floors are relatively young (less than 200 million years). The Atlantic Ocean began to open when the Mid-Atlantic Ridge split North and South America away from Eurasia and Africa about 200 MYA, and spreading still continues at rates of 1.8-4.0 centimeters each year (see arrows). The cross section shown in the plate tectonics diagram extends from South American northwestward across the Nazca and Pacific Plates through Japan.
Courtesy of Paul D. Lowman, Jr., Goddard Space Flight Center

and western Newfoundland to northern Scotland (which was part of North America at the time).

The Silurian Period (beginning 438 MYA) was a relatively uneventful time, during which the Taconian highlands were deeply eroded while the supercontinent drifted slowly northeastward. The accumulated products of this erosion are abundant in Aroostook County in the form of units Sf, Sns, Sspr, Sj, and Ssm. The Late Silurian map shows that by 410 million years ago, western Europe had drifted as far northeast as the equator. At that time, however, its drift direction suddenly changed again as a new subduction zone formed off the "east" coast of North America, initiating what has been called the *Salinic disturbance*. The supercontinent set itself on a relentless collision course with that coast as the plate on which it rode thrust westward beneath the North American plate. In the Presque Isle area, lava rising from above the subduction zone burst forth in a series of explosive eruptions that left a giant hole, or *caldera*, in the ground nearly ten miles across. The rims of that caldera still stand as the resistant, felsite lava ridges of Quoggy Joe and Squa Pan Mountains (unit Dhd). Following the great explosions, a large volcanic island (unit Deh) erupted and grew on the caldera's north rim. Erosion of that volcano produced units Dch and Dsb. Other events related to the Salinic disturbance produced units DSfh, DSfrl, DSus, and most notably, the great mud blanket of the Seboomook Formation (Ds) that still covers vast areas of northwestern and central Aroostook County.

By about 400 million years ago, early in the Devonian Period, the ocean basin between the two converging continents closed as the final, cataclysmic collision took place, crumpling the once-horizontal sedimentary rocks on the opposing coasts. Some mudstones, downfolded to great depths, actually melted and formed great bodies of granite that rose toward the surface through the surrounding bedrock (unit Dl). As a result of this continental collision, a massive mountain range arose in New Brunswick and southern Maine. Rapid erosion of these mountains blanketed the surrounding lowlands with thick deposits of gravel and sand, now preserved only in a small patch (unit Dm) northwest of Presque Isle. This is the youngest rock unit in Aroostook County, all more recent formations, except for glacial deposits, having been removed by long-continued erosion.

After locking horns with North America for about 35 million years, the supercontinent then slid away to the southwest, initiating the second phase of Acadian mountain building in which the rocks of New England were given a powerful clockwise twist. As the map of the Late Devonian (370 MYA) shows, there was one significant piece of evidence left behind in this hit-and-run getaway: western Europe and the northwest margin of Africa were left plastered against North America. All of the spectacular scenery on the coast of Maine, in other words, was actually bestowed on us by Africa!

It was not long, however, before Africa staged a dramatic reunion with its severed coastline. In the Pennsylvanian Period (300 MYA), the restless supercontinent surged northward again and lodged against North America in essentially the same position it had occupied a hundred million years earlier in the Late Devonian. The even larger supercontinent formed by this collision was given the name *Pangaea* (say Pan-*gee*-ah), meaning "all-Earth," by Alfred Wegener, the German meteorologist whose pioneering work in the early 1900s laid the foundations for the theory of continental drift. There is much debate about the extent to which this *Appalachian mountain-building event* affected the rocks of New England, but recent studies suggest that its effect may have been more extensive, and intensive, than it was formerly considered to be. In any case, erosion has removed from New England all traces of any rock formations produced during or after that event. In New Brunswick and Nova Scotia, however, where erosion has been less extensive, sediment derived from this third cycle of Appalachian Mountains is still abundantly preserved in the form of conglomerate, sandstone, and mudstone.

Pangaea remained united for about 75 million years. About 225 million years ago (after the debut of the Triassic Period 245 MYA), a spreading rift formed along the present eastern coastline of North America. Along this rift, first Africa and later Europe separated from North America. In the interval between these two rifting events, a second rift opened between South America and Africa. Thus was born the modern Atlantic Ocean, which continues to widen today at a rate of between one and two inches a year. The map of the Early Cretaceous (125 MYA) shows an early stage of the opening of the Atlantic Ocean basin.

Aroostook on Ice

From the time of Appalachian mountain building until the present, erosion has dominated the geological picture in Aroostook County. Until about a million years ago, flowing water was the only effective erosional agent in the County, but at that time, the climate took a turn for the worse, and flowing ice came to be a significant contributor to the wearing away of the New England landscape.

Ironically, ancient bedrock is far more easily placed in geologic time than are the unconsolidated sediments produced during the recent ice age. There are two reasons for this. First, there was not just one ice age, but at least four of them, separated by complete melting of the glacial ice sheets, and there were several different advances and retreats of the ice within each of the ice ages. The materials by which these separate glaciations must be interpreted are either loose sands and gravels or scratches on bedrock, and consequently the record tended to be scraped clean during the advance of each new ice sheet. Second, there are no radioactive elements suitable for dating within the 50,000-1,000,000 year span during which most of ice age history took place.

In spite of these difficulties, glacial geologists have made much progress in deciphering the more significant events of the *Pleistocene Epoch*—the last 1.6 million years of geologic history. Among their more interesting conclu-

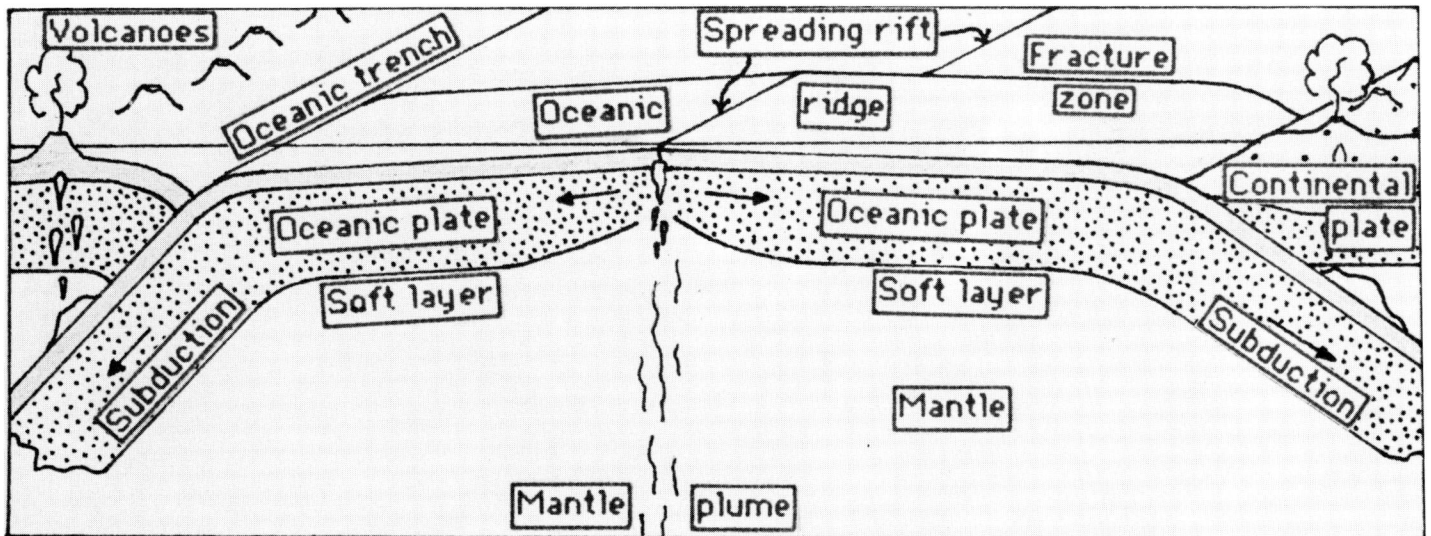

sions, we find that all it takes to initiate an ice age is for more snow to fall in winter than can melt in summer, and that we are probably not yet out of the Great Ice Age, just in a holding pattern before the next onslaught. If so, Canadians and New Englanders might want to ponder the sobering evidence that during glaciations, all of their domains were buried under a blanket of ice as much as two miles thick!

It is clear from scratches in bedrock and other evidence that during the ice ages, ice flowed southward into Maine from a growth center in Labrador. More controversial is the possibility that there may also have been a similar growth center right here in Aroostook County! Within the rubble, or *till*, plastered over Aroostook's bedrock by the last advancing ice sheet are *very* few stones that clearly were derived from Canadian bedrock. These Canadian stones are restricted to a small area of the County north of Caribou. Elsewhere in the state, the till carries only local Maine stones, a fact that Aroostook potato farmers will be only too happy to confirm after hauling them out of their fields for as long as they can remember! This fact suggests that Canadian ice failed to override all but the extreme northern tip of Maine, and that the extensive scouring of the rest of the state must have been accomplished by our very own, home-grown glacier.

A second critical piece of evidence comes in the form of bedrock scratches over a large area in the western part of Aroostook County. Whereas such scratches in the rest of the state point toward the southeast, those in western Aroostook point almost due north. This indicates that the ice that made these scratches must have been flowing northward. Some geologists take these two observations as sufficient proof that Maine did, indeed, have its own glacier, but others argue that the glacier was, indeed, Canadian, and that it simply suffered a reversal of flow direction when the ice warmed and melted down in the St. Lawrence lowland about 12,600 years ago. The question is still unresolved. In any case, it seems clear that between about 12,000 and 11,000 years ago, most of the remaining ice in Maine melted away, allowing the native flora and fauna to

The theory of plate tectonics (literally, "plate structures") explains a multitude of confusing geological phenomena with a relatively simple mechanism. Molten rock rises beneath a spreading rift in the sea floor (center), raising it sufficiently to allow the sea floor plates to slide slowly away from the rift on each side. The plates grow at the rift by the solidification of basalt lava on their spreading edges. Their motion is made possible by a lubricating layer of soft, partially molten rock at a depth of about one hundred kilometers (sixty-two miles). The spreading rift is offset by transverse fractures, one of which is shown here. The far edges of the plates descend into subduction zones beneath oceanic trenches (left and right), causing earthquakes. As the descending plate edges disintegrate, molten rock rises through the overlying plate margins, creating volcanoes. The plate on the right carries lightweight, granitic continental crust, causing it to stand higher than the denser, basaltic sea floor.

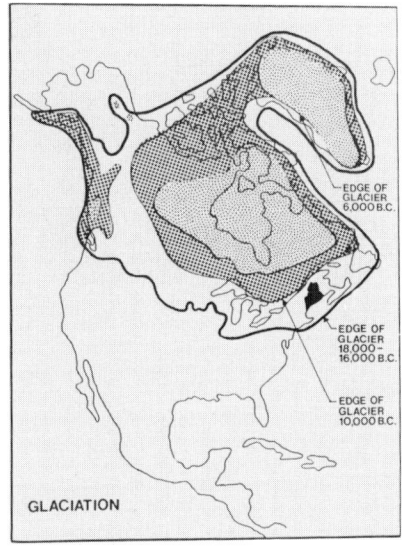

GLACIATION

colonize the land anew.

What did the glaciers do to Aroostook County? Aside from scouring and scratching its bedrock and dumping great quantities of stones on it, the ice affected the land in many other ways. Its passage had greater effect on weaker rocks, such as mudstone and slate, than on more resistant ones, such as felsite lava and conglomerate, and it is to that fact that we owe the prominence of such volcanic hills as Quoggy Joe, Squa Pan, and Haystack, and of Mars Hill (SOmh, taupe) composed of a mixture of lava and conglomerate.

By scouring and filling the preexisting topography, the glaciers also played havoc with the local drainage system, eradicating stream channels, and grinding out lake basins. Wherever lakes abound, glaciers are usually accountable. In the unlikely event that we have, in fact, seen the last of the great ice sheets in Maine, then in time, we would see our familiar lakes fill in with sediment as the stream system gradually reorganized itself.

Another irony concerning glaciers is that most of the features they leave behind are created while the ice is melting away. Most of the County's deposits of sand and gravel originated when glacial meltwater flushed these sediments into holes and channels in the melting ice, especially where the ice had begun to melt away from valley sidewalls. In southern Aroostook, several long, sinuous gravel ridges, called horsebacks, or *eskers,* wind south-southeast through a maze of shallow, swampy basins scoured in limy Silurian sandstone by the glacier's passage. One of these eskers passes just to the west of Houlton.

With the melting of the last great ice sheet, we must conclude our rocky newsreel, but the geologic history of Aroostook County has by no means come to an end. The adventure will continue on far into a future in which humankind will be less than a distant memory. At this time, however, we have the privilege of being able to stop the newsreel for one brief moment, just long enough to take a look at the one special frame in which we live, the Here and Now.

The Life of the County

One of Nature's most remarkable qualities is its ability to regenerate itself. Nowhere is that quality more evident than on the small volcanic island of Krakatao in Indonesia. The island blew up in 1883, obliterating all forms of life. Now, a hundred years later, its reduced remains are covered by a mature and thriving tropical forest brought in piecemeal by wind and wave. Furthermore, the young, patchwork ecosystem functions in perfect harmony, as if its various species had had millions of years to work out their countless interactions instead of a mere hundred.

Here in Aroostook County a similar wonder took place as the land emerged from beneath the Pleistocene ice sheet. As soon as the barren mineral soil was exposed before retreating glacier margin and was thawed by the sun, the seeds of herbs blown in by the wind began to germinate. Among these were grasses, sedges, wormwoods, and pinks.

Following these pioneers, whose decayed remains gradually enriched the immature soil, forests of spruce and aspen developed in the lowlands, while low shrubs such as willow, juniper, and dwarf birch began to appear in the highlands. About 10,000 years ago, alder and birch became common, and a few hundred years later, white pine and balsam fir began to increase. By about 7,000 years ago, hemlock and the hardwoods—beech, maple, and yellow birch—came to form a significant portion of the forest cover, thereby bringing the ecosystem essentially up to date. These various changes in vegetation reflect corresponding changes from a cooler to a warmer climate over time. They are documented by shifts in the relative percentages of the different types of plant pollen preserved in bog sediments.

Looking at Aroostook County's modern natural environment, ecologists have found ten types of forest communities and twenty-two nonforest environments including seven types of open field, six types of swamp, three stream environments, lakes, banks, cliffs, caves, and buildings, both occupied and abandoned. Each of these special habitats has its own special characteristics and its own special mix of inhabitants, which make for a never-failing source of fascination that, according to some, merits far higher ratings than television.

Some of these habitats are more stable and permanent than others, a reflection of the flexibility built into Nature's system. If nothing were ever to happen to disturb that system, a few of these stable ecosystems would come to dominate the landscape. The lowlands would be occupied by a northern hardwood forest comprising mainly sugar maple, American beech, and yellow birch trees with a smattering of other deciduous and coniferous species (see the table of habitats on page 17). In wetter sites, this community would give way to forests of red maple, of northern white cedar, or of both, and on drier sites, to American beech. In some shady ravines, eastern hemlock might establish moderately pure stands. At higher elevations, above about 2400 feet, the northern hardwoods would gradually yield to a spruce-fir forest comprising mainly red spruce and balsam fir. Near timberline, red spruce would yield to a fairly pure stand of balsam fir. Here, lashed by the bitter winds of winter, the trees would be stunted and twisted into an elfin wood. In places where the soil is deep, fertile, and well-drained, a community of white pine, red oak, and red maple would be found at intermediate elevations in the transition zone between the northern hardwoods and the spruce-fir forest.

These stable forest settings would, of course, be interrupted here and there by such natural topographic irregularities as cliffs, caves, rivers, lakes, ponds, marshes, and bogs, which would replace the tree cover with rock, water, and various grasses, herbs, and shrubs.

The northern hardwood and spruce-fir forests and their local variants are known as *climax communities* because they represent the end product of a lengthy process in which short-lived, pioneering plants move in quickly to cover disturbed ground, and are then gradually replaced with more permanent species. Wherever mature climax for-

Loons return to the same nest every year, often selecting such convenient sites as the top of a muskrat dwelling.
Courtesy of the Maine Department of Inland Fisheries and Wildlife

The red fox, an amiable citizen of the County, is often seen patrolling roadsides in search of assorted tidbits on its varied menu.
Courtesy Voscar, the Maine Photographer

ests are established, it can safely be assumed that not much has happened to disturb the land for quite a long time, typically a hundred years or more.

We do have many extensive pioneering plant communities in Aroostook County, however, and they attest to the fact that much of the land has been disturbed in the recent past. Quaking aspen, or popple, is one of the first trees to spring up on disturbed ground, usually sprouting from a network of thin, underground stems. The closely related balsam poplar is often found in association with aspen, as is the similar-appearing but unrelated paper birch, which propagates by seed. Rapidly growing aspen and birch act as a "nurse cover," providing shade for the more slowly growing climax species, which germinate and grow among them. In time, the climax trees overtop the shade-intolerant nurse trees, which then die and decay, returning their spent nutrients to the soil for the benefit of the restored climax community.

Other trees that pioneer on ground disturbed by fire, wind, clearcutting, or by any other natural or human agency that removes the climax forest, include pin cherry, balsam fir, red spruce, and white pine. Some ecologists have argued that many of the extensive stands of white pine that once grew in Maine got their start when Indigenous American bands deliberately burned the climax forest in an attempt to improve hunting habitats. Alternatively, such fires could as well have been started by lightning. Today, white pine often pioneers in old fields, with variable admixtures of red maple, red oak, and many other tree species. In places where the soil is dry and sandy, white pine can even persist as a climax community.

As the table on page 17 indicates, the more stable climax communities tend to have a much greater diversity of animal species living in them than the pioneer communities have. The tallies are based on the preferred habitat of the species concerned. Most occur in other habitats as well, but those listed by name in the table have no other preferred habitat than the one under which their names appear. The reason for this trend is simple, but at the same time profound: because there is greater harmony within the stable climax communities, life is less stressful there, and it allows for the survival of many different kinds of organisms. In the unstable pioneer communities, on the other hand, only a few especially hardy and adaptable species can endure the more stressful conditions that prevail there.

Thus, the climax forests represent an ideal: an expression of Nature's view of the kind of harmony that *should* prevail in Aroostook County under the existing physical conditions. Back in the Ordovician Period, when the County lay beneath a cold, shallow, Antarctic Ocean, the ideal was different, and in the Devonian, when an equatorial sun beamed down on Aroostook's stony soil, it was different again, but for our present place and time, Nature's prescription for a healthy and harmonious forest is expressed in the form of the existing climax communities. Now and then, glaciers, indigenous hunters, or commercial farmers may disturb that harmony, but no matter how intensive or extensive the disturbance, as long as seeds still blow on the wind, the climax communities will always be there, patiently waiting to reclaim the land. Whether we regard that thought as ominous or comforting, it stimulates a healthy respect for the longest-standing tenant and steward of this special land we call Aroostook: Mother Nature.

A familiar winter visitor to the County, the Arctic snowy owl perches on telephone poles and barn roofs, keeping watch for prey.
Photograph by Timothy Finnemore

The bobcat at home. This husky cat prefers bushy woodland for stalking its favored diet of rodents.
Courtesy of the Maine Department of Inland Fisheries and Wildlife

Aroostook's Rocks: A listing of the bedrock geologic formations (Fm) in Aroostook County with their map symbols and colors, and brief notes on their significance. Read from bottom up from the earliest to the most recent.

Devonian Period (408-360 MYA)

Dm Mapleton Fm (blue-green), northwest of Presque Isle: Red conglomerate and sandstone, originally gravel and sand derived from highlands to the east. Less deformed than underlying rocks, but broken by "east-side-south" faults, indicating it was deposited before phase 2 of Acadian mountain building. Contains early land plant fossils dated at 385 MY old.

Acadian mountain building, phase 2: Wrenching of Aroostook's rocks as the supercontinent slid away to the southwest (e.g., the S-shaped fold between parallel "east-side-south" faults west of Presque Isle and the twisted south end of the SOcm belt around Houlton).

D1 granite (blue), west of Houlton: Granite, probably formed by the melting of mudrock thrust to great depths during the Acadian collision.

Acadian mountain building, phase 1: Collision between North America and the supercontinent. All older rock units tightly folded (e.g., the great *syncline between Portage and Van Buren enfolding DSfh within older formations*) and broken by faults (e.g., the region *northwest of Presque Isle*).

Ds Seboomook Fm (blue-gray), southwest of Madawaska and Ashland: Slate, originally mud and sand deposited in a rapidly deepening marine basin as pressure rose from the east.

Dsb Swanback Fm (light purple), southwest of Presque Isle: Marine mudstone, equivalent to Dch, but deposited farther offshore in deeper water.

Dch Chapman Sandstone (purplish-gray), southwest of Presque Isle: Sandstone, originally beach sand surrounding the Edmunds Hill volcano. Contains tropical, shallow-marine fossils.

Deh Edmunds Hill Andesite (light purple), west of Presque Isle: Darker lava erupted from a great, Mount St. Helens type volcanic island on the north rim of the now-extinct Hedgehog caldera.

Dhd Hedgehog Fm (purplish-gray), southwest of Presque Isle: Light felsitic lava and volcanic ash erupted explosively during the Salinic disturbance from a caldera on the shallow sea floor above the new subduction zone.

Silurian-Devonian Boundary (408 MYA)

DSfrl, DSus Fish River Lake Fm and equivalents (light green), southeast of Fort Kent: Conglomerate, sandstone, mudstone, limestone (originally gravel, sand, mud, and lime), and minor lava, derived from a highland that rose in response to subduction to the east.

Salinic disturbance: Formation of a subduction zone off the "east" coast of North America.

DSfh Fogelin Hill Fm (light green), between Ashland and Van Buren: Slate, originally mud deposited on top of S'. Fossil-bearing limestone near top indicates Aroostook trough suddenly became shallow as subduction began in the east.

Silurian Period (438-408 MYA)

Ssm Smyrna Mills Fm (olive), south and west of Houlton: Slate and sandstone, originally mud and sand equivalent in age and origin to Sf, Sns, Sspr, and Sj (some may have come from Miramichia to the east).

Sj Jemtland Fm (green), between Ashland and Van Buren: Slate, originally mudstone deposited in the Aroostook trough as the latter subsided due to rising pressure from the east.

Sspr Spragueville Fm (yellow-green), Presque Isle, Caribou, and Fort Fairfield: Limy mudstone and muddy limestone (like SOcm), same age and source as Sns, but deposited in the Aroostook trough.

Sns New Sweden Fm (yellow), west of Caribou: Limy slate, originally limy mud; same age and source as Sf, but finer-grained and deposited in the deeper water east of Wintervillia.

Sf Frenchville Fm (yellow), west of Washburn: Shallow marine sandstone and conglomerate, originally sand and gravel eroded from *Taconia*, the new landmass created during Taconian mountain building. Truncates eroded folds produced in underlying Om by Taconian collision.

Ordovician-Silurian Boundary (438 MYA)

Taconian mountain building: Collision of Bronsonia with North America (earlier farther south).

SOcm Carys Mills Fm (taupe), between Houlton and Van Buren: Limy mudstone and muddy limestone deposited in the deep marine *Aroostook trough* between two Bronsonia islands: "Wintervillia" in Maine and "Miramichia" in New Brunswick. Effects of Taconian mountain-building not felt this far east. This formation forms the foundations of Aroostook County's fertile agricultural soils.

Ordovician Period (505-438 MYA)

Odms, Odmp Depot Mountain Fm (purple), west of Fort Kent: Equivalent of Om, but deposited to west.

Om Madawaska Lake Fm (pink), west of Van Buren: Low-grade slate with thin quartzite beds, originally deep marine mud and sand-flows derived from erosion of Ow volcanic islands.

Ow Winterville and **Oml** Munsungun Lake Fms (pink), west of Caribou and Oxbow: Lavas (dark basalt and light felsite) erupted as a chain of volcanic islands above a major subduction zone.

Osb Shin Brook Fm (mauve), west of Houlton: Volcanic ash, lava, and sandstone deposited in shallow water around Bronsonia. Contains cold-water (Antarctic) fossils.

Cambrian-Ordovician Boundary (505 MYA)

OCcb Chase Brook Fm (orange), southwest of Portage: Same as OCsd, but formed in subduction zone among Bronsonia islands during **Penobscot disturbance.**

Ocsd St. Daniel Fm (orange), west of Fort Kent: Highly sheared mudstone, sandstone, and limestone conglomerate (*melange,* i.e., sediments caught and ground up in a major subduction zone).

Cambrian Period (570-505 MYA)

Cgp Grand Pitch Fm (gold), west of Houlton: Slate and quartzite, originally shallow marine mud and sand deposited around islands of Bronsonia archipelago. Contains the trace fossil *Oldhamia*.

Natural Communities in Aroostook County

Climax forest communities

Natural community	Associated species	Nature of site	Animal species*	Characteristic animals**
Sugar maple, American beech, yellow birch (N. hardwood)	Red maple, eastern hemlock, white ash, white pine, balsam fir, black cherry, white & sweet birch, red spruce	moist fertile, under 2500'	47	red-eyed voreo, black-throated blue warbler, American redstart, smoky shrew, Fisher
Red maple	Yellow birch, sugar maple, red spruce	wet soils, swamps, muck	43	spotted salamander, northern ringneck snake, great blue heron, tree swallow, winter wren, warbling vireo, northern waterthrush, song sparrow, grackle, American goldfinch, raccoon, mink
Red spruce, balsam fir	Red maple, birches, poplars, white pine, hemlock, larch	lakeshores, riverbanks, mountains, over 2500'	42	northern hawk owl, merlin, pine grosbeak
Eastern white pine, northern red oak, red maple	white ash, sugar maple, beech, black cherry, birches, hemlock	between N hardwood & spruce-fir	29	mourning dove (downy woodpecker, bluejay)
Eastern hemlock	Many species	Various, 0-3000', ravines	15	(great horned owl)
Balsam fir	paper birch, aspen, red spruce	below timberline	(see below)	
Eastern white pine	red pine, pitch pine, gray birch, poplars, red maple	dry, sandy	(see below)	

Pioneer forest communities

Natural community	Associated species	Nature of site	Animal species*	Characteristic animals**
Red spruce	fir, birch, maple, mountain ash, white pine, hemlock	lakeshores, riverbanks, mountains over 2500'	32	rusty blackbird, evening grosbeak
Balsam fir	paper birch, big-tooth aspen, northern white-cedar	blowdowns, clearcuts, beetle kills	26	three-toed woodpecker
Paper birch	poplars, fir, red spruce, white pine, yellow birch, pin cherry	deep, fertile, well-drained	18	Philadelphia vireo, common redpoll
Eastern white pine	various	under 2500'	15	(whippoorwill, crow, hermit thrush)
Aspen	bigtooth aspen, paper birch, pin cherry	various	12	yellow-bellied sapsucker

Natural non-forest communities

Natural community	Animal species*	Characteristic animals
Streambank	25	green frog, barred owl, eastern wood pewee, veery, catbird, yellow warbler, northern waterthrush
Shallow marsh	25	American bittern, great blue heron, green-winged teal, northern harrier, Virginia rail, sora, tree swallow
Grassland	22	vesper sparrow, bobolink, eastern meadowlark
Lake	21	ring-necked duck, goldeneye, hooded merganser, merganser, bald eagle
Bog	19	northern hawk owl, boreal owl, olive-sided flycatcher, palm warbler, Wilson's warbler, Lincoln's sparrow, rusty blackbird
Shrub swamp	17	snipe, yellow-bellied flycatcher
Pond	14	blue-spotted salamander, spotted salamander
Deep Marsh	12	(red spotted newt, eastern painted turtle, pied-billed grebe, muskrat, raccoon, mink, moose)
River	10	(spotted sandpiper, water shrew, beaver, mink, river otter, moose)
Elfin wood	8	blackpoll warbler, white-throated sparrow, dark-eyed junco, pine grosbeak, rock vole
Stable bank	5	(kingfisher, bank swallow, woodchuck, coyote, red fox)
Sedge meadow	5	(northern leopard frog, water shrew, bog lemmings)
Forbs	5	(redpoll, woodchuck, meadow vole)
Cave	4	(little brown myotis, Keene's myotis, big brown bat, porcupine)
Cliff, ledge	2	(common raven, porcupine)

Disturbed non-forest communities

Natural community	Animal species*	Characteristic animals
Cultivated fields	22	killdeer, mourning dove, snowy owl, northern flicker, American crow, American robin, Lapland longspur, snow bunting, brown-headed cowbird
Derelict buildings	15	(rock dove, chimney swift, barn swallow, house wren, European starling, house sparrow, American woodchuck)
Pasture	13	upland sandpiper, American woodcock
Buildings	12	(rock dove, chimney swift, barn swallow, Norway rat, house mouse)
Orchard	7	black bear, yellow-bellied sapsucker, eastern kingbird, white-breasted nuthatch, eastern bluebird

---

* Includes those species that use the community as a preferred habitat.
** Includes those species for which this community is the only preferred habitat. Species in parentheses are not so restricted, but are included because they are conspicuously present.

This bark etching by Passamaquoddy Tomah Joseph depicts Gloosk-ob and his grandmother, Monimquess, in their great stone canoe. She taught him everything he needed to know to survive on earth. The words in the etching mean "woodchuck sitting in stone canoe." From Joan Lester's We're Still Here, *the Children's Museum, Boston, Massachusetts, 1986.*

> The Native People were first in this region. They traversed its beautiful rivers to hunt and fish, and made this land their home.
>
> A world view, based on revelations, informs a civilization and gives meaning to socio-political organizations and beliefs. For the Native Peoples their reliance on, and love for this beautiful land inspired a balance and reciprocity between man and nature. Speaking in awe of this relationship, Henry David Thoreau wrote, in The Maine Woods:
>
> > It was a dense and damp spruce and fir wood in which we lay, and except for our fire, perfectly dark....Getting up some time after midnight to collect the scattered brands together, while my companions were sound asleep, I observed, partly in the fire, which had ceased to blaze, a perfectly regular elliptical ring of light. It was fully as bright as the fire, but not reddish or scarlett like a coal, but a white and slumbering light....I saw at once it must be phosphorescent wood...a piece of dead moose-wood (Acer straitum)....I little thought that there was such a light shining in the darkness of the wilderness for me....The next day the Indian told me their name for this light,—Artoosoqu'—.... Nature must have made a thousand revelations to them which are still secrets to us....It made a believer of me more than before ....that the woods were not tenant-less but choke [sic] full of honest spirits ....I have much to learn of the Indian, nothing of the missionary. One revelation has been made to the Indian, another to the white man....

By the early 1500s hundreds of fishing vessels from France, England, Spain, and Portugal were known to fish off the coast of northeastern North America. Within a few years Basques were pentrating the St. Lawerence for the whales which frequented that river. It was during these years that extensive trading with Native Peoples, especially Micmacs, was begun. Very early, Native People learned to sail Basque shallops and often used Basque sails on their own canoes, such as these drawn by Micmacs on rock in Nova Scotia.
Courtesy of Brian Molyneaux of the Royal Ontario Museum, Toronto

THE SPIRIT IN THE LAND
THE NATIVE PEOPLE OF AROOSTOOK
by Andrea Bear Nicholas
with contributions on the Micmacs by Harald Prins

K'takw-mikw—The Spirit In The Land—According to the aboriginal inhabitants of Aroostook, K'chi-mun'-do, the Great Power, created this land in the beginning and peopled it with many strange, half-human and other-than-human beings. Into this strange world the first human was born. His name was Gloosk-ob, short for gul-u-wusk'-ob, meaning "good man." Since his mother died in childbirth he was raised by his grandmother, Mo-nim-quess, the Woodchuck. As the first teacher she taught him all he needed to know about the world—how K'chi-mun'-do, the Great Power and source of life, existed in the land and all things. She also taught him all the skills he needed in order to survive, as well as all the important values in life, such as sharing, respect, and cooperation. Gloosk-ob learned these things well and became a man of great powers. From then on he traveled all over the world with his grandmother in their great stone canoe doing wonderful deeds.

One day Gloosk-ob decided he would like to make other human beings and animals. Some say he molded them out of clay; others that he shot arrows into a tree and out came a man and woman, then all the other animals, birds, and fishes that we know today. From there they spread out over the land, eventually arriving in Wabanah'-kik or Land of the Dawn. Gloosk-ob now set about teaching all the humans and animals he had created what Mo-nim-quess had taught him. For a long time afterwards the animals and humans could speak to each other, and they lived together as Gloosk-ob taught, in peace and harmony. Meanwhile, Gloosk-ob still had much work to make the world a better place for humans. He had to find Summer, conquer the many evil beings, tame the winds, and bring all the giant animals down to size so they would not harm human beings. When he learned that Og-la-bem'-oo, the Giant Frog, was holding back all the water in his belly and that the people had no water to drink, Gloosk-ob killed him. When he did, all the water flowed out of the frog's belly and formed the Woo-lus'-tukw, the beautiful St. John River.

Before Gloosk-ob left the world to go to the West he performed many other miraculous deeds that transformed the world. In this way each feature of the land that we know today became a sacred landmark, a reminder of the powers Gloosk-ob used for the good of the Wabanakis, the people of Wabanah'kik.

While the oral traditions do clearly describe the origins of our world they have a deeper meaning than that. With all his human strengths and weaknesses Gloosk-ob exemplifies the possible and positive in human nature, while all the evil forces against whom he struggled exemplify the negative, yet also possible in human nature. As such the stories are both historic and cosmic in nature. They hold the accumulated lessons of the past. They are what enabled Native People to survive in the past, and they continue to speak to present and future generations about how to live and survive in the world.

One thing that is remarkable about the oral tradition above is how precisely it describes and parallels the geological periods as determined by scientists only in the last century, ie., the receding of the glacier, the arrival of humans, the warming of the climate, the formation of the rivers, the inundation of land by seawater, the rising of the land accompanied by earthquakes, and the creation of new river channels and outlets to the sea. It appears, too, that the tradition of giant animals may very well reflect actual memories of giant beavers and mammoths—memories brought by the first people to arrive in this area after the last glacier receded. As well, there are other incidents in the oral traditions that readily correlate with the cultural developments as noted by archaeologists over the last 11,500 years of human occupation in this land.

In the past archaeologists tended to dismiss the Native oral traditions and to assume that the different cultural developments in the region reflected entirely different peoples coming and going in the land. It is now acknowledged that this assumption was somewhat ethnocentric in that it denied the possibility of creative or innovative change in the Native population residing here. Today, most archaeologists view the changing cultural history of this region as arising from a combination of factors, including changing environmental conditions, innate creativity and adaptiveness of the resident population, as well as outside influences arising from either travel or the arrival of new peoples. Thus, while different peoples may have indeed come and gone, it is very possible that a core group of people has lived in this land for millennia, just as the oral traditions assert.

The earliest known period of human habitation, shortly after the retreat of the last glacier, is known as the Palaeo-Indian Period and is believed to have lasted from 11,500 to 10,000 years ago. At that time an arctic climate dominated this area and the land was tundra. Caribou were hunted as they traveled in herds feeding on the moss of the tundra. The most characteristic artifacts from this period, known as fluted points, have been found at the headwaters of the Aroostook River at Munsungan Lake and at only a few other sites in Maine, New Brunswick, and Nova Scotia. Artifacts of Munsungan chert have been found at sites on both Penobscot and St. John waters, indicating that people of both rivers traveled regularly to Munsungan for the lustrous chert.

The period from 9,000 to 2,500 years ago is called the Archaic Period. Not many artifacts from the early part of this period have been found in Maine, but many have been found from the Middle and Late Archaic Periods, beginning about 7,000 years ago. Various cultural styles characterize these later periods, but most notably ground and polished stone tools, such as stone axes, adzes, celts, gouges, plummets, projectile points, and ulus, a type of semi-lunar knife. Burials with red ochre were also common to this period, hence the use of the name, Red Paint People. Towards the last part of the period cultural traditions from the south and west began to appear in the region. Archaic Period artifacts have been found along waterways in all parts of Aroostook County, particularly at the junctions of major rivers.

The bulk of all artifacts from the County come from the most recent period, known as the Ceramic Period, which began about 2,500 years ago with the appearance of pottery. The period was distinguished by finely notched arrowheads, the use of birch bark, and possibly the introduction of corn and tobacco. Ceramic Period artifacts have also been found in all parts of the County.

It is said that Gloosk-ob and his grandmother were the first to cross the ocean in their stone canoe to visit Europe, and that they warned the Wabanakis of the eventual coming of the Europeans. About a thousand years ago the Norse were probably the first Europeans to come to North America, but they settled only for a while in what is now Newfoundland. After terrible conflicts with the Native People, they left, and never returned. For several centuries no European explorations in the Americas were recorded. In 1497 John Cabot sailing for England came to the coast of Cape Breton, looking either for precious metals or for the fabled route to the riches of the Orient. He and his backers were hoping to make a discovery that would rival the gold and silver found by Columbus in Central America just five years earlier. While others followed John Cabot to the coast of the Northeast, the Spaniards launched one of the most horrible chapters in human history by exploiting, enslaving, and killing millions of Native People in South and Central America.

Although the history of North America is much different from that of South America, the explorers who came to North America from other parts of Europe seemed to be not much different from the Spaniards. Most seemed to have the same intentions of exploiting the people and the lands they "found," and most would have probably done exactly as the Spaniards were doing had they found the Natives in North America wearing gold and silver. Indeed, many Europeans held the opinion that Native People were something less than human. Neither the French nor English seemed to have any qualms about claiming the lands of the Native People for themselves on the premise that they had "discovered" them, and all, English, French, Spanish, and Portuguese alike, regularly took Native People captive back to Europe.

From the early 1500s Micmacs were in regular contact with Basques and other European fishermen and merchants with whom they initially traded furs for commodities such as steel knives, copper kettles, cloth, glass beads, as well as wine and brandy. In 1534, a French ship commanded by Jacques Cartier coasted along the shores of what is now northeastern New Brunswick. Surveying the area for a western passage to China, the ship's crew encountered Micmacs who waved furs on the end of poles, inviting the foreigners to trade. In 1541, a Spanish sailor reported that "the Indians understand any language, French, English, and Gascon, and their own tongue. . . ." Although most Natives taken captive to Europe either died on the trip or

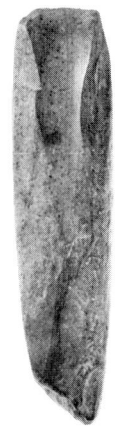
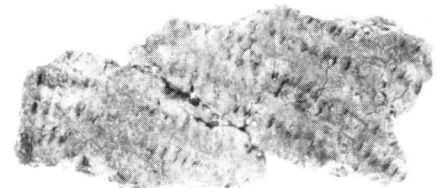

The 11,000 year old fluted point on the left from Munsungan Lake is characteristic of the Palaeo-Indian Period because of the fluting down the middle of each face. Courtesy of Dr. Robson Bonnichsen, Center for the Study of Early Man, Orono, Maine

The ground stone implement in the middle is a gouge from southern Aroostook County. It was made between 6,000 and 4,500 years ago, during the Archaic Period. The fragment of pottery on the right was found on LaPomkeag Stream in southern Aroostook. From the Ceramic Period, it is between 900 and 1,200 years old.

Archaic and Ceramic period artifacts courtesy of the University of Maine, at Orono, and the Abbe Museum. Photograph by Steve Bicknell

were sold into slavery, not all disappeared entirely from history. In the case of one Micmac chieftain named Messamoet, it is known that he lived in the French city of Bayonne for two years in the 1580s, then returned to his homeland.

In 1537 the Pope decreed that Natives were "truly men" and entitled to their lands and freedoms, and that all they needed to become fully human was to be converted to Christianity. Unfortunately, this decree was used to justify continued violence against Natives on the pretext that they refused to be converted. After 1537 converting the Natives became the official excuse for exploration by many nations, thus cloaking the real objectives of exploitation and plunder. Indeed, it was not the missionary impulse but rumors of a fabulous city of gold called Norumbega, somewhere on the Penobscot River, that lured most explorers to the coast of Maine later in the 1500s. When explorers returned to Europe with furs instead of gold, it was quickly learned that there were enormous profits to be had from the fur trade. Soon ships were dispatched just to trade for furs, which have been called "soft gold."

By the beginning of the 1600s France had taken steps to corner its share of the profits from this trade by granting to certain individuals exclusive trading rights in large areas of the Northeast. In return the grantees had to begin colonies in the land, and look for mines of precious metals. In spite of the Papal decree little thought was given to the aboriginal land rights of the Native nations.

In 1603 a Frenchman named Sieur de Monts was granted rights to all of the land between the Restigouche River and what is now New Jersey. The following year, along with Samuel de Champlain and some seventy-seven men, he came to the mouth of the St. Croix River to begin colonizing the land. Their first winter here was a disaster as nearly half died of scurvy or exposure. It was during that year that Champlain wrote some of the earliest descriptions of people native to the Aroostook area, the ancestors of the Penobscots, Passamaquoddies, and Maliseets, whom he referred to as Etchemins.

The Sacred In All Things

A few years after Champlain came to this area a priest named Father Biard, wrote detailed descriptions of the people he met, both Micmacs and Maliseets. Unfortunately, he did not always specify which people he was describing, apparently because the differences were not very great. According to Biard:

"They are nearly all beardless...[and] commonly paint their faces...." "Generally speaking they are of lighter build than we are; but handsome and well-shaped, just as we would be if we continued in the same condition in which we were at the age of twenty-five. You do not encounter a big-bellied, hunch-backed, or deformed person among them: those who are leprous, gouty, affected with gravel, or insane, are unknown to them." (Thwaites 1959: II: 73 and III: 73-5) As for their character Biard recorded this telling comment of one of the Natives:

"...you are always fighting and quarreling among yourselves; we live peaceably. You are envious and are all the time slandering each other; you are thieves and deceivers; you are covetous and are neither generous nor kind; as for us if we have a morsel of bread we share it with our neighbor." (Thwaites 1959: I:173)

The way of life of all Native Peoples of the region early in the 1600s was similar in that all depended primarily on hunting, fishing, and gathering activities. During the fall and winter people dispersed into small family-groups of ten to fifteen in order to hunt moose, caribou, and other animals. At certain times they hunted, trapped, or snared partridge, waterfowl, seal, beaver, rabbit, otter, and other animals, for food, furs, feathers, skins, or quills. In the spring, when shellfish (in particular clams), smelt, herring, and salmon were abundant, the small family groups assembled near the coast in bands of two hundred or more.

Unlike other area peoples Micmacs depended mostly on resources from the sea, and did not grow corn, beans, and squash because of severe winters and a short growing season in their homeland. They did, however, cultivate tobacco, "a thing most precious with them."

Consistently, early Europeans characterized the Native way of life in the entire area as migratory. Speaking specifically of Micmacs, one early visitor described them as "vagabonds...with no fixed abode: for they winter now in one place, now in another, wherever they perceive that chase for wild animals is best." In fact, hunters of all nations generally stayed within established tribal or family hunting areas along specific river systems. Although hunters could move easily into neighboring territories by carrying their light birch-bark canoes over the portages, they usually did so only in times of scarcity or war; and then they generally obtained permission from the family or nation to whom the territory belonged.

Passamaquoddy Song Of The Drum

To the Natives the sacred drum was the means of communicating with the Great Spirit in all things as this Passamaquoddy "Song of the Drum" illustrates:

"I sit down and beat the drum, and by the sound of the drum, I call the animals from the mountains. Even the great storms harken to the sound of my drum.

I sit down and beat the drum, and the storm and thunder answer to the sound of my drum. The great whirlwind ceases its raging to listen to the sound of my drum.

I sit down and beat the drum and the spirit-of-the-night comes and listens to the sound of my drum. Even the great wind-bird will cease moving his wings to hearken to the sound of my drum.

I sit down and beat the drum, and the spirit-under-the-water comes to the surface and listens to the sound of my drum, and the wood-spirit will cease chopping and hearken to the sound of my drum.

I sit down and beat the drum and the great Abbodumken will come out of the deep and hearken to the sound of my drum. The lightning, thunder, storms, gales, forest-spirit, whirlwind, water-spirit, and the spirit-of-the-night-air are gathered together and are listening to the sound of my drum." (Recorded by J. D. Prince, 1901)

At first the fur trade probably did not bring very many changes to the Native way of life since Native People simply adopted and adapted the new goods into their traditional way of life. In time trading brought many consequences, and most of them were devastating. Well before the first detailed accounts early in the 1600s starvation, disease, and war had wreaked major damage in the area. The population in the region prior to the fur trade has been estimated to have been well over thirty-five thousand, but by the early 1600s one priest assessed the population at little more than five or six thousand. If accurate, and in all likelihood it was, then we have only begun to appreciate the enormity of the disaster that befell Native People.

Early trading with fishing crews and explorers introduced Wabanakis to alcohol and spoiled or poor quality food, which drastically lowered their resistance. This made them especially vulnerable to the influx of ordinary European diseases, such as measles, influenza, and smallpox, for which the Natives had no natural immunity. After the European arrival the death rate from epidemics among Wabanakis often reached 90 or 95 percent. With the increasing European market for furs, Natives tried to meet the demand, which often depleted the game. This generally caused starvation unless hunters extended their range into the areas of neighboring nations, which in turn created competition, animosity, and even war between various Native nations. To date, this scenario seems to be the best explanation for the few oral traditions of war between Maliseets and Micmacs, and for the more numerous accounts of war between the Mohawks and all Native Peoples of the east coast. Of the latter, the most famous account tells how a Maliseet woman captive, sacrificed her life for her people by leading her Mohawk captors to their death over Grand Falls.

From very early in the 1600s all the Native territory between the Kennebec and Cape Breton, known as Wabanah'-kik to the Natives, was called Acadia by the French. While the French were the first to attempt to colonize it, the English who had begun permanent settlements in New England in 1620, also coveted it. Three times during the 1600s the English captured the French capital of Acadia, at what is now Annapolis, Nova Scotia, by force of arms. When it was finally restored to the French by treaty in 1667, they began to recolonize the territory. The major part of their plan called for the granting of huge parcels of what was really Native land to titled individuals, called seigneurs. The grant gave the seigneurs exclusive rights to trade, and required only that they colonize or bring settlers to their grants. No provisions were made to reimburse the Wabanakis or to obtain their consent.

One of the larger seigneuries in Acadia, in the middle of Maliseet territory, included a small strip of what is now Aroostook County. This 1684 grant to Rene D'Amours, Sieur de Clignancourt, stretched from Meductic to Grand Falls and included at least six miles on each side of the St. John River. Although Rene did not bring in settlers, as did other seigneurs farther downriver, he became quite notorious at the Maliseet village of Meductic as one who traded illegally in liquor. In spite of the seigneuries and traders such as Rene, the latter part of the 1600s saw the bonds between French and most Wabanakis grow stronger for a number of reasons—proximity and trade being perhaps the most important.

Believing that Christianity was superior to any Native religion, French priests began early in the 1600s telling Wabanakis that K'chi-mundo was the Devil, that spirit was not in all things but only in Heaven, and that Natives must

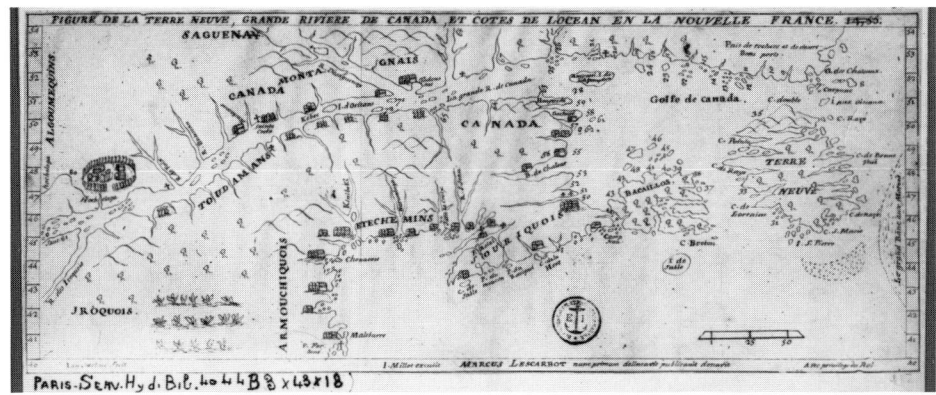

Only on rare maps such as this one by Marc Lescarbot in 1609, was there any recognition of Native rights to the soil. Here the "Almouchiquois" were the Abnakis; the "Etchemins" were in all likelihood the Penobscots, Passamaquoddies, and Maliseets; and the "Souriquois" were the Micmacs.
Courtesy of the National Archives of Canada, NMC, 6321 (original in Bibliothegue Nationale, France)

Transcript map courtesy of the National Archives of Canada, NMC No. 29256; Union of New Brunswick Indians and Maliseet History Project.
At the time of Champlain's first visit to this area Native People obtained most of their food from hunting. Survival thus depended on knowing the animals, and on observing proper rituals connected with this sacred source of life. Conservation, for example, was scrupulously followed, and tahnks was always offered to the spirit of a slain animal. Nearly ever detail of this recent painting of a Penobscot hunter on snowshoes is accurate, except for the bow which should have been illustrated as one piece of wood, not two.
Painting by Langdon Kihn; courtesy of the National Geographic Magazine

cease their traditional practices and throw all drums and sacred articles. Not surprisingly, most resisted. In time, however, more and more Wabanakis became dependent on trade as old skills such as the making of stone tools became lost. With increasing trade and contact the resulting periods of starvation, war, and disease, brought devastation to most native communities, and a growing sense of crisis. Only then did Natives turn in large numbers to the priests who offered hope, as well as food and shelter. That these priests could minister to the sick and not become ill amazed Native People, but above all it was the inability of traditional spiritual leaders to cure the strange new diseases that caused people to lose faith in their traditional spiritual practices. Conversion did not mean that Wabanakis replaced all of their traditional beliefs and practices with Christianity, which was based on an entirely different view of the world than that held by Natives. It is far more accurate to say that Natives consciously combined their old beliefs with the new into a unique blend of beliefs and practices.

Colonial Wars:
Essential To Understanding Aroostook History

In 1675 in southern New England years of mounting difficulties between Native People and English settlers finally broke out into war. Within a year it seemed to engulf all of New England, including what is now southern Maine, and involved Native People from parts of Aroostook. Its causes were complex, but most importantly, it was a war over land. Although English law had required that government consent be obtained before any Native lands could be taken, many settlers had ignored the law and helped themselves to Native lands. There was also a strong bias in English colonial laws that required Native People to respect English law, but did not accord to Natives the same rights and protections enjoyed by the settlers. Native Peoples generally had little recourse, and were often thrown in prison or executed for the slightest cause. When they struck back at these oppressive conditions in southern New England, authorities launched a war of genocide against all Natives, rather than negotiate with any of them. Ironically, the war has been called "King Phillip's War" after the chief who led the struggle.

On the Maine frontier similar biased attitudes guided English policy during this war. Government officials prohibited the sale of ammunition to the peaceful Wabanakis and even ordered the surrender of all their guns. For a people now fully dependent on guns for their survival, this order was like a death sentence, affecting also Penobscots from southern parts of what is now the County. Due to serious trade abuses, some racist attitudes, and the general lawlessness of the frontier, matters quickly escalated. Kennebec and Penobscot leaders tried to negotiate, but they were repeatedly rebuffed and answered by well-documented incidents of treachery on the part of government and settlers, alike.

Out of patience, Native leaders in southern Maine concluded that there was no alternative but war. They were joined by Penobscots, but not Maliseets or Passamaquoddies. Rather than fight, many Natives from all groups fled to the safety of French missions on the St. Lawrence, many by way of routes through what is now the County. Although some settlers and Natives continued working for peace, it came only after Native attacks forced most settlers to vacate the southern Maine coast in 1678.

After the first war in Maine, an uneasy peace lasted only ten or eleven more years, during which disputes festered involving land, abusive traders, biased attitudes, and English cattle that often strayed into Native cornfields. Once again Massachusetts authorities failed to negotiate in good faith. When a Massachusetts soldier fired on a group of Natives who had come to exchange captives, troubles quickly escalated. Once hostilities began, Penobscot leaders tried repeatedly to negotiate with Massachusetts authorities, but were always rebuffed. When trade was cut off with all Natives, including the Penobscots, starvation followed and the war spread eastward. Still refusing to negotiate, Massachusetts called for another war of genocide against all Native People, even peaceful ones, by offering a bounty of ten pounds for every head or scalp of a Native person. Within days Maliseets joined Penobscots and Kennebecs in an attack on Pemaquid in southern Maine.

Since a war between England and France, King William's War, had begun in Europe almost simultaneously (1689), the French were quick to jump into this war in Maine. After the attack on Pemaquid, French officers were sent to the St. John River to build a fort at what is now Fredericton, New Brunswick, and provide war supplies and support to the Natives. Wampum invitations were then sent out to Micmacs who soon joined the effort, and for the duration of the war maintained an encampment on the St. John River.

Only four years after King William's War came to a close in 1699, another war broke out in Europe between England and France, called Queen Anne's War (1703-1713). Although both powers immediately began competing for the loyalties of Native People in the region, Native leaders were determined this time to remain neutral. However, the conflicting pressures made neutrality impossible. Minor instances of violence escalated tensions, and when the French sent officers and war supplies for an attack on Portland, many young Natives joined the effort against the wishes of the chiefs and elders.

When Massachusetts responded swiftly with another scalp bounty (at first twenty pounds, and later one hundred pounds) the war was on. Parties of scalp-hunters or rangers were quickly formed to hunt down and scalp indiscriminately any Natives, both peaceful and warring, including men and women and children, leaving even peaceful groups of Natives little choice but to fight or flee. And flee they did, this time by the hundreds from the Saco, Androscoggin, Kennebec, Penobscot, St. Croix, and St. John to the mission villages on the St. Lawrence, where many of their kin had gone to stay during the two earlier wars. Once again, the routes through Aroostook were witness to another exodus, only this time more massive.

Hoping to regain their land in what is now southern Maine large numbers of refugee Abenakis from the mission villages on the St. Lawrence joined forces with the French and the young Maliseets, Passamaquoddies, Penobscots, and Micmacs. While English forces conducted massive land and sea offenses, the French and their Native allies did what they could to harass English settlements in Southern Maine. At the same time they defended the French fort at what is now Annapolis, Nova Scotia, where many young Native warriors also distinguished themselves at sea in ocean-going canoes and in captured English fishing vessels. In the end, however, the fort was lost to the superior naval forces of the English, thus bringing an end to the war in Wabanah'-kik.

In the treaty between England and France that ended Queen Anne's War in 1713, the king of France surrendered all of Acadia to the English, in total disregard for Native rights to the land, which had never been surrendered. When the Wabanaki leaders learned from the English what had happened, they were outraged and indignant. Said one chief, "He (the French king) can give you whatever he wishes, for me I have my land, which I have given to no one and that I will not give."

The Wabanakis were totally exhausted by more than twenty years of war. Longing deeply for peace, they signed another treaty with the English that they thought contained nothing more than mutual promises of peace.

While the treaty did contain some English promises to respect Native hunting and fishing rights, it turned out to be a document designed to rob Native People of their sovereignty and to subjugate them to the English Crown, thus binding them to respect English laws, even in their remaining lands. Sometime later an English official castigated his colleagues for deliberately defrauding the chiefs with this treaty when he learned that the translators had been carefully instructed not to translate it precisely.

Following Queen Anne's War the two questionable treaties ending that war became the primary cause for immediate problems, and eventually, for three more wars. While the Natives refused to acknowledge the surrender of their own lands to the English and insisted that they had not surrendered any of their sovereignty, French officials and priests in Acadia found themselves striving to restore their reputation among the Wabanakis. Within a few years huge shipments of French goods were again flowing to the Native People of Acadia. To counteract French influence the English now extended the much-needed trade to all Wabanakis, but at the same time slowly began extending their settlements into Wabanaki lands they insisted they had legally acquired from the French king. When combined with the old thorns of abusive traders, stray English cattle, and authorities who refused to acknowledge legitimate Native complaints, the situation quickly deteriorated.

Canoes, wigwams, and containers of all sorts were made of birch bark turned inside out. This painting of Maliseet wigwams in the 1850s could easily have been done in the early 1600s when Lescarbot first visited a Maliseet village at the mouth of the St. John River. Generally speaking, the largest villages were near falls where large quantities of spawning fish, such as salmon, could easily be caught. When people traveled they simply rolled up the bark and carried it in their canoes or on their toboggans.
Painting by W. R. Herries; courtesy of the National Archives of Canada/C-115891, and Maliseet History Project

Mark of a Maliseet chief, Treaty of 1713, courtesy of Massachusetts Archives.

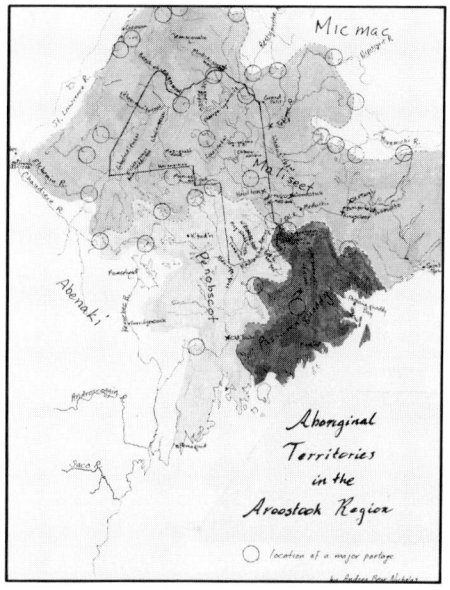

This map of Aroostook County shows the territories of the four Native peoples in the area, (Penobscot, Passamaquoddy, Maliseet, and Micmac) as roughly corresponding to the watersheds of the major rivers. At the time of European settlement the hunting territories of each Native group generally followed the course of major river systems with each family using a particular portion. Authorities, however, are in disagreement as to whether this territorial system was aboriginal, or simply a product of the fur trade.
Map by Andrea Bear Nicholas

Troubles first flared when some Kennebecs killed stray English cattle in their corn; and they culminated with English settlers taking the law into their own hands and killing five sleeping Kennebecs. Once again, the whole area was plunged into another war, its fourth (1722-1725). Although neither Penobscots nor Maliseets had been involved in the hostilities, Governor Dummer of Massachusetts, for whom the war was named, declared war on all Natives and offered a new bounty of one hundred pounds per scalp, frustrated as he was at Wabanaki unwillingness to be subjugated. Dummer now showed a renewed determination to exterminate all Native People in the area, once and for all, and launched a major campaign to destroy Native villages on the Androscoggan, Kennebec, and Penobscot.

After Governor Dummer's War more peace treaties were signed, now including many groups of Micmacs. Once again authorities seem to have taken advantage of the inability of Natives to speak or read English. In Nova Scotia Micmacs and Maliseets were tricked into signing a version of the treaty which did not incorporate any English promises. The English promises were given in a separate document that was subsequently "lost."

Once again, the Wabanakis were unaware that the treaties required them to surrender their sovereignty, and immediately following Dummer's war English encroachments on Wabanaki lands resumed. Firmly believing that they had not surrenderd either their sovereignty or their lands, many Native leaders continued trying to negotiate their concerns with Massachusetts authorities. Their efforts at dialogue, however, failed repeatedly, mostly because of uncompromising English attitudes and designs on Wabanaki lands. Frustrations grew and when combined with a strong French colonial interest in the land, the situation became volatile, needing only the spark of renewed war in Europe to ignite new flames in Wabanah'-kik. This lethal combination of factors occurred not once, but twice more, with the outbreak of King George's War (1744-1749) and the Seven Years' War (1756-1763).

Having failed to negotiate their differences with the

English, most Native chiefs and elders still worked for neutrality prior to both wars, but even that became impossible as it became more and more apparent that the remaining land of the Wabanakis, their access to life itself, was at stake. War became the only option and the Native alliance with the French a matter of necessity. Not the pawns of the French, as so often assumed, the Wabanakis clearly had their own reasons for going to war.

Painfully repetitious, these wars were a tragic strain on the people of the Aroostook region. Bounties, separations, shortages, famine, and disease all took their toll. While every able-bodied man and boy fought in distant places from Nova Scotia, Maine, and Lake Champlain, hundreds of women, elders, and children took refuge at missions on the St. Lawrence. There they were joined for the first time by large numbers of Micmacs who saw their lands on the peninsula of Nova Scotia invaded by thousands of British settlers, soldiers, and rangers.

Called somewhat inaccurately the "French and Indian War," the Seven Years' War in North America was launched largely by the English in 1754, two years before the war began in Europe, as a campaign to defeat the French in North America. Throughout the course of the war the English offensive took place on all sides of Aroostook—on the Kennebec, the Penobscot, the St. John, and the St. Lawrence. Late in 1758 major French defeats bolstered the English and in the winter of 1759 English troops marched up the St. John, destroying everything in their path as far north as a Maliseet village just north of what is now Fredericton, New Brunswick. Fortunately, the Maliseets there had escaped upriver, and many went to Quebec through and around the Aroostook region.

The year 1759 also brought more decisive victories for the English, and some, not so decisive—in the Spring they marched up to what is now Bangor, buried a lead plate, and declared the Penobscots and their lands to have been conquered—all without so much as seeing one Penobscot! Later that year, Quebec, itself, was captured, thus sealing the fate of the French in North America, and with it, the fate of most of their Native allies. Among the defenders in that battle was an unknown number of Wabanakis. Although the terms of the French surrender of Quebec promised peace for all who had taken up arms, and although the British conquest of New France was now assured, Massachusetts forces, one month later, attacked and burned the Abenaki mission village of St. Francis, and massacred many of its inhabitants.

After nearly a century of intermittent wars the Winter of 1759-60 saw the first groups of Wabanakis making their way back to their Native lands over the old river routes. For all it was a somber journey, wondering what would become of them, of their lands, and of their children's children. The peace treaty signed by one Maliseet and one Passamaquoddy delegate at Halifax that Winter was simply a duplicate of the one-sided ones signed at the end of each of the last few wars. It did not include a clear recognition of the aboriginal rights to hunting, fishing, and land, but demanded Native submission to the sovereignty and laws of England.

For the Penobscots the only peace treaty offered to them asserted that they had forfeited their lands by taking up arms against the English, even though the terms of surrender at Quebec promised all who had taken up arms that they would not be deprived of their lands. Only four Penobscots signed this treaty at Boston, and it was never officially ratified by the Penobscots as a people, yet Massachusetts authorities subsequently acted as though it had been.

Although the treaties demanded that Natives recognize English laws, Native People were soon to find out that those laws would not offer them the same protections that non-Natives enjoyed. Before the treaties were signed English authorities were making plans to settle the lands of all Native nations in the area. Before the treaties could be ratified (and they never were), surveyors, speculators, non-Native hunters, and prospective settlers, largely from New England, literally began swarming over the lands of the Maliseets, Passamaquoddies, Penobscots, and Micmacs.

In 1763 the King of England issued a Royal Proclamation which confirmed the rights of Native People to their lands, and declared that no land could be taken from them without their consent. In Nova Scotia and Massachusetts however, colonial authorities claimed it did not apply to them, and proceeded to violate it by rapidly granting away Native lands. On the St. John, which was considered part of Nova Scotia at the time, most lands to above what is now Fredericton were surveyed and granted by 1765 to officers and soldiers of the recent war. When Maliseets complained of encroachments in their territories, they were issued a "grant" of a few hundred acres of their own land! Since people cannot be given what they already own, it was inaccurate to refer to this land as a grant. It was, thus, neither a gift nor proof that aboriginal territory was being recognized. It was a token gesture designed to pacify the Maliseets and conceal the fact that the rest of their aboriginal territories were being stolen. Most of the first English grantees did not dare to take up their grants for fear of Native reprisals, and for this reason Maliseets probably had no idea how much of their lands were being granted away, but their resentment against the British was growing.

Shortly after the first shots of the Revolution rang out in Boston, British soldiers in Nova Scotia, who were still loyal to the Crown, outlawed the sale of gunpowder to settlers and Natives, alike. Realizing that they would now be unable either to trade or feed themselves, Maliseet leaders sought gunpowder for their people at a Massachusetts post on the Penobscot River. In doing so they declared their support for the Revolution, and received the needed powder.

Penobscots, on the other hand, had made their support contingent on the willingness of Americans to curb all trespassing that had been occurring in their hunting territories in the Penobscot watershed. In response Massachusetts authorities showed unusual cooperativeness and outlawed the trespassing, thereby winning Penobscot support. Unfortunately for the Penobscots Massachusetts reserved for their hunting only a corridor six miles on each side of the Penobscot River, and only above the head of the tide,

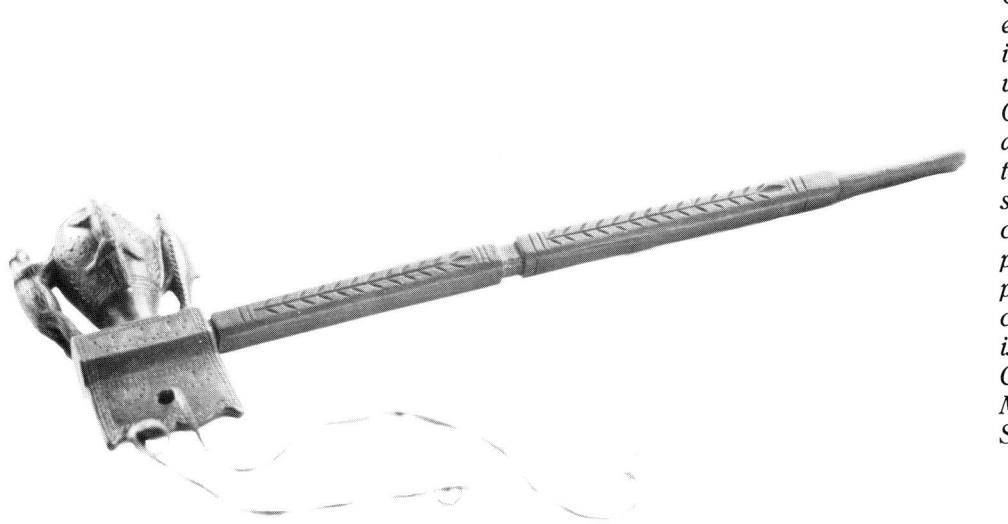

Government among the Wabanakis was esentially democratic. It was based on the idea of consensus, a process of discussion until all serious dissent was reconciled. Great value was thus placed on discussion and oratory. Since tobacco was believed to have spiritual qualities, it was always smoked before any deliberations to bring clarity of mind. An enduring symbol of peace among Native People, the sacred pipe is still smoked before important discussions. This historic Micmac stone pipe is decorated with important game animals. Collection of the New Brunswick Museum, St. John. Courtesy of the Nova Scotia Museum, Halifax.

It was not until the early 1600s that French traders at the mouth of the St. John provided a steady source of trade goods to the Maliseets. Items such as this iron axe found at Masardis and the cloth and glass beads on the right were simply adapted into the traditional way of life and used much as traditional materials had been used. For example, glass beads were used to decorate this Maliseet chief's collar in traditional double-curve designs. Axe photograph by Andrea Bear Nicholas, courtesy of the Nylander Museum, Caribou; collar photograph courtesy of the National Museums of Canada, the Canadian Museum of Civilization, negative No. III-E-27 and Dr. Peter Paul

where Bangor now stands, in effect claiming title to all other Penobscot lands in the lower watershed.

Recognizing that Native support was critical George Washington quickly extended a "Chain of Friendship" to the Penobscots, Maliseets, Passamaquoddies, and later the Micmacs. In the summer of 1776 a delegation of three Maliseets (one a chief) and seven Micmacs attended the historic meeting of the Continental Congress which formally declared independence from England. This delegation also signed a treaty of friendship with Massachusetts during the same trip. The following letter was written by George Washington to the Maliseets just before his famous crossing of the Delaware in December of 1776:

It gave me great Pleasure to hear by Major Shaw that you Kept the chain of Friendship which I sent you in February last from Cambridge bright & unbroken. I am glad to hear that you have made a Treaty of peace with your Brothers and neighbors of the Massachusetts Bay, who have agreable [sic] to your desire established a truckhouse at St. Johns out of which they will furnish you everything you want and take your Furs in Return . . . ." (Printed in Kidder, 1867)

It was the beginning of a difficult relationship with the Americans. Not long after the American agents arrived

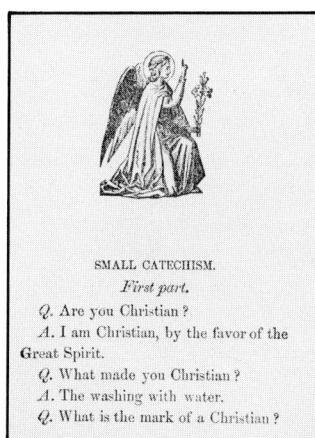 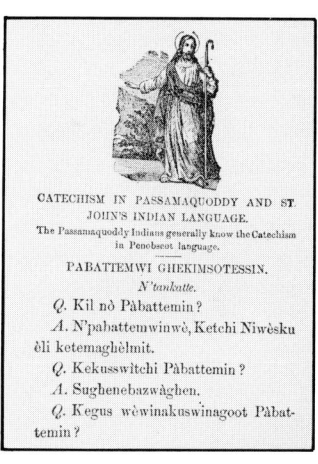

This prayer book in English and several Native languages was printed in the 1800s, but it was derived from manuscripts first written late in the 1600s by French missionaries, most of whom were Jesuits. More than other orders Jesuits placed heavy emphasis on learning the language and customs of a people before trying to convert them. Their goal was to translate the liturgy, thereby hoping to make Catholicism understandable to Native People. From Father Eugene Vetromile's Indian Good Book, *1858*

on the St. John to establish the promised truckhouse, British forces arrived on the river and forced the Americans to abandon the idea. Before leaving, however, the Americans signed a treaty with Maliseets and Passamaquoddies promising them perpetual protection and support in return for their support of the rebel cause. Seriously divided on the matter, some Malisetts chose to remain in their homelands and come to terms with the British. Others, however, nearly five hundred, left with the American agents and passed over the ancient portage to North Lake and Grand Lake (on the border of present-day Aroostook County) to join the rebels in the Passamaquoddy area.

In spite of serious supply shortages and homesickness, a large body of Maliseets supported the rebels in the Passamaquoddy area for the duration of the Revolution, encouraged by the promise that the rebels would later attempt to drive the English out of the St. John River. At one point fully two-thirds of the Native People supporting the Revolution downeast were Maliseets. The rest were Passamaquoddies, Penobscots, and Micmacs. It is fully recognized today that without this Native support most of eastern Maine, including the Aroostook region, would have been lost to the British.

With the final defeat of English forces in 1781 the Revolution was over and a new nation was born. For Maliseets, however, the Revolution was over too soon, since Americans still had not managed to carry out the promised invasion of the St. John River. Now it was not to be. Consequently, the People of the Beautiful River, who still cherished a spiritual attachment to the land of their ancestors, headed back over the inland water routes to an uncertain fate at home. In many ways it was a repeat of another journey made little more than twenty years before. As had occurred after the last war, lands on the St. John were already being selected and surveyed to be given away to new settlers, in violation of the Proclamation of 1763. This time, however, there were to be over nine thousand new settlers, all of them Loyalists, within two or three years. By 1785 many had moved upriver, some as far as what is now Woodstock, to take up parcels of land granted to them without the consent of the Maliseets, as required by the Royal Proclamation. Acadians who had lived in various locations on the lower St. John since well before the Revolution were harassed by the new settlers and finally allowed by British authorities to settle more Maliseet lands near the ancient Maliseet village at the mouth of the Madawaska River, the site of present-day Madawaska, Maine and St. Basile, New Brunswick, without Maliseet consent.

Upon returning to their homelands after the Revolution most of the Micmacs who had aided the Americans found that their lands, too, were rapidly being settled by Loyalists without their consent. For this reason, a number of these Micmacs continued to travel to the Passamaquoddy area hoping for some fulfillment of the promises made by American agents during the Revolution. In 1792 some of their chiefs joined Maliseet and Passamaquoddy chiefs in addressing the following letter to the Massachusetts government: "Since Peace, we have been wandering from place to place. Those spots of ground, which were wont to be our abode are taken up on the American as British side, and when our familys [sic] attempt to encamp thereon are threatened with every insult, so that our women and children are in continual fear—It is to you therefore, that we look as our chiefs—Tho many of us hunt on the English ground, where we formerly resided, and in some seasons obliged still to encamp, yet a place is wanting, where we can assemble unmolested at stated times, according to ancient custom; and for the benefit of such who inclines to sow and plant—It is in this country we wish to make our home—We ask from you to fulfill those promises made in warr [sic],...." (Massachusetts Archives)

It is no exaggeration to say that the Revolution and its consequences contributed directly to an accelerated loss of Native lands on both sides of the border. Before the Treaty of Paris officially ending the war in 1783 there was no clear idea where the international boundary would lie, and the Treaty, itself, defined the boundary only in general terms as somewhere in the Passamaquoddy area. Thus, it was more or less left to authorities on each side of the vague boundary to solidify their claims by occupation.

On the British side there was the added factor of fear that the vital St. John River communication link between Quebec and Halifax might be lost, in addition to the fact that Maliseet and Passamaquoddy claims had not been resolved. This explains the official British policy of settling the St. John River not just by Loyalists, but more specifically by entire regiments of disbanded officers and soldiers on adjoining blocks of land, not only to solidify British claim to the river, but also to serve as military line of defense against both Natives and Americans.

The Americans, on the other hand, had no ready pool of refugees needing to be resettled, nor did they feel quite the same sense of urgency towards the border area as the British. Their drive to settle the lands originated in another need. For Massachusetts, which now claimed the border area, their first concern was to sell the lands to pay off an enormous wartime debt. Only one thing threatened this plan—a newly enacted federal law prohibiting settlement without Congressional authorization on lands inhabited or claimed by Native People, but Massachusetts apparently claimed exemption from this law as one of the original colonies. Without seeking Federal approval the state attempted in 1786 to get the Penobscots to relinquish most of their lands in the Penobscot watershed. When the Penobscots refused, the state still went ahead with a lottery scheme to sell some of their land, as well as land of the Passamaquoddies (see "Lottery Lands" on Osgoode Carleton Map, page 63). The rather slim rationale of the state was that all Native lands in the state had been conquered in 1759, at least to the head of the tide, now Bangor.

This view of Native lands as conquered was typical of most Americans after the Revolution, but by 1789 Federal authorities had come to accept a radically different view, that of "original Indian title" which allowed for lands to be taken from Natives only with their consent or in a just war.

One of the earliest maps showing details in what is now Aroostook County is the deRozier Map of 1699. It is the best evidence we have that Aroostook was still quite heavily inhabited by Native People as the dots clearly marked village or campsites, many of which correspond with known sites of very ancient date. In times of war between England and France the network of waterways through Aroostook saw the added traffic of French soldiers and Native warriors traveling between Quebec, New England, and the St. John River. Sketch by W. F. Ganong in Proceedings and Transactions of the Royal Society of Canada, *1906, from original in the Massachusetts Historical Society Collection.*

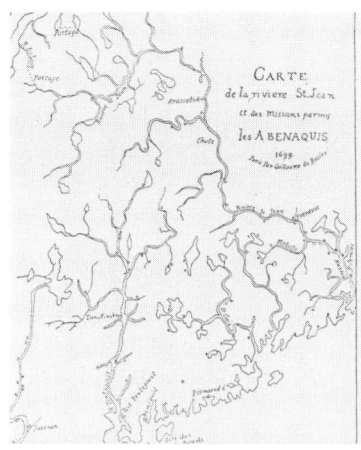

This bark etching of the emblems of the four Native nations in the area shows the animal or fish most typical of each nation. From top left clockwise, Maliseets and muskrat, Micmacs and deer, Penobscots and otter and Passamaquoddies and pollock. During the colonial wars these four peoples formed an alliance known as the Wabanaki Confederacy, which continued to operate into the mid-1800s. Courtesy of the Smithsonian Institution, National Anthropological Archives, Bureau of American Ethnology Collection No. 44315; and Maliseet History Project

Believed to have been the gift of a sacred bird, wampum beads were made of either the blue or white parts of the Quahaug Clam shell. They were then made into "strings" or woven into belts or collars in different designs to record events, decisions, or special instructions. It was the duty of special keepers of wampum to read the belts and preserve their message for future generations. Whenever it was important to inform other villages or nations of matters, such as war or peace, messengers were sent out with belts or strings of wampum. The belt shown here is the Penobscot Council belt. Courtesy of the New York State Museum

During the same year the newly proclaimed Constitution gave all power in Indian matters to Congress. In the following year Congress passed the first of many Non-Intercourse Acts declaring all land acquisitions from Native People invalid unless made with the consent of the Federal Government. Since Congress clearly intended for power over Indian Affairs to reside with the Federal Government, Congress it now seems was negligent in not interceding in Massachusetts' sales of Native lands.

The 1790s, however, were years of land speculation. Just one year after the passage of the Non-Intercourse Act, Major General Knox, Washington's Secretary of War and chief advisor in Indian matters, together with a business partner, bought Mount Desert Island and other parcels of Penobscot-Passamaquoddy lands, now called Lottery Lands.

When Knox's partner later went bankrupt, Knox found another partner, millionnaire speculator and later U.S. senator, William Bingham, who in 1793 bought a million acres of Penobscot-Passamaquoddy lands, including the Lottery Lands, most of which had not been sold. He was also offered the option to buy a huge tract of land in northern Maine, Penobscot and Maliseet land, much of which lay in the future Aroostook County (see Osgoode Carleton Map page 63).

There are no records to explain why Massachusetts bothered to approach the tribes to relinquish their lands after so much of their land had been sold or promised to

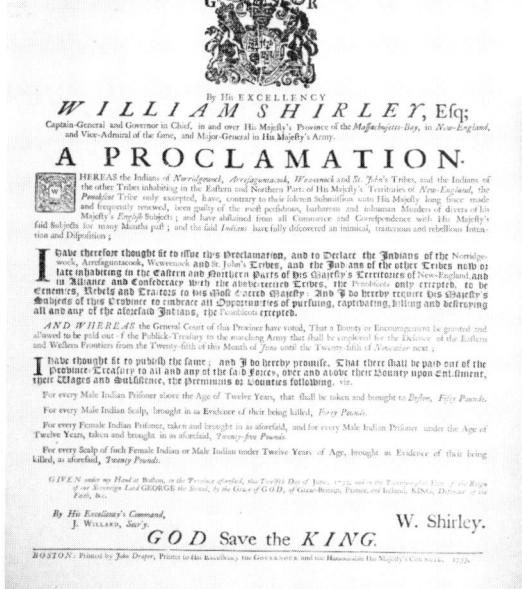

During the last two colonial wars more Natives than ever before fled to the missions on the St. Lawrence. In both of these wars genocide continued to be a major objective of English policy. In this broadside published during the final war in 1755 the Maliseets are named along with the Norridgewocks, the Arresaguntacooks (the St. Francis Abenakis), and the Wawenocks (Abenakis of another mission village on the St. Lawrence). Bounties were later extended to include all Native People of the area, many of whom still have vivid traditions of horrible atrocities committed against them. Courtesy of the Massachusetts Historical Society

Bingham and others, but this is what happened. In 1794 a treaty was dictated to the Passamaquoddies asking them to give up virtually all of their lands (including part of Aroostook County), in return for only a township and a few small tracts of land totalling about twenty-three thousand acres, which Massachusetts promised to protect from further encroachments. It is impossible to know exactly why the Passamaquoddies accepted such an outright swindle, but after years of encroachments and extreme poverty this offer to have some lands clearly reserved to them must have seemed like a reasonable deal, and the fulfillment of promises made during the Revolution.

Possibly the Penobscots knew that some of their lands in the Penobscot watershed had already been sold, but whether they knew of the pending sale of the enormous chunk from Passadumkeag north, to William Bingham, is not clear. They may have suspected as much when surveyor Park Holland passed through their villages in 1793 to survey the lands offered to Bingham. They would not let Holland pass until he said he was only going to mark off their lands to prevent white people from trespassing on them. Bingham never did buy the tract offered to him, but the intent remained to disinherit the Penobscots and Maliseets of those lands.

Under increasing pressure from squatters, the Penobscots finally agreed in 1796 to surrender to Massachusetts all their lands in the Penobscot valley for thirty miles above the head of the tide, retaining for themselves only the islands in the river and, they thought, all of their lands to the north, partly in what is now Aroostook County. In return the Penobscots were to get yearly rations of blankets, gunpowder, shot, and flints, somewhat more than the Passamaquoddies had received, but still no more than a token payment.

At the time of the Passamaquoddy treaty of 1794 Americans believed that the international boundary included most of Maliseet territory on the St. John (see Osgoode Carleton Map, p. 63), and at the very moment that the treaty was being negotiated Park Holland was surveying Maliseet lands in the Aroostook region. American agents had also promised to provide Maliseets and Micmacs perpetual protection in return for their support during the Revolution. Nevertheless, Massachusetts officials disregarded these facts and ordered its agents not to deal with Micmac or Maliseet chiefs who were present at the treaty negotiations, on the excuse that they resided in British territory! In contradiction, Americans allowed Non-American residents, such as British millionaire and land speculator Alexander Baring to own Maine lands in partnership with Bingham and Knox.

Only five years later the first Maliseet lands in Aroostook were granted away by Massachusetts as gifts, mostly to academies in that state to serve as a source of income for them—entirely without the consent of either the Maliseets or congress. The failure to obtain federal consent, of course, is what made these transactions illegal under the Non-Intercourse Act of 1790. In 1980 these and later violations of the 1790 federal law became the basis of the Maine Indian Claims Settlement Act.

Not surprisingly the sudden encroachments in Maliseet territories on the St. John created enormous tensions and at times, moments of violence. In order to quash the unrest and still preserve the loyalties of the Maliseets the new Loyalist government of New Brunswick came up with a plan to educate and settle Native People. The hope was that if Native culture could be eradicated and the Natives taught to make their living entirely off farming and other domestic skills, they would not need their lands, or resent losing them. To be precise, it was cultural genocide, the final step in the colonization of aboriginal people. The first of several schools was opened at Meductic (not far from Houlton) in 1787, and Maliseets from up and down the river were enticed to settle there with regular presents of food, cloth, hats, blankets, and ammunition. At a time of such rapid loss of hunting territories, Maliseets could hardly refuse the offer.

Over the next decades, the early settlers in the Aroostook region, would reap the benefits of these British policies. In continuing violation of the Proclamation of 1763, the New Brunswick government continued to survey and grant away Native lands at will. As squatters, settlers, and lumbermen encroached more and more on traditional hunting and fishing territories Micmacs and Maliseets were pressured to settle down on reserves. That fewer and fewer Maliseets continued using hunting territories in Aroostook is no surprise.

Once settled on the reserves Micmacs and Maliseets experienced other factors that tended to keep them settled and away from their hunting territories. Education in the "civilized arts" of farming and housekeeping handicapped young people in the traditional survival skills of hunting and fishing. At the same time the New Brunswick government tightened its grip over Natives. Alien laws now governed nearly every aspect of their lives. Increased government control, however, did not mean increased protection. When encroachments by squatters continued to shrink even those lands that had been reserved for Natives, authorities turned a blind eye and failed to respond to the complaints of Natives. This pattern of land loss reached a peak in the 1840s when the New Brunswick government, itself, launched a deliberate policy of selling off reserved lands, without Native consent. Native efforts to fight such dispossession appear to have become all-absorbing, and yet another factor serving to focus Native energies on the reserves, rather than on their territories in Aroostook County.

Finally, for Native People in this area the early years of the 1800s were years of devastating famine, disease, alcoholism, and despair—the tragic, but predictable products of colonization and oppression. More than in all the wars combined, death was now ever-present, bringing the population of Native People in the area to an all-time low. More than any other set of factors, these were the most debilitating both to Native People and their traditional way of life, and they explain why the Aroostook region seemed to have been so sparsely settled by Natives when the early

Due to serious shortages and competition from British authorities the Americans constantly feared losing their Native allies, and thus resorted at times to outright bribery and special favors for Native leaders in order to keep them and their people in the Passamaquoddy area. The medal shown here was one of many given by the Americans to Native leaders specifically for this purpose. This one has stayed in the hands of one Micmac family of northeastern New Brunswick since Revolutionary times.
Courtesy of Georgina Barlow, Indian Island, New Brunswick, Canada

Micmac family returning from the hunt, circa 1791. Note the "rough water" style birch bark canoe with rounded ends and humped mid-section, the wigwams, and the box made of spruce root, bark, and porcupine quills.
Watercolor by Hibbert N. Binney, private collection, courtesy of the Nova Scotia Museum, Halifax

settlers arrived. The lands in Aroostook, however, were not entirely uninhabited as early settlers' diaries prove, nor did the lands not belong to anyone.

While some Maliseets successfully adapted their knowledge and skills to these catastrophic events and new conditions, other cherished their cultural traditions and struggled to preserve them. That some succeeded is partly a result of the well-documented abuses and failures of the education program in New Brunswick. This cultural survival, however, is mostly a tribute to the Native culture and to the people, who, against all odds, managed to continue educating their children in their own oral traditions and ways of surviving.

Crucial to the cultural survival of Native People was their spiritual attachment to their lands, without which their communities and culture could not have survived. For many Maliseets it was this concern that led them to wage an endless struggle with authorities to maintain their last few pieces of land on The Beautiful River, the Woolustukw or St. John River. For a few hardy ones, their spiritual attachment to the land led them to continue their more migratory way of life; hunting, fishing, and traveling about in their traditional family territories, whether or not anyone recognized their rights there. (See Maliseets fishing salmon by torchlight, 1836, in color photograph section.)

This latter is the tradition out of which the Maliseets in Aroostook County continued to survive during the 1800s. For them the Aroostook region remained very much a last resort, although by the end of the century there were a very few places left for Native People, even here. As old Newell Bear once told a reporter it was like sitting on a log with a white man. Every time the white man moved over, the Indian had to move until there was no seat for him except on the ground. "I have to sit there," he said, "or else get up and walk away off. You have the whole log, and it is more than you know what to do with, but I—the Indian—I have nothing." (From the *Boston Herald*, 1904)

As settlers took up more and more lands on the Penobscot and St. Croix waters during the 1800s Penobscots and Passamaquoddies, as well, continued using, and perhaps extended, their traditional hunting territories in Aroostook County. During the same period, however, other factors caused these groups to make diminishing use of lands in Aroostook. In fact, Native People on the American side of the border fared no worse and no better than did Natives on the British side. Philosophies and policies regarding Native People were virtually the same.

Under extreme duress from encroachments and deepening poverty the Penobscots in 1818 finally consented to relinquish to Massachusetts all the rest of their territory in the Penobscot watershed (including much of southern Aroostook) except for four townships and the islands in the Penobscot River. In return the tribe was paid four hundred dollars, some trade goods, and a promise of yearly rations. For Massachusetts this was a huge bargain that never received Congressional approval, hence it was another violation of the Non-Intercourse Act.

For reasons that are not entirely clear the state of Maine assumed more extraordinary powers over the two tribes after separating from Massachusetts in 1820. In agreeing to assume Massachusetts' treaty obligations to Penobscots and Passamaquoddies, Maine was supposed to obtain the consent of both. Only the Penobscots gave their consent, yet Maine accepted compensation from Massachusetts for the support of both tribes in the form of the eighteen townships. Ironically, as many as nine of the eighteen were on Maliseet lands in what is now Aroostook County and they had never been relinquished by the Maliseets. Neither Penobscots nor Passamaquoddies saw any benefit from them, either, for they were immediately sold by Maine, and the proceeds placed in the general funds of the state. The rest of Maliseet lands in northern Maine were subsequently divided up between Massachusetts and Maine without either Maliseet or federal consent.

Meanwhile the Penobscots and Passamaquoddies became the object of a nationwide effort to "civilize" Native People through education, a policy similar to that of the British in its design to assimilate Natives and break them of their spiritual ties to the land.

Beginning in the 1830s, just as land speculation began again and as Indian removal policies came into vogue, both tribes were also subjected to ongoing and unrelenting efforts to dispossess them of their few remaining reservation lands. In an 1833 deal involving fraud and forgery the Penobscots were coerced into selling to the state their four remaining townships, two of which bordered on the south line of what was soon to become Aroostook County. Subsequently the state legislature passed resolve after resolve authorizing the state governor and council to lease and sell thousands of acres of remaining reservation lands without the consent of either tribe and without any compensation to either. Meanwhile, the only compensation paid was for timber and hay taken from the reservations, and though put into a trust fund for the tribes, it was seriously mismanaged by the state.

Now deprived of their lands and funds intended for their benefit, Penobscots, Passamaquoddies, and Maliseets found that aid would be given only grudgingly to them, more as paupers than as the rightful heirs to the land. Unfortunately, the overwhelming mood of the century was not sympathetic since the national government was involved in a series of costly wars putting down Indian resistance to American expansion. National legislation, consequently, was designed to disintegrate tribes and assimilate Native People, and the Maine courts reflected this mood with a series of rulings in the last quarter of the century that adversely affected Maine tribes. One declared that Passamaquoddies no longer had any special hunting rights since, in the court's opinion, they were no longer a tribe!

With laws now seriously curtailing Native hunting and fishing rights, and with the expansion of settlers, lumbering interests, and railroads into Aroostook County, hunting and fishing as a way of life for Native People became less and less viable. Like the Maliseets, the Penobscots and Passamaquoddies had little alternative but to accept and adapt to the sedentary lifestyle of their miniscule reservations in Penobscot and Washington counties. With local demand for their seasonal labor in basketmaking, lumbering, guiding, and moccasin and canoe factories, they found less and less need to travel to Aroostook County.

Because of the loss of their hunting territories and consequent famine, disease, and despair, Micmac populations, too, went into sharp decline during the early years of the 1800s, but they rallied and adapted to the oppression they suffered. Increasingly, they turned to crafts such as splint basketry and quillwork, at which they excelled, and to seasonal labor, including lumbering and riverdriving. While some pieces of land were reserved for Micmacs in Prince Edward Island, Nova Scotia, Quebec, and New Brunswick, the dependency and oppression of reserve life was more than many could stand. For them the traditional migratory way of life was still preferable, and with the newly discovered marketable skills, it was still viable. After centuries of trade, disruptive wars, and loss of their land, a wide-ranging mobile existence was nothing new for Micmacs. It simply reflected an ancient tradition of travel and trade established well before European arrival, and an adaptive instinct to survive in the face of upheaval after the coming of the Europeans. That Micmacs continued to appear in territories within the United States, sprang from this migratory and adaptive tradition. It was also the result of a strong oral tradition of the promises made by American agents in return for the loyal services of Micmacs in the Revolution.

The story of Native People in Aroostook does not end in the 1800s. Over the last century and a half since Aroostook became a county, Micmacs, Maliseets, Penobscots, and Passamaquoddies have continued to survive as peoples with their own cultures and traditions, in spite of powerful threats that have continued unabated since colonial times. Among them have been disease, dispossession, assimilation, and racial discrimination. How Native People have managed to survive in this County and still maintain their unique culture is a story that is intertwined with that of Aroostook County. At times a painful story, and at times an inspiring one, it holds lessons for all people of Aroostook, Native and newcomer alike. It is the one story that connects us all with time and the land, allowing us to look more deeply into the past, to understand the present, and to find hope for the future. It is the spirit in the land.

During the 1900s the situation for Native People in Aroostook did not improve much. Extreme poverty, coupled with racial discrimination, seemed to worsen, and the consequences for Natives came in many forms—alcoholism, despair, poor health, shattered lives, and suicide. Rather than recognize these conditions as consequences of their

For Maliseets the feelings of distress and desperation at seeing their ancient lands stolen after the Revolution were most poignantly expressed by one leader, as follows: "You see the situation we are now in and the distress of our families. All this we will submit to if we can be sure to have our hunting secured. We cannot sleep or rest, our women and children are crying about us, all our villages are distressed, we cannot sit down easy in any one place. Our old homes are forsaken and like deer pursued by the hunters leave us no place of rest." From the papers of the Continental Congress, National Archives; sketch by Patrick Campbell.
Courtesy of the Champlin Society, Toronto

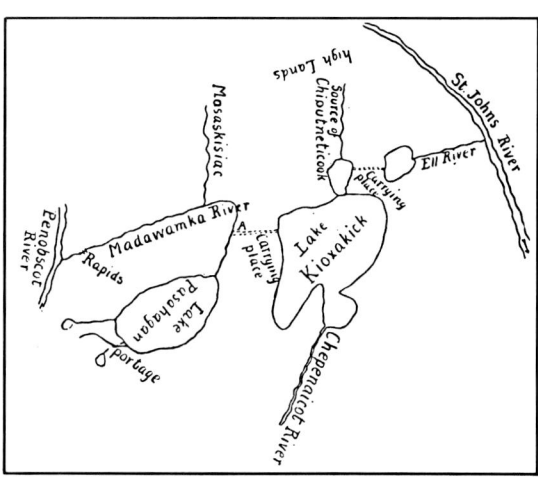

This 1798 map by Passamaquoddy, Francis Joseph, shows the ancient Baskahegan-Grand Lake portage in southern Aroostook, used so extensively during the wars and later by many of the earliest settlers in the County. By way of this route one could travel from Penobscot territory to Kioxakick or Grand Lake, at the head of Passamaquoddy territory, and to North Lake and the portage to Maliseet territory on the St. John. Sketch by W. F. Ganong in Proceedings and Transactions of the Royal Society of Canada, *1901, from original in the Maine Historical Society, Portland, Maine*

dispossession and oppression, the state in 1947 worsened their plight. In that year a decision of the state required all off-reservation Indians to begin paying taxes on their homes. Since the state had reserved no lands for Native People in the County, this law fell heavily on the Micmacs and Maliseets living here. In the case of the Maliseets nearly forty families lost their homes to taxes and the bulldozer, and ended up in even poorer housing than before.

With a situation on the reservations that was not much better, a growing sense of injustice in the 1960s culminated in the Maine Indian land case in which the Penobscots and Passamaquoddies claimed that their lands had been wrongfully alienated by repeated violations of the Non-Intercourse Act of 1790. The Houlton Band of Maliseets subsequently joined in the case, but the Micmacs were excluded even though they had traditionally enjoyed aboriginal rights of land use, hunting, fishing, camping, and mobility in Maine.

To avoid the pain and expense of a protracted court case, all Native parties to the claim agreed to accept an out-of-court settlement. To the tribes it offered land and/or monetary awards for all aboriginal territories lost and damages suffered. For the government the settlement had the effect of legalizing all the dispossession that occurred in the past, whether by treaty or not. It also required, among other things, that Natives surrender their aboriginal rights of hunting and fishing, long guaranteed by treaty.

Valiantly, the Native People of the area struggled to survive the catastrophes in their way of life, and through their own ingenuity, they found ways to adapt. Early in the 1800s they began applying their traditional skills of weaving, quillwork, and leather-work to meet the needs and demands of the settlers. While ash baskets, brightly colored quill boxes, and intricately beaded moccasins found ready markets, sights such as these Maliseet Women *became common.*
Watercolor by John Stanton, courtesy of New Brunswick Museum, St. John, N. B., Acc. No. 5179

*During the Boundary Dispute both British and American surveyors used Native guides for their surveys in the Aroostook region. On the upper St. John one surveyor met many parties of Maliseets, often camped at portages around rapids, as in this circa 1839 watercolor by P. J. Bainbrigge. Describing his Maliseet guide this same surveyor wrote, "Louis' figure is very good, with an old red nightcap on his head, his long black locks hanging below it, and a sort of Indian frock with leggings, made of deerskin...." From McEwen 1988.
Courtesy of the Public Archives of Canada, No. 24163, and Maliseet History Project*

It is important to note that a minority in all Native parties to the claim opposed the settlement from the beginning on the grounds that they had no right to alienate their sacred source of life—their lands in return for money and a tiny fraction of land that was rightfully theirs. To them no amount of money could even begin to repay for the land and way of life lost through the settlement. It must also be mentioned that many other Maliseets not on the Houlton band list, including all those living in Canada, were excluded from the claim even though they had never surrendered their lands or aboriginal rights in the County. At present only a small group of Maliseets now living in New Brunswick is still pursuing the claim that their rights to aboriginal lands in Maine should not have been severed without their consent.

Unlike the Penobscots and Passamaquoddies, the only monies received from the settlement by the Houlton Band of Maliseets were earmarked for land. In 1988 the band purchased a tract on the Foxcroft Road in Houlton, and began construction of a tribal office. An added benefit of the case for the Maliseets has been that they have gained federal recognition as a tribe, and are thus entitled to benefit from federal Indian programs. For the long impoverished Houlton Band this has meant greatly expanded services in the areas of health, education, housing, economic development, social services, and child welfare.

Now relieved of their long struggle for physical survival, the Houlton Band of Maliseets is turning their efforts toward ensuring the survival of their culture and language, which have been for so long under siege. What they hope for now is credit for their role in the history of this region, understanding for the oppression they have suffered, and respect for the unique culture and values that they continue to contribute to the Aroostook of today.

Among the various Wabanaki groups, the Micmacs are by far the most populous—about 12,000—most of whom are organized in twenty-eight distinct bands. Only one, the Aroostook Band of Micmacs, is situated in Maine. The others are in Canada's maritime provinces, Quebec, and Newfoundland. There are also several thousand living in the Boston area. Despite an international boundary that divides their traditional range, Micmac presence in lands on both sides of the border represents an unbroken continuum.

With respect to the heartland of the Micmaq Nationimou (Micmac Nation), which is in Nova Scotia, the Micmac community in Aroostook County occupies a peripheral position. Yet ties of kin and friendship connect Micmacs from both sides of the border. In Canada reservations have long been established for the Micmac. But no tracts of land have

Newell Bear, shown here, was one of the few Natives to be mentioned by name when he and his brother met some of the first settlers in 1811. Newell later worked as a hunter to supply the troops stationed at Fort Fairfield during the Aroostook War. He was known to make seasonal hunting journeys to the Allagash, the Tobique River, and the St. Lawrence, camping often at Ashland, and at the forks of the Aroostook and Presque Isle rivers. Before his death at Maple Grove in 1907 he confided that he did not enjoy making baskets and axe-handles, that he preferred to be in the woods to hunt—be free. "This is no happiness," he said, "only work to get food."
Courtesy of Andrea Bear Nicholas

When the so-called Miramichi Fire of 1825 devastated vast woodlands in central Maine, including much of what was to become southern Aroostook, it was generally believed to have started naturally from extremely dry conditions. However, Lt. Gov. John Neptune of the Penobscots, shown here, believed the fire had been deliberately set to drive his people off their few remaining lands. Indeed, the Penobscots lost one elderly woman in the fire, and all timber and hay on their Mattawamkeag township was destroyed. Portrait by Jeremiah Hardy, circa 1826, in F. H. Eckstorm's, Old John Neptune and Other Maine Indian Shamans, *1945, Marsh Island Reprint, University of Maine Press, Orono, 1980*

The migratory Micmac have ranged throughout this region at least since Champlain's time. In addition to hunting, fishing, and gathering, they also turned to making crafts in the 1800s. By cutting and pounding ash (fraxinus negra) they made thin woodsplints from which ash baskets were woven. Often living in temporary lodges, such as depicted in this nineteenth-century photograph of a Micmac couple in New Brunswick, the women weave the splints and make beautiful baskets.
Albumen print stereograph by J. S. Climo, 1879-1893, Acc. No. 7295, courtesy of the New Brunswick Museum, St. John, N. B.

been reserved for their use in Maine, where they are inappropriately referred to as "Canadian Indians." Collectively, an estimated 1.7 percent of the total population in Aroostook County is Native, numbering between twelve hundred and fifteen hundred, about half of whom are Micmac. Their widespread transience poses a problem in providing a precise demographic picture.

In the 1970s, the impoverished Micmac families in northern Maine formally organized and won limited recognition of their special status as one of the four Native Peoples of Maine when the state agreed to supply them with free hunting and fishing licenses, Indian scholarships, and services from the new Houlton offices of the Department of Indian Affairs (DIA). However, when the Penobscots, Passamaquoddies, and Houlton Band of Maliseets settled their claims against the state in the famous Maine Indian Land Claims Act of 1980, the DIA was closed down, leaving the Micmacs—who received nothing from the settlement—completely out in the cold. Today, the Aroostook Band of Micmacs continues the struggle for cultural survival. As "People of the Dawn," they demand official recognition of their aboriginal rights.

Note: Much of the foregoing has been extracted from a forthcoming history of the Maliseet People entitled *Ktahkw-mikw* by the same author.

*This Micmac man and his Maliseet wife were photographed during the potato harvest in the 1930s. To this day Micmacs and Maliseets continue to travel to the County to work because of an eighteenth-century treaty between England and the United States (Jay's Treaty) guaranteeing to Native People, normally residing in Canada, the right to live and work in the United States without a visa. The treaty also allows Natives to travel freely across borders without having to pay duties for their own goods.
Courtesy of the National Museums of Canada, Canadian Museum of Civilization, No. 75-1881, and Houlton Band of Maliseets, Vincent Erickson Collection*

*This community of Maliseets on the Foxcroft Road in Houlton in 1908 had been more or less permanent since the 1870s when the coming of the railroads brought rapid growth in potato farms and towns, and an end to the traditional way of life. With increased restrictions on hunting and fishing many Maliseets turned to work on the farms and in the towns. Still, work available to most Maliseets was only seasonal, at best—cutting timber, picking potatoes, making Christmas wreaths, which, combined with traditional livelihoods such as basket-making and guiding provided only the barest living, at the bottom of the economic scale.
Courtesy of the National Museums of Canada, Canadian Museum of Civilization, No. 74-17378*

Ed Bear (back row, far right), the coach of this 1939 Gouldville School basketball team, spent his earliest years deep in the woods near Portage and Ashland where his father trapped, made baskets, moccasins, and axe-handles, and guided for sportsmen. After graduation from the Normal School in 1933 he taught in the one-room school on the State Road and later at Gouldville and Cunningham schools. During these years he coached school basketball and baseball teams and played semi-pro baseball with the Presque Isle Indians. Together with Rev. Milton Grant, he dug the first pool in Presque Isle (1936) and under Red Cross sponsorship he taught the first swimming program in the area.
Courtesy of Gouldville School, Presque Isle

Shown here at the signing of the Maine Indian Claims Settlement Act in 1980 is President Jimmy Carter. Standing, left to right, Governor Joseph Brennan, Secretary of State Edmund Muskie, Senator George Mitchell, Chairman of the Houlton Band, Terrence Polchies, and Penobscot Tribal Chairman Butch Phillips. In 1988 the Houlton Band purchased tribal lands on the Foxcroft Road in Houlton where they hope at last to re-establish their ties to their sacred lands and to ensure the survival of their people and culture into the future.
Courtesy of the Houlton Band of Maliseets and the Jimmy Carter Library, Atlanta, Georgia

Micmac craftsman Harold Lafford, is shown here weaving a brown ash splint basket. This photograph was taken during the filming of Our Lives in Our Hands, a documentary about the Micmac People of Aroostook County in October 1984.
Photograph by R. Todd Hoffman, 1984

PERCEPTIONS: A CARTOGRAPHIC UNFOLDING

by Guy F. DuBay

In the beginning, that is in the early days of colonial settlement, Aroostook County with its forested mounds and meandering rivulets served principally as a "lieu de passage," a thoroughfare. To Marc Lescarbot (1570-1634), that lawyer-poet whose drama enlivened the lonely nights of the members of "L'ordre du Bon Temps" at Port Royal, Acadie, Aroostook County remained as some obscure milieu of nomadic Indian narrative. The Native Americans used the rivers, especially the St. John River, to travel a course from the Atlantic to the St. Lawrence Valley.

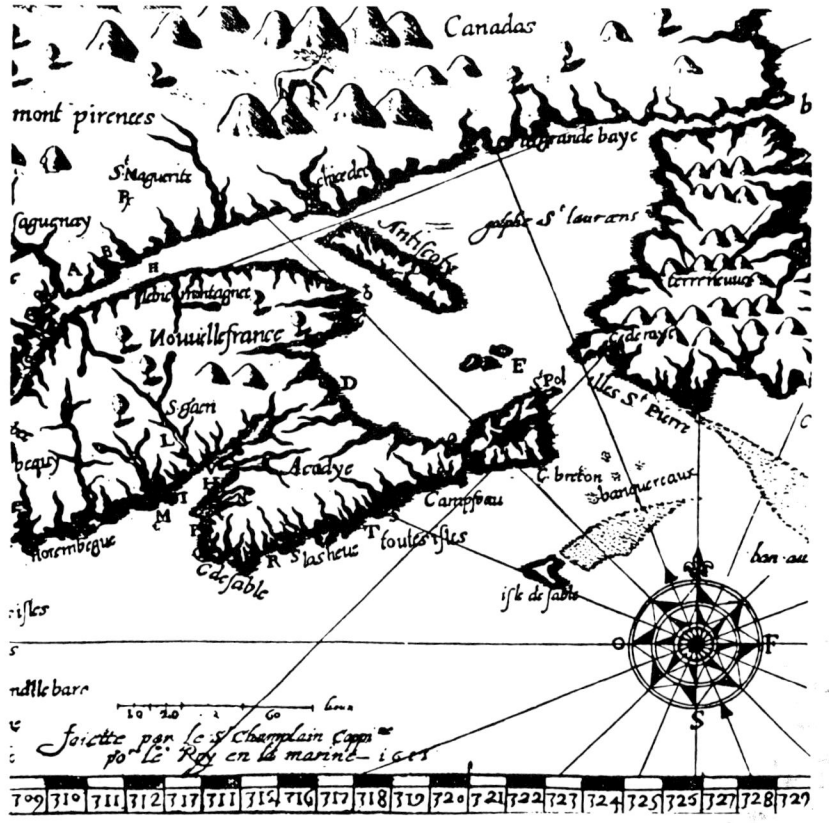

The Royal Geographer, Samuel de Champlain (1575-1635) had wintered on the Saguenay River in Quebec in 1603. The year 1604 found him as a member of the DeMonts Expedition at Ste. Croix in Passamaquoddy Bay. The founder of Quebec (1608) thus personally knew landfalls to either east and west of Aroostook when he sketched his maps of North America in 1612/13.

> Humanity's dream, a return to the idyllic Source, a return to paradise where all of life's necessities are provided. For the Europeans, weary of the excesses and abuses of the established monarchies and churches, of the exhausted soil and overcrowded cities, the New Land, America, was indeed a return to paradise, the dreamed of promised land. Perceptions of the New World by early mapmakers reveal both a growing awareness of its physical features and its potential.

Rival claims to North America on the part of the English and French were on the verge of erupting towards the ultimate clash when a pair of maps appeared in support of each mercantile nation's claim. The River St. John remains as yet the only decipherable land feature relevant to Aroostook County found in the French map of this era by J. B. Danville.

The St. John above Nashwaak is now given multiple tributaries and branches in its headwaters in the western portion of the county near the line which later became the boundary between Maine and Quebec. Portages between the water systems in Maine and those in Quebec are suggested by the proximity of the headwaters of either systems.

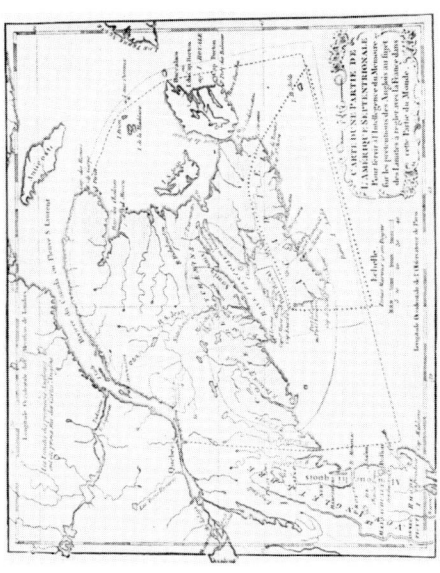

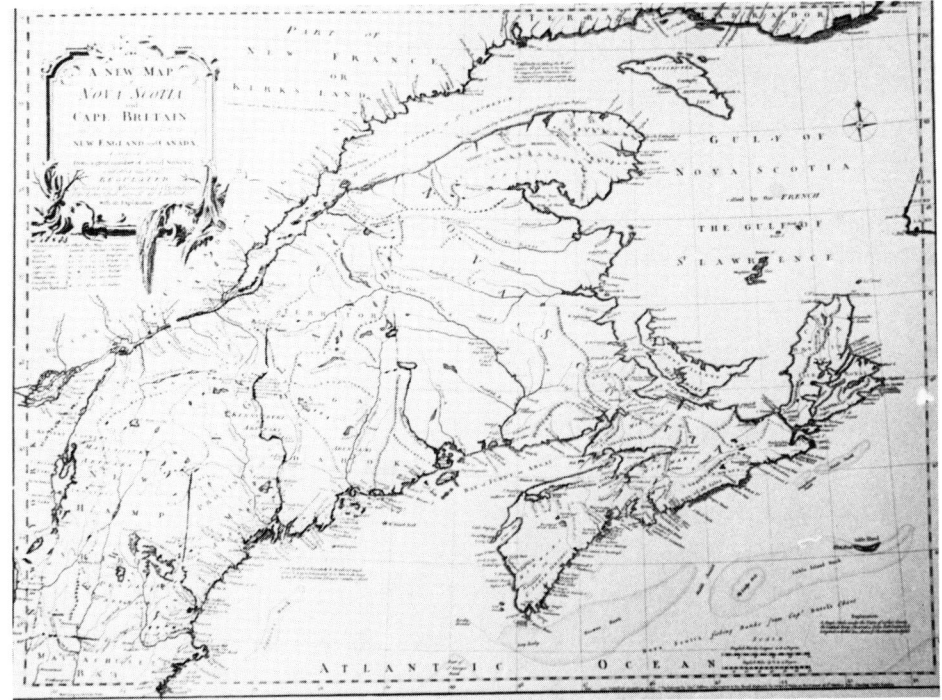

Thomas Jeffreys' new map of Nova Scotia appearing in 1755 concentrated on the presentation of accurate geographical data. Using the longitudinal-latitudinal grid system, Jeffreys' map figures among the first to set adequate land space between the Bay of Fundy region and the St. Lawrence. In addition to the English and French names, Clyde and St. John, Jeffreys lists the river's early Indian name, Wiguidi. The boundary lakes in the upper regions of the St. Francis River (Ourangebena Lake) appears on a map suggesting yet another river passage between east and west from Wolf River (Riviere du Loup) to the St. Francis River. A tributary of the St. John River originating in the lakes region at the head of the Penobscot seems to suggest possible knowledge of the Aroostook Valley. Features from upper reaches of the St. John give evidence that the Native Americans used that region to communicate with the St. Francis tribe on the Chaudiere River in Quebec. The northerly stretch of the Kennebec River in this region evidences the route later made famous by Benedict Arnold's March to Quebec. For the first time the Allagash River flowing south to north from inland lakes to the St. John at approximately the area of the Little Black River appears on a map.

Thus Lescarbot's map (1609) published two years later in his Histoire de la Nouvelle France *shows but northerly courses of our inland waterways.*

Said to have been the most accurate of North American maps sketched up to that time, Lescarbot pens in native huts at river outlets: the St. John, the Ste. Croix, the Nerumbega (Penobscot), and the Kennebec. At this time the Penobscot is identified as the Norumbega, a name associated with a late medieval concept of fabled cities of gold. Across the mouth of the Norumbega, Lescarbot etches the name Etechemins, *that is the Malisett tribe, members of the Abenaki Confederation known as the People of the Dawn, that is the east.*

While the St. John River is drawn in Lescarbot's map with an easterly tributary, very likely the Kennebecassis, or even perhaps Grand Lake above Jemseg, one gleans little factual detail regarding Aroostook County from a survey of this early sketch enclosing all territory we know as Aroostook.

2. Qu'ils étaient beaux, ces jours de notre enfance.
Cher Gabriel, au pays de Grand-Pré,
Car là régnaient la paix et l'innocence,
Le tendre amour et la franche gaîté:
Qu'ils étaient doux, le soir sous la charmille,
Les entretiens du village assemblé!
Comme on s'aimait! Quelle aimable famille
On y formait sous ce ciel adoré.] bis

3. Là les anciens, devisant du ménage,
Avec amour contemplaient leurs enfants
Qui réveillaient les échos du village
Par leurs refrains et leurs amusements.
La vie alors coulait douce et paisible
Au vieux Grand-Pré, dans notre cher pays
Lorsque soudain, notre ennemi terrible
Nous abreuva de malheurs inouïs.] bis

4. Hélas! depuis sur la terre étrangère,
J'erre toujours en proie à la douleur.
Car le destin dans sa sombre colère
M'a tout ravi, mes amis, mon bonheur.
Je ne vois plus l'ami de mon enfance
A qui j'avais juré mon tendre amour.
Mais dans mon coeur je garde l'espérance
De le revoir dans un meilleur séjour.] bis

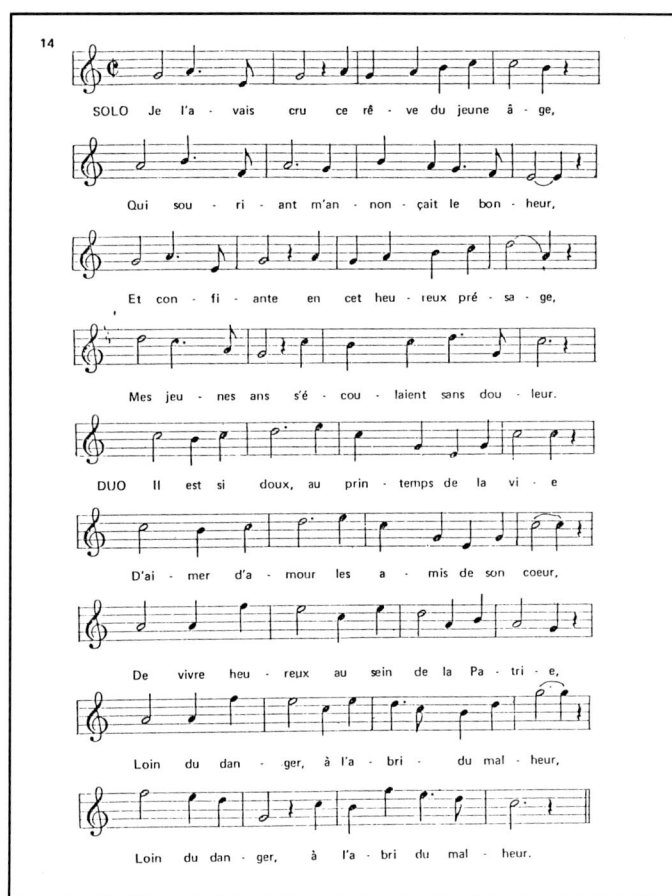

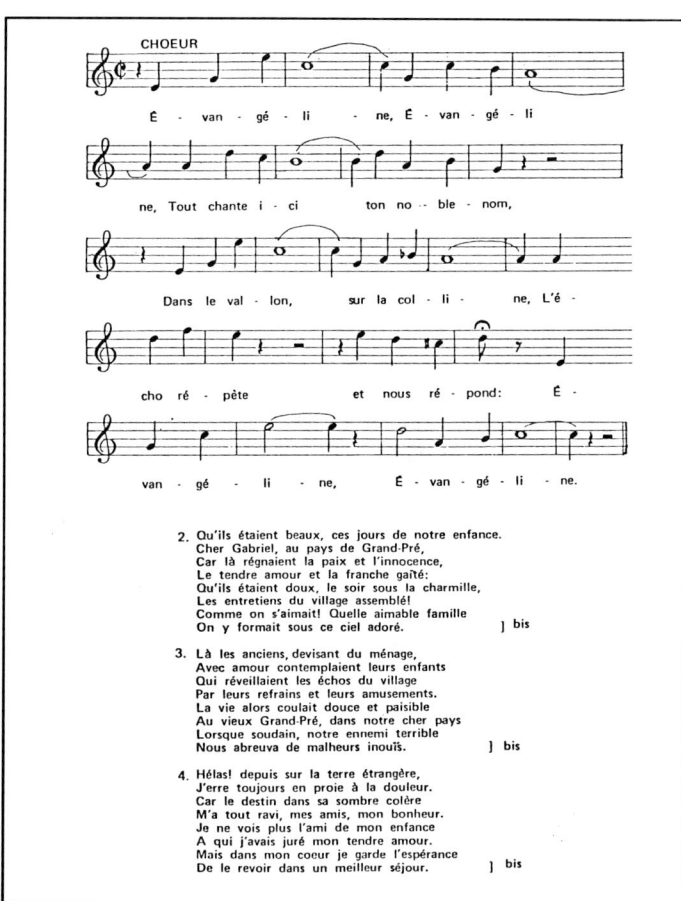

Courtesy of Guy Dubay

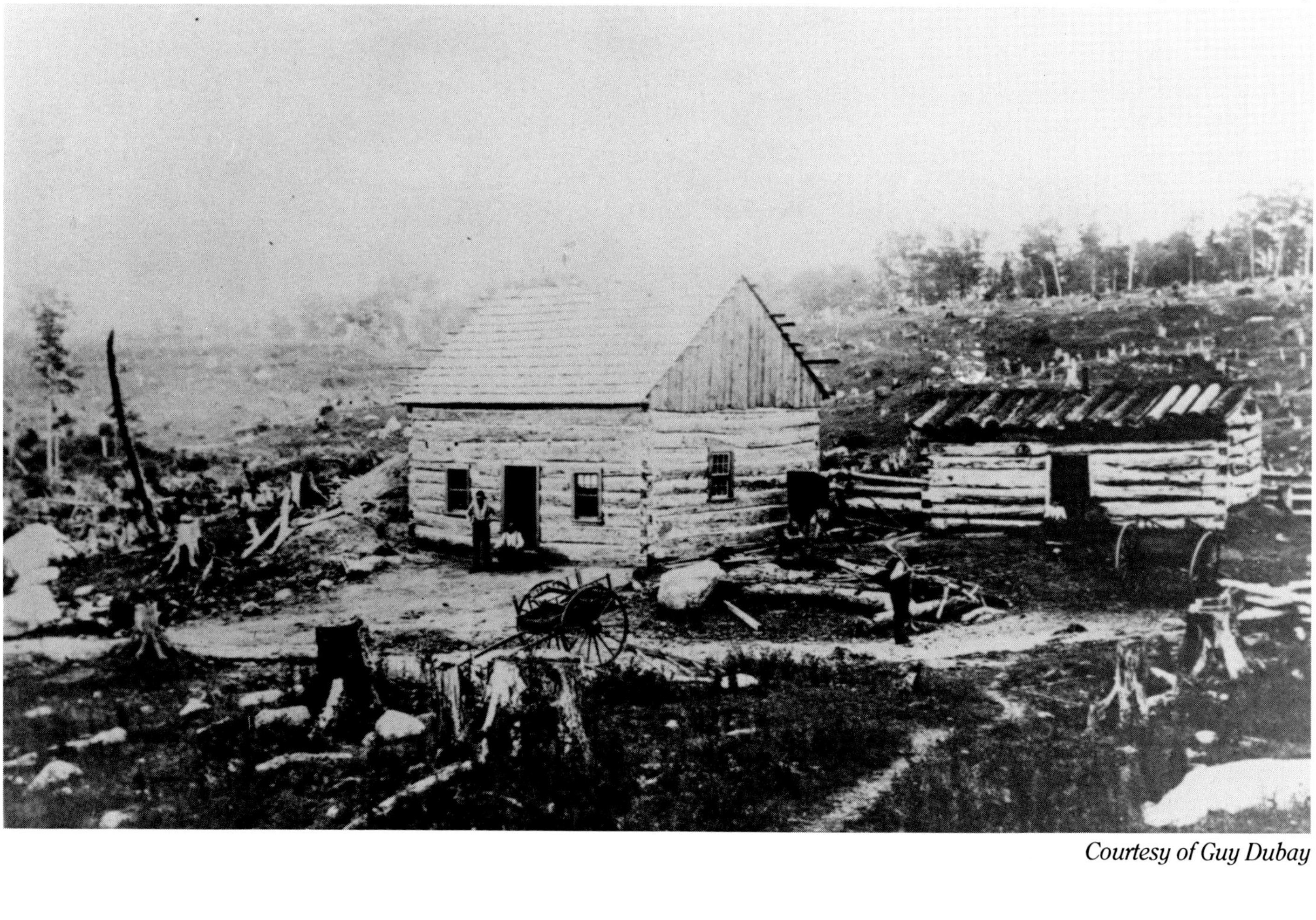

Courtesy of Guy Dubay

Maison Martin, Ste-Anne-de-Pays-Bas, near Fredericton, New Brunswick. The houses of the 1780s in the St. John Valley used this "piece-sur-piece" hand-hewn square log construction. This type of construction dates back to 1604, when the Acadians first came from France. Photograph by Joseph Donald Cyr

THE ACADIANS: A PEOPLE DISTINCT
by Joseph Donald Cyr

The Acadians who settled in the St. John Valley in 1785 were exiled from their homeland by British conquerors in 1755. Their homeland, Acadia, had been renamed Nova Scotia by the British in 1710. This put an end to one hundred years of war between the British and French in North America. New France, which consisted of the colonies of Acadia, Louisiana, and Canada (Quebec), had controlled most of North America. That control was reduced to two small islands by 1763. This was due to a lack of interest in New France by Louis XIV and Louis XV of France.

These people had landed in a region that was very familiar, as the St. John River had been a prime communication route between Port Royale, Acadia, and Quebec, Canada since 1612. The St. John River was discovered and named by Samuel Champlain on June 24, 1605, one year after his arrival in North America in 1604. The Herbert family can trace its lineage back to this first French settlement on Ile St. Croix near what is now Calais, Maine. These Acadians, the first European inhabitants of Maine and the Maritimes, preceded Jamestown Virginians and the Pilgrims of Massachusetts Bay Colony. Their story is an untold part of the history of Maine. Their existence in the Madawaska territory is a testament to their tenacity and sheer will for survival, as well as their desire to isolate themselves in order to retain their French language, Acadian customs, and Catholic religion.

The story of the exile of the Acadians is remarkably complex, and different for each family involved. The exile itself was chiefly due to mistrust and a lack of knowledge of the French language by the British conquerors, as well as inexperience in the rule of a foreign people. The British saw control of Acadia as necessary to protect their shipping with their colonies in America. They also envied the Acadian's abundant agriculture. They inherited a tradition of hate for the French culture and the Catholic religion going back to William the Conqueror, Henry VIII, and Mary, Queen of Scots.

The Acadians who are involved in this story were mostly from the settlement of Beaubassin, near the New Brunswick-Nova Scotia border of today. Because of insurrection, they were exiled to the furthest colony, Georgia. Many escaped into the woods for the first winter and wandered to the Kamouraska area of Quebec, Ile St. Jean (Prince Edward Island), and the lower St. John River. The exiles in Georgia served seven years of indentured servitude and walked back to Acadia from 1763 through the American Revolution. When they arrived, many squatted on land on the lower St. John River near what is now Fredericton, New Brunswick. They were then displaced by the United Empire Loyalists who had been rewarded for their loyalty to England during the American Revolution, by land grants in the lower St. John, after their flight from the American Colonies. The king sought to place them in an area in

Interior of an Acadian house of the 1780s. Notice the bed built into the corner of the house. Because of continuing destruction of Acadian farms by the British, furniture remained simple so houses could be quickly rebuilt. Children slept on straw mats on the floor.
Photograph by Joseph Donald Cyr

The traditional costume for Acadian women consisted of a vertical striped wool dress, usually with brightly contrasting colors. She wore a linen hat, blouse, and collar. The jacket and apron were made of cotton prints traded with their British enemies in New England. Wooden shoes were worn out-of-doors.
Photograph by Joseph Donald Cyr

Basket weaving, use of flowers and herbs for dyes, animal skin lacings for seats of chairs, knowledge of different capabilities of woods, medicine, foods, and animal skins were all learned from the Malecite and Micmac Indians. The Acadians, likewise, had a great influence on the Indians.
Photograph by Joseph Donald Cyr

danger of joining the Revolution in order to hold the land to the Crown. The Acadians there then petitioned the king for land above the Grand Falls. This was approved by the King in order to tame a wild land and to establish a communications link between the colonies of Nova Scotia and New Brunswick with Quebec. The king did this also to put his new subjects in an area where the Malecite (Maliseet) Indians had made a treaty with George Washington to support the Revolution. This would strengthen his claim on the area where the boundary was very unclear.

In the summer of 1785 when the Acadians arrived, they found an area rich in pine and had a resident Malecite population which was friendly, Catholic, French-speaking, and protective. The Acadians had chosen to live near friendly Indians since their arrival in North America because it gave them access to the missionary priests who were paid to convert the Indians. The Indians, in turn, were loyal to Catholicism and their fur trade with France. The Acadians learned much from the Indians, and in turn, greatly influenced the culture of the Indians through intermarriage, trade, and religion.

The early development of the St. John Valley, known as the Madawaska Territory, owes much to the nearby people of Quebec. Many Acadians had intermarried with the Quebecois of the Kamouraska, La Pocatierre, Riviere Ouelle area. This area was instrumental in the establishment of agriculture as was the Riviere du Loup, Ile Verte, Trois Pistoles area for trade and missionary priests. The culture of the Madawaska Territory, thus became a mixture of Acadian, Quebecois, and Malecite elements. The Acadians, however, remained dominant due to their very large families, economic control, and stubborn adherence to oral traditions and melancholic memories.

These people, toughened by the terrible consequences of their history, clung to their medieval French language, their adapted architecture and costumes, their French songs and stories going back before the Crusades, their superstitions and customs shaped by experience, and their religion—the only institution that was able to control them. They grew rapidly in an area that would be claimed by Maine, but of whom Maine had no knowledge until 1817, thirty-two years after their establishment in the area.

Because of the isolation and their relatively few numbers, they were an extended family in relatively short time. Because of their lack of tradition of government, their total adherence to the rules of the Church, and reverence for its priests, the Church acted as temporal as well as spiritual guide. The people tended to respectfully ignore political authority and obeyed only the laws they chose to obey. They were a humble and adaptable people, but were uncompromising in matters of loyalty and principle. They were hard working and hard playing, often choosing the

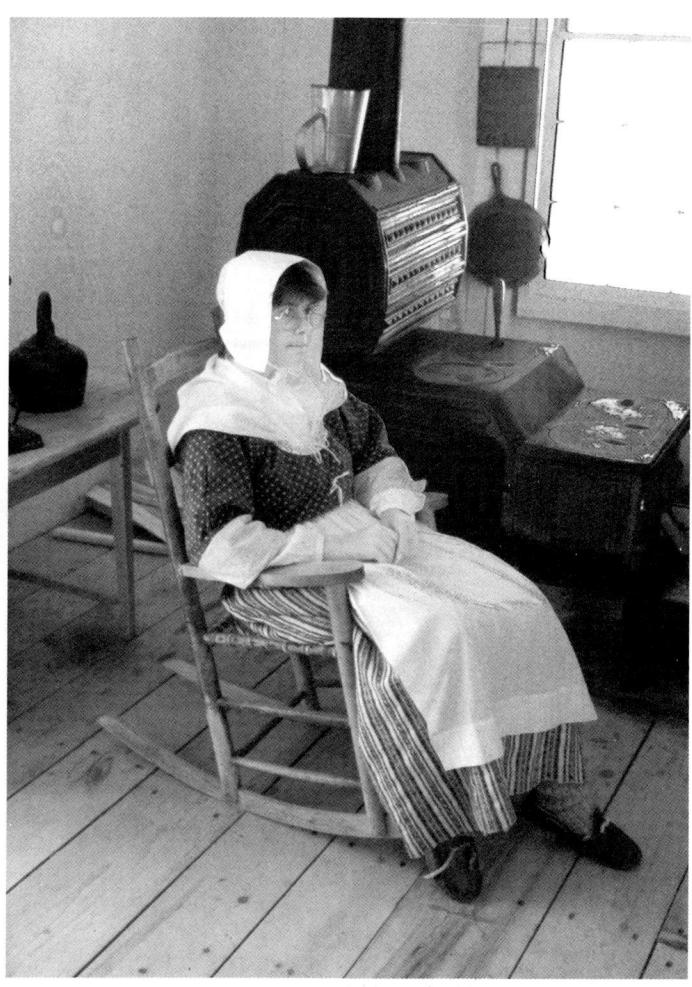

As roads were built into the Valley to avoid the need for traveling on the St. John, there was leisure time to prepare more elaborate clothing, and the importation of luxuries began, including full stoves, eliminating the need for rock stoves. Elaborate homes of this period had plaster walls, hiding the logs and hand-hewn boards.
Photograph by Joseph Donald Cyr

Maison Laurent Cyr of St. Basile was built in 1838. This house is built "en colombage," and was similar to the farms of Touraine, France, with the courtyard framed by barns. To keep poplar wood, used for burning, from drying too much, it was kept full length and stood upright to keep it clear of snow.
Photograph by Joseph Donald Cyr

Interior of the Laurent Cyr house. The rock stove is made at the home, as it was impossible to transport a fully constructed stove in a canoe, only the top plate, door, and pipe were brought. Window glass came from France to Ile Verte, Quebec, and then by canoe to the Valley.
Photograph by Joseph Donald Cyr

The interior of an "en colombage" house with logs fitted to a framework and filled in with other logs, tongue and groove. Furniture was built in the wood joiner's tradition as there were no cabinet makers. These small Acadian houses held an extended family, sometimes as many as thirty people, therefore the house was for work and sleep only, other activities were held out-of-doors.
Photograph by Joseph Donald Cyr

family over worldly ambitions. Women were known by their maiden name even to their graves and held much authority in the family due to the long absences of their husbands in lumbering operations. Children worked hard to keep the farms going and obeyed their parents' unquestioned authority. They had an inherent pessimism, contrasted by a belief in divine providence. Money was scarce and hoarded. They gathered in what nature offered. They brought the pigeon and dandelion from France, and because of them, were never short of something to eat—much to the chagrin of a continent reluctant to accept these "offerings."

The Acadians of the St. John Valley did not experience the stability of land ownership or political allegiance until after 1842 when the boundary question was settled. With the border fixed, those who now found themselves living in Aroostook were given from the British to the Americans. They thought of themselves as Americans whose origins were in Canada, living in a land whose natural geography is Canadian. They have been profoundly influenced by American culture and the English language, but the Valley retains the highest concentration of French people in the United States and has the highest percentage of French spoken in the home. Their folk culture remains intact, and they are recognized as a distinctly different society in the fabric of Maine folk culture.

The Aroostook River. "It was a beautiful river, flowing quietly through the deep forest like a sweet child wandering in a wilderness and dallying with flowers by the way" exclaimed E. Elwell in his account of an excursion by Maine newspaper editors to the Aroostook in 1858. Photo by Connie Tucker

From Hillcrest Farm in Readfield, Maine, two Smith boys, Oliver Carpenter, and Lucius Charles came to Mars Hill (then Soldier's Township) in 1859 to farm the already famous fertile soil. Hillcrest Farm was built by Revolutionary War captain, Matthias Smith, in 1776. Photograph by Iris Brewer

> Pioneers adventurous enough to come to the wildlands of Massachusetts, to the North Woods, were awed by the incredible beauty of the area, as were the editors of Maine newspapers invited to visit the North Aroostook Agricultural and Horticultural Society's Exhibition and Fair in October, 1858. E. Elwell wrote of their excursion in his book, Aroostook: with some account of the Excursions Thither...:
>
> "...arrived at Mattawamkeag Point, a small village at the head of steam navigation on the Penobscot, sixty-one miles above Bangor....At three o'clock in the morning, up and away. One stage coach, one covered stage wagon, and one open wagon, and all aboard.
>
> ...after some travelling through a low-lying region, we climb a long hill—Clefford's Hill—and the whole panorama of Aroostook bursts upon us. Here we pause, we spring to our feet, and join in one hearty burst of admiration. So wide an extent of forest, so brilliantly colored, with so sublime a back-ground we never dreamed of seeing.
>
> ...we met a Mr. J. W. Haines...thirteen years ago ...he headed for Aroostook and when he reached the neighborhood of Presque Isle, he thought himself in sight of the promised land...travelled 12 miles beyond, pitched his tent," and he and his descendants found his first impression to be true.

The Oliver Carpenter Smith homestead in Mars Hill, Maine, has passed down to the fifth genertaion, now owned by Carl W. Smith, owner of Smith Food Distributors of Presque Isle. Another Oliver Smith descendant, Hershel Smith, is a major farmer (potatoes and broccoli), and owner of the landmark Smith's Truck Stop in Blaine, Maine. Oliver's brother Lucius homesteaded in Westfield and left many descendants in the County. Courtesy of Carl Smith

THE LAND OF PROMISE
Introduction by Anna Fields Mcgrath with Philip Turner

"Chosen", a fictionalized account of a piece of Aroostook history.

"Come, come," and then in French, "venez," spoken softly yet firmly. The two tired, dirty, skinny, ragged, and dejected children hobbled down the steel steps of the Bangor and Aroostook night train. The cold wind driving a rain squall and whipping at their clothes forced the small crowd into the warm station house. The shipment of Boston orphans had stopped at all the St. John Valley stations, and the guardian sisters had lined them up to be picked over by expectant farmers—wives and husbands. Now the train had rumbled into Fort Kent for the very first time.

They were the last to be chosen; Pat McTighe and his young sister Mary had clambered off the train and back again all day long. Each time they had been rejected. Now they had been chosen! A smile crossed Pat's face, and he gave Mary's hand, which he had held nearly all day, a little extra squeeze, and said in his very best tones of an older protective brother, "Mary, the Lord hisself has looked after us McTighes."

Young Pat McTighe was only eight years old, and Mary was six, going on seven. They had left Ireland with their eager young parents. The boat was packed as were all sailing vessels and steamships carrying human cargo for profit. This crowding and the lack of sanitation caused contagious diseases to spread quickly so that many succumbed and were buried at sea. Landing at Boston, the ships were met by the Sisters who cared for the orphans until a shipment could be arranged. The St. John Valley was obviously a good place to send Roman Catholic children.

At the Aimant Cyr homestead there were already children ranging in age from six to sixteen, yet room and food were found for the newly arrived. Soon Pat was doing farm chores nearby as well as the Cyr boys. The twisted and deformed left leg slowed him, yet didn't deter him from trying. Now Pat could respond to the love from the Cyr family, and Mary soon was sleeping and not crying from her nightmarish memories. Yet all of Pat McTighe's life he remembered the ocean that had swallowed his Mum and Dad.

From Philip Turner's Rooster: The Story of Aroostook County.

"Saturday-nite Bath"

At the Cyr homestead spring was in the air, and even if the morning still had a sharp nip, Desse ordered up a copper boiler full of water, for now was the time to take off the woolies and slip into summer underwear. The cookstove's water tank was full and steaming, for this family relished Saturday night baked beans with brown bread.

The chores were done early, and a leisurely supper preceded the washtub baths. The tub was wooden, sturdy, and quite large. Aimant had hand-made it a few years after the birth of his son Jean. The girls took over the kitchen with Desse, the older ones soaping the younger ones. Desse was careful that they didn't waste the store-bought soap. She was so very grateful that Aimant had agreed to buy it. The making of soap was tiring and not anywhere near as rewarding as cooking for her lovely children. When all girl children had been packed off to bed under clean linen and aired blankets, the young boys prepared for a scrubbing. Aimant used a heavy hand on the brush for his purpose was cleanliness. Their bodies shone like new snowmen in the sun.

Then Aimant was scrubbed by Desse and she in turn by him. What a glorious feeling to slide between clean bedding with that husband by the unusual name of Aimant. He was what the word implied. He did magnetize her, and he was so loving. Yes he was "Aimant."

From Philip Turner's Rooster: The Story of Aroostook County.

Lumbermen from New Brunswick and New Hampshire searching for pines for the navies of Great Britain and of the colonies followed the trails through the water and forests of the Native People, as had the Acadians escaping from the British. After the American Revolution the new country, the United States of America, was hard pressed for funds, so Massachusetts gave her veterans a choice of land in the eastlands of the district of Maine. Soldier's Township, now Mars Hill, was one grant. Massachusetts also offered the land to finance academies, and the real settling of this area began on the New Salem Academy Grant, now Houlton, Maine, early in the nineteenth century. Dangers were many in the wildlands. One animal feared above all others, the legendary Indian "Devil" who, according to the Indians, feared no man, did not even fear fire. Some said it was a cougar, some a fisher, some a wolverine; but many considered it to be a mountain lion or panther. Wilmot Ashby tells many stories of this creature, in his Complete History of Aroostook. *He recounts a story from a* Maine Woods and Sportsman *of a young man who had gone to see his ladyfriend, became engaged, and left her home after midnight. "The moon was nearing the horizon making weird, dismal shadows along the way. In spite of my new found joy, I could not help noticing that the mare was acting strangely. I often boasted that she would not be afraid of the devil himself, but she shied at her own shadow more than once before we crossed the open field. I had to learn that an imaginary devil with two legs is much less to be feared than a real devil with four. She would hardly wait until I opened the gate at the edge of the wood, I let her thru and turned to close it when a dry branch snapped near by and she started. I was lucky enough to catch the tail*

Henry Lufkin and his family on the long trek north to Aroostook from Rumford to Caribou in 1854. Drawing by Evelyn Kok (from the book Henry, Man of Aroostook County, Maine *by Milton Teague Lufkin. Originally published by the Bond Wheelwright Co., 1976).*

board and then I clammored over the seat. . . . I seized the reins but not to hold her. No sir, I was perfectly willing for her to go as fast as she could. I caught a glimpse occasionally of a long, lithe, tawny brute with a round, catlike head. I didn't need a dictionary to tell me that it was the North American panther, or the Indian Devil. that is the name the Indians give. . . meanwhile the mare made great bursts of speed. the brute was soon beside the wheel, looking up with eager, fiery eyes, then he sprang full at me. I slid to the other side, he landed on the hind wheel and was turned under. He didn't seem to mind the fall, and tried again and again as the wagon bounded over the rough road. I had all I could do to keep the terror stricken mare on the road . . . and all this time I was thinking what must come when the gate was reached. I well knew the mare would keep on over it no matter what became of the wagon and me. . . . Soon I could see the open field through the leafy boughs and tried to nerve myself for the horrible end. I had no weapon. . . . I could hardly believe my own eyes, when the mare dashed through an open gate, straight across the field, and through the big barn doors that were open also. My young brother, upon hearing those frightful yells in the forest, had pluckily acted upon his own impulse to open the gate and doors, and thus saved me."

Painting by Timothy Finnemore

"...the river then became so shallow that we were obliged to haul our canoes half the time upon the bare sand...."
From Thomas Sedgewick Steele's, Paddle and Portage from Moosehead Lake to the Aroostook River, Me., 1882.

Peter Bull's house on the bank of the Aroostook River in Mapleton, photographed in 1965. This was the first frame house in the area and had five fireplaces in its tremendous chimney; three downstairs and two upstairs. When Jackson visited in 1837 he wrote: "...we came to the dwelling of Mr. Peter Bull, who is one of the first settlers on this river, having resided there fifteen years. His first dwelling was an ordinary log hut, but since that time he has erected a handsome house, having a brick chimney, and being well glazed. He informed me that he manufactured his own bricks from the clay found a quarter of a mile below, on the river. His lime, however, was brought from the city of St. John, and cost him $16 per tierce! Very few of the settlers indulge in the luxury of plastered walls and ceilings, on account of the expense of lime. Yet the very rocks under their feet are excellent limestone, but they were not aware of the fact, nor did the people then know anything of the simple process of converting them into lime."
Photo courtesy of Alden Bull

An early settler, Mary Churchill Grant, arrived at an island in the Aroostook River near Crouseville with her husband and little son Job. Mary's husband built a log cabin and gave Mary some fish hooks and an axe then left in his canoe. Her husband had been away for quite some time and Mary was about to give birth to her second child when she saw a canoe coming down the river. Mary hid with her little son and waited to see if the person in the canoe was friendly. While she watched, an Indian woman got out of her canoe and went into the cabin. Night came on cold with dew falling. Mary's labor pains finally prompted her to gather her courage and enter the cabin.

The Indian woman had built a fire and was cooking deer meat on a hot rock. She cut off a piece for little Job who had had very little to eat of late. She then gave Mary juice from the cooking meat and helped her to deliver her baby daughter,

Angeline. The Indian woman wrapped the baby in moss and tied her up in a bark cradle-board. She stayed and cared for Mary for about a week then left in the night. No words were spoken between the women whose language differences prevented it, but no words were really needed. Mary never forget the kind treatment she received.

Her husband eventually returned but he was very ill and finally died. She later married Sam Fox and some of their descendants settled and live today near Washburn. From Mildred Green's All In The Family.
Drawing by Evelyn Kok

Making Camp along the Aroostook River. From Thomas Sedgewick Steele's, Paddle and Portage from Moosehead Lake to the Aroostook River, Me., *1882.*

HEADING FOR THE AROOSTOOK
by Dena Winslow York

Travelers to Early Aroostook

According to recent archaeological discoveries, Native Americans have traveled to and lived in the territory which is now Aroostook County for approximately 12,700 years. French voyageurs, fur trappers and traders, Jesuit priests and hunters arrived next, followed by lumberjacks and surveyors.

In 1804 Charles Turner, Jr., an early surveyor, mapped the townships of Weston and Mars Hill. In 1807 he ran the eastern boundary from Mars Hill north for a distance of eighteen miles. On an early trip Turner went through New Brunswick as most travelers and surveyors did at that time. His job was to survey the boundary lines for Bridgewater Academy Grant. Along the way he had some interesting experiences. His journey entry for September 7, 1802, says:

Travelled on, nineteen miles, to Maductic Falls (so called), passing a considerable stream that comes in from the west, called Pocaock (Pokiok), and put up, in the rain, at Mr. Edmund Tompkins's, where we saw Mr. Tompkins's father, aged 106. He was a tall man, thin-favored, light-complexioned, an agreeable countenance, able to walk out, and to do considerable light labor on the farm; his appetite good and slept well. He, with a number of children, attached themselves to the British Army, when at New York; and although his memory, like other aged persons', had so far failed as that he was not able to tell any particular service he had performed for his king, yet his great consolation, and what he frequently repeated, was that he had been faithful in serving his king.

Two days later, on September 9, Turner went to Major Griffith's, located seventeen miles above Tompkins's residence. He says:

...we were politely entertained, and there was a collection of young folks—nine young ladies and one young widow, and six young gentlemen, who were prepared to spend the evening in dancing, after quilting. The ladies all dressed in white, and all performed their parts in the style and taste of Boston, where, eighteen years ago, Satin's seat was; where the owl and the satyr danced, and no human footstep appeared....

From *Proceedings of the Massachusetts Historical Society.* Vol. 17, 1879-1880, 207-216, reprinted by George Bent in *Acadiensis.* April 1907.

Charles Jackson also made several trips to Aroostook. In 1837 he was employed as a geologist for the states of Maine and Massachusetts when he visited. He states of his mission:

Since it was thought probable at that time that difficulties might perhaps occasion a rupture between the British Provinces and Maine, I was most especially anxious to record the marked topographical features of a country which would necessarily become the theater of action in case of war.

This was not an easy journey. On the way toward the encampment Jackson says:

On entering the forest below, we found ourselves enveloped in total darkness, and it was a most painful task to travel through the woods, stumbling over logs, thrashed in the face by the boughs of trees, or stumbling over rotten logs into a peat bog. The moon, however, soon rose above the horizon, and glimmering through the trees, served to direct our course.

On October 19, after much difficulty with ice, driving snow, and hail storms, Jackson's party reached the Oxbow in the Aroostook river. He comments in his *Geology of The Public Lands:*

...we found that the Indians had there held an encampment, and almost every birch tree had been stripped of its bark to furnish torches, used in spearing salmon.

A little further downriver Jackson began encountering settlers along the river. He talked to them about the extent of their land and the crops they were raising, making notes in his journal. These notes undoubtedly had an influence in helping the states of Maine and Massachusetts decide that Aroostook was worth fighting for.

While he never actually arrived within the boundaries of Aroostook, Sir George Head, (younger brother of Sir Francis Bond Head), governor of Upper Canada from 1835-1837, traveled from Fredericton to Presque Isle (now Centerville) in 1815. Along the way George Head describes incidents which were typical of those experienced by many early travelers into Aroostook as they passed through New Brunswick.

Sir George Head's party left Fredericton at about noon on January 1, 1815. After a difficult drive through deep snow the group arrived at the Upper French village where they passed the night in a single room log cabin. There were only two beds in the cabin. George Head slept in one bed and the man of the house, his wife and four children slept in the other bed. Sir George says in his *Forest Scenes and Incidents in the Wilds of North America,* n.d., that during the night:

The youngest child cried incessantly in spite of all the woman could do to pacify it. Some times the good wife sat up in bed with the little animal hugged between her chin and her elbows, hushing and rocking herself and it; and then she patted its back and it still cried. Then ten times I dare say in the course of the night, out of bed got the poor husband who stood for several minutes at the stove, displaying a pair of lean bare legs, and stirring something in a saucepan with the broken stump of an iron spoon—a picture of obedience and misery! Then he got into bed again. Then came a long conversation and almost a quarrel about what was best to be done. Then at last the other children awoke and the youngest of these began to cry too: the mother said it was the biggest one's fault and beat her. So off she went and we had a loud concert till what with the noise of the children, and the heat, and the dirt and the fleas I felt ready to rush out of doors and roll myself in snow.

At the Old Military Post at the mouth of the Presque Isle, George Head stayed with a Mr. Turner whom he described as:

A tall withered thin man, about sixty years of age, with extremely small legs and thighs, narrow shoulders, long neck, and back as straight as a ram rod. Innumerable short narrow wrinkles which creased each other in every direction covered his face which was brown as a nut; and he had a very small mouth drawn in that pursed up at the corners. His eyes are very little, black, keen and deep set in his head. He hardly ever spoke; and I do not think that while I was in his house I ever saw him smile. He was dressed in an old rusty black coat and trousers both perfectly thread bare and he sat always in one posture and in one place, bolt upright on a hard wooden chair. He seemed to me the picture of a man who from want of interest in the world had fallen into a state of apathy....

There was a small square hole in the center of the door, as there generally is in all Canada stoves, made to open and shut with a slider as occasion required; this he kept open for a purpose of his own, for by long practice he had acquired a knack of spitting through this little hole with such unerring certainty by a particular sort of jerk through his front teeth that he absolutely never missed his mark. This accomplishment was the more useful to him as he was in the habit of profusely chewing tobacco, all the care he seemed to have! And he opened the door of the stove now and then to see how the fire was going on.

After having spent the night with a family whose children had whooping cough and cried incessantly, George Head arrived at the house of a Mr. Long where he spent a miserable night in a room with thirty-six people and six or eight large dogs from a dog team. He says:

...The dogs disturbed us, for they ran about and trod upon us; they growled, and twice before morning there was a battle-royal among them, with the whole room up in arms to part them by throttling and biting the ends of their tails. What with the noise and the shouting and swearing in bad French we were in a perfect uproar. The natural remedy of course would have been to turn the dogs out, but the masters would not allow it as they were of too much use by far on a journey. The gabble of tongues, the smell of tobacco smoke, and the disturbance altogether was really dreadful. There was besides a truckle bed in the room on which two women reposed—the mistress of the house and her sister. These females were not silent; and no matter who slept some where sure to be awake and talking. I quite lost all my patience; sometimes I struck at the dogs as they galloped over me, and I shook one Canadian by the collar, till he roared, who in the company had trodden on my ankles.

In 1817 Col. Joseph Bouchette, Surveyor General of Canada, and John Johnson, surveyor of the United States were appointed under the provisions of the Treaty of Ghent. They were to settle the boundary, a task they attempted to accomplish by surveying what they believed to be the correct boundary.

Two years later, in 1819, John Mann served as part of a survey crew with Surveyor-General William O'Dell from New Brunswick. Mann describes the Aroostook River:

Ascending the river, (which was but shallow,) I never witnessed such abundance of trouts, some of them of great size. The river being low, they gathered in the deepest holes in crowds, so that we could catch as many as we chose. We fixed three hooks, each pointing in a different direction laid them down quietly, and when the fish collected in clusters above them, by pulling the hook quick, we caught very many: some fixed in the head, some in the tail, and in other parts of the body. At first we relished them well, but being so fresh they soon became unpalatable. Meeting with a salmon hole, two of our best spearmen went with their canoes, spears, and torches, and killed thirty-seven in the same hole in one night. We put them in a barrel full of pickle taken off the pork, but it was not sufficient to cure them, and being far from any settlement, we were obliged to throw them into the river.

. . . At every encampment, we found plenty of tall grass on the banks of the river, of which I could, in ten minutes, cut with my knife, as much as would serve the whole company for bedding.

About eighty miles from the mouth of the river, we came to a place where it was divided into two branches. We took the left hand branch, on which we proceeded eight miles farther. The river then became so shallow, that we were obliged to haul our canoes half the time upon the bare sand. Being then ninety-four miles from any house or settlement, and unable to proceed any farther towards the Penobscot, the officers deemed it prudent to return, and take observations on a small mountain which we passed in coming up the river.

One morning being the 17th of August, as we were preparing for dragging our canoes up the stream we were ordered to turn them down the stream which we immediately obeyed, and cheerfully proceeded down the river. When we got down opposite to the mountain, we encamped on the bank of the river; and next day went to its top, which was covered with wood. We commenced working, and cut down about three acres of the wood; which being done, we erected a scaffold of twenty feet high, from which our officer took the necessary observations. Some of us climbed a high spruce tree, from which we had a view as far as the eye could reach, of a desert, excepting one mountain which was situated westward, and naturally bare.

From John Mann's *Travels in North America*. . . .

In 1825 Joseph Norris surveyed the townships in ranges one and two for the state of Maine. In September and October of that same year, Massachusetts Land Agent George W. Coffin was appointed chainman to survey and grant deeds to settlers in Aroostook County along St. John and Madawaska rivers. It was also part of his duty to ascertain the extent of timber which had been cut and to determine who had given permission to cut it.

On his way to Madawaska, George Coffin stopped at Baisley's located about two miles below the Meduxnekeag River. He says in his journal:

This is a most beastly house of entertainment. I had an uncomfortable nights lodging. (I can't say night's rest)

Stores for supplies were one of the first necessities for the early settlers. This store was operating in Blaine in 1895 by Fred and Warren Snow. The great-grandfather, Moses Snow, was one of the first settlers in Mars Hill.
Courtesy of Sandra Barrett Smith Leighton

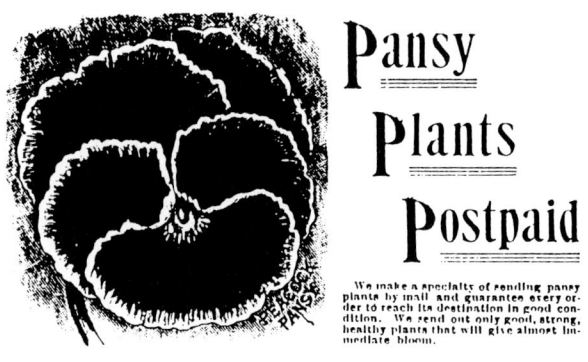

for there was scarcely a whole pane of glass in the windows, and it blowing fresh in the night, a wind mill in my room, might have extended a millers wishes to his hearts content, which together with wood fleas tormenting me, I was glad again to see the light of another day.

25th Sept. Sunday:

I arose this morning in good health, though I cannot say much refreshed. Weather clear, and a fine bracing air. We took saddle horses and rode to Houlton Plantation, about 12 miles, stopped at Esquire Houlton's house—here we found our boatman, they arrived here on Thursday last, we remained at Houlton's this day, found several persons here that had just come through the woods from Penobscot....

Early Settlers in Aroostook

Peter Bull arrived in Aroostook from New Brunswick in May of 1819. He had a land grant from the New Brunswick government for six hundred acres at the mouth of the Presque Isle of the Aroostook which extended to the corners of what is now Mapleton and Chapman. When he and his wife Eunice arrived they built a substantial and roomy log cabin on the bank of the river below the creek, about where the bridge now crosses the Aroostook river on Route 1.

Eunice Bull was one of the first women to come to Aroostook. When she arrived, her husband's clearing was the only one above where the Aroostook bridge in Presque Isle is today. For three months she did not hear another woman's voice. One day an Indian woman came down the river, singing as she paddled her canoe. Eunice later said "That song was the sweetest music I ever heard."

An early newspaper clipping described Eunice Bull as "a woman of rare forethought and energy." At one time, the clipping continues, when her husband was away in the logging camp, a very heavy snowstorm came on. "The most of the hay was in a barn on the island (Bull's Island), while a stronger structure stood upon the main land. With the aid of two small boys and a yoke of oxen, she moved the hay, and as she came up the bank with the last load, the barn on the island crashed in with the weight of the snow."

At the time she came to Aroostook, all trading was done at Woodstock, New Brunswick. There were no stores, no mills, and no post office nearer. Once Eunice had a very narrow escape in the Rips below Aroostook Falls, when going to Woodstock with wool to card and grain to grind, in company with a neighbor. She had a small baby with her, which, as it was near light, she had wrapped in a heavy cloak, which saved its life when the boat upset, for it kept the child from sinking. Eunice Bull was wedged between the boat and rocks in such a way that the waves kept dashing over her, while the force of the current pushed the boat against her so hard that it required the strength of three men to hold it back so that she could be pulled out. She was unconscious when rescued but upon regaining consciousness, her first words were "Where's my baby?" The baby was fine and lived on to a ripe old age. Eunice did reach Woodstock safely, but she had lost everything in the boat and she and the baby were black and blue for days.

Above information adapted from an undated, unidentified clipping, courtesy of Arden Bull.

The Knowlen family of Masardis suffered similar deprivations. The family had run low of provisions in the spring of 1838 and Knowlen along with Eben Bolstridge had set off for Presque Isle, then called Fairbanks, in a boat to obtain supplies. When they left, the men intended to return in three days. Mrs. Knowlen and her four children had only six quarts of corn meal and half a bushel of potatoes in the house along with a cow which gave enough milk for the children. Her husband's thirteen-year-old brother caught fish for the family, and picked fiddleheads. Mrs. Knowlen herself ate only boiled wild chocolate root for three days. Baby Rosewell became seriously ill and Mrs. Knowlen feared her husband had perished when he did not return after ten days. Upon reaching Fairbanks, Knowlen found he could not get the provisions he needed and went on to the Fitzherbert place in Fort Fairfield. There he could also not get provisions and went on to Tobique where he bought one barrel of flour for $22.00, one barrel of salt herring for $19.00, four pounds of tea for $4.00, four gallons of molasses at $1.50 per gallon, and six pounds of tobacco for $1.50 per pound.

On his way down river, Knowlen met a cobbler, a Mr. Cowperthwaite, who had been on a trip down the St. John mending footwear. His trip had been very successful and his boat was loaded with provisions. Knowlen asked him to take provisions to his starving family which Cowperthwaite did, undoubtedly saving baby Rosewell's life.

When Deane and Kavanagh explored the settlements on the Aroostook River in 1831 they told of William Munford from Nova Scotia who had built a house and barn and had cleared seven or eight acres on an island he had purchased from Joshua Christie. In the spring of 1830 the island had overflowed due to jamming ice. Water rose to the eaves of the house and the family was forced to take refuge on the roof all night. In the morning they were rescued by canoes. Unfortunately, Munford's barn was swept away and his cow was lost with it. With the spirit upon which Aroostook has been built, Munford started over on a new location along the river.

As settlement continued to increase, villages began to spring up. As early as 1825 there was a trading post in Blaine which supplied the surrounding territory with edge tools, firearms, clothing, flour, pork, tobacco, and rum.

Just two years later when Charles Jackson visited the area, he called on Dennis Fairbanks in what is now Presque Isle on October 23rd. He says:

We entered the Presque Isle River, and ascended the stream to the farm of Mr. Dennis Fairbanks, who had sent me an invitation to call upon him. His dwelling is a mile and a half up this stream, and he has there established saw and flour mills. On reaching his establishment, we were very cordially received, and our time was spent in explor-

Hugh Jamison was a famous six-horse teamster in his day. Early stage drivers like Hugh were highly respected and stood in a class by themselves. Always having the right of way on the road, their comings and goings were the chief event all along the line of their journey. They were quite a sight to see as they pulled up to a tavern, horses trotting, coach swaying, and dust flying! From a newspaper clipping in Philip Phair's Journal.
Courtesy of the Mark and Emily Turner Memorial Library

A huge load of logs on bobsleds. Courtesy of Dana Cameron and the Ashland Public Library

ing the resources of the country around.

Mr. Fairbanks has dwelt there 9 years, and has brought his estate into a good state of cultivation. He pursues almost every branch of trade required in a new settlement, makes his own agricultural tools, machinery, and even his boots and shoes, showing unusual dexterity in these various occupations.

His mills are three stories high on one side, and two on the other, and the building is handsomely shingled and painted.

In this building is an excellent flour mill, and it is kept in continual operation. A part of the building serves also as a carpenter's shop, where Mr. Fairbanks carries on the work according to his need. He has also a saw mill, and saw boards, which are sent to the boundary line for sale...

When David Hume arrived in Castle Hill in 1860 with his father, he and his brothers helped build their log cabin. At age ninety-one, he recalled: "Those of us who were old enough turned to and helped father build a log cabin. It seems only yesterday that I helped put the shingles on the roof and lay the floor, which was composed of pine boards 18 inches in width. There were three rooms on the first floor and a loft above where we children slept. How soothing it was to go to bed at night with rain beating on the roof, and how cozy it was in winter when we sat before the roaring fireplace with snow drifting against the door!"

From "David E. Hume, 91, Describes Pioneer Life in Aroostook." *Bangor Daily News*, August 24, 1938.

Following is a description of the house of an early settler as it appeared in the *Aroostook Herald* of November 6, 1884:

...It was built of logs, the roof was made of fir trees split in halves and hollowed out with the axe of the woodsman, like a spout. Two of these were pinned to the roof timbers lengthwise, hollow sides up, while the third was then put on upside down over the two, and so on until the roof was complete. The floor was of rough cedar planks, split from the logs, now sawed. The interstices between the logs in the wall were "chinked" with moss and clay, and was rough inside as out, except that inside the bark was peeled from the logs, the fireplace would be a genuine curiosity to the young people nowadays. It was built of rough rocks, and was about six feet wide and four or five feet high, the chimney being built of sticks and mud. There was no trouble about its not drawing, for the flue was large enough to let an ox drop through, if one could get on the trough-like roof. The fireplace would hold something like a quarter of a cord of wood cut in logs four or five feet long. A rock maple back log, two feet in diameter, with a smaller log on top of it, constituted the back of the fire. In winter the occupant hauled his wood on a hand-sled from the woods into the house, and unloaded it on the fire, and when fairly ablaze it was a hot one. Over this fire and before it, the good woman of the house did her cooking, and we have ate at their "cedar-split" table the nicest buckwheat bread, baked in a tin baker before this fire, with

homemade maple syrup instead of butter, and it was good. The buckwheat was ground at Cochran's old grist mill on the caribou stream. This mill stood very nearly where the steam mill stands, in the village of Caribou.

That old log cabin has long since disappeared. The Colonel and his wife are both gone to the other world, but their memory, and the memory of their unique back-woods residence are fresh in mind to-day.

The "Garden of Maine" Begins to Grow

Although Aroostook became a county on March 19, 1839, its northern and eastern borders were not established until the Webster-Ashburton Treaty of 1842.

It was during this time period, and shortly thereafter, in which the growth and development of Aroostook really took off. There were many sorts of folks arriving, including:
"Bluenoses"—Canadian born citizens whose parents were born in the U.S.
"Moosetowners"-Those born in Allagash Plantation.
"Kennebeckers"—Folks arriving from Kennebec County from about 1850 to 1870.
"Canucks" or "Pea-soupers"—Canadians.
"Over-homers"—Peeople with Canadian ancestry who spoke of New Brunswick as "over-home." (These folks are still thriving in Aroostook!)

At first newcomers on their way into Aroostook had come by way of New Brunswick but as crude roads began replacing spotted trails, more and more people headed north. Families already living in Aroostook took in the new folks along their routes. Mary Elizabeth Barker Rogers, an early settler in Island Falls, recalled that the settlers arrived at all times of the day and night and usually stayed with the families having the best accommodations. Her grandparents' house, where she lived, was often full.

Road hotels began to spring up. At the hotels the mother and father of the family took a bedroom with cots and trundle beds provided for the girls and babies. Boys usually slept in a long room above the kitchen called the "ram pasture." Teamsters hauling freight and lumberjacks heading for the woods often slept in the haymows believing any extra comfort was effeminate.

Land in Aroostook was either free or nearly so. A man could buy a farm with his labor on the roads. The lack of available land in southern and central Maine prompted many young families to go north. Along with the early settlers came peddlers and businessmen, ministers, and in 1858 the first editorial excursion, intended to promote the benefits and opportunity in the new land. These were exciting times as Aroostook county began to take on its own unique identity.

Lumbering was one of the most important influences on the developing county. Its influence on the economy was great. Along with lumbering came the growth and development of many communities. Mills were built along most, if not all, waterways. It was said that the trees in Aroostook were so tall that they tore the clouds as they passed over. The cutting of these great trees was first restricted in 1691 when a ban was put on the largest (twenty-four inches and over) and best pines. These trees were marked with the "Broad Arrow" designating them as mast timbers reserved for the British Navy. To get around such restrictions, sawyers carefully turned out boards just an inch or two under the two-foot limit.

Early Aroostook was a land of adventure, of exciting risks, and of uproarious celebrations. It took brave men to break the wilderness and build homes, but it took even braver men to break the log jams in the Aroostook and St. John Rivers.

As important to Aroostook as lumbering, has been farming. Aroostook's richly productive soil earned it the title "Garden of Maine." Orchards thrived in Aroostook and many new varieties were developed such as the Moores Arctic Plumb developed by A. T. Moores of Ashland and the Dudley Winter Apple developed from a Duchess by John W. Dudley of Castle Hill. There was even an Aroostook variety of pansy!

An early method of canning was used to preserve fresh fruits and berries. The fruit was put into crocks and a cloth was tied around the top. The cover was then put on the crock. A layer of mold developed on top and preserved the fruit below. When fruit was wanted, the layer of mold was carefully lifted, revealing the luscious fruit below. After removing the desired amount of fruit, the layer of mold was carefully replaced. Fruit preserved in this manner was said to be as good as if it had been freshly picked.

Food in early Aroostook involved mostly what could be grown in gardens and gathered in the surrounding countryside. The early beginning of spring heralded the maple-sugaring season as it does in much of New England today. When Charles Jackson visited Aroostook in 1837 he commented:

The manufacture of maple sugar is here carried on to a great extent, during the spring season. The process is as follows: Holes being bored into the trees with an auger, a piece of wood is inserted, in which a grove is cut, in order to conduct the sap into receiving vessels, which are made of birch bark, and are called by French name casseroles. Three men can manage 1,000 maple trees, and boil down the sap as it is collected. The sugar season begins about the middle of March, and continues to the middle of May. Three men usually obtain from 1,500 to 2,000 pounds of sugar during the season, and it sells from 10 to 20 cents per pound.

Twenty quarts of sap yield one pound of sugar, at the first tapping of the trees; on the second the same quantity of sap yields one and a half, and on the third two pounds are obtained. The chief obstacle to this manufacture is the want of good evaporating kettles, common iron pots being generally used. If large tinned copper boilers could be obtained, the business could be carried on in a more rapid and profitable manner, while the sugar would be of a much better quality. If good utensils were used in its manufacture, and more skill employed in clarifying the syrup, I

Farming was originally accomplished with horse-drawn plows like this one owned by Francis Winslow of Mapleton. It is pictured in Francis' hop drying house. Hops were raised prior to the turn of the century and provided income for many farmers.
Photograph by Dena Winslow York

Benjamin Wesley Knowles and his wife Caroline Rich Knowles are shown in their orchard near the Aroostook River in Presque Isle circa 1902-1903.
Courtesy of Levi Knowles

Potato farming on the James K. Blackstone farm in Perham about 1900. Notice the unusual two-man potato baskets. Those pictured are _____ Percy, Arthur Blackstone (kneeling), Mark Randall (by digger), Fred Blackstone (on digger), and James Blackstone.
Courtesy of Salmon Brook Historical Society, Washburn

have no doubt that excellent white sugar might be made at a much lower cost than the inhabitants now pay for the foreign article.

No sooner was maple sugaring finished and the plants beginning to bud than it was time to gather fiddleheads and dandelions. Fiddleheads, a delicacy still enjoyed in this area, were originally eaten by Native Americans who showed early settlers how to prepare them. They are the early sprouts of the ostrich-feather fern which grows wild in northern Maine and the Maritime Provinces. Their name is derived from the curled ends of the budding ferns which look like the curled ends of violins. A spring delight to Aroostook natives, fiddleheads are served steaming hot with a lump of butter melting over them and a little squirt of vinegar for added flavor. A good soup is also made from the greens.

Summer's heat brought the need for thirst quenching drinks, and *switchel,* made with molasses and ginger, was one popular drink. Another popular drink was *shrub* made with the wild berries which grow abundantly in Aroostook. Shrub was made by soaking four quarts of berries (usually raspberries) in one quart of vinegar in a covered container for three or four days. The berries were then strained through cheesecloth with all juice squeezed from them. To each cup of juice was added one cup of sugar and the mixture was boiled for about twenty minutes, then poured into preserving jars. This concentrated juice was prepared for drinking by mixing one tablespoon with one-half cup of cold water.

In the fall buckwheat was harvested and made into flour. In the northern sections of Aroostook, among the citizens of Acadian ancestry, ployes were made. These were

Barns have always been a farmer's pride in Aroostook. Members of the editorial excursion of 1878 said of Aroostook barns: "...a farmer, while he is getting his land into cultivation, doesn't care much in what sort of building he lives, but he must have big and well built barns ...(which) he puts his name (on) in big letters." The barn pictured here was owned by G. Howard Nichols of Limestone. It became a tourist attraction with a fee of twenty-five cents for admission and a tour, and he also sold postcards, and had a lunch room for visitors. It stood seven stories high in the main structure, which sprawled over 60 by 120 feet of hilltop, with an ell 44 by 60 feet, and a woodshed 10 by 76 feet. The structure, painted gray, had a bigger-than-life copper cow weathervane, covered with gold leaf that could be seen from miles away. The roof over the horse barn had a six-foot model of a horse, also decorated with gold leaf. There were over two hundred windows, including three stained glass windows, and a sign reading: G. Howard Nichols—Farm of Quality. Howard had dreamed of this barn since he was seven years old, when his folks had moved over the border from New Brunswick. He had been given a hoe and put to work. He never got to school to learn to read or write, however he did learn farming and how to make it pay. In March of 1924, just two years after it was finished tragedy struck, and Howard's barn burned to the ground. He had a smaller one rebuilt, about half the size of the first, but it also burned. *Courtesy of Blanche Beckwith*

Francis Winslow and his wife Angeline arrived in Aroostook in 1858, settling on Creasy Ridge in Mapleton. Among the earliest to farm commercially, Francis' name appeared on an 1874 document committing him to raise potatoes for a starch factory, the first in Aroostook, to be built in Presque Isle the following year. Beside potatoes, Francis raised hops commercially during the late 1800s and sold milk from his dairy herd to the cheese factory in Presque Isle, located on the corner of Park and Main streets. On June 28, 1887, Francis noted in his journal that he "commenced carrying milk to the cheese factory," thus beginning a legacy of dairy farming which continues today.

A man of many talents, Francis was active in the local Grange serving as first Master. He was a school teacher in Maysville—now North Presque Isle, walking a presently non-existent trail from Mapleton to Caribou each day. At the time of his death in 1897 he was chairman of the town board of selectmen.

Today, Francis and Angeline's descendants still live and farm the land they claimed from the wilderness of Aroostook. This photograph of Francis's grandson, Alvin, standing in front of a wagon load of oats, was taken on the farm in 1920. *Courtesy of Flora Angeline Winslow, Francis' granddaughter*

very thin, stick-to-the-ribs pancakes served with all meals in place of bread. They were sometimes served with creton, a spiced meat dish, wrapped inside them. More frequently they were rolled and eaten with the meal, a delicious treat still much relished in Aroostook county!

A winter staple was fried salt pork and potatoes.

The following poem from *Sprague's Journal of Maine History*, vol. 1, September 1913, says much about the character of Aroostook:

Where Aroostook Begins

A director traveling north over the Bangor & Aroostook Railroad was queried recently by a passenger as to where "Aroostook begins," and being unable to answer himself, asked another passenger, a girl living in this hospitable region, perhaps the most perfect combination of scenery and fertility of any county in the United States, says the Boston News Bureau. She wrote on a slip of paper and passed over to him:

Up where the handclasp's a little stronger,
Up where the smile dwells a little longer,
   That's where Aroostook begins.
Up where the sun is a little brighter,
Where the snows that fall are a trifle whiter,
Where the bonds of home are a wee bit tighter—
   That's where Aroostook begins.
Up where the skies are a trifle bluer,
Up where friendship's a little truer,
   That's where Aroostook begins.
Up where a fresher breeze is blowing,
Where there's laughter in every streamlet flowing,
Where there's lots of reaping and lots of sowing,
   That's where Aroostook begins.
Up where the world is in the making,
Where things are new—ideals are shaping—
   That's where Aroostook begins.
Where there's more of singing and less of sighing,
Where there's lots of giving and lots of buying,
And a man makes friends without half trying—
   That's Where Aroostook begins!

These horses walk a treadmill to supply "horse" power to a mill operation in the Ashland area during the mid-1800s.
Courtesy of Dana Cameron and the Ashland Public Library

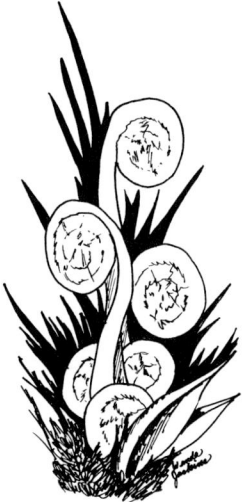

Fiddlehead ferns.
Drawing by Wanda Boyd Jackins

The women of early Aroostook engaged in many of the same activities as their counterparts in other areas. They cooked, raised children, made soap, helped on the farm, and made clothing from wool they had spun and woven into cloth. Their foods were preserved by drying, freezing (in winter and in ice during the summer), smoking, salting, and pickling. In this photograph, Nellie Winslow, standing in front of her Mapleton home, shows off the butter with which she had won first prize at the Northern Maine Fair in Presque Isle.
Courtesy of Bert Winslow

From the earliest settlement of Aroostook, ice from the rivers has been a valuable commodity. The ice was cut when it was fourteen to sixteen-inches thick, in various sized cakes, each cutter having his own idea of what size kept best. After it was cut, the ice was hauled to ice houses where sawdust prevented it from melting. A layer of snow between the cakes prevented the ice from freezing together. In this picture, ice is being separated after cutting. It will next be floated to the conveyors and removed from the river.
Courtesy of Mrs. Joe Gagnon

As Aroostook continued to develop, bridges were built and roads were improved. This covered bridge crossed the Aroostook River in Presque Isle. In the early 1920s the bridge was closed to traffic due to the threat of ice taking it out. Men stationed on the bridge prodded the ice down, thus saving it. This bridge was the second covered bridge on the site. The first bridge was built in 1858. It was nearly four hundred feet long and cost six thousand dollars. The state appropriated three thousand dollars toward its construction and the balance was raised by individual subscriptions. The original bridge was washed away in the spring freshet of 1885 and replaced by the bridge pictured here at a cost of about ten thousand dollars.
Photo by Levi Knowles

Visit to a maple sugar camp in Aroostook. The sap in the maple tree starts to run when the days are warm, but the nights still cold, around the middle of March. After the sap is collected in buckets through spigots driven into the tree, it is boiled down to a syrup, and often dropped into snow for a delicious candy.
Courtesy of ACHS (Aroostook County Historical Center at the Library, UM-Presque Isle)

Early homes in the Allagash and Houlton had a grindstone, as the axe had to serve many purposes and needed a constant edge.
Courtesy of Shirlee Connors-carlson

Willard Jalbert, Allagash guide in the early twentieth century, is shown standing on his head in his canoe as it comes through the rapids on Allagash River.
Courtesy of Shirlee Connors-carlson

Shown here is Cunliffe's Depot, which was one of the brisk places of employment in early times and is typical of woods camps at the time of early settlement. Woods camps were self contained because of their own isolation. Courtesy of Shirlee Connors-carlson

A POCKETFUL OF IRISH SETTLEMENT IN THE WOODS

by Shirlee Connors-carlson

The Irish settlement came about in 1837 according to early records and accounts. Letters written by the first women of the woods settlement tell us that the winters were harsh, travel was by way of the river and early education was at home. Quilts, clothing, shoes, soap, tablecloths, and the needed items for maintaining a home were all done within the household. Water baptisms were held once a year by immersion in the river with the traveling priest baptising Catholic and Protestant alike. The traveling priest recorded births and deaths and left accurate accounts of these events.

From the years 1837 to 1839, John Henderson and Sarah Diamond, John Gardner and Annie Diamond, George Moir and Lucinda Diamond, William Mullins and Elizabeth Diamond, all left Campbelton and came down Green River, put in at the St. John and poled their belongings and children, who were small at the time, upstream to the sites where they had obtained land grants in what is now Allagash Settlement. At that time, lumbering was coming into its own in the north as the pine had run out in the lower portion of the state.

The Walkers, Kellys, Connors, Jacksons, Hughes, and McBraeirtys came a short time later and married into the Diamond line. These families still make up the present-day bulk of the population of the community. Work was provided by woods camps on the St. John River, the Allagash River and the Little Black. The women managed domestic life through the winters, and in the spring when the men came home with the drive, they farmed to provide for the next winter. Life continued in this cyclical way until the present day. By necessity the early settlers were also tailors, cobblers, harness makers, carpenters, farmers, and laborers. Exchange of labor made it possible to survive those early years.

The squatting at Nigger Brook [sic] each summer saw the return of the Indian tribe who were helpful in those early times with medicinal remedies and the utilizing of any and all products provided by nature.

Early homes were built of logs with attached wood shed, barn, or harness shop, with hen houses and pig pens at the outer end. This enabled them to carry on the business of living within closed walls. Life centered around community matters and schooling along with church life in the summer. Food supplies often ran out and required that neighbors fill in from their own diminishing stock in the root cellar. The way of life was such that travelers were always fed and in some winters travel was more brisk than expected. The feather beds were puffed up, clean bedding put on them, and travelers headed for the upper river would be put up overnight.

Flo Henderson, who is now eighty-six, recalls a canoe coming down river one late afternoon. Two Indians disembarked and walked up the path to her home. Being a small child she was interested in the strangers. She recalls

Lillian McBraeirty is shown here on a melting day in spring talking with someone about the tone of this guitar, a common household item, ever-present, hanging on the wall.

that as they came up onto the porch, they exchanged courtesies with her father, stood their rifles on the porch by the door, and came in for the evening meal.

The names of the fifth generation residents gives the immediate clue that one is among the Irish, and when they engage the locals in conversation, it becomes obvious that these are people who have kept their dialect intact with a broad tongue and slow delivery. Storytelling from a generation now gone by tells a present-day traveler that these people have kept their ties to their past. Their music is laced with folk tales of early times and the perils of life on the river. Surrounded by Franco-Americans on the length of the St. John, from St. Francis, Maine to the Grand Falls, the Allagash settlement has not gone through the assimilation that came to the rest of the Valley. By their geographic isolation they have remained a Scotch-Irish community. The school system is not incorporated into a school administrative district. It has its own system and is funded as such by the State of Maine.

Within the entire St. John Valley, the Allagash settlement carries with it a mystique of its own, owing to the continuity of life from one generation to the next.

Allagash is situated at the northern end of the County. Large in land mass, it has always flourished around a forest economy. At the southern section of the County, Houlton, Maine, is also a town that was settled by the sons of Erin.

Many of the early settlers were from New Brunswick, most of Irish extraction and many direct from the Emerald Isle. These rugged men and their women were attracted to the small struggling settlement for the same reasons that launched them across the sea.

Here they found fine productive soil and large stands of timber. The early names in Houlton, according to W. J. Thibodeau, in his book *The Irishman...a Factor in the Development of Houlton,* tells us that the early settlers stayed at an Indian camp on the north side of the Meduxnedeag Stream, and that Mullen made the chopping for Cook's clearing on what is now known as Cook's Brook.

A stream of Irishmen came to the Houlton area, they are recognized as having made a sizeable contribution to the growth and economy of Houlton. The lineage of the early Irish to Houlton can be found in W. J. Thibodeau's book, mentioned above. Houlton's story is rich in the King's Arrow, the broad axe, and timber and sawmills, which stand tall in the structure and the growth of the community.

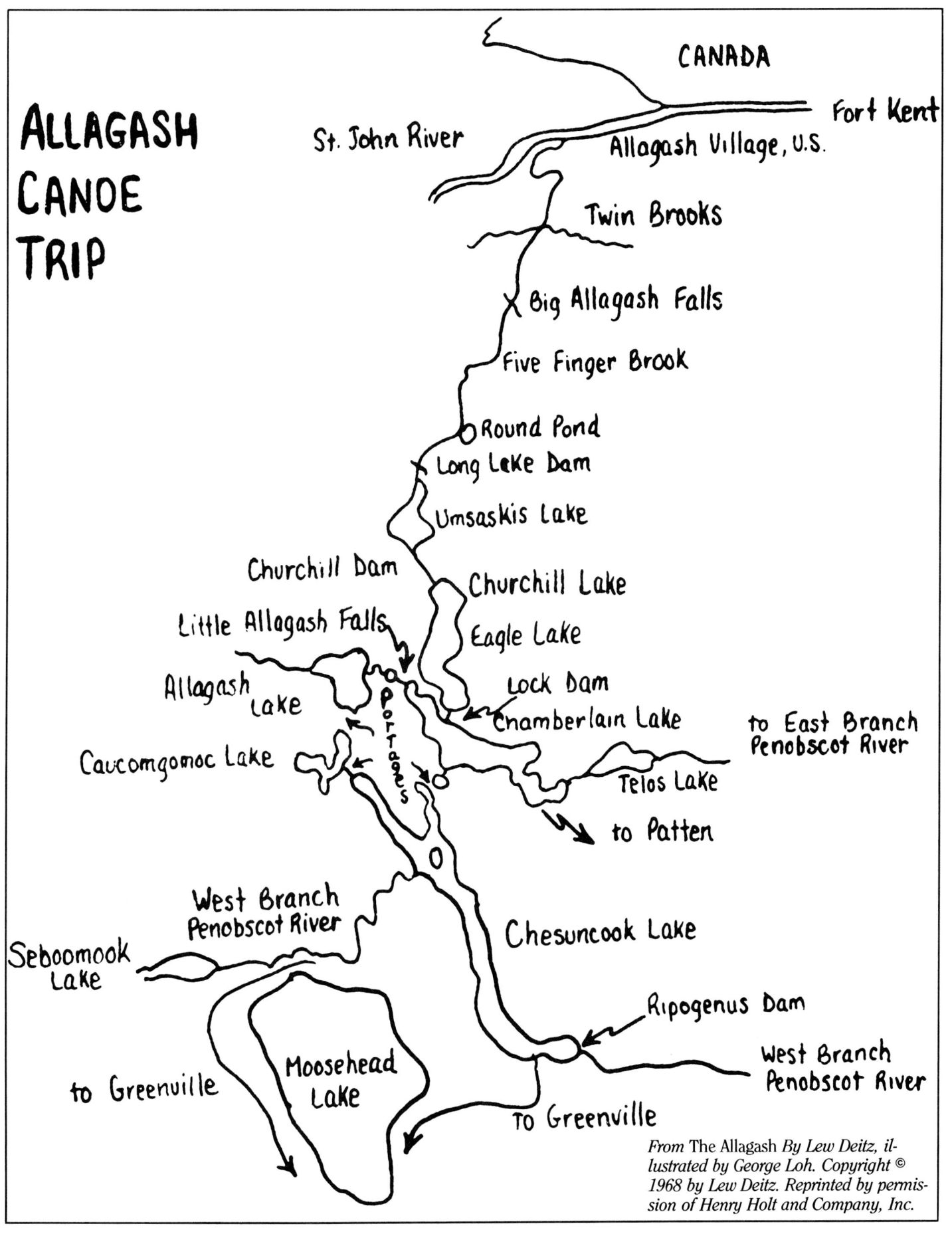

From The Allagash *By Lew Deitz, illustrated by George Loh. Copyright © 1968 by Lew Deitz. Reprinted by permission of Henry Holt and Company, Inc.*

This blockhouse was built at Fort Kent in the summer of 1839, after the Bloodless Aroostook War to maintain the peace on the border until a treaty could be established.
Courtesy of the ACHC

Jonathan Mitchell Map of 1755

When designating the eastern boundary limits at the Treaty of Paris negotiations in 1783, the British and American commissioners relied heavily on this map. Although they may seem to be shown on the map, the "northwest angle of Nova Scotia," the "River St. Croix," and the "Highlands," the three important landmarks, were all completely unknown to the commissioners. While conducting research in Paris in early 1842, Jared Sparks, a Harvard history professor, found the famous "red line" map attributed to Benjamin Franklin, an American commissioner. It was a Mitchell map that had a red line drawn from the Amity area across through the Jackman region, which would have given Britain claim to all waters flowing into the St. John. The map was shown to Webster and Governor Fairfield before the Webster-Ashburton negotiations began, and it made an impression on the U.S. Senate when it ratified the treaty. Another Mitchell map had been red-lined by Richard Oswald, a British delegate, that showed the boundary to be almost exactly as Maine maintained, but this map was kept in secret by the British until after the treaty had been signed. From Henry S. Burrage's Maine in the Northeastern Boundary Controversy.

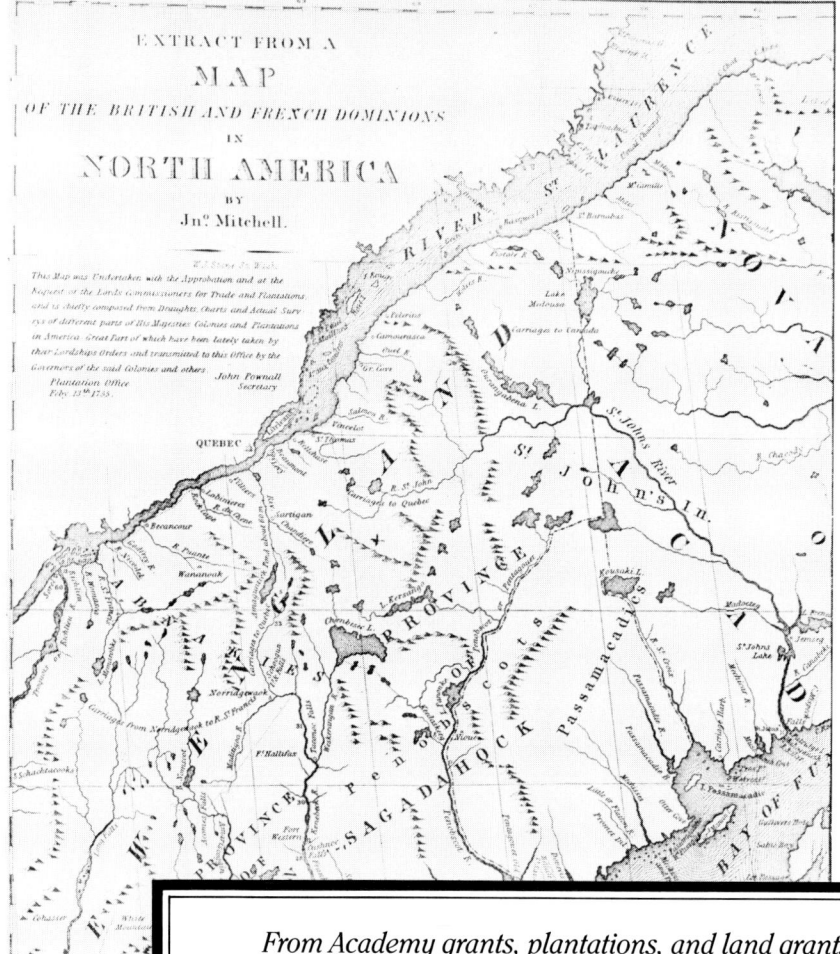

From Academy grants, plantations, and land grants, land earned with labor on state roads, homesteaders farmed, built lumber and gristmills, businesses grew, banks were formed, and political and governmental needs declared the need for a county seat up in the wilderness, and so Aroostook County was born, March 16, 1839.

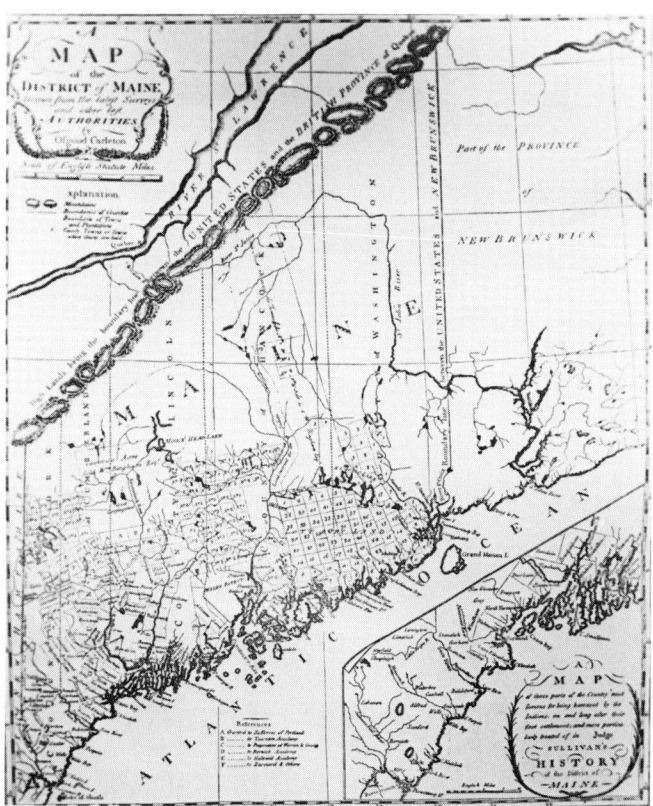

Osgood Carleton Map

This map shows the 1798 American claim that the Magaguadavic River, east of St. Andrews, was the St. Croix and that the Highlands were located close to the St. Lawrence River. Please note the rapid laying out of townships west of the Schoodic River. The British claimed that the western branch of the Schoodic was the St. Croix, which would have put the most northern twelve townships on British soil. This whole area was purchased by William Bingham and Alexander Baring. From Burrage.

AROOSTOOK BECOMES A COUNTY
by Jere W. Green

After many years of disputed claims, national and state neglect, and an unknown border, Aroostook was born amid danger of another war between Great Britain and the United States. Its birth, however, ended any further war between the two countries and inspired the creation of the boundary between the United States and Canada. Under constant harassment by New Brunswick authorities, the people showed again the patriotic zeal of those at Lexington and Concord and forecast the independent frontier spirit of the western pioneer.

The stage was set in 1783 when the Treaty of Paris was signed, ending the Revolutionary War. It stated that the eastern boundary was to be: "From the northwest angle of Nova Scotia, viz.: that angle which is formed by a line drawn due north from the source of Saint Croix River to the Highlands; along the said Highlands which divide those rivers that empty themselves into the river Saint Lawrence, from those which fall into the Atlantic Ocean, to the northwesternmost head of the Connecticut river." This was simple, direct wording, but the signers had no idea of the difficulties those words would cause. At least three rivers had been named the Saint Croix on maps and documents, the northwest angle of Nova Scotia was unknown, and the location of the "Highlands" was to become the big problem.

There were incidents and clashes during the next few years as tensions developed. The territory west of the St. John River became the Province of New Brunswick, Great Britain, in 1784, and the authorities had made some land grants west of the Schoodic River. The Loyalists (Americans who fought for the British during the Revolutionary War) had been forced out of Castine and settled at St. Andrews, which would become American territory if the eastern Magaguadavic River became the true St. Croix.

President Washington appointed John Jay to meet with Lord Grenville to settle differences that had arisen between the two countries since the signing of the Treaty of Paris. Article V of the Jay Treaty of 1794 specified that a commission be established to determine "what river is the river St. Croix, intended by the treaty."

The required three commissioners were appointed, and the St. Croix Commission began work at St. Andrews on October 4, 1796, and ordered exploration and mapping of the Passamaquoddy area. Nothing of importance was discovered, so the August 1797 meeting accomplished nothing. Ward Chipman, the British agent, suggested that Samuel Champlain's maps, concerned with the St. Croix island where the Sieur De Monts expedition had spent the terrible winter of 1604-1605, be sent for in England. The maps were sent to Robert Pagan of St. Andrews who found that Dochet Island in the Schoodic River checked out. Bases of buildings and many relics were found there. This convinced the commission that the Schoodic was the true

St. Croix. Their final decision, in the fall of 1798, was that the northernmost source of the Chiputneticook Lakes was the boundary line. The surveyors, Samuel Titcomb and John Harris, drove a stake by a big yellow birch tree and placed an iron hoop around it with their initials and the date. The southeastern corner of what would become Aroostook County had now been formed.

The War of 1812 stopped any further action. During the war, the British took Eastport, Castine, and Bangor and set up a provincial government over the area between the Penobscot and the St. Croix. They discovered that they needed a direct northern route between Quebec and Halifax, and during the Treaty of Ghent negotiations at war's end, the British tried, without success, to get a boundary change made.

Article V of the Treaty specified that two commissioners be appointed to complete the boundary as designated in the Treaty of Paris. Col. Thomas Barclay, who had served on the St. Croix Commission, was appointed by George III and Cornelius P. Van Ness by President Madison. Chipman was again chosen as the British agent. They met at St. Andrews on August 22, 1816, to approve surveyors and assistants from both countries.

The surveyors traced directly north from the birch tree marking the boundary to a ridge called Sugar Mountain, which they agreed was the point where the Highlands separated the rivers.

When the commissioners met in May 1818, Barclay and Chipman were extremely upset with the surveyor's findings. Sugar Mountain was far enough north to cut off direct access to Nova Scotia. They suggested that the surveyors pay more attention to a survey beginning at the Highlands closest to the St. Croix, a place that they called "that tract of country lying in the neighborhood of the river Restook (Aroostook) and Des Chutes (De Chute) and extending thence toward the sources of the River Chaudiere and Kennebec." Col. Joseph Bouchette, the British surveyor, was fired although he was surveyor-general of Quebec. It was as if he had committed a treasonable act by agreeing to survey results which were not in the political interests of his country.

The next meeting, on May 5, 1819, produced controversy over the surveys. Several more meetings were held between 1819 and 1821, and arguments became more heated as time went on. Each side held firm, the British for the line below the St. John River and the Americans for the line above it. Seeing the hopelessness of any agreement, the commission adjourned and filed their report in April 1822. Maine had become a state on March 15, 1820, and Gov. William King, in his first message to the new legislature, demanded that all of Maine's resources be brought to bear to ensure a just settlement. This reflection of the passionate interest of Maine citizens must have been a strong factor in the impasse reached by the commission.

Settlement by Americans in the disputed area increased rapidly as people learned of the rich soil and valuable timber. Massachusetts made grants to the town of Plymouth and to General Eaton in the Aroostook River area and along the boundary line. A deed granted to John Baker by Massachusetts and Maine land agents on October 3, 1825, read that it was to a lot of land "of a plantation called and known by the name of Madawaska, in the County of Penobscot and State of Maine." Another deed was granted to James Bacon just below Baker's, and others soon settled nearby.

Baker had a farm, sawmill, gristmill, and a store, so his place became a center of American activities and he became their leader. They held patriotic gatherings and had parties which were very annoying to the New Brunswickers.

George Morehouse, a New Brunswick, Canada, magistrate from Tobique, spent most of his time harassing the Americans. He issued warrants for small claims against the Aroostook River and Madawaska settlers which were sometimes resisted by force.

Things came to a head during 1827. New Brunswick imposed an illegal "alien tax" upon the Americans in the disputed area. During the spring, Morehouse tried to prevent them from working their fields, posted notices on the Eaton Grant and elsewhere that they were trespassing on Crown land, and marked their cut timber for seizure. The Americans celebrated the Fourth of July by flying, from their "liberty pole" at Baker's place, a white flag which had an eagle encircled by red stars drawn upon it. Morehouse demanded that the flagpole be taken down, but they refused, so he had summonses sent out for them all to appear at court in Fredericton, New Brunswick. This summons was too much for the Americans to take. They banded together, drew up and signed a compact by which they agreed to settle all disputes among themselves with referees, that they would not accept British authority, and that they would support each other by abiding by the referees' judgment. This was to remain in effect for one year while application was made to the government for regular authority. This civil disobedience toward the world's greatest foreign power by a handful of independent pioneers, neglected by their state and nation, was a remarkable happening in Maine and United States history. It was the match that lit a powder fuse under the feet of politicians that led to dynamite marked WAR.

Morehouse learned of the paper signed by the Americans and demanded it be given to him, but they refused. Baker and Bacon journeyed to Portland to see Governor Lincoln to request that their case be presented to the legislature. Morehouse got a subpoena and had an armed force drag Baker from his bed on the morning of September 25 and take him to jail in Fredericton charged with conspiracy.

Governor Lincoln, after learning of Baker's arrest, issued a proclamation that blasted the New Brunswick authorities for the arrest of Baker and called for restraint so that "the sacred and inestimable rights of American citizens may not be embarrassed by any unauthorized acts." Baker was released on bail by the January court term to appear for trial before the Supreme Court on May 8, 1828. He defended himself against the attorney general, was found guilty, sentenced to two months in jail and fined

St. Croix Monument

This boundary monument was erected to mark the northernmost source of the St. Croix River, as was determined by the St. Croix Commission in 1798. Courtesy of the International Boundary Commission

John Baker's Flag

Baker's flag should have its place in history with other American and Maine patriotic flags. It was the symbol that began Maine's serious and continued pressure for land rights.

George Morehouse, testifying before the New Brunswick Supreme Court at Baker's trial for conspiracy for flying the flag, said, "I observed a flag hoisted—a white flag with an American eagle and a semicircle of stars, red. I pointed to the flag and asked Baker what it was. He said, 'the American flag, Mr. Morehouse; did you never see it before, if not, you can see it now.' I asked him who planted it there; he said, 'he and the other Americans there.' I requested him in His Majesty's name to pull it down. He replied, 'no, I will not; we have placed it there, and we are determined we will support it, and nothing but a superior force to ourselves shall take it down; we are on American territory; Great Britain has no jurisdiction here; what we are doing we will be supported in; we have a right to be protected and will be protected, in what we are doing, by our Government.'" From State Papers, Second Session, Twentieth Congress, 1828-1829, Document No. 90.

Drawing by Evelyn Kok

twenty-five English pounds, but he did not serve the jail term.

Tensions started to run high. The 1828 Maine State Legislature passed strong resolves that called the situation a crisis and they looked to the United States government "for defense and protection against foreign agression," and that "if new agressions shall be made by the government of the Province of New-Brunswick upon the territory of this State, and upon its citizens, and seasonable protection shall not be given by the United States, the Governor be, and he hereby is requested to use all proper and constitutional means in his power, to protect and defend the citizens aforesaid in the enjoyment of their rights."

This "frontier" area now had the attention of Washington where it had been politics as usual since the 1822 impasse on the boundary question. Each Maine governor had raised the question of the boundary settlement. Governor Paris, in 1825, had pointed out "that depradations, to a very considerable extent, have been committed on our timber lands, lying on the Aroostook and Mawascah and other streams... by British Subjects." The Maine and Massachusetts Congressional delegations included outstanding men, but the government was unmoved. Now it turned to Article V of the Treaty of Ghent which called for impartial arbitration of the boundary claims by a foreign sovereign. President Adams, in his annual message to Congress, December 2, 1828, announced that by agreement with the British the king of the Netherlands had been chosen as the umpire.

George Fields' Affidavit

The following affidavit by George Fields, dated December 31, 1827, taken from the Historical Society of Piscataquis County, *Collections*, volume 1, page 420, shows the extreme harassment undergone by the Maine settlers through the constant efforts of George Morehouse and other New Brunswick officials. It also shows the law-abiding nature and tenacious spirit of these pioneers. Morehouse was especially heavy-handed during 1827, because of the John Baker affair and general opposition of the American settlers:

I, George Fields, fifty years of age, now of Houlton, was born in Pensacola, where I lost my father. My mother married again and moved with me into New Brunswick. I continued there excepting two or three years in Canada until about four years ago. I then went to the Territory of the United States. William Piles, an American, went on the same year with me. I found there the two Johnson's, Lewis and Charles, and a man by the name of William McCrea. I settled about twelve miles up the stream, about nine miles above the line. The first year, a Deputy Surveyor General by the name of West came up from Prince William, and seized all my timber on the Aroostook, and made me pay a duty of two shillings a ton. The next year James Sisson of Tobique Settlement got a license to cut timber, and I with a number of others cut under him and other people who had obtained licenses—and from whom we obtained our supplies. Afterwards we worked for ourselves. Last March, George Morehouse Esq. came to the settlement with John Davidson to mark timber to be seized and forbid the people from working or occupying any further. I was then preparing to come away.

Two years ago I was arrested by Daniel Craig, a Deputy Sheriff of New Brunswick for a debt of 65, on the suit of William Hallet, and carried down the river almost to the St. Johns, a mile and a half below the lines—where I met one of my sons who gave bail for me—and I returned home—and afterwards settled the debt by letting Hallet have a farm belonging to me on the St. Johns, a few miles below the Aroostook of which I had a grant from the government of New Brunswick.

Early last March I was sued by Patrick Connelly before Justice Morehouse for three days work which was to be paid in work by me. The writ was served by Stephen McNeal, a constable. A yoke of oxen were also taken by the constable at the same time out of my shed on a warrant for a debt of three pounds against my son and driven on to the river and he returned and told me. I agreed to settle both demands and give my note for the amount, and promised to pay the costs to the justice. I went down the next day to pay the costs which I did and complained of being sued and came home again. I thought the note was written payable in three months, which Connelly and I agreed upon.

On a week after my return, the constable came with a writ from Esq. Morehouse on the same note, and took my body—about sunrise as I was going to the mills—and as I could not get bail, carried me before the justice, who directed me to attend the next Friday—and released me on my promise to do so. On the Friday appointed I attended to stand trial because I considered it was in the States and they had no right to sue me there, and so told Mr. Morehouse and talked hard to him about it. He said it was a cage of unclean birds and he did not pity me. I ought not to have gone there—that I knew it was considered to the States when I went there, and that William Piles and I (who are brothers-in-law) did it to get into the American government. Also, he said that I spoke disrespectfully of the government, and that if he had not known me from a boy he would have sent me to Fredericton. I told him he could not send me there—He said he could tie me neck and heels and send me there.

The next day the constable came up with the execution and seized a yoke of oxen, five hogs, a couple of two year old bulls and my cow. He got to my house before I returned from Tobique—I met him about three miles below driving them down—they were carried to Tobique and sold, but for not enough to pay debt and costs, as I found afterwards. How much it was I did not stop to ask and never knew. My son bought the cow at the sale and brought her back to me—I was afraid they would take me next. I then set out with my family to come away, and was on my way on the river with my wife and five children under ten years of age and the cow. Nearly opposite Mr. Morehouse's I met the constable with a fresh execution for the balance of the costs, upon which he took the cow again. My wife cried and advised me to give the money we had, which was twenty shillings, to redeem the cow. Mr. McNeal said he would take it and pay the rest himself—Mr. McNeal was very civil to us and let me go.

All the property I have is some household furniture which I brought from Aroostook, with about 10. I owed some debts upon the river. I had a horse that had gone to pay an honest debt. My sons are on the St. Johns—they are used to the river and do not like to leave it. I am afraid of returning to my sons on account of my creditors—I should have come away, if I had not owed a dollar. I left the Aroostook because they would not let me live there in peace. They took everything away as fast as I got it. I have a very large family and not very good health, and if I got a little timber or anything to procure supplies they would seize it. . . . I now live in Houlton.

his
George X Fields
mark

From: *Collections*. Historical Society of Piscataquis County, page 420.

Agents of the two governments made their presentations to the king on January 10, 1829, and the king announced his decision exactly two years later. He had decided that the boundary line ran along the St. John to the St. Francis, then northwest to a ridge, and then southward along the height of land. Maine had gotten the larger and better part of territory and Great Britain had gotten the line of communication that it wanted. Great Britain approved the decision, but it was not ratified by the United States Senate, mainly because of Maine's violent opposition. The 1831 Maine State legislature met in secret session and passed strong resolves against acceptance which were sent to the president, all Congressional members, and all governors. One resolve stated that "No decision made by any umpire under any circumstances, if the decision dismembers a state, has or can have any constitutional force or obligation upon the State thus dismembered unless the State adopt and sanction that decision." The same session passed an act to incorporate the town of Madawaska, including area below the St. John and the disputed territory north of the river. Houlton, organized as a plantation on April 21, 1826, was now incorporated as a town. Maine had become very interested in what was happening in the northern area.

U.S. Army troops had been assigned to Houlton in 1828 and constructed the Hancock Barracks on Garrison Hill. They then worked on the building of Military Road. An excellent road for that time, it connected Houlton with Mattanawcook (Lincoln) where a state road led to Bangor.

Map of Northern & Eastern Part of Maine

This map, from Hale's map of New England, shows the two ranges of townships surveyed west of the boundary line for Washington County, and a line of dashes that depict the boundary claimed by Maine. Showing how little was known about the northern area as late as the 1820s, note the large mountainous area shown between the Aroostook and Allagash. The Alexander Baring township, now the Alexander and Baring townships west of Calais, was part of Lord Ashburton's million-acre tract. From Burrage.

Dashiell's Map of 1830

This map shows the American boundary claim nearly to the St. Lawrence River, the British claim of a line west from Mars Hill, and the king of the Netherlands' line going up the St. Francis River. The lines descend along the Highlands to the northernmost head of the Connecticut River in New Hampshire. The present shape of Aroostook, decided by the Webster-Ashburton Treaty of 1842, is 893 square miles less than that allotted by the king, but Webster got the Hall's Stream decision, which gave New Hampshire one hundred and fifty square miles. Webster also acquired Rousse's Point on Lake Champlain, which was of more military value than the high ground northwest of the St. John River, and also, unknowingly, 6,500 square miles of the extremely valuable Vermilion and Mesabi iron ore regions of Minnesota. From Burrage.

Hancock Barracks

Built during 1828 and 1829, Hancock Barracks was advantageously located on Garrison Hill just east of Houlton and about one and one-half miles from the border. It was built and first occupied by four companies of the Second Regiment, U.S. Infantry that also helped to build the Military Road. They were relieved by artillery in 1838 which remained until 1845. As U.S. troops, they were under orders not to participate in the Aroostook War unless attacked. Esther Orr Faulkner created this remarkably accurate watercolor from the recollections of James Pierce. Pierce stated that the chimney bricks from the Barracks were hauled to town and used in the construction of the Houlton Elks Lodge in 1906. The Faulkner painting and a scale model of the Hancock Barracks, built by Houlton High School industrial arts students from original plans obtained in Washington, are located at the Aroostook Art and Historical Museum.

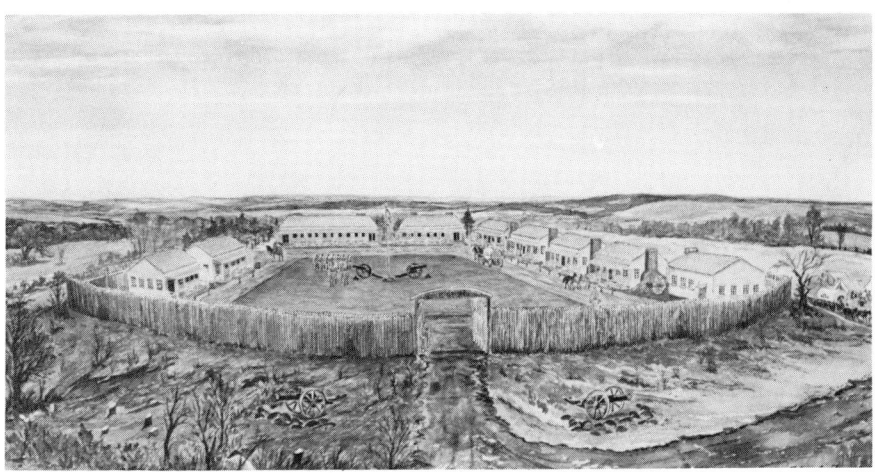

Area residents worked with three companies of soldiers to build it in just three years. It was important not only for military purposes, but because it provided a direct route through Maine for the area's commerce and mail and opened up the region to a large influx of settlers from central Maine and elsewhere. The presence of the troops brought stability, cash, and a new sense of sociability.

Sometimes called the only casualty of the Aroostook War, Pvt. Hiram T. Smith actually died while building the Military Road. Officially, he died of "exposure," and many stories have been told about how he may have died. Smith was buried, near Haynesville, where he had perished. The Lydia Putnam Chapter of the Daughters of the American Revolution from Houlton placed the monument in his memory near the burial site. Checking on Smith's military record in Washington, the D.A.R. was told that he had died at the Madison Barracks in New York and had been a deserter. Research proved that Smith died here. Records must have been very inaccurate at that time, as other Hancock Barracks soldiers that were buried at Houlton were listed as deserters.

The Ballad of Hiram Smith

Oh, Hiram Smith was a worthy lad
Who made his parents both proud and glad
But in eighteen hundred and twenty eight
This young man met with a sad, sad fate!

(Refrain)
Poor Hiram died in those days of yore
While on his way to Aroostook's War!
Yes, deep in the woods by the Haynesville road
He dropped at last live's weary load!

(Refrain)
Now many folks did falsely say
That he deserted and ran away;
But years of study and careful tho't
Finally proved that he did not!

His comrades' letters were there to show
It was pneumonia that laid him low.
So now the D.A.R. we thank
For his honored grave on a Forkstown bank.

So here's to the memory of Hiram Smith.
We know not one of his kin or kith;
But just as sure as his soul has flown
If he hadn't of died, he'd 'a never been known!

(Refrain)
Refrain:
Upon his grave may flowers grow sweet,
But the stones lie cold on Hiram's feet!
—Clarence Hatch

Sir Archibald Campbell, the new lieutenant governor of New Brunswick, countered by increasing troop strength in Fredericton, building up the posts at Grand Falls, Woodstock and Temiscouata, and beginning work on Royal Road to Grand Falls. An uneasy stalemate was now formed that would last for a few years.

During this lull, Houlton voters started proposals for the organization of a new country with Houlton designated as the shire town. On January 5, 1833, it was decided to have Alpheus Felch, the town clerk, write to Shepard Cary, a Houlton resident who was now a state representative in Augusta, that the voters were unanimous in wanting to establish a new county in the region and wanted Cary to try to accomplish the task. Cary failed to move the legislature to action.

Four years later, a formal petition, dated February 3, 1837, signed by Aaron Putnam and twenty-five prominent Houlton men, was sent. It reads, with the original spelling and grammar intact, as follows:

To the Honorable Senate and House of Representatives of the State of Maine in Legislature assembled,

The undersigned respectfully represent that the inhabitants of the Northern District of the County of Washington are subjected to numerous inconveniences in consequence of their connexion with the Southern section of that County, they being so far distant from the shire town, that parties cannot attend Court with thier witnesses without incurring great expense, jurors in addition to the fatigue of a long journey do not draw fees sufficient to defray their expenses, while the sum allowed to them is a heavy charge upon the County, the Officer is subjected to many risques in conveying prisoners to goal, which render necessary the employment of aids, which together with the means of conveyance require him to make disbursements to a large amount, which the sums allowed are rarely ever sufficient to meet, they would further represent that settlements are being made in many townships in the North part of the County of Penobscot the inhabitants of which will suffer like inconveniences with those in the North part of Washington County, and that the only remedy for these burthens and inconveniences is the organizing of a new County.

The legislature did not act upon this petition, perhaps because it did not include Madawaska and did not have a name for the new county.

The "inhabitants of Township Number Six in the third range from the East line of the State" (Smyrna) had other ideas. Thirty-four signed a petition which they sent to the 1838 legislature that stated, in part, the following:

...that they concive [sic] a county composed of the five ranges of townships as prayed for in the petition of Aaron Putnam and others....But in their opinions these objects would be more surely attained by having the Shiretown in the centre of the proposed county, that said Township of No. 6 is more central than any other tract on which settlements have commenced. That the rapid increase of population, the superior quality of the soil and its advantagious situation induce the undersigned to hope that said Township will erelong become a Town of much importance.

Wherefore your petitioners pray that the territory before described may be constituted into a county by the

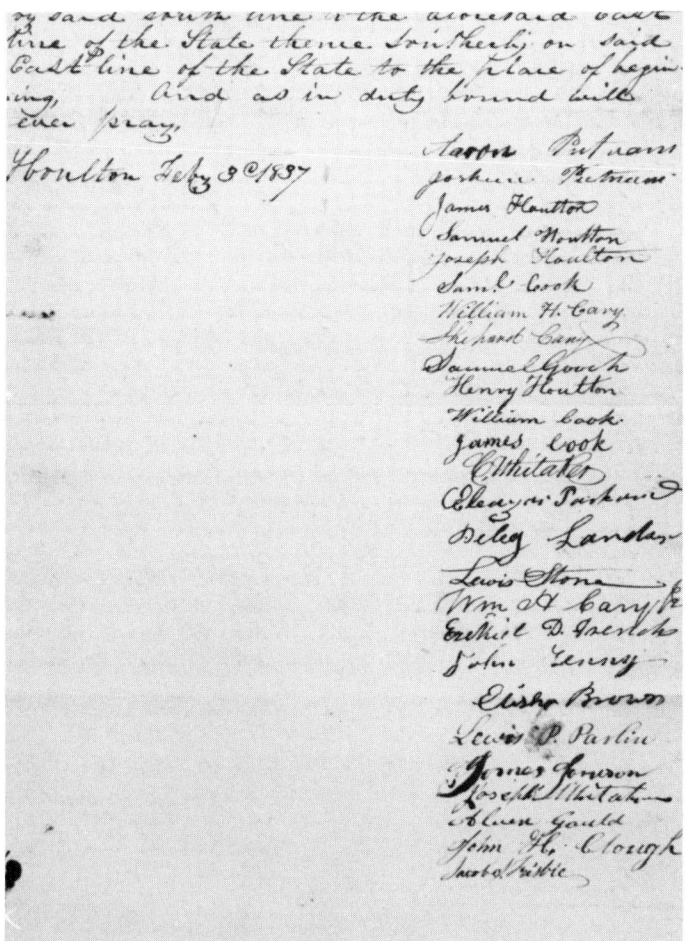

The Houlton Petition Signers
This shows the signatures of Aaron Putnam and the other twenty-five signers of the February 3, 1837, formal petition to the Maine State legislature for the formation of a new county.
Courtesy of the Maine State Archives

name of Aroostook and that said township may be the Shire Town thereof.

The name, Aroostook, had now been proposed for the new county.

With this unexpected competition, the Houlton town fathers seem to have acted quickly to put down the opposition to their plan and get petitions favorable to them sent by other towns. They sent a petition to the State Legislature in January 1839 that was similar to the petition of 1837 except for the statement that "all of the territory in the State north of the Fourth Range of Townships, north of Bingham's Township and east of the Senecott Range of townships, from the East line of the State may be set off." William H. Cary and the other forty-eight signers now agreed to include the Madawaska area should it become part of Maine. The name for the new county was left blank. Petitions that were almost exactly worded to that of Houlton were sent by Hodgdon, Bridgewater Academy, and Linneus. They also asked that "all of the territory in the State north of the Fourth range of Townships north of Bingham Purchase and east of the Seventh range of Townships from the East line of the State may be set off from the Counties of Washington and Penobscot and constituted into a County by the name of _____ and that Houlton may be the Shire Town thereof." Like Houlton, they wanted the new county to be six townships wide, including a one-township strip from Penobscot. They didn't seem to know of the name, Aroostook, that was suggested the year before by their neighbors in Township Six, Range Three, but the area was called "The Aroostook," the name of the river in its midst.

At this same time, January 1839, a convincing and farsighted petition opposing the formation of a county was received by the legislature. The thirty-five signers' argument was so persuasive that, if it had been adopted, the history of Aroostook might have changed considerably. The complete text of their petition, with original grammar and spelling intact, was, as follows:

The undersigned inhabitants of Penobscot County settled on the Aroostook Road having seen a petition published in the Democrat *a paper printed at Bangor praying for a new County of which Houlton is to be the Shire Town would ask the consideration of the Legislature of such objections as they may urge against the measure.*

The contemplated County it is true embraces a large territory of as fertile soil perhaps as any in the State. This territory however has but a very small population, a few towns are partially settled but the central part of it is now a wilderness. The land is good and destined at no distant period to sustain a population inferior to few if any sections of this State of equal extent. Along the Eastern line of the State some considerable settlements have been made in a few Towns. Thriving settlements have recently been commenced along the route of the Aroostook road and in the valley of Aroostook bordering on the River. The westerly line of the contemplated County map is the Aroostook Road twice leaving two Ranges of Townships which would be cut off from all communications westerly by the Kataadn and other Ranges of mountains the lakes and a tract unfit for settlement & cultivation. These two ranges of townships are mostly settling land of the first quality. It appears to the undersigned that the strongest argument in favour of a new County "The distance of their shire town and consequently the great expense incurred in carrying on suits at law" would operate with equal force against it as placing these two ranges of townships in a situation precisely similar. That the interest of all concerned would require whenever a new County is established here, that it should extend from Kataadn to the eastern line of the State they believe few would pretend to deny. They however believe that the time has not yet arrived when the interest of the State or the convenience of the settlers require a new County. The policy of constituting Houlton a Shire they think may well be questioned. It is on our extreme Easterly boundary adjoining the Province of New Brunswick and can never accommodate any considerable portion of the County. Most of the land near the central part of this territory and where the centre of population must eventually be is public land.

The measure contemplated would operate unfavourably as regards the settlement of those lands as it would subject them to the inconvenience cited above in attending suits at law. Should the petition be granted in a few years, as soon as the central parts of the new County had become settled the Legislature would be petitioned to remove the Courts. A more central and convenient location would be asked for. All the excitement trouble and vexation to the inhabitants· time of the Legislature and expense to the State must be incurred which your experience will teach you is attendant upon the settlement of similar questions.

That we suffer some inconvenience on account of the distance we have to travel to attend our courts of law we are willing to admit. This operates in some degree to prevent litigation. We had much rather this state of things should continue than to main the wishes of a far greater will by having a new County established at this time and we would most earnestly and respectfully remonstrate against establishing the new County petitioned for and as in duty bound will ever pray—

These gentlemen envisioned the area as a promised land, the center of which would become most highly developed. They also felt that all of northern Penobscot County should become part of any new county for better representation of the people.

Having received these many petitions, the legislature acted. The original draft of the Act of Establishment gave the county the old name of Restook after crossing out the previous names of Arestook and Jackson. Restook was later amended to Aroostook. The Senate referred the bill to the next legislature on March 4, but it was reconsidered the next day and passed to be engrossed as amended on March 6 and sent to the House. The House concurred and passed it on March 9, and Governor Fairfield approved it on March 16, 1839. It stated that it was "to take effect on May 1 next." Aroostook was now a county, a narrow five townships wide, extending to the northern border, wherever that might be.

The 1839 legislature and Governor Fairfield had many more pressing problems than the county petitions. Maine-New Brunswick relations had become increasingly hostile, and the outbreak of another war between the United States and Great Britain was imminent. The legislature may have decided to establish the new county then, instead of postponing the decision, because of the dangerous situation in the area.

Trouble began when Ebenezer Greeley of Dover, who had been appointed by the commissioners of Penobscot County, through an act of the legislature, to take a census in the Madawaska area, was arrested on May 29, 1837, taken to Woodstock and then released. Returning to his work, he was arrested again on June 6 and imprisoned at Fredericton. Governor Dunlap asked Pres. Martin Van Buren, who had just taken office, to intercede, and Greeley was released. He returned home, but was told by the commissioners to go back and finish his work. After returning, he was promptly arrested again and lodged in the Fredericton jail on September 11. Dunlap appealed again to Van Buren without success. Maine people, the press, and Edward Kent, the new Whig governor, were aroused. Greeley was released on February 9.

The 1838 legislature resolved that if Congress did not pass the bill to survey the northeastern boundary, then the governor would appoint commissioners and surveyors to carry it out. It also called for Congress to erect more military posts and forts in eastern Maine and plan for a defense of the disputed area, as Sir John Harvey, who had become Lieutenant Governor of New Brunswick the previous June, was aggressively building up the military forces there.

Maine and Massachusetts land agents appointed George W. Buckmore to investigate timber violations by New Brunswick loggers in the Fish River area. In January 1839, he reported that large numbers were trespassing on state land and defied the government to stop them. Buckmore found that more than two hundred men, forty-eight yoke of oxen, and sixteen pairs of horses were working the area, and he estimated that more than one hundred thousand dollars' worth of timber would be cut illegally that winter. The fiery John Fairfield, who had been elected governor again, recommended that an agent be employed with enough men to "seize the teams and provisions, break up the camps, and disperse those who are engaged in this work of devastation and pillage." The legislature approved and appropriated ten thousand dollars.

Fairfield appointed Rufus McIntire, a four-time congressman from Parsonfield, as agent, and Maj. Hastings Strickland, sheriff of Penobscot County, and a two-hundred-man posse were employed to help. On the night of February 12, McIntire's camp on the Madawaska River was surrounded by forty armed New Brunswick men, and he and two Penobscot County magistrates were captured and jailed in Fredericton. Major Strickland escaped and, using fast horses in a Pony Express type ride, traveled rapidly to Augusta through harsh winter weather to brief Governor Fairfield. Two prominent New Brunswickers were captured and taken to Bangor. Over two hundred New Brunswick loggers broke into the Woodstock arsenal and armed themselves to repel any invaders.

Sir John Harvey issued a proclamation that was taken as a declaration of war by Maine. He called for the return of arms to Woodstock, saying that he was ordering military forces to the area and was calling for companies from two battalions to be in readiness.

This was it. The Maine State legislature appropriated eight hundred thousand dollars to be used for protection and ordered 10,343 militia men to be ready for immediate action, and within a week ten thousand troops were in the Aroostook region or on their way there. Washington finally comprehended the situation, and Congress authorized the president to raise fifty thousand troops to aid Maine and appropriated ten million dollars in case of war.

Harvey was busy on his side. He had nearly one thousand troops in the area and others in Fredericton as reserves, and most of them were British regulars.

The Bangor *Whig*, a daily newspaper, sent a "war correspondent" to Houlton, and colorful accounts of the

Rufus McIntire

Rufus McIntire was appointed by Governor Fairfield to head a two hundred man posse to break up the lumber camps, seize the teams and provisions, and disperse the New Brunswick loggers who were cutting timber illegally on Maine land. He and two Penobscot County magistrates were captured on the night of February 12, 1839, and taken to be jailed in Fredericton. This action precipitated the Aroostook War. From John Francis Sprague's The North Eastern Boundary Controversy and the Aroostook War.

Strickland's Ride

Maj. Hastings Strickland, who accompanied Rufus McIntire and his posse, was not captured and rode nonstop to Augusta, a three hundred-mile distance in a reported fifty hours, to inform Governor Fairfield of the severity of the situation. From Sprague.

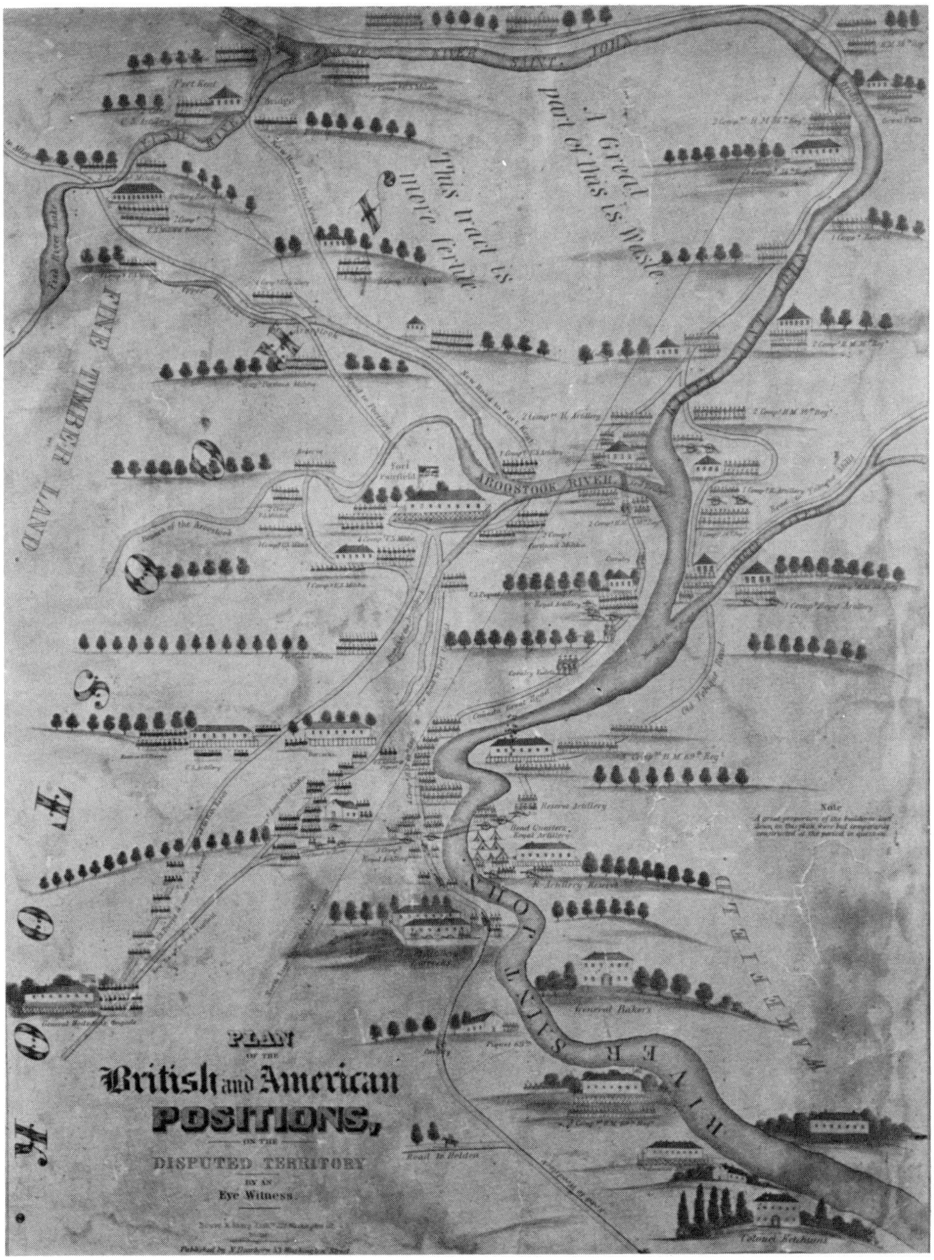

British and American Positions

This excellent map shows the severity of the situation where a skirmish would have started bloodshed. Maine quickly put one thousand militiamen into the area and another one thousand were on the way. Many may have been using Revolutionary War guns and swords, but they were itching for a fight. On the New Brunswick side, most were professional British troops. Part of the Sixty-ninth Regiment came from Quebec, and four companies of the Thirty-sixth Regiment came with artillery from Fredericton. The Forty-second and Fifty-second Regiments and the remainder of the thirty-six were moving into the area, and there were about 350 New Brunswick militiamen. The British had 350 men at Madawaska, 90 at Grand Falls, 90 at Tobique at the mouth of the Aroostook, and about 600 at Woodstock. Artillery was located at Madawaska, the Aroostook, and at Woodstock, and more men were positioned every two miles to act as road-watchers and messengers.
Courtesy of the Aroostook Art and Historical Museum, Houlton, Maine

Boundary March and Quickstep and Soldier's Song

War seemed certain. It was to be the "Red Shirts" of Maine against the "Blue Noses" of New Brunswick, and it was going to be great. Spirits were high, there was much flag waving, and patriotic war songs appeared in the early 1839 daily papers. The "Boundary March and Quickstep" shows that music was written for the occasion. The "Soldier's Song," sung to the tune of "Auld Lang Syne," gives an indication of how high Maine war sentiment was running.
Courtesy of the Aroostook County Historical Center, at the Library, University of Maine at Presque Isle

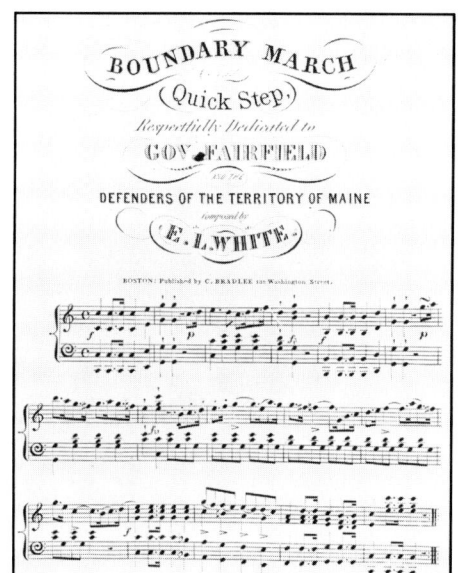

"war" scene appeared in the paper for several weeks.

Acting quickly, President Van Buren sent Maj. Gen. Winfield Scott, Commander of Northern Forces, to Maine to try to defuse the situation. Scott told Fairfield that he was "specially charged with maintaining the peace and safety of the entire northern and eastern frontiers." He also had the power to mediate and negotiate a settlement between Maine and New Brunswick.

War was being demanded by the people and press, and Fairfield was hard pressed. Scott quickly took charge, won Fairfield and public sentiment over to a more peaceable frame of mind, and established contact with Harvey. He persuaded Harvey, whom he had known during the War of 1812, to agree that there would be no armed aggression to try to control the disputed area and that an armed Maine civil posse would not be expelled. Fairfield agreed, in turn, to withdraw Maine troops if a land agent and an armed civil posse could remain to secure the seized timber and prevent any further lumber encroachments. Harvey issued his declaration of agreement. The legislature passed Maine's resolution on March 20. The Governor's Agreement, written by Scott, was signed by Harvey on March 23 and by Fairfield on March 25. The "bloodless" Aroostook War was over before it had started, and only nine days after Aroostook had become a county. Scott had done a remarkable job, considering how high feeling for war were running in Maine when he arrived.

Harvey was careful to abide by the agreement, knowing that the slightest excuse would start the Maine war fever again. Through no fault of his, a detachment of British troops was sent to Madawaska in the fall of 1839. The part of the Maine posse that was at Fort Kent threw up breastworks and began building the fort. Fairfield protested the troop assignment, but he was soothed by Harvey and tensions relaxed. The British government now pressed the United States for a boundary settlement, fearing that something might happen to ignite the situation again, and Pres. Van Buren sent Daniel Webster to London to consult with British authorities.

Pres. William H. Harrison was inaugurated on March 4, 1841, and he appointed Daniel Webster as secretary of state. Harrison was much in favor of settling the boundary dispute and told Webster to start negotiations with Great Britain. Harrison died a month later, but John Tyler, who succeeded him, retained Webster as secretary of state.

Webster knew that the attitude of Maine was the big stumbling block, and that Maine would have to consent to any compromise before it could be ratified by the U.S. Senate. He began to influence prominent Maine people with his ideas and kept Governor Kent and the Congressional delegation informed of his progress. In return, he got a feel for any changes of thought in Maine about a settlement.

Lord Alexander Baring Ashburton was chosen by the British government as a special minister with full powers to settle boundary matters. Ashburton held a million acres of Maine timber, located west of the St. Croix River, which, as Alexander Baring, he had bought in 1795 from William Bingham, the Maine timber magnate from Philadelphia. Baring later married Anne Louisa Bingham, Williams's daughter, and became Lord Ashburton in 1835. He was a friend of Webster's, and Webster was a legal advisor to the Baring Brothers, one of the largest European business firms. Their friendship was to lead to a harmonious and quick settlement.

Webster proposed that a commission be appointed that would be empowered to resolve the controversy by unanimous agreement. Maine was to select four prominent men equally from both political parties, and Massachusetts was to provide three members to make a seven-man commission.

Governor Fairfield, again in office, called a special session of the legislature to discuss the situation and appoint commissioners. William Pitt Preble and Edward Kavanagh were nominated to represent the Democrats and Edward Kent and John Otis, the Whigs. Massachusetts appointed Charles Allen, Abbot Lawrence, and John Mills.

The arbitration went on during the summer months. Bit by bit, Webster put a boundary line together, using the king of the Netherlands' decision as a guide. A line below the St. John River between Grand Falls and Fort Kent, so that the Madawaska area would not be divided, was not

Governors John Fairfield and Edward Kent

Fairfield, a Democrat, and Kent, a Whig, took turns as governor of Maine during the turbulent years leading up to the Aroostook War and the final signing of the Webster-Ashburton Treaty. The towns of Fort Fairfield and Fort Kent were named for them. From Burrage.

Daniel Webster and Lord Ashburton

These two friends were the architects of the 1842 Webster-Ashburton Treaty that ended the northeastern boundary controversy and assigned the United States-Canada border. From Jones in bibliography

allowed. Maine was to have the upper St. John and the rivers flowing into it. The Highlands northwest of the St. John were an obstacle because they gave Great Britain military advantage if Maine were ever to be invaded, but the land itself was of little value. Free navigation rights to the St. John for the transport of timber and agricultural products to the ocean was a must on the agenda of the commissioners, so they agreed to give up the Highlands area for the water rights and a monetary payment.

Ashburton agreed with the Webster declaration and both signed the treaty on August 9, 1842. The United States ratified it on August 20 by a vote of thirty-nine to nine, and it was ratified by the United States and Great Britain on October 13.

Maine felt that Ashburton had gotten the better of the deal, but Webster had done his homework and played his cards well, and the commissioners must have felt that he had obtained all that they reasonably could have expected. The United States was assigned 7,015 square miles and 5,012 went to Great Britain, but Maine had received 80 percent of the best land.

Maine had to go along with the deal. The controversy had gone on much too long and could not have been put off any longer. Townships were being laid out in the area, Maine people were pressing for more fertile land to settle, and timber was needed for lumber and shipbuilding. A new leaf in the pages of American history had been turned, and Aroostook could now look to its future.

On March 21, 1843, Penobscot County gave up its three-township wide section north of Township 8, but it refused to release the remaining three-township wide strip between Aroostook and Mount Katahdin as the "inhabitants of Penobscot County settled on the Aroostook Road" had requested in 1839. Then on March 12, 1844, Aroostook was completed when all the townships north of Township 10 in Piscataquis and Somerset counties to the west line of the state were added to make Aroostook a county of 6,453 square miles, larger than the combined size of the states of Connecticut and Rhode Island.

Major General Winfield Scott

General Scott quickly arbitrated the Aroostook War controversy before another war began between the United States and Great Britain.
Photograph by William Duncan, courtesy of Irene Bradford, Patten, Maine

"The County," Aroostook County, Maine

Secluded and isolated in the Northwoods, the Aroostookans developed a strong sense of neighborliness with each other, while maintaining the strong sense of independence and patriotism that made them feel a people apart, with the rest of the world as "Outsiders." They were surrounded by the seemingly impenetrable forest, rivers that though navigatable, were treacherous in the spring, frozen in the winter, and too low to navigate in the fall, with only spotty trails and logging roads until the Military Road was built from Bangor to Fort Kent. Lack of communication with the "Outside," and few doctors or other community professionals, encouraged community interdependence. A sense of self-reliance and responsibility for others grew, with a work ethic that continues to this day.

Spiritual *relates to sacred matters, to those things of ultimate importance;* spirituality *relates to a sensitivity or attachment of religious values, while* religion *relates to the divine and things of utmost importance, writes Webster. The spirit is the animating, vital principle, giving life to physical organisms. Cultivation of the spiritual is nourishing and nurturing whatever one deems divine or sacred, or of utmost importance. Aroostookans did and do nurture and protect, cultivate with energy and awe, the spirit that gives life, the animating sacred spark that gives meaning to this adventure, this celebration we call life.*

The Aroostook work ethic starts early, this little potato picker in a Monticello potato field is just two years old, had come to the fields to help mama get "picked up," in 1951. Courtesy of the Imogene Holmes Estate

A. The First Baptist Church of Houlton was organized March 25, 1863, and a church was built during the ministry of the Reverend R. C. Spaulding with six men and seven women. By 1867, the church membership had increased to sixty, and the Sunday School numbered over one hundred. The old building was enlarged and reconstructed from 1894 to 1901.
Courtesy of the ACHC

CULTIVATION OF THE SPIRIT IN THE GARDEN OF MAINE

by Iris Fields Brewer with Joseph Donald Cyr

The variety of religious expression throughout the County is practically limitless, but these four churches represent some of the differences. There have been many humble, unassuming houses of worship that were built over one hundred years ago, but they have grown and changed along with the community and are still in use today, such as the Bridgewater Baptist (B). Others, like the Houlton Baptist (A) are a bit more elegant, reflecting a certain calm dignity, a certain tranquillity that suggests a "shelter from the storms of life, a haven of rest." Some of the rural churches in use today are found off the beaten track but still active, neat, and well kept, such as this Lake Road Church in Monticello (C). Some of the County's churches have been quite elaborate, suggesting an individuality that borders on eccentricity, reflecting the free thinking, independent spirit that most County folk prize, such as this early view of Fort Fairfield's Congregational Church (D).

Religion has been a major influence here in Aroostook County for many, many years. The Native American Indians worshipped their Creator according to their own traditions long before any white man set foot on the land of this geographic area.

Later, when the Acadians were forced out of Nova Scotia, to come up the Riviere Saint Jean, they brought their French Catholic traditions with them as integral facets of their daily lives. That religious orientation is still sufficiently strong to be influential in bringing people back to the valley every summer, quite literally by the thousands, either for family reunions, to celebrate the "Foire Brayonne" or simply to return to their roots—to "come home."

Joseph Donald Cyr, a native of the St. John Valley, has contributed the following account of the development of the Catholic religion/influence in the northern St. John River Valley.

The Catholic Religion in the St. John Valley

Roman Catholicism has had such a profound influence on the attitudes and culture of the Acadians of the St. John Valley that it is difficult to separate the two, and impossible to remove its mark from the Acadian character.

The Acadians had a lot of input into their church. Historically, the missionaries who served them were primarily concerned with converting the Indians. The Acadians reaped the benefits of the missionaries as a result of being close to the Indians. The Acadian settlements were spread out along the marshlands and rivers, some settlements spanning one hundred miles or more. Because of this, many seldom saw a priest, but steadfastly practiced their religion. Often a White Mass was said by an elder. This service was complete except for the Eucharist. Marriages were announced to the elders who also baptized the newborn children and buried the dead. When they did get resident priests, the role of those priests extended to settling civil disputes as well as interpreting political messages. (This led them to considerable difficulties in Old Acadia as the priests were appointed by the Bishop of Quebec, an enemy of England.) The priest, being knowledgeable in Latin, Greek, some Hebrew, French, Micmac-Malecite, and English, served many roles because he was the only educated man in the region. He educated, interpreted, and lead the people whom he regarded as his children. In this respect, his family was large for there was only a handful of priests for all of Acadia.

The Catholic religion prospered. The proximity to Catholic Quebec was the reason for the settlement of the St. John Valley. The people were devout. They proved this devotion when most of the colony traveled one hundred miles to receive communion on Easter Sunday 1792.

The first Parish was St. Basile, now located across from St. David. It was named by Bishop Hubert of Quebec on November 12, 1792, after St. Basile, the great Bishop of Caesarea, doctor of the church whose feast day is June 14. The priest of St. Basile had missions in Frenchville, Van Buren, and Houlton, all established in 1826. From those parishes other parishes grew, covering all of Aroostook. The first resident pastor was Father Ciquart in 1794. He had entered Canada when French priests were forbidden to enter Canada by the British government. He was deported to England where he left for Bourges, France. He was then deported from France in 1792 due to the French Revolution. Bishop Carroll of Baltimore sent him to Old Town and he came to the St. John Valley in 1794 at the invitation of Governor Carleton of New Brunswick.

In 1870 the Catholics on the American side separated, becoming part of the diocese of Boston. They had petitioned Pope Pius IX and Rome created the Diocese of Portland because of their request.

The churches of the St. John Valley are large and seem oversized for the small communities where they are found. To many, they seem too rich and elaborate for the perceived wealth of the community. The people of the communities are, first of all, almost all Catholic. The church serves as an expression of community pride, often built with contributed materials and labor, thus costing only a fraction of what it should have. The church was often the only public building in town, fulfilling roles in the Valley that it was not required to fill in other areas. The government of Maine was very slow to organize schools in the St. John Valley so that responsibility fell to the church. Convents were constructed for such purposes, as well as for hospitals. In 1884, the Mariest Fathers from Quebec established a convent and taught school while vastly enriching the cultural life of Van Buren. In 1898 the Holy Rosary Sisters of Rimouski taught school in Frenchville. In Eagle Lake the Little Franciscan Sisters of Mary opened a hospital in 1905. The Daughters of Wisdom of Sevres, France, had a hospital and Academy in St. Agathe, and schools in Lille and Edmundston. There were many other convents established later and many large ones on the Canadian side. St. Basile, with three orders, had an Academy, a hospital, and the largest convent in the Valley. Edmundston became a diocese. There, the church built the schools, a college, an orphanage, and even a community center. It was also their responsibility to keep birth, marriage, and death records.

Catholics in Southern Aroostook

Along with the arrival of the military garrison at Houlton came a stronger interest in religion as well as all other aspects of social life. According to Cora Putnam's well researched book on the early history of Houlton, the acting colonel of the Second Regiment of the U.S. Infantry invited a Father McMahon of Eastport, Maine, to visit the soldiers at the Hancock Barracks the year after the War Department established that post. By 1838, the groups of Catholics had grown so that the Bishop of Boston sent the Reverend Manasses Dougherty to investigate the possibility of building a church. Reverend Dougherty celebrated Mass at the home of Alice Mullen, but as the congregation grew they moved to a building nearby until a church could be erected. Several people contributed money at that time, and more money came in later from surrounding towns, and especially from the soldiers at Hancock Barracks. In 1839 there was quite a revival. One featured sermon was "Temperance In All Things," undoubtedly a rather relevant concern under the circumstances. At this time there were eight companies of artillery and a strong threat of war as the controversy over the contested boundary was reaching its peak.

Many of the priests at Houlton have been Irish Catholic, rather than French, as one might have expected. Several have listed Ireland as their place of birth. At times when there was no local priest in residence, a priest from Woodstock, New Brunswick, would serve as interim pastor frequently. The cooperation by the people on each side of the border has been exemplary most of the time except for the brief years of strife and military intervention. Mars Hill's resident Catholics had to "make do" with services in private homes at first, just as so many other groups did. By 1914, regular services were held in Snow's Hall, a rented facility, until, in 1917, a church was bought just across the line in Blaine. This served the parish until the present church was completed in 1928.

The Puritans Arrive

In the 1700s and early 1800s, one of the major influences on pioneering exploration of the New World was the notion of giving grants of land to various groups who would, in turn sell off these grants and use the profit as financial support for the group. Many of the groups were religious organizations trying to generate financial support for church sponsored schools and/or academies. Many of the towns in Aroostook County are named for the academy or group which was to be the beneficiary of such sales.

The Town of Houlton Established Earlier Than Aroostook

The earliest settlement in the Aroostook area, then under the sponsorship of the Commonwealth of

B. The Bridgewater Baptist Church was one of the early churches in the County. In the very early years Bridgewater apparently had two settlements, one where the village is now and another near the Canadian border.
Courtesy of ACHC

C. Many small churches are still active in rural areas of Aroostook. This Lake Road Church in Monticello is neat and well-kept, and apparently heated with wood, as there is a good-sized wood pile to the right of the driveway.
Courtesy of Iris Brewer

D. The Congregational Church at Fort Fairfield is a unique sample of the care and planning the early settlers lavished on their churches. Their own personal lives were limited in extravagances, but in their churches, they could show their skill in craftsmanship and at the same time let their imaginations "take wings," because it was done with the intention of glorifying the Creator.
Photograph by Tucker; courtesy of ACHC

This is the Church of Ste. Luce, Frenchville. This tintype shows the second church in the parish, constructed in 1847. The first church was a mission of St. Basile in 1826. Bishop Benedict Fenwick of Boston mentions the construction of this building on his visit to the area in 1846.
Courtesy of Joseph Donald Cyr

Massachusetts, was Houlton, started in 1807 for the purpose of providing financial support for the New Salem Academy. (The boundary between the United States and Canada had not yet been settled; Maine was not a separate state; the boundary was believed by many people to be "somewhere" between the area that this first group came to settle and the mountain some twelve miles to the north that we now know as Mars Hill Mountain.)

Since Houlton was founded by dedicated pioneers attempting to finance their beloved Academy, it is only reasonable that church related activities would serve as the primary focus of social interaction. The resources were extremely limited, with private homes serving as the only early meeting places.

The first group of people to organize themselves into a formal church society came about in 1811, less than four years after the first trees were cut for the first homestead. They were so strongly influenced by the Puritan teachings that they chose to be known as Puritan Orthodox Congregationalist. (The Puritan movement was intended to purify the church of any Catholic or Anglican orientation.) There was no official hierarchy in the early Congregational Churches, perhaps a reaction against the strictly observed hierarchical organization of the Catholic Church of the time.

Houlton had no actual church edifice until 1837, and by that time many of the original group had converted to the new religious movement called Unitarian. In most New England Puritan towns the church was one of the very earliest needs to be met. No doubt this was influenced by the fact that the General Court of Massachusetts required sufficient interest and money to erect a church building and pay a minister's salary before making application for the founding of a town.

One vitally important factor may have played a crucial role in the delay of the building. The Reverend Alpheus Harding was called to the mother church at New Salem in 1807, the very year that Houlton was founded. Reverend Harding, a Harvard Divinity School Graduate, had been strongly influenced by the more liberal interpretation of Holy Writ, as had much of the Harvard Divinity School in its teaching, although not until later years in name. The Reverend Mr. Harding had been a schoolmate of one of the town's founders, Aaron Putnam; so Harding's word and opinions must have carried considerable weight in the early days in Houlton. The Unitarian Association was actually founded in Boston in 1825 and some ten years later (about 1835) Reverend Harding visited Houlton. After a few days of discussion with some of the local people, several families withdrew from the original organization of 1811, and started plans for a Unitarian church. It was erected in 1837 on North Street, on a lot donated by Aaron Putnam, just above his big frame house, now commonly known as the Black Hawk Putnam Building. This church was used quite regularly until 1842, although there were times when no local Unitarian pastor was available. At such times, the meeting house was made available to various denominations, and Sunday School was lead primarily by the Unitarians. In 1864 the church building was repaired and put on a new foundation. A rear extension for the choir was added and the interior was renovated. On August 15, 1864, it was dedicated and the women of the parish formed a sewing circle. A ways and means committee was chosen to raise funds for the purchase of an organ. The attempts were successful, and their efforts were celebrated with a pipe organ recital on March 4, 1865. In 1888 this church was struck by lightning and partially destroyed, then later abandoned. Houlton's second Unitarian church was built in 1890, but was destroyed by fire in 1902. After the fire a larger lot was purchased, and the present Unitarian church at the corner of Kelleran and Military was built.

The Congregationalists

Congregationalism was embraced by a variety of denominations of Protestant Christians. This doctrine advocates that a group of people who get together to worship make up a complete church in itself, with no need to subject itself to control from other groups for its governance. Their formal governmental hierarchy is practically non-existent, since they feel that the body of people joined together should be independent of outside influence.

The original church society in Houlton (formed back in 1811) had started out as a Congregational Church, but the group who would be called Unitarians broke away. The original organization, now known as the First Congregational Church of Houlton, has really had a continuous history to the present. A missionary was sent by the Evangelical Missionary Society of Massachusetts to the Houlton settlement as early as 1818, before Maine became a separate state. Records are lacking until 1829, when one report states that the minister, Rev. Samuel B. Wetherall, "visited 125 families on this side of the line, many of whom have not heard a sermon for four years." Reverend Wetherall returned the following summer for a three month stay. When there was no minister in residence, they often met in the school or in homes, but they did meet and made an attempt at holding their society together.

Artist William McGregor, who was serving in the U.S. Army at the barracks painted the Ten Commandments on tablets which adorned the church walls for years. Between 1843 and 1848, a Reverend Mr. Savage served as pastor. He acquired an enormous eleven hundred-pound bell for the church, and was instrumental both in obtaining the charter for the Houlton Academy and in establishing an Auxillary Bible Society in Aroostook County even though serving during that same time period as a member of the state board of education.

Deacon Kendall and his family left Houlton around 1850, creating a great loss for the community. (The original records apparently had been lost in a fire at the home of Deacon Kendall, since they decided to reform and write up new guidelines in 1831.) For about eleven years there was no pastor, but attempts were made to hold the group together and in 1859 a missionary, Rev. Elbridge E.

Ste. Marie, Eagle Lake, was designed and built by Father Joseph Marcoux in 1907. He also constructed a school-convent and a hospital as well as designing many other religious buildings in the region.
Courtesy of Joseph Donald Cyr

The interior of St. Bruno de Van Buren shown decorated for Easter Sunday. The mission of St. Bruno de la Grande Riviere was created in 1827. The second church pictured here was designed by Father Stanislas Vallee and opened in the fall of 1873. Courtesy of Joseph Donald Cyr

The Grotto of Our Lady of Lourdes on the grounds of St. Mary's College in Van Buren was run by the Marist Fathers. The grotto was built by Father Thomas.
Courtesy of Joseph Donald Cyr

The Church of St. David was organized as a parish in 1871. This building, built by Father Louis Huot, was opened in 1913.
Courtesy of Joseph Donald Cyr

Carpenter, came to Aroostook County. He was noted for his sermons, and under his guidance many improvements were made. Beginning in about 1870, there was no pastor nor even a supply minister. The church was closed for a time, but a few faithful women kept the Sunday School in operation and held weekly prayer services. In 1876 a new minister came, and had to hold services in the vestry as the building was too dilapidated to be fit for worship. As the membership grew, so did the need, and the building was moved to a location on Court Street and major improvements were added. In 1956, the building burned and the Unitarians and Congregationalists found themselves worshiping together again.

Unitarians and Universalists

The Unitarian/Universalist influence was very strong in Aroostook County, perhaps based on the friendship of Rev. Harding (of Harvard) with some of the earliest settlers of Houlton.

The Saga of the Stolen Church

In Masardis, as in the other early settlements in Aroostook, the first church services were held some place other than a church, since there were so few churches. The earliest services in Masardis were held in a little log schoolhouse on the Point. There were only itinerant preachers, or circuit riders, because no one community could support a minister, let alone a church in those hard times. The denomination represented was not as important as the fact that there was a minister in town to hold services of some sort.

The first actual church edifice in Masardis was paid for by George Sabins, and the labor was provided by local volunteers. It was used by many different denominations, and was first called a union church. Some of the local Congregationalists thought it might be a good idea to move this church into the village, but, according to Paul Maureau, in his tale *The Masardis Saga*, they neglected to discuss this idea with the other good folk who used the building. In the dead of night, as the story goes, they somehow managed to get this large building onto rollers, and using eight teams of horses, they managed to get it to its current location. They had a sign all prepared, which read: Congregational Church of Masardis 1915. (The same church had originally been beside the old cemetery.) Once they got it up on posts, it apparently was there to stay, in spite of the claims by other denominations that it had been stolen.

A gentleman by the name of Pat Reed is quoted by Maureau as having said of the local worshipers involved in the conflict, "They goddam near kicked the slats out of each other." The sign boards (more than one) kept disappearing but services continued, and the name stuck. It is still referred to as the Congregational Church. The Episcopalians refused to attend, or even to use the building for their services; instead, they traveled ten miles to Ashland, usually by wagon or carriage, to hold services there at the Emanuel Episcopal Church until their church in Masardis could be built. All Saints Church, reported to be a beautiful chapel, was consecrated in 1916 by the Bishop of Maine. The locally produced woods are simply but elegantly exhibited, and many local people provided the many lovely appointments, some in memory of local people for various reasons. A Dr. Favor, uncle to the actress Bette Davis, was a particularly well-loved Anglican priest. He drew folks from far and wide with his special accomplishments at the organ.

The church has since been closed by the Diocese, as a result of a series of problems, and the furnishings passed on to other groups. For a time it was used as a recreation hall, since the building and land were given to the town. It was later used by members of the union from the local paper mill, then closed.

The Church of England/Episcopalian

Here in Aroostook County, many people who chose the Church of England or Episcopalian form of worship crossed the border into Canada for church services at first, although there was an Episcopal Church organization in Presque Isle by 1875, and in 1904, the Methodist Episcopal Church was organized.

The first Episcopal church services in Houlton were conducted in 1841, by Rev. John Blake, chaplain at Hancock Barracks. He bought the land for the church and rectory, and, at the time of his death, he left twenty thousand dollars to the Parish. The mission at Houlton, known as "St. John's Church," was dependent upon other clergy, frequently from New Brunswick, after Reverend Blake left. In 1887, the name was changed to "The Church of the Good Shepherd."

Methodism

Some of the earliest ministers in Aroostook County were Methodist circuit riders who made their rounds before there were any roads on which to travel. One of the earliest was the Rev. Sullivan Bray, who converted Mary Frisbie in Houlton. She became the leading spirit in Methodism in the Houlton area for many years. Others were the Rev. Joseph Lull, in 1832; the Rev. Alphonso Rogers of New Hampshire, in 1833; the Rev. Mark Trafton, in 1834; Able Alton in 1834-35; David P. Thompson in 1836; and Richard H. Ford in 1837. In 1839, the Rev. John G. Pingree came to "Aroostook Mission." No bounds were set, and his circuit covered Houlton north to Fort Fairfield, west to Presque Isle and Ashland, and south to Masardis, Patten, and back to Houlton. Following a spotted trail along the Aroostook from Fort Fairfield to Ashland was a long trip, sometimes covered on snow shoes, other times on horseback or on foot. He lost his trunkful of belongings and sent a letter, listing his loss and itemizing the value, to the hotel in Ashland. (See letter on p. 88)

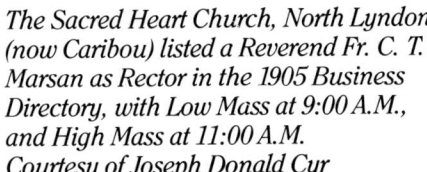

*The Sacred Heart Church, North Lyndon (now Caribou) listed a Reverend Fr. C. T. Marsan as Rector in the 1905 Business Directory, with Low Mass at 9:00 A.M., and High Mass at 11:00 A.M.
Courtesy of Joseph Donald Cyr*

*Through the subscriptions of the soldiers at the Hancock Barracks and other volunteers led by Mrs. Collins Whitaker, funds were gathered to build a Catholic Church in Houlton in 1838. Anthony Mullen, Francis Bird, and James McKenna volunteered to haul the rock for the foundation and John McGrority and Michael Tobin volunteered to hew the frame for the building. The foundation was laid and the frame boarded in during the year of 1838 for St. Mary's Catholic Church.
Courtesy of ACHC*

This is believed to be the first Catholic Church at Fort Fairfield. By 1840 there was a small building, humble and unassuming, made of rough boards and shaved shingles, on Boulier hill about a mile and a half from what is now Fort Fairfield along the spotted trail toward what is now Caribou. It was the first Catholic Church between Indian Point on the Tobique River in Canada and North Lyndon, some twenty-nine miles north on Violette Brook. Most of the Catholics in this area were Irish. Later, this little church was moved nearer to what is now the town line between Fort Fairfield and Caribou cemetery. Because it was the only place of worship for people of that faith, they came from far distances to solemnize births or pronounce the last sad rites along the river.

One Anthony Cain was reported to have lost a leg as a result of a fire, and that leg is believed to be buried there in that peaceful resting place.

*Because there was no Protestant church nearby, this church served their needs as well, and many of them helped with the materials and work in rebuilding the little church.
Courtesy of the Fort Fairfield Public Library*

*Benidicta, now a plantation, rather than a town, was started as the dream of Bishop Fenwick, apparently in 1834. It has always been a strongly Catholic community, and at one time high hopes were held for its success. The bishop had expected people to flock to Aroostook by the thousands, in view of its wonderful potential. Unfortunately, his hopes were dashed. The college building was dismantled in 1871. The original rectory was destroyed by fire in 1975, and a new one built in 1975, and the interior of the church was renovated. Most of the families in the area are still strongly Catholic, and were most supportive in restoring the Church of St. Benedict.
Courtesy of the Church of St. Benedict*

*The First Unitarian Church in Houlton was erected in 1837 on North Street on a lot donated by Aaron Putnam, just above his big frame house now commonly known as the Black Hawk Putnam Building. This church was used quite regularly until 1842, although there were times when no local Unitarian pastor was available. At such times the meetinghouse was made available to various denominations and Sunday School was lead primarily by the Unitarians.
Courtesy of the Aroostook Art and Historical Museum*

A home missionary came to Mars Hill in 1870 but there was not much progress until 1884, when a minister was sent. A Sunday School was started and cottage meetings were held, with no real organization until 1895. In 1896, Joseph Lincoln gave the lot for the present church and by 1905, the people wanted a parsonage. Henry Frost donated the stumpage on Mars Hill Mountain and the trees were cut and hauled to a lot donated by Coleman York. The actual money for the necessities of building other than the lumber itself was raised by the Ladies Aid by serving suppers at ten cents a plate and selling cookbooks at twenty-five cents each.

According to the *Atlas of the Christian Church*, the camp meeting became a dramatic influence on the ever-moving frontier around the late 1840s. Camp meetings "offered entertainment and education, companionship and courtship, all under the umbrella of a democratic gospel powerfully proclaimed." This movement became extremely evident in the early days of Aroostook County. As a result of the sparsely settled areas, it was difficult for the early church to gain enough support to keep them going; indeed many churches disbanded briefly, especially around the time of the Civil War. The various camp meetings made it easier for an itinerant preacher to speak in one area for a week or so, then move onto the next site. Just as many of the early churches were open to various denominations, so were the early campgrounds used by whatever speaker, or in some cases, entertainer, who happened to be in the area. Glenna Walton Alwood, in *Paper Talks* (1987), gives an account of a concert presented at the Littleton Methodist Campground by a William Chapman of New York in 1918. Chapman brought with him Beatrice Belkin as a singer and a violinist named Rubinoff who was only nineteen years old at that time but already famous.

The Methodist association opened this campground during the year of 1894, apparently having moved to this location from Hodgdon, perhaps as a result of its proximity to the railroad. The campground had its own special station and the train officials ran special excursion trains to accommodate the people wanting to attend. Some came from as far away as Bangor to spend the day, or a few days. The grounds had a tabernacle, a hotel, a large dining room, and over two hundred cottages. The tabernacle was reputed to be the largest one around, but frequently the crowds were large enough to overflow its capacity.

(Information from: Doris Tardy, daughter of the late Howard Wotton. Wotton acquired the deed to the campground when the adjoining farm was purchased in 1946.)

The Riverside Campground at Robinson also had special excursion trains, and some of its most loyal supporters come from as far away as Moncton and St. John in Canada. In July 1919 the evangelist was David Anderson of New York, who stated that the camp meetings were purely evangelical and non denominational. He stated that the first Christian camp meeting was held at the River Jordan by John the Baptist, and that there were two baptisms; the first, with water for repentance; the second a baptism with the Holy Ghost. At Riverside, this was called a Feast of Love. Riverside still holds meetings each summer, and there are still many faithful followers who meet there. The train no longer makes the special excursion runs that brought some of the four thousand or more people to the open-air meetings. The tracks have even been lifted, and there are no more trains in this area. For many people, the Riverside meetings were considered the great religious event of the year. Don and Leitha Tompkins have been attending for many years, maintaining a summer cottage. Don said the first time he attended, he walked across the border from Canada, about eighty years ago, as a youngster. Many people remember the open-air meetings on the hillside with great affection. (See photos, page 88)

The Whited Campground in Bridgewater is still active just a few miles from Riverside on U.S. Route 1. It was started in the 1940s, by Rev. Harold Bickford. Reverend Bickford was very active and influential in starting and encouraging many of the Pentecostal churches in central and southern Aroostook.

Easton had a campground at one time as did Caribou. Mapleton's Baptist Park is still active, and there is a campground along the Aroostook River north of Presque Isle although these are of Baptist orientation.

The Salvation Army organization, another product of the Methodist ministry, celebrated its one hundredth anniversary on September 8, 1988. They are well-known throughout the County for the support services they provide for the poor and needy, but also for emergency help in a variety of ways. Sometimes the help is in the form of food and shelter for homeless people, other times it might be clothing and other help for a family after a fire, or food for a rescue operation of some sort. We are all familiar with their supportive programs at Christmastime.

The main reason for being, though, is to provide church services. Bible study programs are available, as well as special youth programs. The denominational orientation is Protestant, favoring Methodist traditions, but not restricted to any denomination, doctrine, or creed.

The Houlton office is the only management center in the County but there are now a total of fourteen outreach programs in various communities, including a thrift store in Presque Isle. The group has been at the same location in Houlton for about fifteen years.

In the early years, they were not well received in Houlton, and it must have been a struggle to earn the positive reputation they now enjoy. Some of the people of the town felt that the Army would draw membership away from the established churches, at least at first. The editor of the Houlton paper wrote in the Christmas issue of his paper some very negative comments, urging the selectmen of the town to discourage the Army's activities and suggesting that the jail should be prepared for more boarders. In February he again complained of the unpleasant influence, suggesting that he would rather be afflicted with diphtheria then take part in their activities. After several other negative comments were published, many of the local people had turned against the Army, even to the point where rotten eggs and garbage were thrown at one open-air meet-

A new Unitarian Church was erected on Military Street on land donated by Hudson T. Frisbie. It was dedicated on September 10, 1890, by the Rev. Minot J. Savage of Boston. This church and two others were destroyed in Houlton's great fire of 1902.
Courtesy of ACHC

After the great fire, a larger lot was purchased and the present Unitarian church at the corner of Kelleran and Military streets was built.
Courtesy of Cathy Craig

The Unitarian Church of Presque Isle was started in 1887. Unitarianism had gained considerable popularity by this time. In 1919, a Rev. D. F. Mowery was filling the pastorate for the Unitarian churches, apparently county wide. (At one time there was a Unitarian/Universalist Church in Washburn. Washburn was a very important spot in the early economy of the County, undoubtedly because of its strategic placement along the waterway.) Priding themselves on the notion of being free thinkers, they frequently built churches with styles that were a trifle unusual.
Courtesy of ACHS

The church now owned by St. Anne's Episcopal Mission near the town line between Mars Hill and Blaine was purchased from The Congregationalists, but used at one time by Catholics, before their church was built.
Courtesy of Iris Brewer

Many of the earliest churches were Unitarian/Universalist by denomination, such as this church in Caribou. (current view)
Courtesy of Timothy Finnemore

The Congregational Church of Presque Isle was officially organized on July 25, 1865. For several years before that, Congregationalist services had been held in schoolhouses between 1848 and 1863. The Congregationalist Church of Presque Isle is reported to be the first church edifice in Presque Isle, even though this group was the third to be organized as a church. The same John Allen who bought the town clock to be placed in the (now) United Baptist Church became a member of the Congregational Church in 1870 and rented his home to be used as its parsonage.
Courtesy of Iris Brewer

ing, and, on one occasion, a shot was fired; the bullet narrowly missing the finger of a drummer as it passed through the drum during a parade. One *War Cry* reports that in Houlton the Army had an encounter with the devil in the shape of the local editor, as the editor tried to run down some members of the Army, even striking out at several members and hitting one sister with his whip. The conflict was pretty much an ongoing thing, apparently, as the captain and twelve others were jailed in 1894. However, by 1950 a different editor commended the activities of the Salvation Army, and currently they are greatly appreciated for their war against sin, poverty, and evil. No doubt in these times, the progeny of that early editor would be somewhat embarrassed if apprised of his persecution of these well intentioned, compassionate people. (See photo, page 88, Aroostook Times Building)

Baptists

The following excerpt is from a poem by Anna J. S. Tarbell to commemorate the sixtieth anniversary of the State Street Baptist Church in 1903:

> We've met tonight with heart so light
> With those we love in this dear home,
> From far and near we've gathered here,
> Our Diamond Jubilee has come.
>
> Yes here we meet in bonds most sweet
> To celebrate that gladsome day,
> When like a star whose beams shine far
> Our church first started on its way.

(two verses from a poem with thirteen verses)

The poem above exemplifies the attitude of many of the early religious leaders of this area. They had a faith in the Creator that was strong enough to see them through incredible hardships and to give them the courage necessary to approach obstacles that must have appeared as almost insurmountable. That faith was a guiding influence throughout the area, and the influence is still extremely strong. The specific interpretations and doctrines vary, but each denomination appears to respect others more because of the foundations of faith and belief in a power higher than self.

The United Baptist Church of Presque Isle (commonly called the State Street Baptist Church) has a long and very interesting history. It was originally known as the First Baptist Church, and the date of its organization was March 19, 1843, the fourth anniversary of Aroostook as a separate County. The earliest meetings, according to a history of this church written in 1933, were held in a log schoolhouse in what was then called the Moses Rose district, some three miles south on the Houlton Road. The County was newly organized, and homesteads were far apart. There were no roads and no village, only trails spotted on trees, many of them from one mill to the next. The records for the first nineteen years were lost. The first church edifice was built in 1872 on the east side of Main Street on what is now the Griffiths lot. Then the church suffered a decline in membership until it was closed in 1886, and the building sold to the Catholic Society. This building was later destroyed by fire.

Then on September 19, 1887, Rev. H. L. Caulkins became pastor, and during his ministry a second church edifice was built on the corner of Church and Second streets. This church was dedicated on June 27, 1890, and on Thursday, March 19, 1903, the sixtieth anniversary of the original organization was observed. (During these exercises, the poem mentioned previously was read by its author, having been written specifically for this occasion.) In 1915, this group united with the Free Baptist church of Presque Isle to become the United Baptist church.

The First Free Baptist church of Presque Isle had come into existence following the October 1859 session of Springfield Quarterly Meeting when a Council of Ministers was chosen for that purpose. Nine people presented letters and became charter members; three from Lyndon (Caribou), two from Fort Fairfield, two from Phillips, Maine, and two from Vienna, Maine. They voted to adopt the covenant and articles of faith of the Free Baptist Denomination. Prior to 1880, there had not been a Free Baptist church edifice owned exclusively by that organization north of Houlton.

One day in February 1880 a group of people were gathered in the home of Deacon Thatcher Smith. Rev. G. M. Park, who was then pastor, was present. The need for a house of worship was discussed, and some offers of help in building were made and by June a building committee was chosen. Several lots were considered, and the present lot chosen. It was purchased at the then considered high price of four hundred dollars. The man who sold the lot, gave one hundred dollars toward its purchase price; the remaining price was made up by subscription from the group. The largest subscription, three hundred dollars, promised by the Ladies Aide Society, was the result of the encouragement of the pastor. There were no plans for a church vestry, and some thought it was preposterous to even consider one, but the pastor wanted one, so the Society was persuaded to assume the expense. They managed to meet that commitment before it was dedicated at the Christmas entertainment. In many areas throughout the County, it has been the Ladies' groups that have raised the money for the "extras" that mean so much to our beautiful churches. In some instances the Ladies' groups have actually raised the necessary money for the buildings themselves, many of them by box socials and church suppers at a charge of ten to twenty-five cents a plate. Their hard work is not always recognized publicly, but it is always appreciated by the people who benefit from it.

The Baptists (with many variations, i.e. Reformed, Free, Faith, United, etc.), were responsible for many of the early churches, some quite elaborate and others quite simple. As might be expected, the churches which drew from a larger number of people had larger and more elegant churches. Having such "extras" as stained glass windows, a pipe organ, and other finery, were frequently the result of donations in memory of some beloved pastor, elder, or deacon, or, in many cases, the result of the diligent efforts

According to *Reflections of Early Ashland*, in 1871 a Bishop Neely performed the service of consecration at the new Episcopal Church which was now completed, free from liabilities, and even had a fine bell presented by interested people abroad. The name of the town had evolved from Number Eleven to Aroostook to Ashland and now to Dalton. In 1876 the name was changed back to Ashland.
Courtesy of ACHC

This is the St. John's Episcopal Church in Presque Isle.
Courtesy of Rev. Thomas Knox

The First Methodist-Episcopal Church in Aroostook was founded in 1839, and the building completed in 1855, in Hodgdon. Houlton also had a Methodist Church, built in 1861. This church had been organized in 1838, previous to the organization of the one in Hodgdon, but did not get a church building until later. Perhaps that was a reflection of the fact that in 1837 the Unitarians had completed their church, and it was available for use by other groups when a Unitarian minister was not available.
Courtesy of Clovis A. Frame

In 1889 a Methodist Church was built in Spragueville, Presque Isle, near the outlet of Echo Lake. Andrew Sprague was the first to contribute lumber, and his son Elbridge sawed it. George F. Whidden was appointed architect, and his son, the Reverend Cassius C. Whidden, whose actual appointment was Easton and Mars Hill, was asked to preach part time at Spragueville as well. His salary for the Easton and Mars Hill was seven hundred dollars per year, and the folks at Spragueville agreed to pay one hundred dollars of that. On July 2, 1890, the First Methodist Church of Presque Isle was dedicated. After the organization of the Presque Isle Church in 1909, that group supplied the pastor for Spragueville, until the original church was sold in 1944. The bell dated 1889 was sold to Ross Kitchen's son-in-law for his church in Connecticut.
Courtesy of Lois Jarvis

This is the Methodist Episcopal Church at Fort Fairfield. Note the double winding stairs leading to the second-story main floor.
Courtesy of the Fort Fairfield Public Library

A Methodist church was built in 1861 in the Porter settlement of Houlton. Soon after that Houlton was taken from the Western Circuit and joined with Linneus and Hodgdon. The church built in 1861-1862 was enlarged and repaired in 1881, but destroyed in the fire of 1902. The present structure is built on the same lot.
Courtesy of ACHC

of the women's groups.

One of the Baptist groups took shape in 1852 in the village we now know as Blaine. (In 1852 Blaine was called Alva Corner, and was a very strategic place in the County, because of its proximity to the Canadian Border.)

The earliest church in Mars Hill is the East Ridge Union Church. It came about as a result of the East Ridge Sewing Circle, which had started in 1877. These ladies wanted to have a meeting house, and, by ice cream sales, quilting bees, and various other fundraising techniques, they raised enough money to get started.

The United Baptist Church in Mars Hill had its beginnings at about the same time period, when a council appointed by the Aroostook Free Will Baptist Quarterly Meeting proceeded to form a Free Will Baptist Parish. The new group applied for fellowship and was admitted on November 23, 1878. On May 27, 1882, a Sabbath School was organized, but it only lasted for about one year until it was disbanded. This group joined the East Ridge group and they were known as "The Mars Hill East Ridge Sabbath School." Later the Mars Hill village group reorganized into a church on April 5, 1895, and the church was erected in 1896-1897. For a time this group was known as the Free Baptist Church, but on June 8, 1917, the present church name, the United Baptist Church, was adopted. The bell was donated by James Gilman.

Deacon S. W. Tabor reportedly came to Washburn in 1859 from south China. Reverend Tabor conducted Sunday school classes in the first schoolhouse near the ferry. The early religious preference appears to have been either Congregational or Baptist (as related by the late Ray H. Carter in his book *An Informal History of Washburn, Maine.* Reverend Tabor, having no quarterly papers or Bible Study Guides to use in his teaching had to use the Bible, but he managed to organize other study groups by his inspirational missionary spirit. He was frequently asked to perform final rites as well as praying for the sick.

Traveling missionaries sometimes preached in the early schoolhouse, and if the crowd was too large, overflowing that building, services would be moved to a nearby barn. In 1860 an Adventist traveling minister came through, bringing a different approach to religious worship, and baptizing five converts. A church was organized in East Washburn as a result of this influence. Baptist revival services were held at about the same time, and some former Methodists and Congregationalists became Baptists. By 1871, a Baptist church was organized, but they remained dependent on itinerant preachers until 1873. In 1880, a church and parsonage were started and the church was dedicated in 1885. The Maine Missionary Society, presently known as the Maine Baptist Convention, was instrumental in supplying preachers here as well as in many other areas. Perham also had a Baptist Church, and the same minister served both groups at times.

In Crouseville, the Advent group was prospering. In 1883, evangelist "Aunt Abbie" Wood drew people from as far away as Ashland, even though many had to walk that distance. Between 1911 and 1914 the Caribou Praying Band held special services, even to the point of establishing their own special group, a Crouseville Praying Band. Interest in religion was so great that Washburn came to be called the "Holy City." The church in Crouseville was organized as the Christian Church, and it continued as such until the present building was constructed in 1885. It was reorganized in 1896, and the official name was changed to the Second Advent Church.

Special meetings were held in Ashland by I. H. Lidstone and soon a Methodist Episcopal Church was organized. By March, 1894, the Lidstone Methodist was planned, and by December of the same year the church was in use, although unfinished.

There were a few Catholics in Washburn, but no organization until a medical doctor, Dr. H. B. McManus, arrived in 1894. Catholics had the choice between the Holy Rosary Church in Caribou and St. Mary's in Presque Isle. In 1922, plans were made to establish what is now St. Catherine's Mission Chapel.

In 1915, Pentecostal services began in Mapleton, which were soon followed by similar services held in the Town Hall. This revival was influential in the establishment of the Washburn Church of Pentecostal Power and the first organized Pentecostal assembly in Maine. Rev. Nelson Magoon and his wife, both ordained ministers, had been leaders in this movement, along with her brother, Harold Bickford of Mars Hill, who was both an excellent musician and a much admired preacher. The Pentecostal influence has spread greatly since the turn of the century, and currently appears to be very popular.

Presbyterians

In 1872 occasional meetings were held in Houlton for Presbyterians. A Rev. Kenneth McKay, pastor of the church at Richmond Corner, New Brunswick, would come across the border to hold services in the little red schoolhouse on the Foxcroft Road, since there were a few Scottish families in Houlton by that time. In 1880, a lot was deeded by Thomas and Catherine Campbell, some three miles out of Houlton on the Foxcroft Road. The local Scottish, Irish, and English Presbyterians combined their money and efforts and built a church. The cost was ten thousand dollars, which was a sizeable sum of money for those times. Those who could not afford to give money paid their share in labor. Prime pine plank lumber was used for the pews, and the effort was called a "labor of love."

By 1886, there were enough families in Houlton village to try a church of their own. A lot was purchased at the corner of High and Military streets, and the first service was held on June 26, 1888. This time, their church came under the presbytery of Boston, whereas the previous one, on Foxcroft Road, had been supervised from Canada. In 1896 a new church was built, the former one having been outgrown. In 1919 the Presbyterian church joined the Congregational church and the Presbyterian church building was sold to the Christian Science Society, (See photo, p. 92, First Church of Christ Scientist)

A Methodist Church was built in 1887 in Caribou on the south side of Sweden Street. A Methodist Episcopal Church is listed in the 1905 Business Directory, with Reverend A. E. Luce as pastor. Courtesy of ACHC

The Presque Isle Methodist church was dedicated on Sunday, January 10, 1909, with special services running until January 15. Boston area Bishop John W. Hamilton and Bangor District Superintendent Rev. J. W. Hatch were in attendance to lead these special services at the corner of Academy and Epworth streets. Photo by Iris Fields Brewer

The only time a conference met in Presque Isle was in 1914, with Bishop Hamilton presiding. Rev. J. W. Irvine was pastor at the time the church was built but left soon after, and Rev. Aaron Kinney served as interim pastor from January until May, when the new pastor Fred G. Gamble arrived to serve until April 1912.

This apparently was the same Aaron Kinney who served the Christian Endeavor group in Westfield in December of 1918. Reverend Gamble was succeeded by Rev. G. Edward Allen, who was reported to be a man of wide learning with great ability as a preacher. Rev. Harry Whitely served from 1934 to 1936, during which time the Spragueville Church was repaired and regular services were held there. The Spragueville Church was sold in 1944, but the pulpit chairs and flower stand were refinished and are still being used. Courtesy of Iris Brewer

Quakers

The Society of Friends became active in the Fort Fairfield area. An active group was well established before the Civil War, and they apparently were active in the underground railroad that played such a large part in the slavery issue. Reportedly, there was a house near the border that had a rollaway wall, which was used to hide Negroes seeking freedom in Canada. As the story goes, a family in Kent, New Brunswick, were reported to have come through Fort Fairfield by way of the underground railroad. The General Meeting House was said to have a boarded up door to an area that had been used as part of this underground railroad and an antique dealer in Houlton had served as a very important link in the chain. (See photos, pp. 90 and 91)

Seventh Day Adventists

The Seventh Day Adventists have a long and varied history here in the County. The group that now meets in Presque Isle, near the Gouldville School, actually had its beginnings in Blaine on December 24, 1887. The charter members met first in a hall at Blaine Corner, then later met in the Blaine School. After this group became organized they received members from Monticello in 1892 and 1893, and in 1900 more members were accepted from Washburn. In 1908 some transferred membership from Oakfield. For a time the Blaine group met on Saturdays at the Westfield Baptist Church at the corner along U.S. Route 1, in the same church where, on Sundays, the Baptists were holding services. In the autumn of 1917, they moved to Westfield village and meetings were held in the home of Fred and Nellie Smith. Later a Seventh Day Advent Church was built next door to that home. (Fred was a carpenter; that was probably a strong influence, but there is no record of who actually built the Church.) By 1933 the folks in Presque Isle were planning to build a church, and it was dedicated on December 30, 1944. On June 30, 1945 a new church in Oakfield was in place and many of the earlier group in Westfield and Mars Hill had moved away from the area. On December 8, 1954, the Westfield group joined the Presque Isle Church, and the Westfield Church has now been sold and renovated and is currently beingd used as a private residence. (In fact, the woman who has done much of the typing for this chapter, Carolyn Rigg, lives in that former church now.)

Spiritualist

The Spiritualist movement has sometimes been called more para-Christian than Christian. It actually started in the second half of the Nineteenth Century and is associated with the Fox sisters in Rochester, New York. In 1908, the Universal Church of the Master started in Los Angeles. At first it was strictly a West Coast concern, but it has since spread all across the continent.

Many people appear to believe that the "New Age Movement" is an outgrowth of Spiritualism. Shirley MacLaine has lent authenticity to some unusual beliefs with her unabashed devotion to her beliefs. She works with faith healers, space travelers, channelers, and crystals, but mainly encourages people to have faith in themselves and their own powers, especially by stressing such principles as encouraging people to look closely at their own mind, body and spirit. Perhaps the main ingredient in all beliefs is the "faith of a grain of mustard seed."

The campgrounds obviously required a large parking lot for the horse-drawn vehicles as well as another place to tether the horses where they could be provided with food and water.
Courtesy of Frank Dunn

Reverend Pingree, circuit riding Methodist minister, traveled amongst the Aroostook settlers by stage in 1838. This letter requests compensation from a stage driver who lost his trunk. You will note that some books were more valuable than his clothing.
Photograph by Tucker; from the George "Pete" Sawyer collection

This turn of the century photograph features the train station and a group of passengers at the Littleton Campground.
Courtesy of Doris Tardy

The octagonal tabernacle at Riverside Campground was built in the early 1900s and used until it was replaced in 1972 with the present auditorium. Much of the financial support came from a loyal follower in St. John, New Brunswick.
Courtesy of Leitha Tompkins

The editor of the Aroostook Times *at Houlton was violently opposed to the Salvation Army when it was first organized and used his editorial position to influence others in his attempts to rid the community of this disturbing element. Ironically that very building later housed this benevolent group in its upstairs rooms.*
Courtesy of Frank Dunn

The same John Allen who sold the lot for the church now commonly known as the State Street Baptist Church, also donated one hundred dollars toward starting it. He spent his winters in California with one of his sons. In 1881, on his return trip, he stopped in Boston and purchased a clock. Soon after that the local people raised money by subscription to buy and install a bell in the tower along with the new clock. At the town meeting in March of 1882, the town accepted by vote both the clock and the bell and agreed to keep them repaired and insured.

The building that is now called the Bethany Baptist Church of Presque Isle appears to have had a very interesting history. Seemingly, after having organized in 1843, they built a church edifice on Main Street in 1872, but suffered a decline in membership, and sold that building (later destroyed by fire?) to the Catholic Society in 1886. Then, in 1887, the group got a new pastor and some new enthusiasm, and a second church edifice was built at the corner of Church and Second streets. This building was dedicated in June 1890, but in 1915, the two groups of Baptists joined to form the United Baptist Church of Presque Isle, and the building in question was sold. Later, it was purchased by the group who organized as the Bethany Baptists, and it is currently operating under that name.
Courtesy of ACHC

The Military Street Baptist Church in Houlton was organized as a Free Baptist church on May 8, 1867. The planning council met in the vestry of the Congregational church. A building was rented on ground later occupied by Ricker Academy. In 1893, the church was moved to its present location and renovated, when the Ricker Trustees bought the first lot. During the renovations, the group met in the YMCA hall then later in the Methodist Church. The original church was destroyed in the fire of 1902, but a new church was rebuilt on the same lot.

The First Baptist Church in Caribou was organized in 1863. It was finished in 1880 on High Street with the Rev. I. E. Bill as pastor. In 1905, the Business Directory lists Rev. T. J. Ramsdell as pastor, and the schedule of services: Sunday Services 10:30 A.M., Sunday School 11:45 A.M. Evening Services 7:00 P.M. in winter and 7:30 P.M. in summer time. (Many churches apparently did not hold evening services, especially in winter.)
Courtesy of ACHC

First Free Baptist Church of Blaine
The first church group, consisting of seven people, met at the home of Joseph Bubar in February 1852 and organized the Free Christian Baptist Church. A lot was donated by Joel Valley, and in June 1886 the church building was erected. The bell, a gift of "Uncle" Fred Hewitt, still peels forth the Sunday morning services.
Courtesy of Gail Beals

East Ridge (Union) Church. Thomas and Mary L. Banks deeded land to the East Ridge Sewing Circle in 1879 for the construction of a meetinghouse. Cyrus Shaw's oxen hauled logs cut from the nearby mountain. The lumber was sawed at Wilson's Mill in Kings Grove. The sills were hewn by hand. The little church has had some hard struggles, even being closed for a time, but it is active and thriving now.
Courtesy of Cathy Craig

The Westfield Free Baptist Church like many others stressed the importance of appropriate guidance for youth. As a result the Young Peoples Society for Christian Endeavor was formed with local people acting as Laymen Leaders. Different individuals agreed to lead meetings, following a supplied text, with each leader being assigned, or volunteering for, a particular topic of discussion.
Courtesy of the Lauretta Corey collection

The Oxford Presbyterian Church at Maple Grove was originally a Quaker Church, built in 1890. Quakers are opposed to violence, but are not afraid to take a stand when it omes to equality. In 1826, Quaker Jonah Dunn, formerly a politician in both the General Court of Massachusetts and the Maine Legislature, came to Houlton. When he saw the injustices taking place as the British made arrests over the Border dispute, Dunn was the first to petition the governor for a military post to protect the settlers in the Houlton area.
Courtesy of Cathy Craig

Wingate Haines and his wife are believed to have been the first Quakers to arrive in the Fort Fairfield area around the 1840s. Fred Haines was an early farmer in the Fort Fairfield area and was also a Quaker. Since Quakers were opposed to war and violence, one farmer reportedly told his sons that if they fought in the Civil War, they would not inherit any property from him, but if they agreed to refuse to fight, they would automatically be given some of his property with no charge. As the story goes, this farmer physically restrained one young son from volunteering for service, but when the young man reached the age where he could go against his father's wishes, he volunteered anyway, and was disinherited.
Courtesy of Lois Haines

Seventh Day Adventist churches were very popular as part of the Millerite movement. Since the predicted date in 1843 passed and the Second Advent did not occur, they have lost some of their popularity. There is still controversy as to whether the Sabbath, as the day of rest and worship, should fall on the first day or the seventh day.
Courtesy of Iris Brewer

The B'nai B'rith, a Jewish organization, was formed in Presque Isle at the Northeastland Hotel on May 2, 1938. A temple was built in Presque Isle because of its central location.
Photograph by Maureen McGrath Murchison

An attempt was made to organize a Jewish group in the St. John Valley, but it was short lived. Called the Congregation Beth Israel, they took shape in 1914. At one time, they had a synagogue, but in 1940, Harry Escovitz was responsible for its dismantling. Because a congregation must have at least ten male members over the age of thirteen in order to continue, and they could no longer maintain that number, they were forced to disband. In its place he erected this memorial plaque on a rock.
Photograph courtesy of Madawaska Times

This postcard, issued by the Northern Maine Lutheran Parish in 1982, shows the only three Lutheran churches in Aroostook: one in New Sweden, on the left; one in Stockholm, on the top right; and one in Caribou, on the bottom right. The first church edifice in New Sweden was dedicated July 23, 1880, as the First Swedish Evangelical Lutheran Church. In 1896 it was renamed the Gustaf Adolph Evangelical Lutheran Church. The church was organized in August, 1871, two months after the arrival from Sweden of the regularly ordained Lutheran minister, the Rev. Andrew Wiren. Between 1870 and 1880, church services were held in the community's public building, called the Capitol. Mr. Nels Olson was a Baptist layman who arrived in New Sweden with the first Swedish immigrants. Swedish Baptist Church was organized with eight members on March 4, 1871. The first Baptist church was built in 1881, converted to a parsonage in 1895, and burned in 1907, while it had been replaced by the current larger building in 1892. On November 27, 1886, the Free Christian Gospel Mission Church of New Sweden was organized, and the edifice dedicated five years later. Several other religious persuasions flourished in the Swedish colony for a time, including the Advent society, but no buildings or active congregations remain. Trinity Evangelical Lutheran Church in Stockholm was organized in 1906 and built in 1907. Lutheran services in Caribou started in 1954, and Faith Lutheran Church in Caribou was organized in 1956. The current sanctuary was built soon thereafter. *Courtesy of Richard Hede*

Some of the people of Houlton became interested in Christian Science in 1894 when Mrs. Samuel Putnam received a copy of the Mary Baker G. Eddy textbook after he had experienced what was considered "a remarkable healing." Mrs. Putnam and her brother Addison P. Smith and his wife became interested in the new idea, and the Smiths started holding meetings in their home. During the "Great Fire of 1902," when much of the town was destroyed, many people noticed that the Smith residence, which was directly in the path of the flames, survived relatively unscathed. In 1916 a group met at the Smith residence to plan the formal organization of a Christian Science Society. Twelve others joined Mr. Smith in electing officers and adopting bylaws. The Presbyterian Church Society on the corner of High and Military streets had joined with the Congregationalists in 1920, so the Christian Scientists bought their building to use as a meeting place and school. They maintain a Reading Room in the Masonic Temple building. In 1951 the name was changed to First Church of Christ, Scientist. The group was quite active for several years, with its influence spreading as far as Island Falls and Monticello as is evidenced by a letter at the Aroostook Collection dated March 26, 1936. In 1939, the Maine Register lists twenty-seven Christian Science Churches in Maine, but it has not proved to be a strong influence in Aroostook County. *Courtesy of ACHC*

*The Church of Jesus Christ of the Latter Day Saints in Caribou, as an officially organized body, saw its first members baptized in 1951; however, it was not until about twenty years later that the first services were held in the present building, on the first Sunday in January, 1971. The original building has been expanded several times, and it now contains not only the spacious auditorium for church services, but also classrooms and a stage for various presentations, in addition to the library (described in the caption accompanying the picture of its interior), as well as a gymnasium with a regulation sized basketball court, and the necessary facilities for showers, and such.
Courtesy of Elder Willey*

*The library of the Mormon Church at Caribou now has five microfilm readers and five microfiche machines. The library is open to the general public every Saturday from 8:00 A.M. until 4:00 P.M., with trained staff available to assist in research efforts. There is a family registry where interested individuals can seek information relevant to any family name, worldwide. The library provides access to over two million roles of microfilm regarding this information, on a loan basis as a rule, but the information can be purchased in most cases. Access to most of the services are free; however, a small charge is necessary to cover shipping, handling, and processing for some items. Currently, attempts are being made to develop a permanent record of information pertinent to the local area and its families. There are over 150 films in stock, and several video presentations explaining how to use the various services efficiently.
Courtesy of Elder Willey*

John R. Braden, "The Little Iron Horse from Tennessee," and driver-trainer John Willard brought cheers and tears to the eyes of Aroostook. Purchased by the Mooseleuk Club in 1921 to represent the city of Presque Isle, Braden captured the hearts of the populace, inspiring loyalty from his fans that prompted thousands to gather when he raced: along the rail, overflowing the grandstand, even watching from rooftops. Small in stature but big in heart, this spirited little pony-pacer competed in meets throughout Maine and New Brunswick, Canada, winning forty-five out of fifty-five races with the frenzied cheers of the crowds ringing in his ears; often, to be declared a winner, a horse had to win the "best of" three or five heats/dashes. So enthusiastically was this horse embraced by the citizens of Presque Isle, that he was honored with many tributes: a street, a theater, and a cigar were named after him; and a banquet was held at the Northeastland Hotel with Braden as the guest of honor. His career ended in 1926; his retirement was financed by his own bank account, which his owners had set up to support him in his old age. When he died in 1929, he was laid to rest in the infield of the Northern Maine Fairgrounds; a monument gives lasting tribute to this fine animal that brought neighbor closer to neighbor and helped to make Presque Isle one big family.

"Aroostook is a racing realm unto itself . . . ." (From Charles Wilson's Aroostook: Our Last Frontier) Though most popular as summer recreation at various meets and county fairs, harness racing was not limited to fair weather. Frozen lakes and ponds were utilized to extend the season throughout the year. "In winter season, a race course was kept cleanly swept upon the icy surface of the St. John, and here many notable contests were engaged in between the fast-steppers of the town." (From Edward Wiggin's History of Aroostook) Many communities had trotting parks in the early years of Aroostook County settlement; over the years, they have fallen into disuse or found another purpose. The exception is the track at Presque Isle, home of the Northern Maine Fair, which is still utilized for harness racing. In addition to the fair meet, many organizations have established extended meets during the summer; these have all fallen by the wayside. The latest endeavor is County Raceways, founded in 1986 with Dr. Alroy Chow as president for the 1986-87 season. Dirk Duncan was president the following season, and Michael Murchison presently holds the position. Courtesy of Paul Mullen

THE GARDEN BLOOMS

The promise of the seed can be realized only in the soil, the water, the air, and the sun. The soil, in meadows, intervales, and other centers; the air, with refreshing winds; the springs, ponds nourishing the creative idea; and the energy of the sun contribute to the blossoms, to the fruit of the soil and the mind. Blooms, and other artifacts develop naturally with the proper conditions, and so the mind with its own natural creative instincts develops artifacts and products, blooming in the minds and hands of all who will attend to the cultivation.

The early settlers had little time for pleasure-seeking. Sustaining life in the wilderness required long hours of arduous labor. The hardy pioneers needed release from the strains of daily life and were compelled to rely on their own resources for enjoyment. Communal work projects were an excuse for merry-making; the rewards of wrestling, dancing, and games after the task was completed were motivation for the work of barn raising and similar activities.

"When the barn framer had done his work, and the great event of 'raising' took place, the boldest and best men climbed the unsteady skeleton, ax in hand. Up went the pioneer athletes, from one piece of timber to another, balancing themselves on the small girts and big beams while they caught the wooden pins tossed up to them from below" (Wiggin) This barn raising took place in Easton in the mid-1860s; note the food-laden table in the foreground.
Courtesy of the ACHC

SUNSHINE AND MOONLIGHT—RE-CREATION
by Maureen McGrath Murchison

Recreational experiences are sought to lend balance to our lives. Whether mentally stimulating, such as participation in the arts, music, or a literary club; or a physically demanding sport such as running, racing, or swimming, we choose activities that meet our physical, psychological, and/or social needs. Play is an important socializer; expressing, developing, and teaching the dominant values of a culture. The play instinct serves to prepare the child for adult life by enabling him/her to develop respect for democratic rules, and providing awareness of the necessity for cooperation within the society. As noted by Elias and Dunning, "...although the structures of such activities and the meanings to the participants vary, no human society has yet existed without some form of modern sports." The continuing development of sports activities indicates a societal attempt to control aggressive behaviors: the liberating effect of a mock battle/sports contest as a tension releasor has been achieved without overt acts of violence. Recreational experiences allow the participant to express emotion that might otherwise explode in hostility; they also provide an outlet for the expression of the highest emotions. Awe and reverence as experienced by the hiker "at-one with mother nature"; or the exhilaration of an athlete as he realizes his potential in a hotly contested sports event.

In primitive cultures, the lines between work and play were not sharply drawn; most recreational activities had utilitarian or survival value, such as hunting, fishing, or weaving, which modern day enthusiasts pursue on a purely recreational basis. Life for the earliest inhabitants of Aroostook, the Micmac and Malecite (Maliseet) Indians, was a struggle for mere physical existence; as it was for the first white settlers, the Acadian refugees from Nova Scotia, and for the settlers of New Salem, or Houlton Plantation. The aforementioned Indians were nomadic by nature, following a seasonal trail of hunting, fishing, and trapping as a means of survival. Their recreational experiences reflected this lifestyle through game playing that sharpened survival skills, such as spear throwing in a game of T'so-ha-ta-ben. The business of survival left little time for pleasurable pursuits for the early white settlers, also, so they took advantage of ordinary activities by making them into social events. Most families had a Bible, which they would read together as a family, or gathered together at a prayer meeting; the necessary task of sewing provided an opportunity for quilting bees and sewing circles. Perhaps the best example of communal work would be that of a barn raising, a major event attended by young and old, and a cause of much merry-making when the day's work was complete. The highlight of the event was the barn dance; the folk dances that were experienced on these occasions were spirited and informal. The music was provided by a fiddler and perhaps a piano or organ accompaniment to the various

Card playing, which has long been a popular pastime, knows no social, economic, or political barriers. Lumbermen, physically exhausted after a long, arduous day in the woods, would look to a game of cards—forty-five, poker, or spades—for mental stimulation. Social clubs were formed, such as the Meridian Whist Society pictured here in Caribou in 1907, to provide an opportunity for an evening of any one of a number of games such as bridge, as friends gathered in a convivial atmosphere of rivalry and camaraderie. At family reunions, a game of cards provided a prime opportunity for young and old to comingle, strengthening and preserving family ties.

Other recreational diversions included a game of chess or checkers; both games inspired tournaments which were well-attended and commonplace. Later board games, such as Monopoly, Life, and others, joined these aforementioned games as a popular leisure pastime among family and friends.
Courtesy of Images, *ACHC*

"This festival is the big thing of the year, reaching far beyond the borders of the county in attracting crowds hitherward …[to enjoy] varied attractions.… These scores of visitors derive their impressions of the wealth and productiveness of the county through this annual visit and report back to others. Thus, the fair is probably the greatest asset we have."

(Collins) Founded in 1850 as an institution for and by farmers, the Aroostook Agricultural and Horticultural Society was the major event of early years. Families would travel from all over the state and the Canadian province of New Brunswick to camp at the fairgrounds for the duration. This annual event provided an opportunity for farmers to exchange ideas and engage in friendly competition for the best potatoes and/or beef critters. Thus, the Northern Maine Fair, as it came to be called in later years, was in a large part responsible for the success of the farms and maintaining the population of Aroostook. In 1858, J. B. Hall, as editor of the Presque Isle Pioneer, *invited the editors of the leading journals of Maine to visit the Northern Aroostook Agricultural Society (N.M.F.) for the purpose of acquainting themselves with the resources of the territory. Specifically, he hoped they would write glowing editorials to entice the railroad to expand the County. The endeavor was ultimately successful with the arrival of the Bangor and Aroostook in 1894. This view of the Northern Maine Fair, taken in the 1920s, indicates the attendance of this popular event. Among the favored attractions are harness racing; horse pulls; a horse shoe pitching contest; or, more recently, truck pulls.*
Courtesy of Levi Knowles

reels, jigs, and square dances. Also known as a "junket," or "kitchen raket," depending on where it was held, the barn dance is indigenous to America. Dance has long been an integral element of society, maintaining and preserving customs and family ties, and has been recognized by historians as an important vehicle of cultural preservation. Simple pleasures are the best, and folk dancing was and is a favorite pastime; other favorite pastimes were card playing, a family picnic, or a scenic ride through the countryside— first by horse and buggy or sleigh, later by automobile. As the physical development of the county occurred, first with the Military Road to Houlton in 1838; then the arrival of the railroad in the mid-1800s; and the automobile in the early 1900s, the citizenry of Aroostook had more leisure time. An essential element to the development of the County were the county fairs, particularly the Aroostook Agricultural and Horticultural Society, later known as the Northern Maine Fair, which attracted thousands of people from downstate, as well as from Canada. The leisure time created by these developments resulted in an increase in the popularity of spectator sports, such as football, baseball, and basketball. Arriving in the county in 1900-1901, basketball quickly caught the favor of the locals and has reached "mania" proportions in terms of popularity both as a spectator sport and as a favored form of exercise. Other preferred recreational diversions included attending circuses, participating in local festivals, and enjoying the parades that often accompany these attractions. Aroostook has also proven itself to be a center of activity for hot air balloon enthusiasts. Of the many ascensions taking place in the County, the most famous and well-attended were the first trans-Atlantic balloon crossings occurring in Presque Isle and Caribou. Recreational opportunities have continued to expand, with the development of parks and other facilities, as well as organized recreational programs available in most Aroostook communities. Presque Isle was the site of the only U.S.O. in the County; the building has since been incorporated into the municipal recreational program. Aroostook State Park, the first in the state park system, became available to the public in 1939, and has been a popular locale for outdoor enthusiasts year round, with winter and summer activities available. The thousands of lakes and streams found in the County have made attainable a variety of water sports, including swimming, boating,

Thousands of out-of-state people travel to "the County" each year to hunt and/or fish in the vast bountiful wilderness. Shown here, left to right, in March of 1879 in Island Falls, are guides William W. Sewell and Wilmont S. Dow with Theodore Roosevelt who hunted and fished in the Oxbow region. Taking time out each day to read the Bible, Roosevelt would go alone to a certain spot in the woods, the beautiful point of land at the confluence of the West Branch Mattawamkeag and First Brook. This spot came to be known as "Bible Point"; and the 27.4 acre point was named to the State Register of Historic Places in 1970, and donated to the state in 1971, to be preserved as a natural area.

Theodore Roosevelt was fond of telling of the wet spring he was there. While proceeding along a rocky road he said to his guide, "How do you tell the road from the river?" "No beaver dams in the roads" was the reply. Without humor, life in remote communities would have been dull. Often, the village "wits and wags" would gather at the general store, which has proven to be a forcing ground for humor; men went there as to a club, for relaxation and entertainment. (From Edwin Mitchell's It's An Old state of Maine Custom.)
Courtesy of Jean Sawyer

Some of the most picturesque, natural scenery in New England is found in Aroostook County. The St. John River in northernmost Aroostook has been referred to as the "Rhine of New England"; Oakfield with its mountainous, broken terrain has been referred to as the "Switzerland of Aroostook." (Wiggin) Many leisurely hours have been spent enjoying the beauty of nature, whether with horse and buggy, in a sleigh, or in an automobile as Elber Fields and friends, out for a Sunday drive in Westfield in 1913. "Autos vastly increased the scope and extent of social and business intercourse in the county, making life richer and more worth living ....Probably nowhere else in the United States is there a section of equal population where autos so abound as Aroostook. Gas stations are busier than saloons used to be. Aroostookans overrun any place that has a show or a holiday with their generous patronage and it's the spirit, and the fact that thousands of autos make it possible to exercise it, that has boosted such institutions as the Northern Maine Fair." (Written by Collins in 1922.) "He goes there not to find the pleasures or refinement of the town or city but to create them for himself...." said Holmes in describing Aroostook. Simple pleasures, such as a family picnic by a stream, in a grassy meadow, or in one's own backyard; hiking on Haystack Mountain; or biking on a dirt road on a hot summer day, bring much enjoyment to the citizenry of the County.
Courtesy of Albert Fields

fishing, water skiing, or participating in one of the many river races held each year. Winter sports are also plentiful, from sledding down a hill, skating at the local rink, snowmobiling across the vast open fields, or skiing on the numerous cross country trails or down the slopes of various hills and "mountains". The business aspect of recreation has not been overlooked; as entrepreneurs have understood the need for re-creation to replenish the soul, they have made available a variety of attractions. Guides and outfitters provide opportunities for back-to-nature buffs; other recreational diversions include the Vacationland Estates resort in Island Falls; numerous campgrounds throughout the County; Funland amusement park in Caribou; various country clubs which provide golf courses for the many golf devotees; bowling alleys; roller skating rinks; stock car races; harness races; or, for a more quiet time, a rented video tape (which is in direct competition with movie theatres); or time spent in a video arcade, there is something for everyone in the County. A lively evening of dancing is offered in "night spots" as well as the modern version of the barn dance, the "garage" dance.

According to Stan Brakhage, as quoted in *Northern Lights studies in creativity*,..."the problem with play as a concept in this society is competitive sport...Play is absolutely joyful and quite serious...is crucial to developing ones abilities; but putting it into competitive context destroys much inate behavior." The creative process of re-creation of one's self: through fabrication/resolution of a crisis, such as participation in a hotly contested sports event; skydiving; driving too fast on the highway and surviving; or (an antidote to this form of escapism) through the arts: writing, painting, music...even humor...is necessary for the health and well-being of the soul. "There is an urgency about the creative process that derives from the survival instinct...isn't limited to just physical...but includes 'mental and spiritual survival.'" As noted by Stan Scott, editor of *Northern Lights studies in creativity*, "Karel Appel's 'inner lights,' which go on in the creative process, and Larry Woiwode's 'northern lights' are...examples of ...archetypal use of metaphoric imagery to name the primordial creative power that heightens and transforms consciousness." Another metaphor for creative energy, used by the Living Theatre, is the image of light itself; a member of the company speaks"...we all are/suns and stars/and Function as Celestial/Lights."

Festivals serve an important social function in the ordering of time; winter carnivals, harvest festivals, New Year's celebrations, religious and "fun" holidays. Because we are social animals and require order in our lives, we create intervals in our social life through festivity: to order time through the suspension of orindary social time. Festivals provide an opportunity for participants/attendees to disguise their social personality, such as at a Halloween/masquerade party, or participating in the potato wrestling contest at the Maine Potato Blossom Festival in Fort Fairfield; or to emphasize it, such as at a wedding, or at religious services. Parades, an event in and of themselves, were often the indicator of upcoming events and festivals,

such as this circus parade used to entice the populace to spend an evening at the circus in Ashland in 1917. Aroostook was the mecca of big circuses in the early 1900s.
Courtesy of ACHC

Basketball was invented in 1891 as an indoor alternative to the fair-weather sports of football and baseball; it has been a mania in Aroostook County since it arrived in early 1900. The Presque Isle girls were among the first to organize a team, under the direction of Myra Vickery. The uniforms worn by these girls' teams, as seen on the Aroostook State Normal School girls team of 1909, brought shock and outrage from the general populace of the County. The boys quickly caught on to this popular new game, both as a form of physical exercise and as a spectator sport. Early basketball games were held wherever a large enough hall could be found. Rules were not universal in early games and teams found themselves playing under "boys rules in Presque Isle... and girls rules in Caribou." (Nathan White) Presque Isle became the first Aroostook team to win an undisputed state title in 1932; until the inception of play-offs, teams would simultaneously claim the title of "Champs." Basketball activity increased greatly over the years, with most schools incorporating it into their physical education programs. Teams were not limited to high schools, however; clubs and organizations formed their own leagues; before long, prep schools, grammar schools, and towns had their own leagues. A few towns had semi-pro teams, but high school basketball has remained dominant in the hearts of Aroostook fans. Although the rivalry among themselves is fierce, when a County team makes it to the tournament, everyone pulls for the "home team."
Courtesy Nathan White Collection, UMPI Library

During the years of the Second World War, the many airmen stationed at Presque Isle Air Force Base, and later Loring Air Force Base, had the opportunity to fraternize at the only U.S.O. in the County, located on Main Street in Presque Isle. It was dedicated in March 1944 with volunteers devoting many hours to ensure the happiness of the many strangers who were stationed at P.I.A.F.B. and Loring Air Force Base, some seventeen thousand soldiers who otherwise would have no place to go. After the war years, the building was no longer needed for these purposes. The city of Presque Isle purchased the building for a community center; it fulfills that purpose to this day, offering a variety of activities, including basketball, dances and lessons in gymnastics and ballet. Seen here are Ellaika Grant, Amanda Murchison, Sarah Knowles, and Kara McGrath.
Courtesy Donna Cain

Humans have long held a fascination for the wonder of flight; hot air ballooning is one of the earliest attempts to achieve this end. Aroostook is famous for hot air balloon ascensions; Houlton was the site of many in the early 1900s. Perhaps the most famous occurred in Presque Isle on August 11, 1978, as the Double Eagle II ascended from a clover field under the capable hands of Ben Abruzzo, Maxie Anderson, and Larry Newman. They landed in the history books when they completed the first trans-Atlantic crossing, touching down in a barley field in Miserey, France on August 17, 1978, just 137 hours, 5 minutes, and 30 seconds later.
Photograph by Voscar

The first balloonist to make a successful solo crossing of the Atlantic was Ret. Col. Joe Kittinger, who left Caribou on September 14, 1984. He landed in the little seacoast town of Savona, Italy, approximately 84 hours later, arriving on September 18, 1984, in his helium balloon, the Rosie O'Grady Balloon of Peace. Joe Kittinger, of Skylab fame, and Douglas Palermo had wanted to make a race out of the first balloon crossing in 1978; the crew of the Double Eagle II declined the offer, according to Charles McCarry in Double Eagle.
Photograph by Brenda Ketch

Early gardens, the forerunners of today's parks, were essential for survival in pioneers days. Although we are no longer obliged to maintain a garden for subsistence, we still seek opportunities to "get back to the basics." Most communities in Aroostook offer some type of park or recreational facility, such as the Bi-Centennial Park in Presque Isle. There is always room to run, jump, and play in "Wonderful Aroostook the Garden of Maine."

The city of Presque Isle donated one hundred acres of land near Echo Lake, including Quaqua Jo Mountain to the state in 1938, thus forming the first State Park in Maine. The work was done by the Works Progress Administration (W.P.A.), a governmental agency, as the state had funds for maintaining, not developing state parks. Summer and winter activities were incorporated into the facilities, and County residents as well as non-residents find much enjoyment swimming, picnicking, camping, and boating in the summer; and snow sledding, cross country skiing, and skating in the winter. (See photograph in colored section.)
Photo by Maureen McGrath Murchison

When the glacier left Maine, it left in its wake 2,503 lakes and ponds, thousands of streams, and the only Atlantic Salmon rivers in the country; which have proven to be irresistible bait for many out-of-state enthusiasts. Whether fly-fishing, trolling, or using live bait, hopes run high for the capture of this and a number of other varieties of fish, including trout and togue. Not limited to warm weather, devotees brave the cold to try their luck at ice fishing with the comfort and protection of a fishing shack, as pictured here.

A variety of other water sports are available, including canoeing; boating; water skiing; swimming; or lounging on the beach near the water's edge. Swimming is no longer limited to warm weather since the construction of several indoor pools, including those located in Limestone, Island Falls, and Presque Isle. Many communities have incorporated water sports into their festivals, such as the 'Roostook River Raft Race,' an exciting part of the Maine Potato Blossom Festival, held in Fort Fairfield each year; the Meduxnekeag River Canoe Race in Houlton; canoe races at the Lumberjack Roundup in Ashland; or the Regatta in Van Buren.
Photograph by Voscar

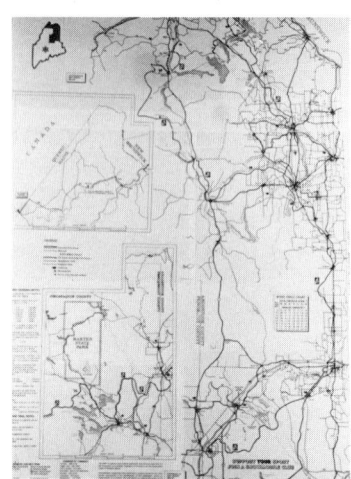

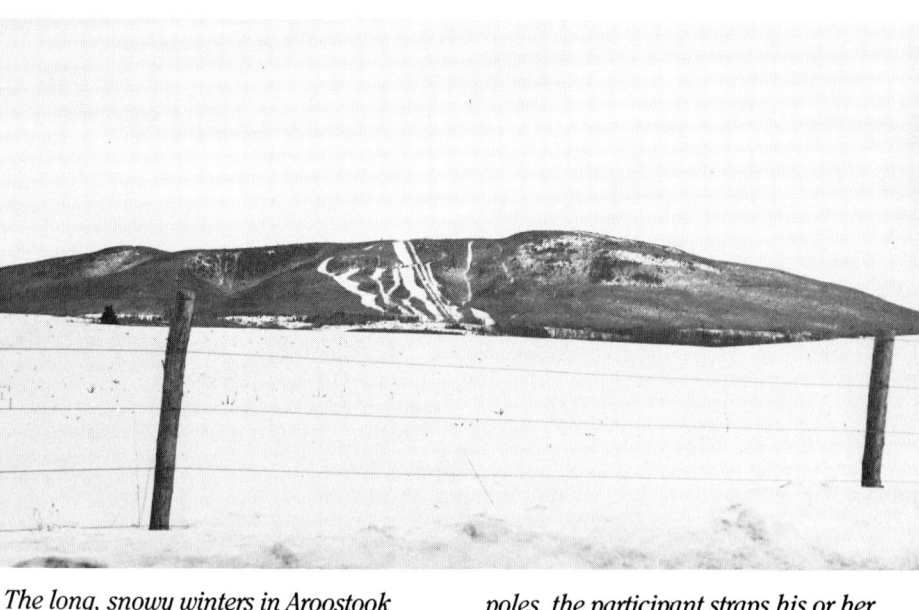

Snowmobiling has been extant for many years, but didn't gain popularity as a winter sport until the late 1960s. As more and more people bought snowmobiles, the necessity for a place to ride them became an increasingly difficult situation. It was then that snowmobile owners organized into groups and clubs and cooperated with the private land owner in the construction and maintenance of snowmobile trails. All winter long Aroostook County residents and down-state visitors take advantage of Maine's best kept secret, the many miles of groomed trails criss-crossing the County.
Courtesy of Presque Isle Chamber of Commerce

The long, snowy winters in Aroostook provide ample opportunities for outdoor enthusiasts. Among the more popular activities are downhill and cross-country skiing. Although we do not have any large mountains, the downhill aficionado encounters many fine ski areas throughout the County, from Madawaska to Island Falls and in-between. Shown here is Big Rock in Mars Hill, which has slopes for the novice as well as the experienced skier. A new winter sport that is rapidly gaining in popularity is snow boarding. Using a single short, wide ski and no poles, the participant straps his or her boots onto the board and manueuvers it skateboard style down the slopes. This new sport promises much excitement and exhilaration for the inspired athlete.

Cross-country skiers take advantage of the numerous, well-groomed trails that are maintained throughout the County. The opportunity to participate in these sports is available to many, as these activities have been incorporated into the curriculum of most schools.
Photo by Maureen McGrath Murchison

Ice skating has long been a pleasurable pursuit easily accessible to County residents. Most communities maintained an ice rink, or kept a pond, lake, river, or a portion thereof, shoeveled to accommodate local families. Less hardy souls had another option available when Presque Isle began operation of Maine's first "recreation department indoor skating and hockey rink and the second curling facility in the state of Maine." (William Haskell) This indoor rink was available from February 1964 to January 1969 when the roof of this facility caved in due to snow and ice accumulation. Indoor skating again became available in January 1979 when construction of the Forum in Presque Isle was completed. Formal instruction in ice skating became available in 1982 with the formation of the Aroostook Ice Skating School, a recreational skating organization affiliated with the Ice Skating Institute of America. Under the professional guidance of Terry Huff, the members of Aroostook Ice Skating School perform in an annual ice show, "Music on Ice" as well as participating in I.S.I.A. competitions in Natick, Massachusetts, since 1987. Amanda Murchison skates in the 1987 musicale.
Photo by Maureen McGrath Murchison

The Forum, a modern facility in Presque Isle, provides an opportunity for events and functions that would otherwise be unavailable. A multi-purpose building, it is host to eighteen annual large-scale events and fairs as well as a dozen or more smaller events. The installation of new hockey boards in 1987 made it possible for exhibition games to be played by Class A teams, such as this Blue/white exhibition game by the University of Maine Black Bears shown here.
Photo by Mark Putnam

Childhood games have remained virtually unchanged since pre-historic times; climbing trees, cavorting in streams and rivers, playing with pets, and participating in games of exploration. The play instinct served to prepare the child for adult life by teaching the art of survival, whether the enemy in mock battles was animal, human, or alien. With the development of electronic and computer games, such as Nintendo® and Atari™, and video arcades, the enemy has a whole new connotation as players attempt to prevent inter-galactic wars. The programs for these games come in varying degrees of difficulty, thus allowing the child/player to first save the Earth before trying to save the Universe.

Many educational programs are also available for these electronic devices, providing the user the opportunity to sharpen basic skills such as reading, math, music, co-ordination, and manual dexterity; or more challenging programs to stimulate the intellect and mentality of the user. These "modern" games enjoy a great popularity, however, they have not supplanted the age-old games of baseball, soccer, skipping rope, and other outdoor activities. Left to right are Amanda Murchison, Joshua Tompkins, Derek Tompkins, Adam Murchison, and Kara McGrath.
Photo by Maureen McGrath Murchison

One of the earliest settlers hereabouts was lumber entrepreneur and Loyalist Nathaniel Churchill who built this homestead in 1839 at Rum Rapids on the Aroostook River near Crouseville. It is now the residence of Clifton Boudman. The 1890's picture is courtesy of Clifton Boudman.

Joseph Wingate Haines and wife Mary (See photo p. 91) came to Maple Grove (now Fort Fairfield) in 1844 and built the first sawmill in return for a grant of one thousand acres of land. He also brought the first Devon cattle into Aroostook. This Haines Homestead, built with a beautiful mansard roof, is still occupied by Haines descendants. This photograph was taken in 1875.
Courtesy of Herbert and Lois Haines

The Snell House in Houlton, hotel for early travelers in Aroostook, shown here decorated for the one hundredth anniversary of Houlton in 1911.
Courtesy of Eugene Jackins

> Meadows and intervales interrupt the forests and waterways of Aroostook, naturally inviting areas where people can come together, build homes, meetinghouses, and theaters to share in this celebration we call Life.
>
> Architectural style in Aroostook has been called "helter-skelter," and there is certainly a wide variety of styles. From the temporary log homes of the early pioneer to the estates of today, our homes both reflect and influence our basic values, our need for security.

*The Paige House in Presque Isle was built as a private residence. Note the barn in the rear. This picture was taken at the turn of the century.
Courtesy of the Presque Isle Historical Society*

MEADOWS AND OTHER CULTURAL CENTERS
by Clifton Boudman

After the Presque Isle Opera House burned in 1946 and Perry's Theater burned, the Braden Theater opened in 1950, and the handsome State Theater on State Street opened in 1947, designed with modern seating that was the last word in style, but it burned in 1961. The Cinema opened in Presque Isle in 1970 and closed in 1986. The Braden in Presque Isle remains as one of the few theaters in Aroostook, including a Cinema in Caribou and one in Houlton, as home videos cut into the market.

The Universities at Presque Isle and Fort Kent have consistently provided live theater, and art and foreign films are as part of the Fine Art program at the University of Maine at Presque Isle. The UMPI art program was started in 1966 by sculptor, film/art historian Clifton Boudman, and in 1971 the first professional art gallery in northern Maine opened at the university. In 1972 the first annual six-credit European Art Study Tour to England and the continent began. Ceramicist Joel Dana joined the faculty in 1973, painter Anderson Giles in 1979, and ceramicist Mark Huff in 1981. A BFA was offered in 1986. The university's Hudramics Club was expanded into the Association of Performing Arts, followed by Pioneer Playhouse. A Center for the Performing Arts opened in Caribou in 1988.

"No other region of Maine is so openly defined by its landscape as Aroostook County.... The vast north woods are given mental definition by the clothing of trees, the forest itself.... But in the County there is no escaping the primacy of land. Here and there the gentle roll of the land is interrupted by the abrupt forms of aging Silurian volcanoes like Haystack and Quoggy Jo mountains outside Presque Isle.

"Remote, isolate, this 'other Maine' is fertile artistic ground. The few maverick artists who abide here, however, are less inclined to examine the physical landscape than they are the psychic landscape, to cultivate images and visions rooted in the soil." From Ed Breem, the *Maine Times*, October 1987.

1820 to 1850
French Acadians, British loyalists, and southern New Englanders came north, cleared land, made spaces, constructed homes, and formed villages and towns—the beginnings of a northern Maine identity, of the Aroostook culture.

1850 to 1890
Most larger homes, with modifications were based on earlier Neo-Classical designs. Expensive clapboard made locally was augmented with some shipped in from downstate and from Boston. First Presque Isle Opera House was constructed.

Main Street, Fort Fairfield circa 1905 with the Frontier Trust in the center.
Courtesy of Ft. Fairfield Public Library

Main Street, Presque Isle, in the 1950's.
Courtesy of Presque Isle Historical Society

Opera houses were found in the larger towns by the turn of the century and the numbers increased in the early 1900s. These scenes of the Ashland Opera House and the interior of the Presque Isle Opera House exemplify similar scenes in Houlton and Van Buren. Artists from Chataqua, New York, brought their music to the County and were well received.

The second Presque Isle Opera House was built in 1913 by Hadley V. Mooers of his design, for John Hone, pioneer motion picture operator. Its stage was sixty-five-feet wide, and forty-three-feet deep. It burned April 26, 1947.
Courtesy of the Turner Memorial Library

Perry's Theater.
Courtesy of the Presque Historical Society

The Presque Isle House was a turn of the century hotel with Perry's Theater next door.
Courtesy of Blanche Beckwith

1890 to 1900
Town opera houses brought culture and performing arts to northern Maine in the form of legitimate road shows, touring acting companies, and early film presentations. Some acting troupes stayed all winter performing a different play each week. Luanes Opera House opened in Ashland.

1900 to 1940
Art and culture arrived in the form of imagery projected in various operating motion picture theaters throughout the County. Hone's Opera House was built in 1913. The Gem Opera House and Rudy's Theater were opened in Caribou in 1920s. The Gem became the Powers Theater which closed in the early 1970s. Perry Theater was built in Presque Isle. A devastating fire destroyed this beautiful structure in 1946.

1940 to 1970
Many film theaters were constructed between the late 1930s and the 1950s, the Golden Age of film attendance in northern Maine. Van Buren had the Marilyn and the Gayety, Fort Kent the Community and the Savoy, and Caribou the Caribou Theater and Rudy. A terrible fire destroyed the Rudy on September 4, 1952. Films were shown in Eagle Lake at Martin's Hall; in Madawaska the Modern and the State were in operation until recently, and Hussy's Theater operated in Mars Hill until the 1960s.

The Paramount Theatre block was built in Fort Fairfield by Downing Company of Presque Isle for Raymond R. Johnston. The theater was leased to a division of Paramount Pictures. On March 5, 1930, the Fort Fairfield Review *states, "The Paramount, Fort Fairfield's great new theatre to open Wednesday, April 2nd... best and most modern picture house north of Portland... brilliant opening exercises... excursion trains from all over Aroostook County and New Brunswick." The opening attraction was* Honey *starring Nancy Carroll.*
Courtesy of Gilbert Titcomb

NORTHERN FLORISTS

- STATE -

HAPPY COOKING

OPERA HOUSE

Enchanted Forest

Boy's Ranch

Gilda

ATTENTION FARMERS

Northern National Bank

We have just received

"Just Common Sense"

Sue Valentine Thompson

PINE TRAIL INN

HOME BAKED BEANS

Aroostook Co-Operative Company

JOHN GARFIELD GERALDINE FITZGERALD NOBODY LIVES FOREVER

The Mysterious Mr. Valentine

The State Street Theater, *Presque Isle, operated from 1947 to 1961. Typical theater offerings in the mid 1940s were:* Gilda, *starring Rita Hayworth; The* Enchanted Forest, *including a sportscope, cartoon, and newsreel; and* Nobody Lives Forever, *starring John Garfield and Walter Brennan. Courtesy of the Presque Isle Historical Society*

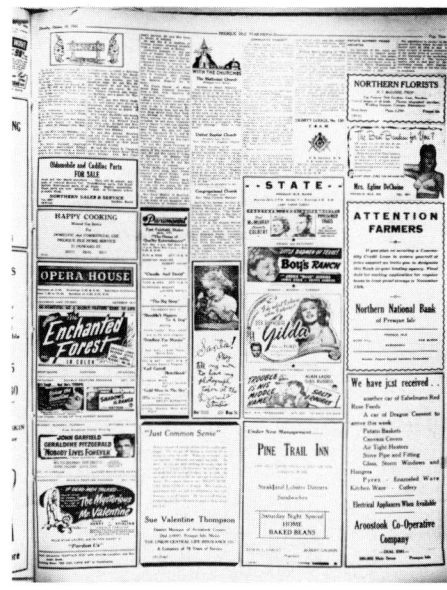

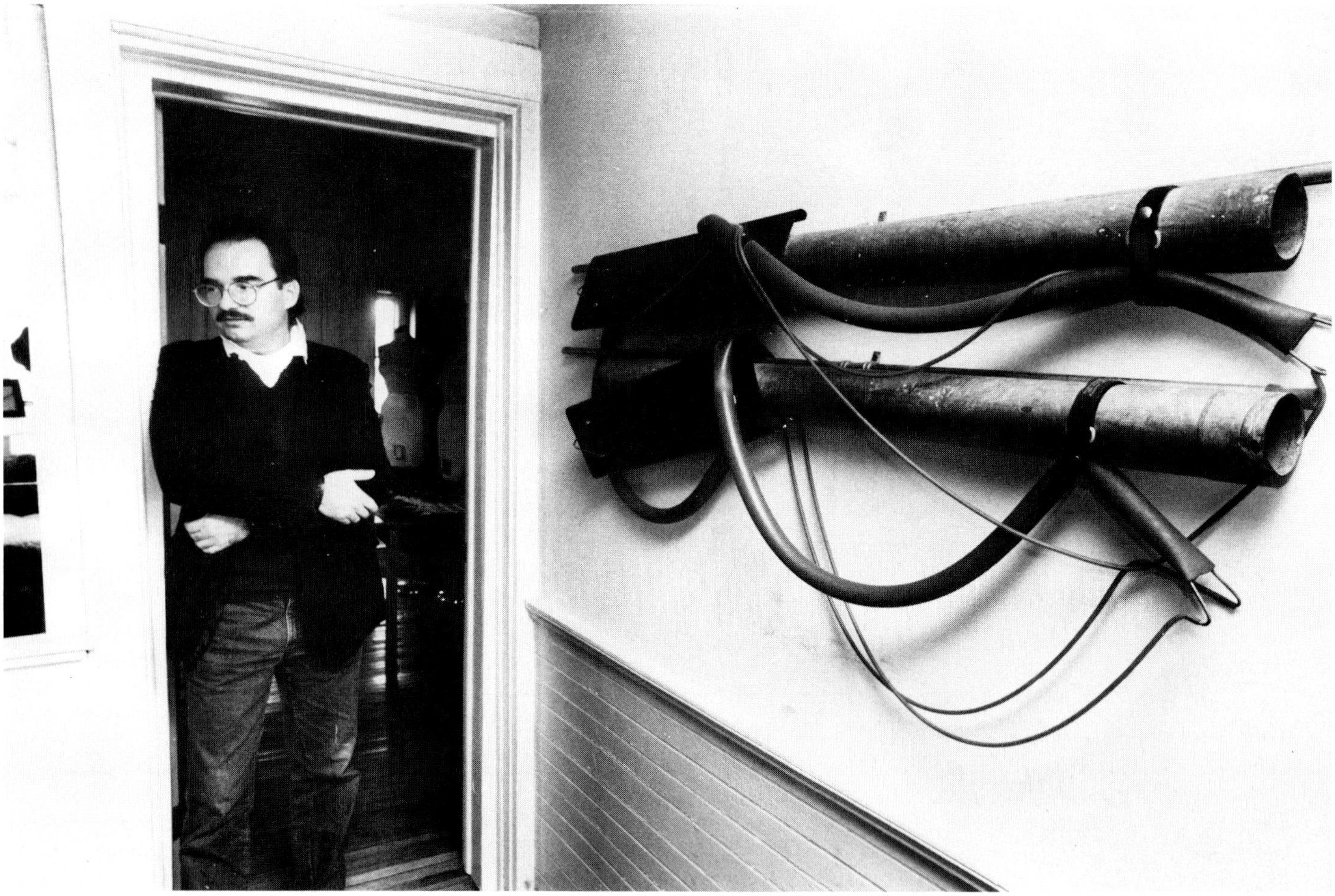

Clifton Boudman, senior professor of art at the University of Maine at Presque Isle lives a few miles upriver from Presque Isle at Rum Rapids, Crouseville. "He inhabits a nineteenth century farmer's home, one of the oldest homes in northern Maine, built circa 1839. Boudman, who variously refers to himself as a sculptor, imagist, and alien, has fashioned for himself a glitzy, hi-tech soul-hole of white-washed walls and mirror tiles. With Dada as his decorator, he has populated his cool retreat with semiotic beings—humanoid sculptures . . . saddlery, old jewelry and rubber. The grounds of Boudman's riparian estate are spiked with stiff metal sculptures, creations of his earlier life as a junk sculptor in the Richard Staniewicz/ David Smith/Mark DiSuvero tradition. The overall effect of Chez Boudman is an imaginative affirmation of the life of the mind." Boudman came to Presque Isle from Maryland to develop his own art program, including a three-week European Art Study Tour each year. He is also a delegate to the Edinburgh (Scotland) Film Festival each year. He has attracted attention for his "elegant black and white drawings, works cryptic and clinical, combining sparce geometric forms and passages of free drawing." From Ed Breen, the Maine Times, *October 1987. Photo by Scott Perry*

Anderson Giles, associate professor of art at the University of Maine at Presque Isle came to Presque Isle "to combine his two artistic loves by teaching both painting and photography. He paints with an emotional expressiveness evocative of deep psychic space and hot with the residue of myth and mysticism; employs images suggested by temples, pyramids, and crystals. Thematically it is consistent with Giles's expressed concern with apocrypha and the disappearance of advanced civilizations. His paintings seem like direct transcriptions of intuited experience. Mythology has always fascinated Giles, but he also acknowledges a more arcane influence on his art—the occult thought of psychic healer Edgar Cayce, the Sleeping prophet of Giles' hometown of Virginia Beach." From Ed Breem, the Maine Times, *October 1987. Photo by Scott Perry*

Mark Huff, associate professor of art at the University of Maine at Presque Isle and ceramic sculptor also paints, draws, writes poetry, and "creates his own one-of-a-kind multi-media books. The spirit of surrealism runs through all that he does. While acknowledging a stylistic affinity of his work with West Coast funksters, Huff is very serious and contemplative." From Ed Breen, the Maine Times, *October 1987. Photo by Scott Perry*

The works of Aroostook hermit and folk painter Donald Ashby Clark have recently been discovered by Ruth Reed Mraz of Fort Fairfield. A group of dusty watercolors had been stored in her mother's cellar since she had purchased the adjoining property where Clark once lived.

Clark, who painted familiar barnyard scenes, horses, and cows, also drew exotic animals. A recluse since childhood who never married, Clark lived alone during his adult life, mostly in a tiny log cabin with no conveniences. Born in 1893, Clark died in 1970 and is buried in an unmarked grave in Union Cemetery in Fort Fairfield. Although he lived in extreme poverty, he left money to charity. Photograph by Jan Kok

Micmac quillwork, these boxes and cradle were made with porcupine quills dyed black, white, and red. The cradle was made by Christina Morris of Halifax in 1868. The design features the moose, the mysterious "flyfot" (or Basque origin?), and the eight-pointed star or "Kagwet" starfish, often considered the most distinctively Micmac motif.
Courtesy of the DesBrisay Museum, Bridgewater, N.B., photo courtesy of the Nova Scotia Museum, Halifax

Is creativity the gift of a few, or inherent in all? Right brain/left brain studies seem to confirm that the creative potential exists in all, and is manifested in a wondrous variety of ways. Some paint, some photograph, some sculpt, some work with needles and fabric or fibers, and some create order, symmetry, and beauty in their surroundings. The aesthetic imperative finds expression in Aroostook as everywhere else in our world.

The aesthetic sense, with its urging to appreciate beauty, to create and recreate objects expressing those urges must be inate in humanity as its expressions abound in every culture. The quest for the beautiful, and the need to express the emotional response to living are manifested in visual arts, performing arts, and in living.

From the painstaking porcupine quill work and the beadwork of the Native Peoples, to the paintings for today's hospital loan programs, the need for artistic expression seems to flow in an outpouring of a shared vision, to create a reflection of the beauty of life.

A watercolor-enhanced pen and ink drawing of the now razed Northland Hotel in Houlton was done by Esther Orr Faulkner of Houlton.
Photograph by Jan Kok

SPRINGS, RIVERS, AND ARTISTIC FLOWS

by Anna Fields Mcgrath with contributions by Evelyn Kok, Kathy Finnemore, and Harald Prins

Ruth Reed Mraz, a Fort Fairfield native, creates porcelain dolls as a hobby. They are dressed authentically in period costumes, copied from photographs of her own ancestors. Their clothes are either antique or reproduced from old fabrics. She also has studied doll sculpture and has created portrait dolls of her three grandchildren. She is a member of the Doll Artisan Guild of America.
Photograph by Jan Kok

John Holub, a self-taught artist came to Westfield in 1975. He specializes in watercolors of Aroostook County scenes. He is one of many local artists who has displayed his work in the lobbies of the Aroostook Medical Center in December, 1988. One-man shows are a monthly event at TAMC, with shows arranged and sponsored by the Art Loan Program. Proceeds of sales of works on display go to community service projects.

Local artist and florist Bessie Higgins is shown at a senior art show exhibit at the gallery of the University of Maine at Presque Isle for Don Cyr in 1979. Higgins has given private art lessons to two generations of Aroostookans, and is loved and admired by all who know her. Courtesy of ACHC

Cary Hospital in Caribou sponsors an art program featuring the works of local artists, such as this scene by local artist Gloria Wilcox. Phyllis Belanger, Dorothy St. Peters, Shirley Ayer, Eileen Bernard, and Laura St. Peter look on as Eileen Bernard is presented with the painting in appreciation for her work on the program. Photograph by William Flagg

Local artist Bernice Cyr exhibits her paintings at the Northern Maine Medical Center, through the Hospital Guild of Fort Kent. Local artists exhibit on a rotating basis at the hospital. Courtesy of the Northern Maine Medical Center

A Thanksgiving mural was created by the second grade at Mapleton Elementary School in the fall of 1988. Support for creative expression by school children has been sponsored by the American Association of University Women in The County. For over forty years, they have sponsored art contests, and other events. Another sponsor of creative visual arts has been the Northern Maine Fair where booths have been well stocked with paintings and other handiwork of County residents of all ages. The children are from left, front, Erica Voisine, Melissa Saucier, Deanne Pulcifer, Elizabeth Richardson, and Amanda Leonard. Second row, Jenny Wood, Jennifer Nichols, April Michaud, Alanna Clair, Danna Beaulieu, and Erin Kennedy. Third row, Buddy LaCombe, Matt Clifford, Derek Nickerson, Joshua Alley, Anthony Gamblin, Joey Lyons, and Jamie Smith. Back row, Andrew Dyer, Lewis Chase, Ryan Burnett, and Jeffrey Nault. Photograph by Chase; courtesy of the Star Herald

"In Fashion" in Aroostook
by Kathy Finnemore

One robes oneself for protection from the weather, for modesty's sake, for status, for enhancement of body attributes, to reflect a need for self-expression, or some combination of these. From the fig leaf, grass skirt, and animal skins, to the beautiful, hardy fibers and fabrics of this late twentieth century, being "in fashion" both reflects and influences the social history of any region. This is most certainly true in Aroostook County.

The Acadians of the Madawaska Territory (pre-Revolution) grew and spun flax to make linen for clothing, bed clothes, tablecloths, towels, and other needs and found a market throughout the area in the first half of the nineteenth century for their linen, called "Madawaska crash." They also carded and spun sheep's wool, and wove or knitted it into clothing and bed clothes.
Courtesy of Ann Michaud

This is the 1911 wedding party of Ada May Chase and Dr. Frank Tarbell of Smyrna Mills. The bride and attendants' gowns reflect the practical but elegant silhouette of the time, with slim, fitted waists, and skirts draped loosely over the hips and gathered at the back. The dresses were probably made of silks and satins, and are lavishly trimmed with lace and embroidery.
Courtesy of Jane Tarbell Brown

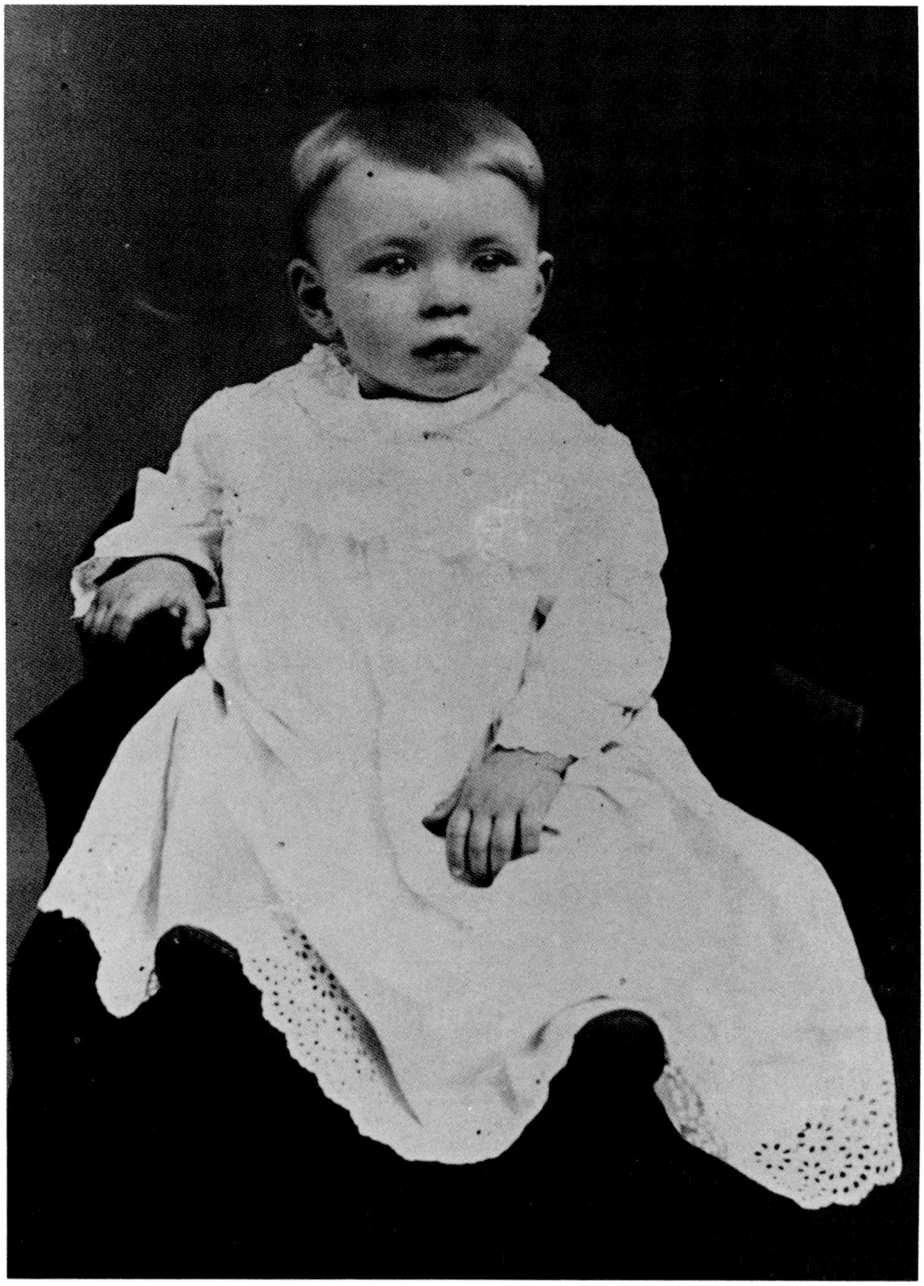

This christening gown for little Lucius Charles Tarbell was made in 1888 from his mother's wedding gown (note the lace).
Courtesy of Albert Fields

An unidentified young lady has dressed for cold weather, in her luxurious fur coat and muff ensemble, completed by a large hat embellished with feathers, popular during the first few years of the century.
Courtesy of the David Dorsey Collection

Edward G. Perrier, Bertha Irving, and E. J. Dorsey on a trip to Boston, were dressed for winter in fur, tailored woolen coats, and felt hats, typical of the 1930s.
Courtesy of Edward J. Dorsey

Presque Isle-born and raised designer Jessica Hedrick McClintock of Jessica McClintock, Inc., is shown at work in her San Francisco studio in 1988. She specializes in romantic yet up-to-date apparel. Starting with five thousand dollars and a lot of determination, she directed her vision into a multi-million dollar business. Jessica credits her New England upbringing for her success. She was taught by her mother and grandmother to work hard, and learned to make decisions at a young age. Jessica provides an example of the Aroostook qualities of determination and hard work in the complicated world of fashion design. Her lines include: Jessica McClintock, sophisticated ready-to-wear and bridal clothes; Gunne Sax, for children and teenagers; and Scott McClintock, sportswear named for her son. Jessica and her assistants turn out five hundred new designs five times a year.
Courtesy of Verna Hedrick, Presque Isle

The role of the university in fostering art in this area is apparent in Kathy Finnemore's show at the University of Maine-Presque Isle's Pullen Gallery, entitled "Silk." Pictured is her 1980 line of contemporary women's suits and dresses. Kathy has established a business designing and making clothes in Caribou.
Photograph by Kathy Finnemore

Hunter Davis at Shin Pond, cooling his fiddle around 1910. This old trapper was one of many who traveled through the woods, bringing news, stories, and folk songs to the woods crews, and fiddling for parties and dances.
Courtesy of Shirlee Connors-carlson

Leon Michaud with his "White Lady" banjo, and the Rhythm Kings
Courtesy of Evelyn Kok

> When the first settlers arrived in this wild new land, music probably assumed an even greater importance than it did in their own homelands. It brought them together in fun and shared nostalgia with much gaity and dancing, which served as vital courting rituals. There were also hymn-singing meetings for those whose leaders believed that dancing was a ploy of the devil, especially to the music of a fiddle. Judging by the popularity of the fiddle, most people ignored this warning.

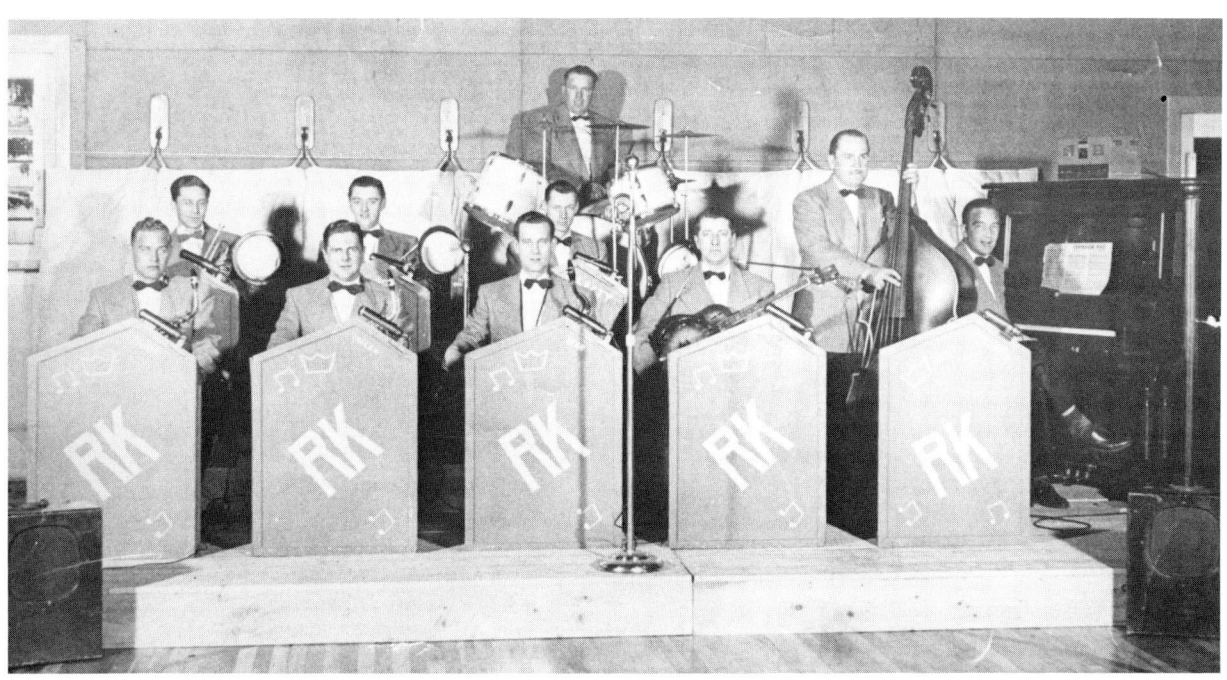

NORTHWINDS AND HUMMING STRINGS MUSIC IN AROOSTOOK

by Evelyn Kok

Laura Flint's Diaries, 1867-1876

What was it like to be a teenager in 1867? From an early diary kept by Laura Flint, who lived in Fort Fairfield and Ashland over a hundred years ago, the fascinated reader is transported back to the days when young people traveled great distances by good-old Dobbin-power to musical gatherings and dances. The girls wore dresses hand-sewn from cloth with old-fashioned names, dresses so long, full and cumbersome that they limited the type of dancing on those important and poignant occasions when they had dates.

At the musical gatherings they sang "The Bold Sojer Boy," "Flow Gently, Sweet Afton," "Carnival of Venice," "Blue Bells of Scotland" and "Robin Adair." Laura tells in her diary that her friends sang "Pop Goes the Weasel" and "Yankee Doodle" on comb and jew's harp during school recess. Simple fun! At every dance, the musicians played "Money Musk." Virtuosos on every instrument (especially trumpeters) played "Carnival of Venice" with triple tonguing, bellows shakes, and endless variations for better or for worse.

Many young people went to dancing class to learn waltzes, polkas, round dances, quick-steps, "chases," quadrilles, squares, and grand marches. They looked forward to being invited by their favorite friend, and when no invitation was forthcoming, some cried in their pillows.

Laura writes (the grammar and spelling are hers):

"Mon. Dec. 16th Heard there was going to be a dance tonight. No one came after us, so I suppose they did not have any.

Tues. Dec. 17th, It snowed almost a foot yesterday. It is very light and will not make very good roads. One week from today is Christmas—talk of having a good time.

Fri. Dec. 21 Went to dancing school last night. I danced with George McNally and Jake Mosher. Ed Gardner, extra, dances with Walter Hawes, L. C. Mooers, one dance, refused eight. H.N.I [?] Edna is going Christmas with Lew Bearce. I have not had any invitation yet—of course I shall have to go with some old fool tomorrow night. There is to be a dancing school for the benefit of the poor waltzers (sugar) Edna and I had to dress four chickings something I never done before in my life."

Many people of the county today owe their names, existence, and identities to the romances and marriages formed during those musical gatherings and dances recorded in Laura Flint's diary.

Leon Michaud Remembers the Old Dance Pavilions and the Bands that Played There

Leon Michaud and his group called Lewie Boy often played in Presque Isle during the 1930s. He played a Fairbanks "White Lady" banjo in the group that also featured

Lew Michaud with Alma and Guy Beaulieu on piano and guitar. Later, the group expanded to become Lewie Boy and the Commanders, with Pee Wee Ramo on drums, Doug Grant on trombone, and Carol Spear as "Maine's Trick Violin Player." Some old-time fiddlers who would often drop in on various bands were Bary "B-B" Brown, Johnnie Coty, Joe Sweat (already in his eighties), and Dana Rafford of Ashland playing contra violin.

The Rhythm Kings were a County dance band of the 1940s. Freddie Boyce, Sherwood Kelso and Dean Silvia played saxophone, Leon Michaud played guitar, Frank Chase (from Caribou) played bass, Rene Levesque played the drums, Dennis Terriault played trombone with Doug Grant, and Harold Delano played trumpet. Among the County pavilions where they played were: Queen Esther in Oxbow; Silver Slipper in Ashland; Ginn's Pavilion in Fort Fairfield; Riverside Pavilion in Houlton; Venetian Garden in Edmunston, New Brunswick; Acadia Hotel in Fort Kent; Hammond Hotel in Van Buren; and Paul's Arena, Maple Grove, Fort Fairfield. Paul's Arena had a concession stand, and those requiring further refreshment met out back in the cemetery during intermission for some "white lightning" to rejuvenate weary dancers. (This information was provided by Leon Michaud).

Dorothy Dingwall Remembers Presque Isle's Musical Past

During the 1920s, Chataqua used to come to Presque Isle for a week each summer. My first experience with it involved a sneak approach. Their tent was behind what was then the Training School, and on a pleasant summer night I was caught lying flat on the ground with my head inside the tent, listening quietly. Other young people who crashed the gate more boisterously were driven away, but I was invited to come in and listen. That might have been about 1923 or 1924. For the next few years after my sneak approach, my parents purchased a ticket for me.

There were several prominent musical organizations in Presque Isle. The Barbershoppers had a beautifully balanced male chorus of good voices for many years. The Community Concerts Association, which started in 1945, brought three or four concerts to the city yearly until 1986.

The Clef Club was a women's chorus. It started before my time and continued to about 1956. Here are some of the leading lights of the group during these years:

Miss Alice Kimball—vocal teacher. Her home was on the Parsons Road. She had a great garden. She studied and traveled in Europe. I heard her sing for the memorial service for President Harding in 1923. Sylvia Weinberg in her teens was one of Alice Kimball's students.

Mrs. Isadore Stevens—organist and choir director for the Baptist Church and then for the Congregational Church. I participated in two vesper services that she arranged and directed—as choir singer the first time and as pianist the second time, when we did several piano-organ duets.

Mrs. Ivan W. Waddell—graduate of the New England Conservatory. She was a very fine pianist and teacher. She did more than any other musician to alert me to the importance of interpreting music.

Miss Evangeline Tubbs—faculty member of the Aroostook State Normal School. She taught music to prospective teachers and directed concerts.

Several prominent musicians from the big cities came to Presque Isle through the years. One of them, William R. Chapman (of New York?) brought one or two soloists whom he accompanied each time they came. He also directed choruses of the Clef Club, Fort Fairfield's Nordica Club, and music clubs from Caribou and Houlton. I attended one of his concerts in Littleton at the campground around 1925. I was tremendously impressed. Hearing professionals made a big impression on a music lover who had never heard anything professional before.

(Dorothy Dingwall, herself, has been a leading pianist, accompanist, and teacher in the County for many years.)

A Variety of Musical Groups in Aroostook

The high schools and the institutions of higher learning in Aroostook had, and have, many and varied musical groups performing at school functions and for the public. The All-Aroostook Music Festivals, sponsored by the high schools through the Maine Music Educator's Association, continue to be big events. The Northern Maine Chamber Society, now under the direction of Harrison Roper of Houlton, made its debut in 1986 and provides an opportunity for those whose tastes and interests lie in orchestral music of the past. The Presque Isle Barbershoppers were active and popular for many years during the mid-century. Its chorus and its individual quartets won many honors in state and regional competitions.

The Caribou Choral Society, under the direction of Dan Ladner, was formed on the occasion of the nation's bicentennial celebrations. It gives at least two performances a year at several communities in Aroostook and in Canada and flourishes today undiminished in popularity.

"Music Theater"
Maine's First E.T.V. Program

Before 1958, many rural classrooms had little or no music instruction and no music supervisor. When the new possibilities of television burst upon the Maine scene, three men in the education field, Phil Annas (State Department), WarrenHill (commissioner of education), and Clifford O. T. Wieden (president of Aroostook State Teachers College), sent Prof. Jan Kok south to Augusta for a year to write and teach a live-in school educational television series for the early grades (kindergarten through third grade), and for the middle grades (fourth through ninth grade).

Maine at that time had no ETV station. WENH-TV at Poland Springs donated the use of its facilities, staff, and air time. WABI-TV in Bangor and WAGM-TV in Presque Isle donated air time for transmission to the eastern part of the state and to the County.

"Music Theater" was a big success. It leaped across the borders into New Hampshire (and Canada) where it was

At a reception of the Community Concerts Association, Mrs. Nathaniel Barker pours tea for tenor Richard Tucker, left, while Howard Hrushka, along with Tucker's accompanist, and Emery Skillin wait their turn.

Mrs. Barker, Howard Hrushka, and Emery Skillin were officers and workers in the organization for many years. The paintings shown on the walls are by Lucy Hayward Barker, whose work is in the collection of the Farnsworth Museum and the Aroostook County Historical Center at the library of the University of Maine at Presque Isle.
Courtesy of the ACHC

The Presque Isle Barbershoppers Chorus gives a public performance. Left to right, front row: Bill Campbell, Elliott Farwell, Henry Gagnon, Jasper Bull, John McNally, Emery Skillin, John Gorman, Al Erickson, Lou Michaud, Ted Dubay, Doc Unger, George Chase, Neil Michaud, Charles Everett, John Sluka, Roy Smith, and Fred P. Stevens. Second row: Bob Hayden, Cobby Downing, Clarence Benjamin, Herb Sprague, Larry Crockett, John Philpot, Ivan McLauflin, John White, Merle Oak, Dwight Vance, Bill Haskell, Maynard Miller, Earl Dow, and George Kesip (?). Third row: Earl Crawford, Phil McGauflin, Willie Moreau, Ray Rafford (?), Mike Roberts, Gilbert White (BUN), Ron Cyr, Fred Culberson, unknown, Jack Downing, unknown, unknown, Fred Lavaway, and Walt Holder.
Courtesy of Jim Willette

Contemporary string and wind ensembles performing at the University of Maine at Fort Kent.
Courtesy of the University of Maine at Fort Kent

Director Dan Ladner and the Caribou Choral Society with members of the Northern Maine Chamber Society at the 1988 Christmas Concert in Caribou.
Courtesy of Evelyn Kok

Jan Kok in the studio at Poland Springs where his year-long ETV series for in-school use was originally televised. Courtesy of Jan Kok

Some scenes by Evelyn Kok to illustrate the song, "Three Pirates Came to London Town," in the ETV series. Courtesy of Evelyn Kok

received so enthusiastically that the New Hampshire School of the Air (University of New Hampshire at Durham) offered its facilities to the Maine Department of Education to put the early grades series on tape with a grant from the Ford Foundation. These tapes were played for the next seven years.

The songs that Professor Kok taught in the series were chosen from *Songs to Grow On* and *More Songs to Grow On* by Beatrice Landeck, published by Edward B. Marks.

The TV illustrations were done by Evelyn Kok. Even today, people who watched the program when they were children remember "Three Pirates Came to London-Town," "Risselty Rosselty," and "B-I-N-G-O." Some of these children are now parents and teachers, and pass the songs along to new generations with an early-acquired understanding of pitch and time reading and an interest in how musical instruments produce sound.

Musical Contributions by Service Clubs

The Lion's Club of Presque Isle presented its first Minstrel Show in 1947, with the Rhythm Kings providing music. These shows continued annually until about 1964 when social attitudes toward minstrel shows changed and the Lions switched from Deep South to Broadway. Joe Olore directed all the performances of the Broadway shows, which were a highly popular annual event from 1965 to 1977, including such shows as *Man of La Mancha, The Sound of Music,* and *Gigi.*

The Kiwanis Club of Presque Isle started its annual *Kiwanis Talent Revue* in 1952 to raise money for the Kiwanis Child Health Clinic. Students and other people from the County try out for these shows, which have been directed by Jan Kok since their inception.

Recreating the Musical Past

Several groups and individuals in Aroostook are interested in recreating the musical past in a variety of ways. There are families who play old-time or historical music for their own enjoyment, as past Governor John Reed's family used to do. There are instrumental ensembles such as the Presque Isle Recorder Consort, which was organized in 1975 and performs ensemble music for recorders. There are also makers of traditional and historical instruments, such as Jay Witcher. A former aerospace engineer, Jay Witcher relocated his harp workshop from California to the Houlton area in 1980 to take advantage of the northern hard maple that grows in this area. He makes reproductions of ancient harps, and also modern harps of his own design. His harps are in use world-wide by well-known performers and recording artists, and by people from other walks of life who "just want to play a harp."

Then there are groups who enact the musical past. The people of one such group put on a show called *Antics with Antiques,* sponsored by the Friends of the Aroostook County Historical Society at the University of Maine at Presque Isle in 1986, to celebrate the County's cultural heritage. This show included old zithers, fifes, and other musical oddities in Evelyn Kok's collection, and skits and musical performances in old-fashioned dress and with antique props.

Sylvia Weinberg as the Mother Abbess sings "Climb Every Mountain" in The Sound of Music.
Photograph by Voscar, the Maine Photographer

These metal newspaper offset printing plates are part of a cherished wall display in Joe Olore's menswear clothing store, Presque Isle.
Photograph by Voscar, the Maine Photographer; courtesy of the Star Herald

Jay Witcher's harp shop.
Photo by Cathy Brewer Craig

The Sound of Music *with Phronie Bouchard and a bevy of school girls.*
Photograph by Voscar, the Maine Photographer

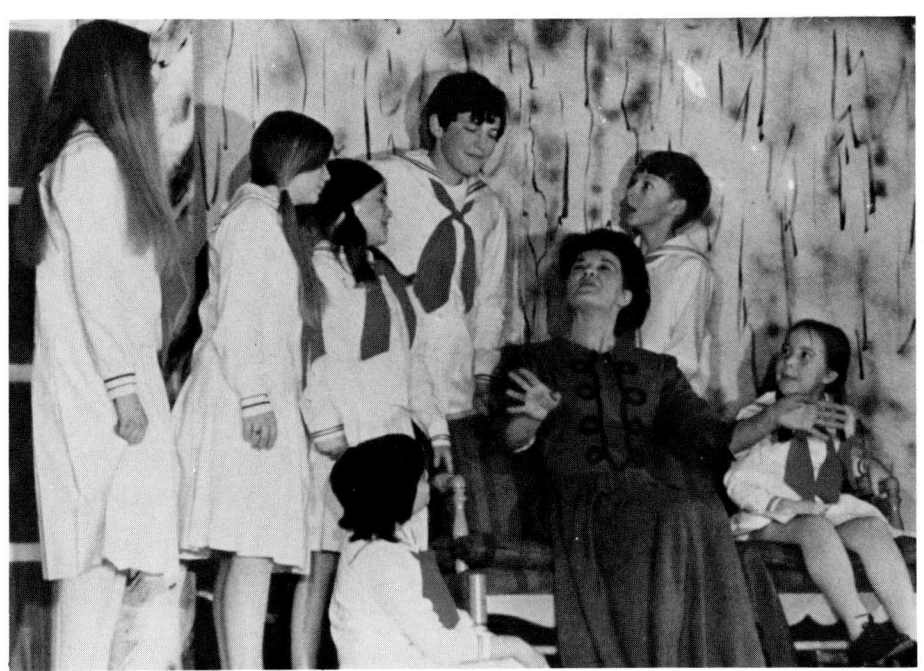

The musical Nadeau family in Aroostook at the turn of the century.

Gov. John Reed of Fort Fairfield enjoys a musical evening with his family at the Blaine House in the early 1960s. Daughters Cheryl (violin) and Ruth Ann (piano) join their parents.
Courtesy of Albert Fields

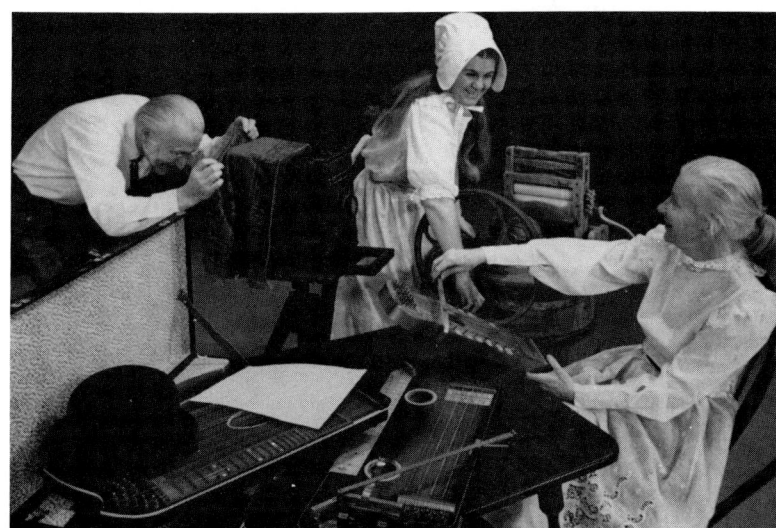

The Presque Isle Recorder Consort. The flat-backed lute on the table was designed and made by Evelyn Kok in 1963 "to play like a guitar, and look like the music sounds." The group includes, left to right: Jan Kok, director, recorder, guitar and voice; Evelyn Kok, guitar, flute, percussion, voice; Roberta Griffiths, recorder, voice; Dick Kimball, recorder, voice; and Jean Hamlin, recorder.
Photograph by Julian Turner; courtesy of Jean Hamlin

Preparing for the show, "Antics with Antiques," in 1986 to celebrate the County's cultural heritage, sponsored by the Friends of the Aroostook County Historical Center at the Library of the University of Maine at Presque Isle. Left to right: Prof. Jan Kok peers through an early view camera, Dena York operates a very antique washing machine, while Evelyn Kok plays The Black Hawk Waltz *on a bow zither.*

All-Aroostook band members in 1988
Courtesy of Evelyn Kok

The early schools in Aroostook were held in homes; the first frame house built in Houlton, the first English settlement, kept one room for school, with young children attending during the day, and older ones at night. And when Dennis Fairbanks built his mill on the Presque Isle Stream, and had attracted a few families, a room above the mill was used for a school room. But the early schoolhouses in Aroostook were typically log cabins, such as this one on the St. John River close to Schoolhouse Rapids near Allagash. *Courtesy of Shirlee Connors-carlson*

This group of students at the Westfield Grammar School in 1923 appears to be taking their education quite seriously. *Courtesy of the Lauretta Corey Estate, from Sylvia Grass*

RULES FOR TEACHERS

DUTIES
(Before or After School Session)
* Wash windows & clean classroom with soap and water once a week.
* Check outhouses daily. *(Plenty of old catalogues are available at School Board office.)*

APPAREL
(Forbidden Wear in Public at All Times)
* WOMEN: (1) A bathing costume
  (2) Bloomers for cycling
  (3) Skirts slit to expose ankles
  (4) Bustle extension over 10 inches
* MEN: (1) Detachable collar & neck tie removed from shirt
  (2) Shirt sleeves unlinked & rolled
  (3) Hair closely cropped *(unless bald or have disease of the scalp)*

CONDUCT
(Cause for Immediate Dismissal)
* Smoking of cigarettes, use of spirits, frequenting of pool or public dance halls.
* Marriage or other unseemly behavior by women teachers.
* Joining of any Feminist Movement, such as the *Suffragettes*.

Superintendent—Sept. 15, 1886

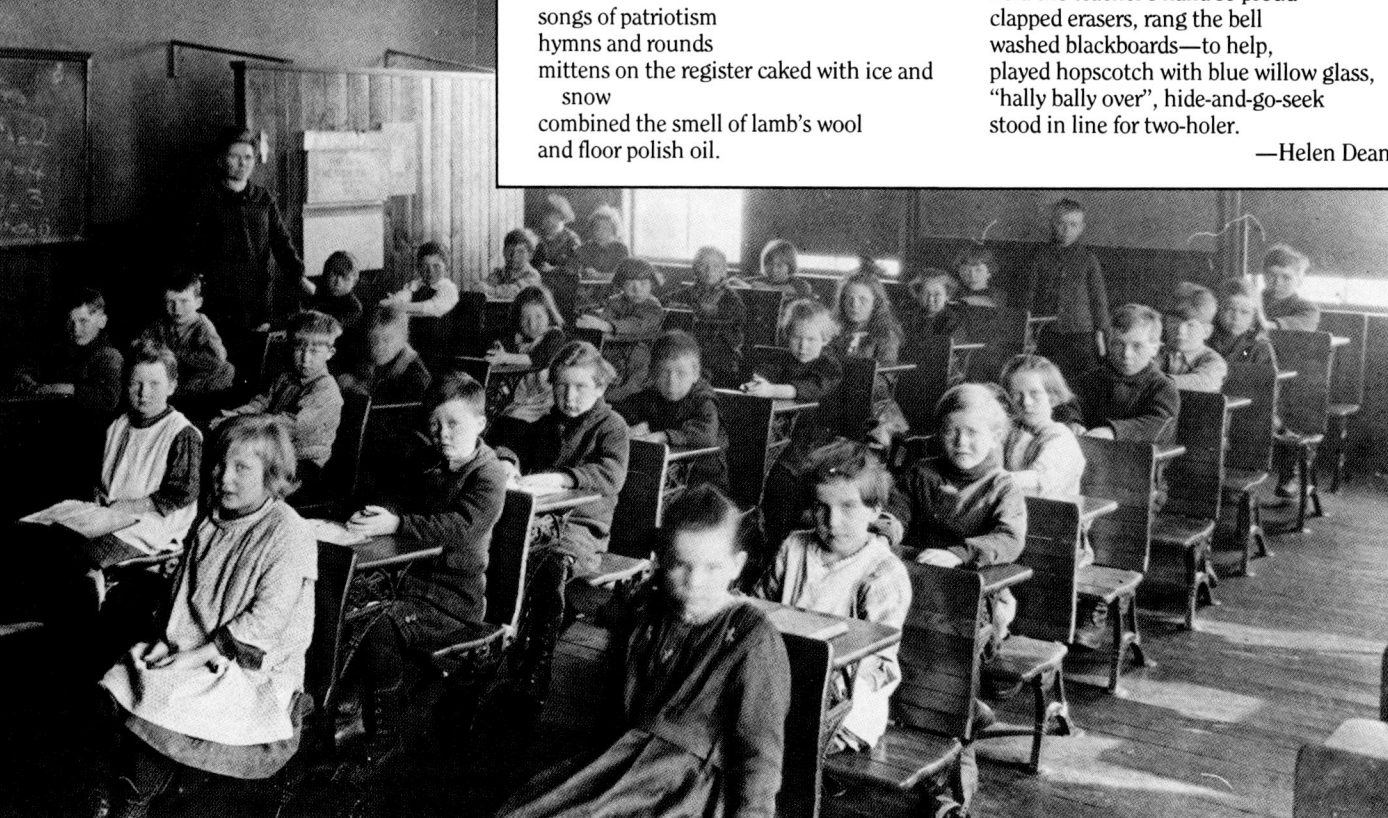

One-Room School—Blaisdell Farm

Cream colored clapboard

a sunlit room
songs of patriotism
hymns and rounds
mittens on the register caked with ice and snow
combined the smell of lamb's wool
and floor polish oil.

at recess we

held the teacher's hand so proud
clapped erasers, rang the bell
washed blackboards—to help,
played hopscotch with blue willow glass,
"hally bally over", hide-and-go-seek
stood in line for two-holer.

—Helen Deane

Maj. William Dickey came to the Madawaska Territory in the mid-1800s for health reasons, saw the plight of the French Acadians, and set about to do something about "this deplorable situation." He worked relentlessly to bring a specialized training school for teachers to the Madawaska area, which finally came to fruition in 1878. The plight of the Acadians was ever present in his thinking, as they spoke only French, and poorly understood what went on in the mainstream of life, in a land to which they had been departed. He devoted his energies to bringing a training school that would train teachers to teach in French, as well as teach then to speak fluently in English. the Madawaska training school operated one year in Fort Kent, and the next in Van Buren, alternately, for years. The first principal of the Madawska training school was Vital Cyr, followed be Miss Nowland, who revoiced in 1913 when electricity was installed at the Normal School to replace the kerosene lamps.
Courtesy of the Fort Kent Historical Society

CULTIVATING THE MIND: EDUCATION IN AROOSTOOK

by Shirlee Connors-carlson

Civilization as we know it is the result of ageless educative processes, instigated and supported by individuals, groups, nations: at home, in schoolrooms, in halls of higher learning, in research laboratories, and in mentor relationships around the world. We stand today on the shoulders of those who have learned, remembered, and shared the products of their minds, as we pursue understandings of our origin, perceived directions, and purposes, as Sir Julian Huxley and Teihard du Chardin have said, with possibilities and limitations and patterns of interaction, and deduce future trends. We learn the need for cooperation and the place for competition, but mostly we learn the need for participation in our own individual cycles of learning.

Civilization is increased and promoted through the Teacher, the teacher who creates, in the mind of the Pupil, a wonderment of life, its processes and expressions, and who also creates an ambiance, and facilitates the necessary processes and situations to attempt to satisfy that wonderment, and to create new ones.

Probably no state took the education of its young as seriously as Maine, according to the *Population of the United States* in 1860. At mid-nineteenth century Maine led all states in its white population in school (and its population was almost entirely white), and in 1860 Maine had the highest literacy rate in the new nation. This concern for education was reflected in Aroostook.

From early times on, education was placed in a position of importance in Aroostook. All grants of land, such as the one in Hodgdon, specifically had a stipulation that three lots be set apart for municipal and school purposes. The deed for Hodgdon was recorded September 12, 1782.

The early schools in Aroostook were typically log cabins in the woods or in the settlements. The early log cabin school was replaced by the one room school at the turn of the century.

After funding was established by the state of Maine for education, a set of rules was established and these rules were expected to be adhered to. Shown here are the rules set forth in 1886, and in 1915.

Rules for Teachers
1915

1. You will not marry during the term of your contract.
2. You are not to keep company with men.
3. You must be home between the hours of 8 p.m. and 6 a.m. unless attending a school function.
4. You may not loiter downtown in ice cream stores.
5. You may not travel beyond the city limits unless you have the permission of the chairman of the board.
6. You may not ride in a carriage or automobile with any man unless he is your father or brother.
7. You may not smoke cigarettes.

Two-room schools became fairly common in the late 1800s and by the turn of the century pupils in grades kindergarten through grade four were in one room, and pupils in grades five through eight in an adjacent room. A pail of water with a common dipper was a normal occurrence, as was a wood stove in the middle of the room, and an outhouse, often connected to the building. This two-room school at Westfield opened in 1907, and the first class is pictured on the stairs.
Courtesy of the Lauretta Corey Estate

The James School was built in Spragueville, Presque Isle, in 1917 to teach local children through grade eight until 1948 when it was closed with the consolidation of all elementary schools in Presque Isle, Westfield, and Mapleton under School Administration district No. 1. It was used as a non-denominational church by the Hillside Gospel Mission for ten years, then left to deteriorate until Julian Turner and local residents resolved to restore it, and completed restoration in 1987. It is used for educational and recreational activities, including "A day in a country school" visits by local elementary scholars.
Courtesy of Julian Turner

8. You may not dress in bright colors.
9. You may under no circumstances dye your hair.
10. You must wear at least petticoats.
11. Your dresses must not be any shorter than two inches above the ankle.
12. To keep the school room neat and clean, you must: sweep the floor at least once daily; scrub the floor at least once a week with hot, soapy water; clean the blackboards at least once a day; and start the fire at 7 a.m. so the room will be warm by 8 a.m.

Education in Aroostook has always been an important part of life. Schools of the past vanished, that were used for prayer meetings, annual town meetings, box socials, or other unexpected functions. But today they are used for adult education classes, for English as a second language, both for children coming to school where the adults still speak French, or for the dependents of airmen at Loring who marry Vietnamese, Korean, or other Asian women. Alternative Education classes are available for those who cannot attend regular school. And with the accelerated social, cultural, and economic changes, many non-traditional people are returning to high schools, or entering a vocational-technical school, or the university for a baccalaureate or master's degree for a career change.

Aroostook is fortunate to be able to receive Maine Public Broadcasting Network programs which provide a vast array of educational and informative programs to schools and to homes. Truly, we live in an age when life-long learning is a given.

Sherman Elementary School for grades three, four, and five. It is one of the few remaining wooden structure school buildings still in use.
Courtesy of John Johnson

With the opening of Limestone Air Force Base in 1950 (renamed Loring Air Force Base in 1959), federal monies were available in the 1950s to serve dependents of the airmen, enabling Limestone to build this modern high school with an Olympic-sized indoor pool, the only such school in Aroostook.
Courtesy of Limestone High School

Parochial schools, such as St. John's Episcopal School in Presque Isle, shown here, Saint Mary's College at Van Buren, and St. Mary's Convent at Houlton served those who wanted a religiously-oriented education for their children. Saint John's was purchased by the town of Presque Isle and donated to the state for a Normal School in 1903. Saint Mary's, the first convent school in the area, operated from 1885 until 1926. It was operated like the Lycee or French college system, and was somewhat elitist. Courses in liberal arts and commercial studies were offered. Students enrolled after completion of grammar school, and finished with a college education.
Courtesy of ACHC

Before state funding was established for education, a fee was collected from families for each student attending classes to pay teachers. This made education a privilege, rather than a rule. When Easton, Maine, established their high school in 1877, fees were still collected for the cost of maintaining teachers. The "Free High School" came into being in approximately 1873, and was the subject of much controversy for some years. In the yearly report of the State Department of Education, the Free High School was reinstated after a year's suspension by the Maine state legislature. By 1879, over eighty-six towns had free high schools, and were attended by 6,215 pupils. After the suspension, enrollment reached 14,900, and the controversy abated. Early high schools were often made of wood, as this one at Fort Fairfield, built in 1887.
Courtesy of the Fort Fairfield Public Library

As funding for education progressed to cover more expenses, conveyance of pupils was budgeted and a hired person was paid for conveyance. Here we see a public mode of transportation in Caribou for the purpose of transporting children to school about 1910.
Courtesy of ACHC

The University of Maine at Presque Isle, one of seven campuses of the University of Maine System (1970), developed from a state normal school for teachers, it opened in 1903 by an act of legislature, following efforts of local citizens led by Reverend Park. Buildings on the site of the former St. John's School were purchased, and a dormitory and dining hall named Normal Hall were built in 1905-1906. As the school grew, more buildings were added: Preble Hall, to house administrative offices and classrooms; auditorium, gymnasium, and library in 1921, followed by South Hall, a dormitory, in 1924. Wieden Hall, a gymnasium and auditorium, was built in 1960, allowing for expansion of classrooms and library facilities. A new dormitory, Emerson Hall, was built in 1963, followed by Kelley Commons Dining Hall in 1967. More new dormitories followed; Merriman Hall in 1967 and Park Hall in 1969. The new library was completed in 1975, and Merriman House, the president's home, was altered for office space, and a home for the president, Dr. Stanley Salwak, was purchased in the community. A private home near the campus was purchased in 1974 and used for offices until renovated for a home for Pres. James Roach in 1987. The university plans an extension for Kelley as a student union and conference

Former Governor of Maine, State Senator, and Secretary of State Edmund Muskie discusses plans for a new building with Aroostook State Normal School Principal Clifford O. T. Wieden. The building housing an auditorium, gymnasium, lunch area, classrooms, and offices and it was named after Dr. Wieden, and completed in 1961.
Courtesy of the Library, University of Maine at Presque Isle

The Wording Hall of Ricker Classical Academy was originally opened as Houlton Academy in 1848. Until 1858 it was the only school beyond the grammar schools in Aroostook. With state funding for free high schools in 1873, Houlton Academy would have lost its students and closed but Dr. Joseph Ricker arranged for an endowment from Colby College, and it was renamed Ricker Classical Institute, and operated as a normal school, training teachers. The Philip Mansur home was purchased for a library, a gymnasium/auditorium was added in 1947 and it was renamed Ricker College in 1949, serving as a junior college for the area. The College grew with the return of the veterans of World War II and the arrival of many foreign students. The campus was expanded with a new library and dining hall, and the college commenced awarding baccalaureate degrees. But unfortunately it closed its doors in the late 1970s and was sold. It was renovated into apartments for the elderly and is known as Ricker Plaza. Some of the other buildings were sold and some remain empty, a sad reminder of this once proud institution.
Courtesy of the Cary Library

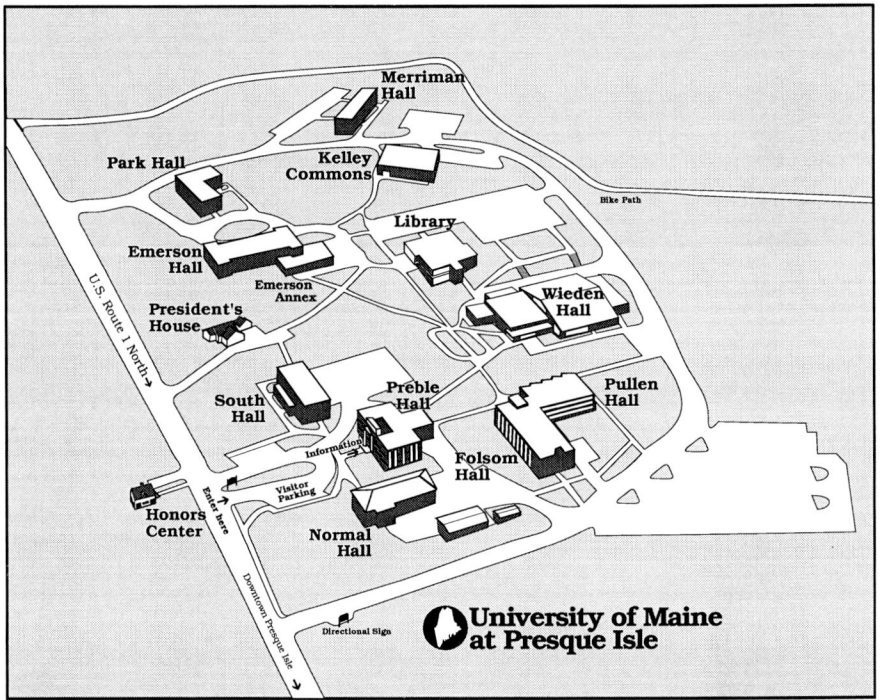

center.
The University of Maine at Presque Isle recently received a grant to become the Northeastern Dissemination Center for the National Center on Deafness. The project not only places Aroostook County at the center of concern for the hearing impaired, but may include the Maritime Provinces of Canada through potential cooperative arrangements. The Center is a resource for children with hearing impairment, their parents, and teachers, but also for the elderly hearing impaired.
Courtesy of the Office of University Relations, University of Maine at Presque Isle

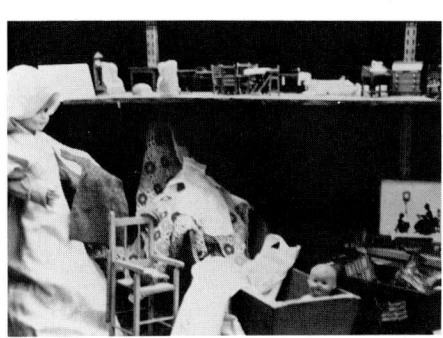

Acadian life in northern Aroostook is part of the cultural background that is rich in history and folklore. The University of Maine at Fort Kent celebrates Acadian Cultural Heritage each spring with a festival. This display of old toys and a doll dressed in authentic clothing a typical Acadian child would have worn is at the university.
Courtesy of Shirlee Connors-carlson

The University of Maine at Presque Isle has initiated interactive television courses with its outreach sites at Loring Air Force Base (1988), and Houlton (1989). In an interactive mode, students at an outreach site can see, hear, and converse with the students and faculty at the originating site. With ITV, courses not normally available at outreach sites can be provided with little adverse effects from distance and weather. Current planning includes links between the universities, vocational-technical institutes, public libraries, and some high school libraries.
Photograph by William Duncan

The University of Maine at Presque Isle offers a variety of undergraduate degrees, from education to liberal studies, including an honors program. As with many institutions for higher learning, many students are non-traditional, and are retraining for career changes, but the campus is inviting for students of all ages. These students relax on a dormitory lawn, with the UMPI Owl sculpture in the background. The owl was sculpted by Bernard Langlais. Outreach sites include Loring

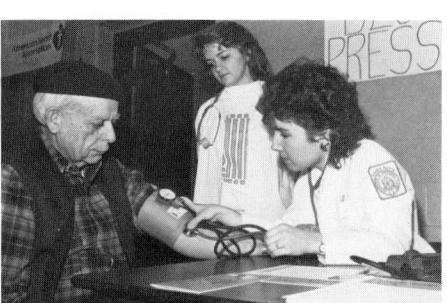

The Aroostook School of Commerce was established in 1946 in Presque Isle, and operated through 1951, one of several business colleges throughout Aroostook,

Air Force Base and Houlton, now reached by interactive television. The campus is itself an outreach site for graduate courses from the University of Maine, Orono, and the University of Southern Maine. The university will join other campuses and other institutions including high schools in a state-wide community college system, connected by interactive television.
Courtesy of the Library, University of Maine at Presque Isle

Bridging the gap between differing philosophies has always marked Speaker of the House John Martin (Democrat), as an outstanding contributing citizen of Maine. That spirit is evident here as we see Speaker Martin and Governor John McKernon (Republican) strolling on campus at the University of Maine at Fort Kent on commencement day, 1988.
  The UMFK has always stood for the tradition of blending cultural differences. As Commencement Day, 1989, approaches, the face of campus life will say good-bye to those graduating, and will thank them for their contribution to this tradition.
Courtesy of the Office of University Relations, University of Maine at Fort Kent

Shown here is a health conscious citizen taking advantage of a blood pressure clinic, sponsored by the Student Nurses Organization at UMFK.
Courtesy of the Office of University Relations, University of Maine at Fort Kent

especially popular after World War II.
Courtesy of the Library, University of Maine at Presque Isle

A dedication for the preservation of their heritage is obvious in this restored bedroom in the Caribou Historical Society's "log cabin," built in 1986 with money from Caribou native, Mericos Whittier, who went to California and made his fortune in real estate.
Photograph by Richard Strelka

The Caribou Public Library was a dream of the Women's Christian Temperance Union in 1888, they located a library in the back room of a store in 1906. With a ten thousand dollar grant from Andrew Carnegie, New York steel magnate and philanthropist, the Caribou Public Library was built in 1911 on a lot donated from the Nathaniel Bartlett estate. A new wing was added in 1964, leaving the Carnegie building intact. Present holdings include the local newspaper, the Aroostook Republican *(from 1887 to 1930 also available on microfilm)*, with an index to the years 1887 to 1949, as well as a fine collection of fiction, non-fiction, and children's books and periodicals.
Courtesy of the Caribou Public Library

Cary Memorial Library, the first library in Aroostook County, originated with a literary society, the Instructive Companies, founded by Samuel Kendall, Jr. (son of one of the first settlers of Houlton Plantation) in 1821, just ten years after the first home was built in the wilderness. Books were collected and in 1850 the Forest Club loaned the collection through the Houlton Library and Literary Association, incorporated in 1868. A room was made available at the Reform Club Reading Room on July 1, 1876. In 1896, the Fact & Fiction Club and the Houlton Women's Club rented a room in the George B. Page store for the collection. In November 1899, Dr. George Cary left much of his estate for the erection and maintenance of a free public library, to which was added a grant of ten thousand dollars from Andrew Carnegie. John C. Stevens designed the building, built entirely of gray granite from a Smyrna quarry near Cochran Lake, by John Chadwick of Houlton. The library opened in 1905. It was expanded with a wing in 1969, which houses most of the collection of forty-one thousand books, periodicals, and audio and video tapes. The original building is used for conferences, meetings, and offices. The library has been a regional center for Talking Books since 1968.
Courtesy of the Cary Memorial Library

Fort Fairfield Public Library was organized in 1895 and had as a nucleus about three hundred volumes which were kept in a small room in the rear of a store. Both the room and the service connected with it were practically given by the proprietor. After a few years, the books were moved to the offices of C. E. Holt, who served as librarian. In 1913 the town received the sum of ten thousand dollars from Andrew Carnegie for the purpose of constructing the present library building. It is an especially beautiful building with elaborately carved woodwork and a handsome brick fireplace in the reading room, both trademarks of a Carnegie library. The building remains unchanged, but the collection has grown to over twenty thousand books, and patronage keeps increasing.
Photograph by Helen Deane

WELLSPRINGS AND IRRIGATION POOLS: LIBRARIES, HISTORICAL SOCIETIES, MUSEUMS, AND OTHER EDUCATIONAL SUPPORT SYSTEMS

by Anna Fields Mcgrath

The intellectual curiosity of a people, and the expressions of its manifestations often result in the gathering and preserving of collections by both individuals and institutions. This has been true in the County, where the outpouring of the need to share these collections has resulted in a wonderful array of libraries, museums, historical societies, and educational organizations throughout the entire area of settled country.

These organizations in Aroostook have often been built on the collections of individuals, or of clubs and societies originated for the purpose of building libraries and museums, from the first library at Houlton, to the society just building its museum at Limestone.

As Shakespeare said "Instructed by the antiquary times, He must, he is, he cannot help but be wise." A library's raison d'etre is to collect, preserve, and dispense information and ideas so the people can pursue wisdom, and advance the frontiers of human knowledge; and the museum's forte is to preserve and protect the artifacts of the culture; while the educational organization's focus is to promote and expand the educational enterprise of the community.

Ashland Community Library, opened on June 1, 1961, serves Masardis, Portage, Garfield, Oxbow, and Nashville, with nine thousand books and over one hundred cassettes. A library association was formed in 1904, and a collection of books was housed at Mrs. Bearce's store on Exchange Street. The books were moved to the Seeley Store on Main Street in 1920, then to the Andrews Building on Exchange Street, then to Mrs. William Theriault's clothing store. In 1944, the books were put into storage until the Ashland Community Association was formed in January 1949 with Rev. James Johnson as librarian in the Old Exchange Hotel. In 1951 it was moved to the second flood of the fire station. The Rotary Club of Ashland voted to contribute money until a library was constructed, which occurred in 1961. It is governed by a board of trustees, and is subsidized by the town.

The Robert A. Frost Memorial Library, Limestone, Maine, was initiated by the Limestone Women's Civic Club in 1937, and built in 1941 with a gift from Aubrey C. and Stella Frost, in memory of their son who was killed in a motorcycle accident. The collection was started in 1899 with a gift from the Honorable T.H. Phair to the town. The collection now totals over ten thousand volumes, and the library is supported by the town.

The Fort Kent Public Library was originated with a public library movement, begun in 1929. In 1936 the Business and Professional Women's Club decided to work for a public library as a project. The Rotary, Lions, American Legion, and superintendent of schools joined them. They commenced collecting books which were shelved in the town office, moved to the Morenault building, then to a small room in the fire house in 1938, run by volunteers. Work by the committee continued until a library building was built and dedicated in 1960s, with a collection of three thousand volumes. A wing was added in 1965, and a second wing, plus basement conference room were added in 1984. The collection now totals over twenty thousand volumes, and is heavily used.

The Madawaska Public Library originated in the St. Aquinas Catholic Church under the direction of Father O'Neill, in 1945. After several moves, the present library was built in 1973. The collection includes twenty thousand volumes, and houses the Madawaska Historical Society headquarters.

The Library at the Northern Maine Vocational Technical Institute at Presque Isle, Maine, is located on the former U.S. Air Force Base in a newly constructed addition to the Christie Complex. The first permanent library was operated in the former Non-Commissioned Officers Mess Hall in 1968, then moved to the old air force gymnasium in 1980, before being built in its present location in 1987. The present library holdings total over thirteen thousand volumes. A media center, as well as an automated circulation system is planned, expanding the presently installed automated catalog system, MaineCat.

The Library, at the University of Maine at Presque Isle was built in 1975. This modern three-story building houses a collection of academic books, periodicals, serials, microfilm, phonographs, government documents (since 1979), a media center, and a TV studio. Special collections include: the Aroostook Collection, the Maine Collection, Rare Books Collection, Forbes Geological Collection, Fine Arts Slide Collection, and the Juvenile Books Collection. The library participates in the University of Maine System's automated library network, with interactive access to the holdings of all libraries in the System. The present library has grown from one room in the administrative building serviced by faculty to the present collection serviced by 4½ professional librarians and 4½ support persons.

The building housing the Blake Library of the University of Maine at Fort Kent was constructed as a gymnasium in 1928, extensively remodeled and converted to a library in 1966. Before that, the library was housed in Cyr Hall. A major addition to the first floor was built in 1988. The library holds over fifty thousand books, and has three hundred periodical subscriptions. The library also provides audiovisual facilities, computer work areas, a microfilm collection, and professional services that make it the center of information resources at the university. It is a participant in the new automated circulation and catalog network linking the seven libraries of the university system.

The Washburn Memorial Library was started when Governor Israel Washburn, for whom the town is named, donated two hundred books from his personal collection to the town for a library. Unfortunately these volumes were lost in the fire of 1864. The town has budgeted for a library in town meetings since 1883. A collection of books was instituted and a library maintained in several locations in town, until the present building was completed in 1950.

The library was dedicated to the men and women of Washburn who served their country in World Wars I and II. An addition was constructed in 1988 which doubled the size of the library. It houses a collection of over twelve thousand volumes, including a collection of Maine books, children's books, and craft books. Town records, town reports, and yearbooks are available.

The time, money, and effort by historical societies seems to reflect the value the group places on its heritage, and Aroostookans preserve their heritage in a wondrous variety of ways, as evidenced from town to town.

Allagash Historical Society was founded in 1976. Their collection of artifacts of Allagash are housed in a log cabin, two-room museum, with a military section, and a frame building, the Lumberman's Warehouse.

The Bridgewater Historical Society was formed in 1984. They meet in the town hall, built in 1894, which they are restoring. Long-range plans include preservation of the town's history on videotape.

The Haystack Historical Society was formed by Daniel Turner in June 1981 to serve Mapleton, Castle Hill, and Chapman. It was originally called the MCC Society, but the present name was adopted later in 1981 when a constitution and by-laws were accepted by the members. Donated books and magazines are in the UMPI Library. Plans to acquire an historic building to restore as a museum are underway, with a promise of family heirlooms and artifacts when exhibition space is available. Haystack Mountain is a landmark for central Aroostook, and was part of the Indian trails across the state.

The Limestone-Caswell Historical Society, initiated by the Limestone Women's Civic Club, was incorporated in 1980. A planned museum will be built on this site on Foster Avenue. The society has been preparing oral tapes of citizens in the town, and is collecting artifacts for the museum.

The Stockholm Historical Society and Museum was founded in 1975, a product of the local conservation commission and the United States Bicentennial Committee. The museum building was the first store and post office in Stockholm, and contains an excellent collection of photographs and artifacts. One of the rarest artifacts is a huge and ponderous hay press, circa 1900, a forerunner of the modern hay-baler.

The Ste. Agathe Historical Society owns the Ste. Agathe Historical House which dates from the 1850s to 1860s. The collection consists of household and everyday items used by a typical Franco-American family of the late nineteenth and early twentieth centuries. The society was founded in 1978.

The William Dalton Historical Society was formed in 1987, the sesqui-centennial year of Ashland. It was named for the first name of the town, and the assumed first settler. The society collects, records, and preserves the history of Ashland, Masardis, Garfield, Oxbow, and Nashville Plantations, and Portage. The collection now includes photographs, letters, and other memorabilia including Dr. Hagerthy's medical books, bookcase, and doctor's bag with all his tools, as well as census records. A major project is

The Mark and Emily Turner Memorial Library, Presque Isle, was dedicated in April 1967. This modern library building includes the original Carnegie library, built by Astle and Paige, which opened on July 1, 1908. The first library association in Presque Isle, the Half & Half Club, was organized in 1874. They collected books for loan and placed them first in George Powell's Drugstore, moved them to the post office, then to Laila Smith's Millinery Store, then to Holmes Jewelry store in 1905. A lot was purchased by Thomas H. Phair, who visited New York with Senator William Frye and Eugene Hale to ask Carnegie for a ten thousand dollar grant, in 1906. The library holds more than fifty-four thousand volumes, with a special emphasis on Maine and local history, including microfilmed copies of Presque Isle local newspapers from 1857.
Courtesy of the Turner Memorial Library

The W. T. A. Hansen Memorial Library in Mars Hill, Maine, was founded in 1937 by Pauline Colbath Hunter who started collecting gifts of books, and opened the Mars Hill Public Library in 1938. It was located upstairs in the Hussey Block, and four years later moved downstairs in the same building. In 1948, Walter T. A. Hansen, a prominent Mars Hill businessman, left a bequest to build a new public library for the inhabitants of Mars Hill and the surrounding communities. The new library was opened in 1952.
Courtesy of the W. T. A. Hansen Memorial Library

The Aroostook County Historical Center at the Library, University of Maine at Presque Isle, contains a collection of material on Aroostook County, Maine. It was initiated in 1984 from a collection the had been growing since 1978, and has developed rapidly since. It includes books about Aroostook, or by Aroostook authors, local newspapers, postcards, photographs, letters, diaries, musical scores, phonograph records, censuses, annual reports, staff-produced videos, vertical file material (including the research files of the late County historian Charlotte Lenentine Melvin), maps, and artifacts (such as a civil war uniform), the Images of Aroostook *photographic collection, the Bradford House photographic collection, and oral history tapes. Current activities include indexing the local newspaper in Presque Isle.*

Anna Mcgrath and Nancy Roe are seen here examining maps in the Special Collections Room.
Photograph by William Duncan

L'Association Culturelle et Historique de Mont-Carmel—Museum and Cultural Centre in Lille, Maine, was opened in 1984. Formerly a Roman Catholic church, Notre Dame du Mont-Carmel, it was built in 1909 in Baroque style from the design of Daoust, of France. Due to a significant decline in population, and to the sale of the building (seating capacity of over 450), Bishop Edward C. O'Leary of Portland, Maine, decided to close the church in 1977. Joseph Donat Cyr, local artist, had recently purchased the former Lille Rectory built in 1896, next to the Mont-Carmel church. In an effort to preserve the church building, Cyr and Boyd Pryor proposed to Bishop O'Leary that the building be made into a museum and culture center, and this was approved in 1982. Cyr is presently working to restore the

building. The museum and cultural center will hold concerts, historical exhibitions, and educational programs as soon as possible.
Sketch by Joseph Donat Cyr and Boyd Pryor

The Aroostook Historical and Art Museum of Houlton, Maine, was founded by the late Hon. Ransford W. Shaw in 1938. It was located in a room in the Nickerson Block. In 1943 Mr. and Mrs. S. L. White donated the McIntire-Donworth House, built in 1902 at 109 Main Street, to house the growing historical collection. The building, located next to the Cary Memorial Library, holds a collection of diaries, letters, account books, photographs, books, household and pioneer tools, muskets, Indian relics, a flax wheel, looms, restored clothing, posters, and a model and artifacts of the Hancocks Barracks, built to defend the area against the British in the Northeastern Boundary Dispute. The Museum includes the Ricker Room, with artifacts, photographs, and memorabilia of Houlton Academy, afterwards called Ricker Classical Institute,

and later called Ricker College.
Photograph by Cathy Brewer Craig

cleaning headstones in the Ashland Municipal Cemetery, shown above. Another project is continuing research to expand a 1987 publication *Reflections of Early Ashland, 1837-1937*. The society meets in the Ashland Community Library while planning for a building.

The Woodland Historical Society, incorporated in 1978, was given the Snowman School by the town in 1982 to be used as a museum. The school had been built in 1895 by David Snowman, a local carpenter. The building was restored in 1983 by the society and the Kiwanis Club. The building includes antiques and historical items donated by townspeople and others interested in the preservation of the cultural heritage of Woodland. The society also sponsors parades and antique shows, the latter held in the Consolidated School.

Although the natural history centers, garden clubs, extension clubs, and 4-H clubs are not collectors and preservers of our cultural heritage as libraries and museums are, they are transmitters of that heritage, and of the values that inform our activities, for our values are reflected in the activities of our minds and hands.

It was to no small degree intellectual curiosity and the quest for intellectual freedom that induced many of the first settlers of central and southern Aroostook to escape the "narrow, uniformed and countrified minds... in the southern towns..." of lower New England to venture into the unmapped land of promise to the north, as Henry David Thoreau wrote in *The Maine Woods*.

Thoreau, on one of his trips to the North Woods, stopped at "Uncle George" McCausland's for supplies. On the shelf of this logger supplier, many miles from "civilized towns," Thoreau found *Parrish's Geography*, calendars, and novels. Thoreau said, "The deeper you penetrate into the woods, the more intelligent... do you find the inhabitants, for always the pioneer has been... a man of the world."

The Caribou Historical Society was organized in 1974 by Clara Piper, and the group met at the Nylander Museum, Key Bank, and Rose Acres while they worked to obtain a museum building, and collected artifacts, books, and other paraphernalia. They commenced publishing a series of booklets entitled Gleanings in 1981, and volumes are published irregularly. The society, with contributions by the family of former Caribou native Mericos Whittier, was able to have this log cabin constructed by R. F. Harris Company, and the S. W. Collins Company, on land donated by Mildred Hatch. It is furnished with artifacts from a variety of time periods, and also contains photographs.
Sketch by Bethany Chambers Smith

The Fort Fairfield Historical Society and the Bicentennial Committee of Fort Fairfield had a replica of the blockhouses (built to protect the border in 1839) erected on Main Street, not far from the original site. The museum houses artifacts including this loom used by the early settlers of this town named after Gov. John Fairfield.
Photograph by Helen Deane

The Fort Kent Historical Society, formed in 1925, has its headquarters at the B&A Railroad Station on Market Street, Fort Kent. Present fundraisers include a fall breakfast and a historical ball in the spring. The Fish River Railroad, which ran along Route 11, opened access to markets to Fort Kent in 1901, and was added to the B&A system in 1903. The station was built in 1903, and deeded to the FKHS in 1980. The line is still active.
Courtesy of the Fort Kent Historical Society

The annual Fall Foliage Plane Ride during the height of fall foliage color is the major fundraiser for the Friends of the Aroostook County Historical Center at the Library, University of Maine at Presque Isle. The Friends is a group of County people who formed in 1984 to assist the Aroostook County Historical Center at the Library in the acquisition, preservation, and promotion of material on the cultural heritage of the County. The Friends publish an ACHC Newsletter, edited by Jere Green. They are one of the sponsors of the Sesquicentennial of the County, 1989. Mike Kelley, representative of Key Bank, a regular sponsor of the Fall Foliage Plane Ride holds young Kristina Tompkins, ready for her first ride. Anna Mcgrath holds Timmy McGrath before his first plane ride, in 1988.
Photograph by Maureen Murchison

The Madawaska Historical Society, organized in 1968 to celebrate the one hundredth anniversary of Madawaska, is forming the Madawaska Historic Centre in St. David Village. The Centre now includes a log cabin, the Tante Blanc Museum with all the equipment needed to turn flax into Madawaska crash (sold throughout the County in the mid-nineteeth century) a restored one-room schoolhouse built in 1870, and the Acadian Landing Site and Cross, commemorating the original cross planted by the Acadians when they landed at the mouth of the Madawaska River where it empties into the St. John River, seeking escape from British exploitation. The Tante Blanc Museum is named for Marguerite Cyr who brought food and clothing to fellow Acadians during the "year of the black distress," 1816, when famine threatened the group because crops failed from early frosts, followed by a severe winter. She spent her life in service to her "family." The Madawaska Historical Society publishes a newsletter, and books, and sponsors a family reunion each year focusing on one Acadian family.
Courtesy of the Madawaska Historical Society

The New Sweden Historical Society was organized in 1925 as "The Sons and Daughters of New Sweden, Maine," continuing an existing tradition of annual celebrations of New Sweden Day, in commemoration of the founding of the colony, July 23, 1870. The museum, dedicated in 1974, is a replica of the Capitol, an original building of the colony which served as a school, church, store, and immigration office. The museum has a fine collection of skis, including Jemtland skis (with one ski in each pair longer to keep one's balance when hitting a snow drift) also a collection of axes, and a velvet-seated sleigh. Recent additions to the museum site include an early log cabin, restored with many of the original furnishings and the Lindsten Stuga. The society is currently restoring the Lars Noak Blacksmith Shop which has the original forge and many items from the Johnny Johansson Blacksmith Shop.
Courtesy of the New Sweden Historical Society

Notre Heritage Vivant—Living Heritage Historical Society was incorporated in 1973, and serves the communities of Grand Isle, Van Buren, and Hamlin and Cyr Plantations. The Acadian Village was started when ten acres of land were donated by Mr. and Mrs. Charles Ayotte of Van Buren. Then Mr. and Mrs. Addis Beaupre donated her great-grandfather's family home, known as the Morneault building, constructed in 1857. A country schoolhouse, circa 1880, from Hamlin was added, followed by two houses built in 1860. Aided by participants of the Comprehensive Employment Training Act, and the Maine State Bicentennial Commission, the Acadian Village was dedicated on May 8, 1975, with more donated buildings being prepared for restoration at the site, and furnishings and historical research materials arriving at the society. Construction continued with a chapel, and a barn now being restored and furnished with early machinery. The Acadian Village is registered in the National Register of Historic Places, 1973, and is known as an Historical National Landmark. A general store-information center has been added as an outlet for hand-made Acadian articles.
Courtesy of Martine Pelletier

The Presque Isle Historical and Genealogical Society, renamed in 1972 from the Presque Isle Historical Society, was incorporated in 1964. This Clarence Town Coach, hung on C-springs, dates to about 1860-1870. It was donated to the society by William Flora, and is one of the many artifacts stored in the basement of City Hall awaiting restoration for exhibition. The collection of the society includes clothing from the turn of the century, photographs, and artifacts from local homes and barns. Planning is underway for a museum.
Photograph by Margaret Cook Duncan, courtesy of the Presque Isle Historical and Genealogical Society

Two museums that seek to recreate the past, the Anderson Toy Museum of Fort Fairfield, and the John E. and Walter D. Webb Museum of Vintage Fashions in Island Falls.

The Salmon Brook Historical Society was organized in 1980 by a group of interested citizens of Washburn, Wade, and Perham. The Museum Committee was charged to collect items for a museum and to find a suitable building for a museum. Through the generosity of interested people, they were able to buy a home that had been part of a mid-1800s farmstead, constructed in 1852 by Ben Wilder who was the first official postmaster of Washburn, and a nephew of Issac Wilder, the village's first resident in 1842. The home has been restored (including a slate sink and pump), with furniture and clothing of the mid-nineteenth century. A prized possession is a replica of the flag of the United States circa mid-1800s, with a large star in the center, surrounding by thirty smaller stars.
Photograph by Dennis Harris

The Anderson Toy Museum houses a collection of antique dolls, dollhouses, toy furniture, and toys. Most of the dolls are from Germany with human hair wigs and antique clothing. Ruth and John Anderson have been collecting antique and home-made toys since 1971, and have filled seven rooms of the top floor of their home with these toys, including a 1911 American Humpty-Dumpty circus by Shoen Hutt.

A tea party for antique dolls, dressed in children's clothing. The boy doll (with his back to the camera) wears boys' clothing with a "Best" label, and has an antique pocket watch. The doll with a straw hat is thirty-six inches tall. The exhibit is completed with antique screens, a Japanese willow tea set, and linen tablecloth and napkins.
Photograph by Maureen Murchison

The Museum of Vintage Fashion, displays a collection of men, women, and children's antique clothing collected by Frances Webb Stratton since 1951 in a house built by A. L. Hamilton in 1894. It was rebuilt by Bryon Noyes in 1910 to become the Webb Museum of Vintage Fashion in 1983. The structure of seventeen rooms has twelve filled with displays of antique fashions in a home-like atmosphere. The bridal room contains gowns representing styles from 1865 to 1930, a Hat Boutique with hats representing styles of 1900 to 1960 (including hats that belonged to Sewell, the first settler in Island Falls), and a red velvet bodice that Alice Sherman wore to Teddy Roosevelt's inaugural ball. Mrs. Delmont Emerson of Island Falls wore the black velvet dress trimmed with pearls to Governor Milliken's reception in 1916 (note photograph on floor). There is a bedroom with straw and feather ticks, and assorted dolls and clothing. Tea is served in a pink Victorian tea room by appointment.
Courtesy of the Webb Museum of Vintage Fashions

The child, as the child in each adult, needs to have an opportunity to immerse him/herself in nature, and although towns and cities are invading the forests of the early settlers, areas and institutes are reserved to ensure our appreciation of the earth and the heavens.

The Arthur E. Howell Wildlife Educational Foundation of Amity, Maine manages the Wildlife Management Area contained on over sixty-nine acres, and the Spruce Acres Refuge. The Refuge has a trout pond, and recently planted spruce and Norway spruce trees as well as trails to view many species of area wildlife in their natural habitat. The area was donated by Arthur E. Howell, a retired policeman from Massachusetts, who manages the Foundation with assistance from faculty and students of Ashland Community High School. The Foundation keeps a fox, tamed to visit area schools interested in wildlife conservation activities. An injured American bald eagle named Bell is a permanent resident.
Photograph by Maureen Murchison

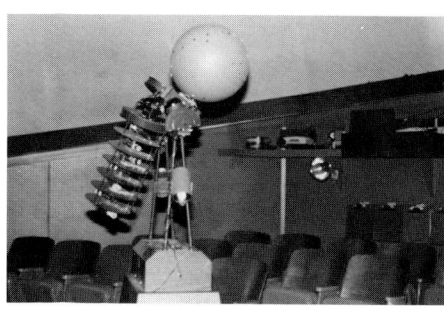

The Francis Malcolm Institute, Easton, Maine is a multi-purpose facility housing a planetarium, laboratory, exhibit area, and conference room on 260 acres of land which includes a mile-long self-interpretive bog trail, and a two and a half mile-long cross-country ski-snow shoe trail. The Institute was made available through a bequest of Francis M. Malcolm in 1977, who had been born and spent his early years in Easton, then left to serve as a school administrator in Vermont and Alaska, before retiring to California. The major focus is outdoor education for school children, but all are welcome.
Photograph by Rebecca Hayden-McGrath

(Martha) Chambers was curator from 1967 to 1983, and coordinated exhibits and classes for the Caribou Art Club for many years previous to that.
Courtesy of the Nylander Museum

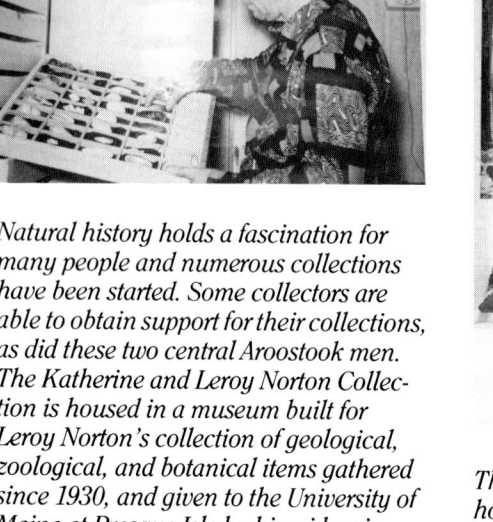

Natural history holds a fascination for many people and numerous collections have been started. Some collectors are able to obtain support for their collections, as did these two central Aroostook men. The Katherine and Leroy Norton Collection is housed in a museum built for Leroy Norton's collection of geological, zoological, and botanical items gathered since 1930, and given to the University of Maine at Presque Isle by his widow in May, 1971. The collection contains thousands of shells, including such rare shells as the Scarlaria Pretiosa, or Precious Wentlehorp, and a large man-eating clam shell weighting 650 pounds. Norton, a Presque Isle rural mail carrier, was a self-taught taxidermist, and his collection contains preserved birds, reptiles, and small mammals.
Photograph by Maureen Murchison

The Nylander Museum of Caribou, Maine, houses the extensive geological, marine, and natural history collections of Olof O. Nylander. He was born in Oremolla, Sweden, and was a boy protege of Swedish geologist Sven Nilsson. After migrating to America in 1883, he was hired by the United States Geological Survey, and was an associate of Dr. John M. Clark in 1905 and 1906 at SUNY Albany. He contributed to many professional geological and scientific works, and was awarded an honorary master of science degree by the University of Maine. The Caribou Garden Club and citizens of Caribou, with the Maine Development Commission and with labor provided by a Works Progress Administration, had the museum built in 1938. On his death in 1943, the city of Caribou assumed the property. Mrs. Asher

Aroostook County Extension Homemakers Groups were started in Maine in 1915 as the Maine Farm Bureau Federation to facilitate efforts of the Home Demonstration Agents of the land grant university, University of Maine, to bring educational programs to rural community families in the preparation and preservation of food, updates on nutrition, child care, sewing, and making craft items for the home. The Houlton Women's Group was founded in 1918, and there are nineteen flourishing groups in Aroostook County today.
Courtesy of Bernadette Campbell

Scout's mottos: "Be prepared" and "Do a good turn daily" reflect the concern of the older generation that enhanced opportunities for the development of the younger generation be consistently available from mothers and fathers.

Aroostook's 4-H clubs were formed soon after Dr. Leon Merrill, director of the University of Maine's Agricultural Extension Service, appointed Harold Bickfor as the first director of boys and girls' clubs in agriculture and home economics in 1913. Frank Hussey of Presque Isle, prominent businessman, joined in 1915 with a gardening project. The oldest Aroostook Club is the Aroostook Valley Beef Club started in 1948, and the Aroostook Valley Dairy Club started in 1951. The 4-H pledge is: I pledge my head to clearer thinking, my heart to greater loyalty, my hands to larger service, and my health to better living, for my club, my community, my country and my world.
Photograph by Shirley McHatten

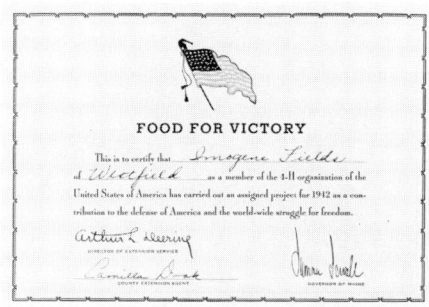

During World War II, 4-H clubs rallied to help, as this certificate indicates. Maine 4-H clubs produced and preserved foods valued at over $100,000 during 1918 and over $117,200 in 1944.
Courtesy of Fielda Holmes Webber

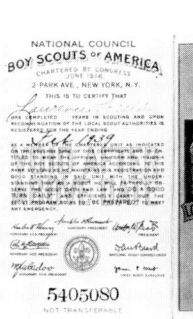  

Girl Scouting in Aroostook County began in the middle to late 1930s, although Juliette Low started it in Georgia in 1912. The first independent troops were formed in the early 1940s; councils were formed in Houlton and Presque Isle to administer troops in these areas. In 1962 the Abnaki Girl Scout Council was created. Girls learn skills that help them in a constantly changing world, as they live by the Girl Scout Promise: On my honor I will try; to serve God and my country, to help people at all times, and to live by the Girl Scout Law.
Courtesy of Mary A. Hunter

Boy Scouting in Aroostook commenced in the late 1930s and early 1940s, and the movement has grown until most towns have one or more troops. Boy Scouts were active in paper drives during World War II, and continue to contribute to society.
Courtesy of Nancy Tarbell Fields Estate

The Bear Hill Grange chapter in Houlton is typical of the many grange chapters that were formed in Aroostook during the late 1800s and early 1900s, to support educational and social values of the farmers. Chapter 16 formed in Houlton in 1874, and by 1924 had the largest Grange sponsored cooperative store and mill in the world. Women voted at the Grange before they were allowed to vote in state and federal elections. Grange Halls, used for meetings, were also used for family gatherings. The Grange was one of many efforts to support farm life through cooperative buying. Aroostook granges had their own abatment insurance company at the turn of the century.
Courtesy of Frank Dunn

In the remoteness of woods camps the men would welcome anyone who was traveling who would bring news of life in the settlement. The crew stayed all winter at the woods camps and followed the drive in the spring, which brought the men back to the communities. The "Bull cook" reigned supreme in the woods camps, and allowed no boisterous talk or laughter at the table. He would converse with the parish priest, game warden, or trapper, and after the evening meal, tell the news.
Courtesy of Shirlee Connors-carlson

"What is most striking in the Maine wilderness is the continuousness of the forest...it is even more...wild than you had anticipated...an intricate wilderness...the aspect of the country, indeed, is universally...savage... the lakes are something which you are unprepared for; they live up so high, exposed to light, and the forest is diminished to a fine fringe on their edges, with here and there a blue mountain, like amethyst jewels set around some jewel of the first water...and fair as they can be. These are not the artificial forests of an English king... here prevail no forest laws but those of nature," wrote Henry David Thoreau in The Maine Woods. Indeed, thick forests, that had been growing since the glaciers retreated, greeted the visitors of this land, the hunting grounds of the Native Peoples; the wild Eastlands of Massachusetts—now the North Woods of Maine. The first pathway into this forest was by the river St. John, after the boundary controversy was settled with part of that boundary down the middle of the river, and with the boundary controversy came the Military Road to Houlton and on to Fort Kent, to be followed by railroads, and telephones, then jets, and now satellite communications. The beautiful rivers, the clean pure air, and new interstate highways are pathways to the still-wild forests dotted with contemporary cities, and still bring the fortunate to the land of promise.

Courtesy of Shirlee Connors-carlson

PATHWAYS IN THE GARDEN AND OTHER COMMUNICATION ROUTES
by Shirlee Connors-carlson

In the early days of settlement of Aroostook, communication outside each settlement was not an easy matter. The Native People, the Acadians, and the first settlers in New Salem (Houlton) used the "riverhighway," the St. John and its tributaries into the "sea of trees," to communicate with each other and with the "outside." Traveling priests were "common carriers" as were lumberman going from woods camp to woods camp, for supplies, messages, and mail. Lumbering outposts were established—a depot on Seven Island in the St. John, Clifford's Depot on the Allagash.

Travel on the St. John was disrupted during the Aroostook War, but the Webster-Ashburton Treaty included the stipulation that navigation on the St. John should be free to Americans and Canadians. Daniel Webster later said he considered that this is one provision of the treaty was of greater value to Maine than the lost territory north of the St. John. The war also brought the Military Road from Bangor to Houlton and Hancocks Barracks, and was extended up through Monticello, Presque Isle, Ft. Fairfield, and on to Fort Kent. The west Aroostook road from Molunkus through Patten and Masardis to Fort Kent was connected to Presque Isle through Ashland. (The road north from Van Buren left much to be desired.) Roads means mail and mail means post offices. The *Main Register* for 1837 lists post offices at Haynesville, Hodgdon, Houlton, and Linneus. The *Register* for 1843 adds Amity, Conway (in Benedicta), Molunkus, Number Three (Sherman), Orient, Smyrna, and Weston. Masardis was the only post office listed north of Houlton.

Stages used the roads as they developed, followed by the railroad, telegraphs, telephones, radio, TV, and now satellite, cable, and interactive TV—from the water, to the earth, and now through the skies.

Newspapers and newspaper editors in Aroostook seem to have changed with the times, from being a voice for a particular viewpoint, to a more eclectic, local news format. The following list of best-remembered newspapers that have been published in the County indicates the interest of both newsmen and subscribers in the happenings of the County.

NEWSPAPERS

Daily Paper
 County Times

Weekly Papers
 Aroostook Democrat—Presque Isle, 1863-
 Aroostook Herald—Presque Isle, 1860, 1884-1889
 Aroostook Pioneer—Presque Isle, 1857-1868; Houlton, 1868-1935
 Aroostook Republican—Caribou, 1880-
 Aurora—Fort Fairfield, 1875-1876
 Beacon—Fort Fairfield, 1892-1895

Dog teams were a common means of transporting supplies and mail through the forests of Aroostook in early times. Courtesy of Rose Nadeau

The telegraph office was located in the railroad station in Fort Kent and typifies the way of communication in the early days of northern Aroostook. Courtesy of the Fort Kent Historical Society

County Times—Presque Isle, 1972-1973
Fort Fairfield Gazette—Fort Fairfield, 1891-1892
Fort Fairfield Review—Fort Fairfield, 1902-?
Gazette—Ashland, 1905-1922
Houlton Pioneer—Houlton, ?-1935
Houlton Pioneer Times—Houlton, 1935-
Houlton Times—Houlton, ?-1935
Independent—Presque Isle, 1902-1906
Katadhin Kalender—Sherman, 1876-1879
Limelight—Limestone, 1953-
Loyal Sunrise—Presque Isle, 1863-?
Mars Hill View—Mars Hill, 1908-1916
News—Mars Hill, 1917-1922
North Star—Caribou, Presque Isle, 1872-1901
Northern Leader—Fort Fairfield, 1892-1901
Rolling Stone—Ashland
Rogue—Presque Isle
St. John Valley Times—1956-
Star Herald—Presque Isle, 1890-
Sunriser—Presque Isle
Voice—Patten/Sherman Mills, 1869, 1871-1874

Weekend Papers
   Aroostook Sunday Herald
   "County Page," *Bangor Daily News*—Bangor

Journals
   Echoes—Blaine, Maine, 1988-
   Northern Lights—University of Maine at Presque Isle, 1983-

This restored mail stage is typical of those in Aroostook after the military road was completed. Weekly trips from Bangor to Houlton brought the mail to the federal troops beginning August 8, 1829. Courtesy of the Bangor Daily News

The White Mountain Telephone Company was organized in 1895 in Blaine, with the first telephone in John Ramsey's law office in Blaine, and the second installed in Guy Wilson's drugstore in Mars Hill. On February 6, 1906, the name was changed to Aroostook Telephone and Telegraph Company. An office was later established in Mars Hill, and sold in 1932 to the New England Telephone and Telegraph Company. The dial system was developed and installed in 1941. Aroostook T&T connected thirty towns and had five thousand subscribers. By 1895, the Fort Kent Telephone Company was formed and telephones were installed in the outreaches of Aroostook's small towns and woods camps, such as this one at Seven Islands in 1910. Although the telephone was used in the larger woods operations, there were many camps that relied on foot messengers as late as the 1930s.
Courtesy of Shirlee Connors-carlson

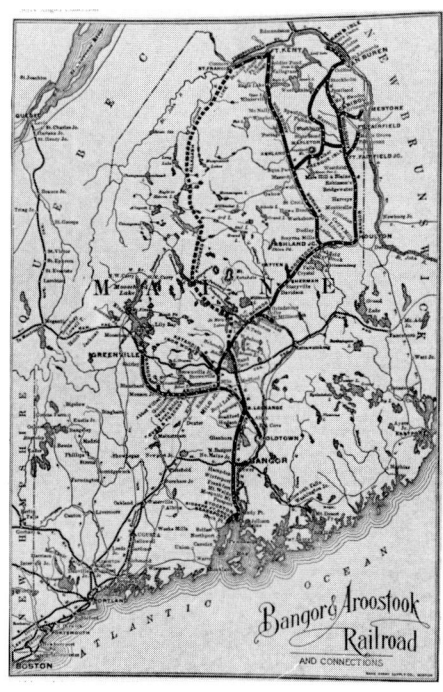

The railroads came to Aroostook through Canadian "spur" tracks from their railways to Houlton and Fort Fairfield in the 1870s, and the Bangor and Aroostook Railroad came in the 1890s, thanks to the efforts of Joseph Hall, editor of the Aroostook Pioneer *in Presque Isle, who invited all the editors of Maine to come up and visit the North Aroostook Agricultural and Horticultural Society's fair in 1858. They came, they saw, and they reported on the beauties of Aroostook, but this was not sufficient to induce development of a railroad until much later. The railroads did bring mail on a regular basis, but they have been replaced by airmail and trucks, and the railroad beds torn up. Mail service by rail ceased in 1965. This map is from J. and Cleaves H. Angier's* Bangor and Aroostook: The Maine Railroad, *Flying Yankee Enterprises, Littleton, Massachusetts, 1986, page 50.*

This fine post office building was opened in Houlton in 1858. Mail in Aroostook in the years of settlement came from St. John or Fredericton, New Brunswick. It was sent for, and paid for, by the receiver of the goods, packages, or correspondence. When Maine became a state, post offices were established in most towns, and after the Aroostook War, mail came through the new Military Road. James Lander was the first mail carrier, he traveled first on foot, then on horseback, and lastly by carriage as the road improved. First post offices were in private homes, but buildings such as this were built by the late 1880s; in Presque Isle in 1863, in Fort Kent in 1879.
Courtesy of Eugene Jackins

These two newspapers owner-editors were well-known throughout the County as rugged individualists. King Harvey, recently retired owner-editor of the Fort Fairfield Review was instrumental in keeping interest alive in a muder case of a young newsboy and waitress until it was solved fifteen years later. Edward Perrier, owner-editor, of the Presque Isle Star Herald *from 1946 to 1960 was active in the post-war industrial renovations of Presque Isle.*
Photograph of Perrier, courtesy of Edward Perrier.
Photograph of King Harvey courtesy of Voscar, the Maine Photographer

The radio, operated by battery, was one of the necessities in every home or at the woods camp, as a source of connection with the outside world. Commercial radio stations began to proliferate after the first, WAGM, started operating in Presque Isle in 1935. We now have the following radio stations that blanket the County with music and local happenings: WKZX (formerly WAGM), WCXU, WDHP, WEGP, WFST, WHOU, WLVC, WOZI, and WSJR as well as university stations WUPI and WUFK.

In 1927 Houlton, due to its superior atmospheric conditions, was the only long wave receiving station in America to connect with the continent. By 1930 there were between twenty-five and thirty million telephones connecting Belgium, Germany, France, Sweden, Switzerland, and Spain with American Telephone and Telegraph Company going through Houlton. More recently, the Aroostook Amateur Radio Association, using a two-meter radio repeater in Presque Isle communicates throughout the United States through a packet system, in addition to the many ham radios in use by individuals throughout Aroostook.
Courtesy of Shirlee Connors-carlson

A road across the southern part of Aroostook, connecting Quebec and Ashland has been encouraged for many years. This group of hardy souls in 1957 are getting ready to follow logging roads across the eighty-mile stretch through the forest.
Courtesy of the George "Pete" Sawyer Estate

Northeast Airlines served the Aroostook area with runs to and from Presque Isle throughout the 1940s into the 1970s, and included the "Yellow Bird" jet in their timetable. This plane is bringing Dr. West, president of the Boy Scouts of America, for an inspection tour. Eastern Air Lines presently serves the area.
Courtesy of ACHC

Aroostook's only television station, WAGM-TV, has been in operation since 1956 in Presque Isle. Although other television stations are available through cable, and via satellite, WAGM-TV brings home news and weather, and is first choice for most native Aroostookans, especially during harvest, when "Potato Pickers Special" comes on the air at 5:00 A.M. helping connect farmers and harvest workers who want a job, a babysitter, but most especially to keep the pickers/harvesters aware of weather conditions and when the farmer expects them in the field. This program originated with Wayne Knight on WAGM radio and continued on radio stations WKZX and WFST. This is weatherman Jim Myers in 1957.
Courtesy of Buddy Price

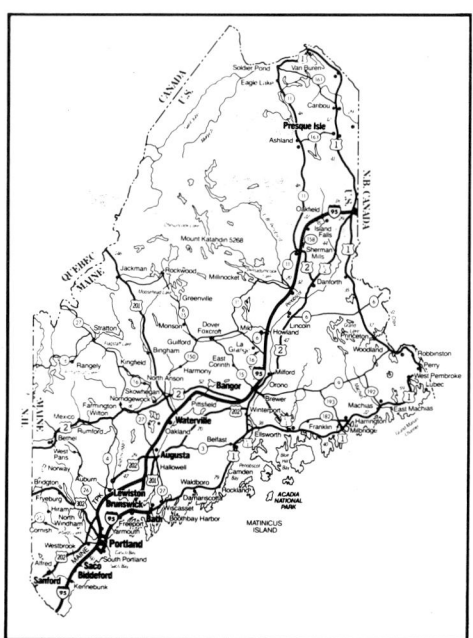

Contemporary map shows the major roads in the County, and the vast tracts left with only woods roads and secondary roads into the still forested areas.
Courtesy of ACHC

Lumbering in Aroostook in the late 1800s.
Courtesy of ACHC

Posing circa 1917 at the landing at the start of the drive, this fresh crew "ham it up" before the back-wrenching work begins. Youthful and in the prime of life, drivers each wielded the essential tool of log driving, the peavey or cant-dog. But not all young men were ready to be a pulp driver. (See page 148)
Courtesy of Shirlee Connors-carlson

> The universal dream is to live out one's life, especially one's final years, in the land of birth. It's almost as though the odors, the scents of the homeland are imprinted into us. The Land of Dreams, where the soil is always fertile, the rivers always sparkling, and the air clear enough to "see forever." For some, it is the Motherland, or the Fatherland, or the Garden of Eden, or mystical places like Mount Olympus, or Delphi, or Power Sites to the New Agers. It may be only a psychological response to the territorial imperative. But for many, this land, this garden is that Special Land, whether we live here, or only visit, the Land calls loud and clear.

Stumpage buyers who cut and shipped timber to market were often paid in timber operator scrip money such as Jewett & Pitcher of Boston and St. John, New Brunswick. Aroostook ton-timber was driven to New Brunswick to be manufactured and shipped to New England markets. Courtesy of Robert Sawyer

THE LAND: IN COMMON AND UNDIVIDED
THE LUMBER WORLD OF WESTERN AROOSTOOK
by Guy F. DuBay

If the map of Aroostook might be compared in outline to two humps of a camel's back, I'd say under the easterly hump are the agricultural lands, the "Garden of Maine" and under the westerly hump are the timberlands, those lands held "in common and undivided."

The easterly townships running along the border of the state of Maine and New Brunswick were pioneered by homesteaders who followed hard on the heels of timber interlopers of the Aroostook War. To the yeoman and husbandsman, the forest was an impediment to be overcome. Bringing with them the Jeffersonian ideals which held the agrarian society to be the epitome of civilization, these homesteaders responded to the challenge of the forest by burning it. A clear burn yielded its own natural fertilizer as ash blended in with thick loam. By such methods, a few short years broad oat fields spread where a thick cover of fir and hard woods once shielded the land.

West of Route 11 in the fifth and sixth ranges of townships, in lieu of parceling townships into individual homesteads, the state granted stumpage and cutting rights to lands in complete or entire townships to those who could thereby assist the state to fill its coffers by means of such stumpage revenue. The owners of these townships each held rights to a share of the revenue—from the whole and not just a parcel or divided lot in said township. That is, land was held in common and undivided.

This resulted in the preservation of the forest through several phases of cutting history and several generations of ownership. As heirs came into the picture, each was given a proportionate share of the whole. The common interest then resulted in none of the owners developing portions of the township oblivious to the interest of others. The benefit of common ownership came from the revenue which was held in common and undivided. Such was the single most important factor contributing to the maintenance of the forest character of western Aroostook to this day.

That the region described developed as it did may largely be attributed to a distinctive factor—that the land in western Aroostook has been held not in individual proprietorships but in common and undivided. That is, unlike the homesteader settling patterns in the eastern part of Aroostook, townships in western Aroostook were granted in whole by the state which held them in trust for the people. When a partnership ensued, owners of a township did not parcel out the land among themselves but shared fractional interests in the whole—whence comes the phrase: in common and undivided. When such land devised upon heirs passed in succeeding generations, each owner came into interest of a complex fractional share of the whole as opposed to the mere part of it. The impact of land held in common and undivided on partnerships was to lead to a curious blend of fractional interests such as in a Civil War era agreement between E. G. Dunn of Ashland and

E. S. Coe of Bangor with timber operator A. S. Flint. Dunn's share comprised 3/8-31-52 of 1/8 and 31/52 of 1/2 of the two portions of the townships owned to which they are granting timber cutting rights. Ebenezer Coe's shares comprised 21/52 of 1/8 and 21/52 of 1/2. This tended to encourage the preservation of the forest wherein each proprietor might secure his fractional share of the revenues generated from the wildland yet never individually developing a component of it, without considering the needs of others. That man indeed changes the nature of all he touches is obvious as the reforested land takes on the stock of a less variable forest. What the western sector of Aroostook will become cannot be accurately predicted on the record of the past alone, but a general premise remains: regardless of who tends the land, it will maintain a certain distinct characteristic so long as it continues to be held in common and undivided.

In 1860, Aroostook had a population of twenty-two thousand and it was a time of prosperity. The intense exploitation of forests brought wealth, employment in the woods, and a market for farm products. Every fall heavy barges came up the river, filling with joy the hearts of the colonists at harvest. As soon as winter came, every available man left for the *chantiers* or lumber camps.

All winter long they cut and hauled, searching for trees of outstanding value in the face of danger, frostbite, and sudden death. Sharp axes slipped on icy surfaces and hard thrown chips or falling timbers sometimes knocked a man unconscious.

The standard ton weight of pine was a hewn log forty feet long and one foot square, with the average virgin pine squaring five tons to a tree. Without rivers, yellow pine could never have been the golden harvest that it was, floating logs by the millions to mills and ports where it was in great demand, especially for the building of British vessels.

The loggers' first job was to shape a way to the water. Sometimes they used dry sluiceways down a hill, made by laying large trunks of trees together the whole length of it. Logs were rolled into the upper end, and descended at such speed that smoke and bark would fly. At other times, a hemlock with its limbs cut about a foot from the trunk was used as a drag which the oxen drew, while a log was attached to it by strong chains. The stumpy limbs prevented the team from being pushed forward too fast, but if that chain had broken it would have meant certain death for them. The best cutter was surrounded with general consideration, as was the pair of horses that could haul the heaviest load.

The crew ate boiled or frozen pork and beans, which they washed down with tea sweetened with molasses. Buckwheat pancakes, of course, were a staple, and sometimes they had salt codfish and potatoes. The evenings were long and the storyteller was at his best.

When the ice went out, tons of timber started moving toward the ocean. The crew followed the drive down, camping along the shores. With courage often borrowed from the rum in their hip flask, they rode timbers, jumping from one to the other amidst boiling rapids. Balancing themselves on their pick poles, wet from icy spills, some even met death when they were crushed between jamming timbers or against rocky ledges. Each log was branded with a hewn mark to identify ownership, and most started on the St. John River about ninety miles above Fort Kent.

There was wild rejoicing when the men reached the town, spending their money on barrelsful of whiskey, rum, and gin. With long hair and beards, in heavy woolen trousers cut off above the ankles as a safety measure, they celebrated for days on end. Red strips of flannel, the remains of colorful shirts, were fastened to tall poles and to the yokes of oxen.

It is no wonder that young ladies were kept inside by their mothers, at least until the boisterous festivity had given way to the inevitable gigantic headaches that followed.

Though set south of the Aroostook Border, Telos Lake figures vitally in Aroostook affairs. Located three hundred rods from Webster Pond on the Penobscot watershed, Telos Lake which empties in the Allagash Waterway allowed in 1839 the reach of Penobscot River Lumbermen to stretch out into the Allagash headwaters which normally flowed into the St. John River. The diversionary canal constructed between these two bodies at the head of waters, each flowing in opposite directions, was constructed by Amos Roberts of Bangor, Maine. Two years later in company with Maj. Hastings Strickland, he added dams at the outlet of Lake Chamberlain to raise its water level and so divert its flow through Telos and the Penobscot watershed. Selling the operation to Rufus Dwinal of Bangor, who put a toll on lumber passing through the canal, lead to a controversy among lumbermen, yet the East Branch drive of the Penobscot went to the mills on Allagash water. In 1847 when the lumber drive of Aroostook lumber operator Shepard Cary and New Brunswick lumberland John Glasier hung up at Round Pond on the Allagash, the men drove up toward Telos Cut to Churchill dam and blew a hole in the Penobscot built works which sent the Allagash timber scurrying downriver to the Fredericton and St. John destinations. Bangor rivermen soon repaired the dam and recovered Allagash headwaters for the Penobscot. Two years later in a practical reenactment, the Cary crew hoisted the dam gates in lieu of blowing them. Washouts eventually took favor with the St. John River operators and by the Civil War the project was abandoned.

Lakes with natural outlets generally have broad beaches and sloping shorelines but any dammed body such as this produces shorelines with cluttered banks. The inundation of shorelines leads to creation of dead wood characteristic of man-made lakes in wildlands.

Approximately a mile upstream from the Fish River's outlet into the St. John River where the Fort Kent Block House of 1839 yet stands, a sawmill stands on the site of the early water-powered mills that had timbered the lumber used to construct the wooden framed buildings on Military Square. William Dickey early invested in these mills following his arrival at Fort Kent shortly after the settlement of the border conflict. These sawmills gave rise to an economy

The flower of Aroostook Valley commerce at the turn of the century were, left to right, standing: George B. Dunn, Charles Daggett, and E. G. Dunn, Jr., and seated, Rev. Marcus Keep (?), and Thomas H. Phair. The Dunn brothers commanded an early lead in the lumber trade in Aroostook Valley following the pioneer efforts of the late E. G. Dunn, Sr., who operated American-owned sawmills in St. John, New Brunswick. Phair, owner of some seventeen starch factories throughout Aroostook, was recognized as the County's "Starch King."
Courtesy of George "Pete" Sawyer Estate

The Aroostook River, like the St. John, is an undulating river with high water especially at the spring freshet. This scene portrays the Elbridge G. Dunn estate at flood stage. Dunn purchased this homesite at the confluence of the Big Machias and Aroostook rivers in Ashland from Dalton, Township 11, Range 5's pioneer settler. From this supply farm, Dunn headquartered his Aroostook River operations until 1870 when he moved to St. John, New Brunswick, where Aroostook lumber was manufactured into timber.
Courtesy of Robert Sawyer, Ashland, Maine

Until the arrival of the railway on the Aroostook, lumber was driven to St. John, New Brunswick, to be sawn and marketed. With the possibility of shipping manufactured lumber direct from Aroostook via rail, the Ashland Lumber Comapny was formed to do just that. Shown here is an 1898 construction scene at Ashland.

At the construction of these mills, Ashland Lumber Company's sawmills were considered the largest lumber mill operation east of the Mississippi until 1904 when the St. John Lumber Company built its own in Van Buren, Maine.
Courtesy of the Ashland Public Library

Teamsters played a key role in timber operations, especially as distances from cutting site to river landings increased. Early pine lumbering along the rivers did not involve as much toting as did turn-of-the-century work. The original pine stand, bordering on the riverways and felled close to shore, called for quick switching of lumber to the river landing. However, as operations receded onto the ridges away from shorelines, teamsters using bobsleds such as that shown here, bridge the work of the lumberman and the river driver.
Courtesy of Shirlee Connors-carlson

which led to the construction of Fort Kent Village which by 1870 had a population of 1,034 persons. James Jenkins of Boston (Dorchester), Massachusetts, who was president of the Falmouth Bank there provided the venture capital to operate the business enterprises here. Since there were no banks throughout all of Aroostook, venture capital had to come from distant sources and lumber operators who accessed such capital played a key role in financing commerce here.

A Little Pulp Driving

ONE SPRING, Dad and I were waiting for the pulp drive to go by so that we could start trapping. We would set our traps on logs and dead trees that were tied to shore. The pulpwood would have carried the traps downriver if they were set before the drive.

I told my father "I guess I will join the drive until it goes by." I was sixteen then, and he said, "You damned fool! You don't want to have anything to do with any pulp drive." I still thought it was better than hanging around. I poled up the river until I met the drive and hired out. The boss said, "Did you ever do this before?" I answered that I didn't, but that I thought I could do it. He just smiled.

We had supper just before dark and the crew went to bed shortly after. They were sleeping in tents. I had to pick boughs or sleep on the ground. On a drive, the men were generally in a different place ever night. The cooking was done outdoors. The bread, cakes, and what-have-you were baked in a reflector oven, placed before a fire. We were eating at 4 A.M. and soon after we were going downriver in batteaus, which looked like double-ended dories. They were very seaworthy and were used to carry men and supplies. The ice had gone out early that year, but there was a good deal of snow in the woods. We came to a sideplace, which wasn't boomed. A boom is a bunch of logs, chained end to end, and are placed in front of these places, to keep the pulp out. This place was full of pulp and the crew went over the side like rats. They had all gone, except me, and the big French boss said, "What's the matter with you?" I thought I had better go before I got thrown in. I said nothing.

This was early in spring and that water was cold! You could not get up on the shore as the snow was too deep. The water was up to my waist. Once in awhile, I would step in a hole, or slip, and go in over my head and come up spitting and blowing. After the pulp was back in the river, it was 10 A.M., and time to eat again. I found out that they ate four meals a day. That night, I decided I wasn't a pulp driver and drew my pay of $1.00, took my canoe, and left.

My father said, after I arrived, "You're late!" I guess he had expected me back sooner. (From: "A Little Pulp Driving" by Jim "Grizzly" Lynch, *Tales of an Old Maine Guide*.)

Madawaska—The Town Fraser Paper Built

1925 was an important year for both the town of Madawaska and Fraser Paper Limited. Fraser Paper located in Madawaska and ventured into paper manufacturing. This provided much needed employment for the people and the surrounding towns.

Up to that time, Madawaska was a rural community. There were few scattered farmhouses and one general store. After the establishment of Fraser Paper, the town rapidly developed into one of the most prosperous towns in the state of Maine.

Fraser Paper Limited was incorporated in March of 1925 as a wholly owned subsidiary of Fraser Companies Limited. Construction of a mill to house two bond paper machines began in May and by October 25, 1925, the No. 2 Fourdrinier paper machine was completed and began producing bond paper. Four months later, No. 3 paper machine came on line providing more employment. The influx of people moving to Madawaska created an acute housing shortage. Fraser included a housing program with the mill construction at a cost of twenty-five hundred dollars, which provided housing for the construction workers and paper machine personnel.

Fraser expansion continued. By April of 1928, two additional paper machines had been added and the population of the town of Madawaska had reached two thousand. These four paper machines produced bond, fanform, register, and waxing paper. In November of 1928 and February of 1930, No. 5 and No. 6 catalog machines were installed at a total cost of eighty-five thousand dollars. This compares to today's cost of approximately twenty to twenty-five million dollars for one machine of a similar type. Sears Roebuck Company was Fraser's primary customer for catalog paper.

Expansion and modernization has continued through the years. Today the Fraser Paper complex houses five bond and three groundwood paper machines, two super-calendars, and two off-machine blade coaters. Online computers for the papermaking process have been added. Automated stock preparation, roll wrapping and computerized labeling and shipping systems are now part of the producing process.

Fraser Paper Limited has grown from a one-mill operation of two hundred employees with an annual production of eleven thousand tons of paper into a specialized company employing nearly eleven hundred people and manufacturing in excess of forty thousand tons of paper annually.

In 1983, Fraser Paper was named American Legion Employer of the Year. Fraser received the top award at the national convention for high employment of veterans.

The economy revolves around Fraser Paper. No publication is big enough to tell all Fraser has done for this town. It pays approximately 70 percent of the town's taxes, a 3.2 million dollar tax revenue. The average annual salary is thirty thousand dollars and Fraser draws employees from the entire St. John Valley.

Fraser's Madawaska-Edmunston Complex
A Unique Relationship

The two Fraser operations are only one mile apart. They are in two different countries and lie in different time

"At the Hulling Machine Falls (who named that ugly chasm chose well), where Dead Man's Strip begins, the haste of the drive took horrid toll of flesh. 'Old Stove-Snipe' as he was called. The ancient hermit who long had claimed for his own the cave and the gray cliff above the narrow trail of the strip, chiselled that year, the names of three men of the XK crew. That was his single hobby, his constant task in summer heat and winter cold, clinking away with mallet and chisel on the face of the cliff, sinking Bible text deep into the rock and adding the names of the men who were victims of the Hulling Machine." From Holmman Day's The Rider of the King Log, 1919.

Allagash Falls, a challenge to canoeists today who portage around it, was the bane of early lumber drives as the drive, often moving in clusters of a million board-feet, would frequently tangle up here. A solution to the problem posed by this natural phenomenon lay in reservoir damming.
Photograph by Dana Shaw

William Cunliff (1858-1941) pictured here with his wife, Cora Dickey Cunliff (1854-1926) at Cunliff Depot above Round Pond on the Allagash River, represents the second generation of lumber operators in the County. William Cunliffe, Jr., was the son of William H. Cunliffe (1820-1895), New Brunswick native who entered in the employment of Shepard Cary (1805-1866) of Holton who sent him up to Fort Kent in 1896 to manage the interests of the property of what later became the firm of Cary & Cunliffe. The firm drove large quantities of lumber down the St. John to the Fredericton, New Brunswick, boom where the lumber was manufactured for the foreign trade. In the second generation Cunliffe drove Allagash timber down to the sawmills of the St. John Lumber Company in Van Buren, then the largest sawmill works east of the Mississippi. Considered to have been a demanding employer, author Lew Dietz wrote of him: "He was a hard man and a tight-fisted one....Any man who ever worked for Will had a story to fatten the legend of his unpopularity. One logger who went out of the woods to attend church on Sunday was asked upon his return what the priest had given him for penance. The reply was prompt and wickedly telling, 'To go into the woods and work for Will Cunliffe.'"

Mrs. Cunliffe, pictured here in as much finery as a lady might be expected to carry into the deep forest, was the daughter of Maj. William Dickey (1810-1899) who served as Fort Kent representative to the state legislature for a dozen terms between 1869 to 1897. Dickey figures among the early logging operators on the Fish River. His name is retained to the current day in the place name of Dickey Village in Allagash and Dickey Hall on the campus of the University of Maine at Fort Kent.

The Cunliffes operated in the upper reaches of the Big Black River where Cunliffe Pond in Township 13, Range 16 and Cunliffe Brook farms a tributary of Depot Stream. As such the Cunliffe influence was broad throughout the forested region of western Aroostook.
Courtesy of the Allagash Historical Society

First generation Lombards were steam-driven such as this one here. Gradually this noisy monster of the forest came to be replaced by the more versatile and smaller diesel powered log haulers. Lombards did the work of several toting teams. With one operator and conductor (the latter seen here on the load), Lombard crews could tote in one run the equivalent of that hauled by a dozen teamsters using as many pairs of horses and bobsleds.
Courtesy of Shirlee Connors-carlson

The work of sorting gap crews lay in reading log marks to sort out logs by owners. Each log was ax-marked on the end and black marked in order to be read and sorted before being sent to sawmills. Here, downriver logs with marks designating ownership by New Brunswick operators were driven out of the gap into the main channel of the river. Upriver-owned logs were sorted and driven into company holding booms abreast of the riverside sawmills. A similar gap operation had been organized at Fredericton, back in 1844. There the function had been to sort out logs by owners to be rafted for the last stretch of the drive to St. John. Rafting was a necessary process required to avoid lumber washing out to sea. Sea rafting could not take place on the extreme upper river ways of the County due to obstructions presented to the drive by Grand Falls on the St. John and Aroostook Falls above Aroostook Junction on that river.

The sorting gap at Van Buren, Maine, on the St. John proved to be unique in the sense that it was structured for nighttime operation as well as daytime sorting. Because of the rapid rise and fall of the St. John River in the spring freshet, the river driving season is particularly abridged in comparison to the summer-long driving seasons on the Kennebec and Androscoggin rivers in southern and central Maine. In order not to obstruct downriver commerce, logs manufactured at the upriver mills needed to be sorted rapidly from those logs of such operations as Murray and Gregory: Stetson and Cutler of St. John. Lighting then was brought to bear on the sorting gap operation to permit sorting to occur through a nighttime shift as well as a regular daytime crew.
Courtesy of Martine Pelletier, Van Buren, Maine

"From earliest times, those who have lived in Maine have been an enterprising people, getting the idea of a worthwhile undertaking for themselves or their community, planning it carefully and thoughtfully in advance, and then giving their best to bring the project to full success. Enterprise in Maine has taken various forms.

"Many successful settlers did all their farming, lumbering, carpenter work, and blacksmithing for themselves. The tanner was one of the first to specialize. An enterprising farmer found that he liked the work of tanning and had good success with it. He cut the hemlock trees on his farm, peeled off the bark, ground it up, and placed it in a clay-lined vat with the hides. He poured water over all, added more as it evaporated, and kept the skins there for months while the tannic acid from the bark was doing its work. When

the hides came out of the acid bath, they were washed and made ready to be worked into hard, thick leather for soles, or into softer leather for clothing, bags, and many other items needed in colonial homes. There was less demand for footwear, because most people went barefooted, except in the coldest weather. Sometimes this man offered to tan any skins which his neighbors would bring, keeping half the leather as his pay. Other farmers were glad to agree to this. The tanner did less farming and spent more time at his special work. He soon had a supply of leather to trade for things he wanted." (From: H.B. Clifford's, Maine and Her People)
Courtesy of Irving Randall, Wayne, Maine

zones. The St. John River flowing between them is the international boundary. The two operations are diverse in nature but dependent upon one another. A multiple pipeline system connects Fraser Paper Limited with the Edmundston pulp mills. This system transfers the bisulphite and groundwood pulps from Edmundston to Madawaska to feed the eight Madawaska paper machines.

Recently, another dimension has been added to this unique relationship. High-pressure steam produced at Edmunston is transferred through a seven thousand foot stream pipeline to the Madawaska mill, reducing oil consumption by 377,000 barrels annually at both the Madawaska-Edmundston complex. An international bridge across the St. John River was constructed to carry the steamline. Regardless of the international boundary, the people have the same roots and remain one and the same nearly 150 years after the two Madawaskas were politically divided.

A good view of "the slip" or gangway for logs into a sawmill, shown here with a sawmill scene from Mapleton, Maine. Courtesy of Jim Willette, Presque Isle

Turn-of-the-century lumber operations witnessed a significant change in the variety of timber harvested. Pioneers had selectively sought out the virgin pumpkin pine for masting and spars shipped to foreign buyers. Second generation operations drew out spruce and some hemlock in the long lumber trade and especially cedar for split rails and fencing. Hardwoods of the cut-over lands provided in the third generation early twentieth-century operations stock for the plywood and veneer mills such as this outlet in midtown Houlton on the Meduxnekeag. Unlike softwoods of the evergreen variety, hardwoods cannot be as readily driven on the rivers but were rafted down to the millsites on the softwoods. Courtesy of ACHC

With the ever lengthening tote roads, the wild lands of western Aroostook gradually opened up to sports and hunters. Locals such as Willard Jalbert developed a reputation as a reliable guide and a fine spinner of folk tales and yarns. Posing here before a sportsmen's party prizes, Jalbert lets it be known that the wilds of Aroostook, even as late as 1958, had not quite yielded to plow, harrow, and civilization. At a later time, contemporary with our own, value systems would becry scenes such as these as tasteless slaughter and a sample of man's destructive work on the natural environment. Others responded that the hunt served to keep the deer herd in balance with available food supply, obviating the tragedy of painful starvation in the heavily snow-capped forests. Once the game was shot, the load had to be brought home. The trusty teamster could be relied upon to help (for a hide quarter perhaps?). Courtesy of Edwin Jackins

In addition to the tote roads into the Maine woods, the sportsmen's world has adapted modern conveniences to suit their needs. Here shown is a piper cub airplane used in the 1950s to reach the innermost favorite fishing holes of western Aroostook. Courtesy of Paper Talks

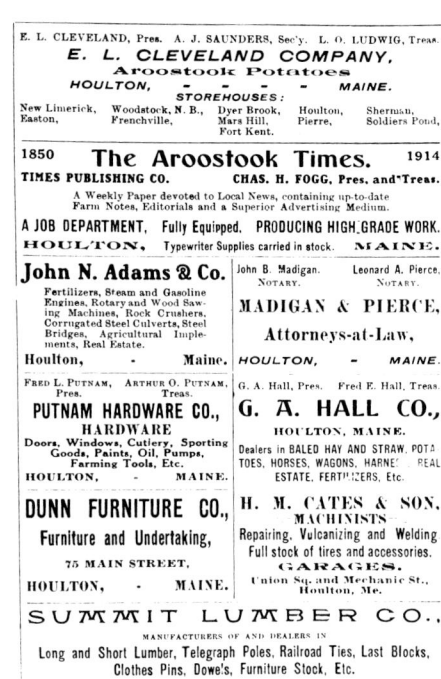

Railroads and starch factories were followed by a variety of businesses new to Aroostook including Edward L. Cleveland's consolidation of the potato shipping industry.
Courtesy of ACHC

The present Fred P. Stevens Clothing Store in Presque Isle had a long history pre-dating this century. The 1892 Maine Register lists D. A. Stevens as manager of S. Friedman & Company. The 1899 Register indicates that Stevens had branched off on his own by that date. Stevens was born in Aroostook, educated in Houlton, and opened this store in 1886 for S. Friedman and Company, remaining as manager for ten years and becoming proprietor in 1896. Business in Presque Isle apparently was brisk and Friedman, a German immigrant who established his first store in Houlton in 1880, must have regretted his move of selling out his manager. In 1904 Friedman returned to Presque Isle as a competitor of his former employee. Friedman and Company is noted as listing in the local directory until 1944, however the Stevens Firm continues to this day.
Courtesy of Maggie Niles, Presque Isle

With the Canadian rail link, first at Houlton in 1870, then at Fort Fairfield in 1875 and throughout the St. John Valley from Van Buren to Madawaska in 1876 (rail connection by ferry crossing of the St. John) and on to Presque Isle in 1881, the agricultural economy surged upward. Starch and cheese factories sprang up everywhere, but as late as 1891 the Canadian Pacific, buyer of the New Brunswick and Canada Railroad, could boast in its advertisement, "The only line between Aroostook and Washington Counties and Bangor, Portland and Boston." That year, the Bangor and Aroostook Railway Company was incorporated with the intention of driving a rail line directly into Aroostook. Houlton native Albert C. Burleigh presided over the organization and finance of the plan. Canadian Pacific responded by adding a full schedule to its ads listing fares from Aroostook points. A generation argued for a railroad to Aroostook and an array of solutions were offered but none seemed to fit the bill until the Burleigh Plan of 1890 led to the formation and capitalization of the Bangor and Aroostook. Albert A. Burleigh, a native of the County Shire became the rail line's first president in 1891.
Courtesy of ACHC

Street scenes showing Aroostook farmers hustling their potatoes to the starch factory in Houlton. Courtesy of the Eugene Jackins

THE GARDEN OF MAINE
by Guy F. DuBay

Aroostook County is so vast a territory that it is possible to grow up here without becoming familiar with all of the lumbering scene described and to live oblivious of the transnational factors central to a lumbering economy. Indeed there has been a tendency of County residents in the eastern townships to speak of anyone coming from areas south of the Haynesville woods to be regarded as being from "the outside." Back in 1858 when the Northern Aroostook Agricultural Society invited the editors of newspapers in Maine to tour Aroostook, the editors took note of the fact that in many instances they were introduced to local businessmen as "Gentlemen from 'the outside.'" Correspondingly Aroostook residents meeting their peers in state-wide conventions and associations are often met with the remark, "Oh, so you're from THE County!"

Given the five ranges of townships lying immediately west of the eastern line of the state, where homesteading succeeded the original "timber interlopers," the economic history of the area turns toward Yeomanry, husbandry, and homesteading. To the pioneers who settled here, the forest provided an impediment to be conquered. True to the Jeffersonian view which considered the agricultural economy as providing the epitome of civilized status, the early homesteaders in Caribou attacked the forest by burning it to yield pasturage and meadow:

On this warm May day the sun beat down through the treetops with their delicate young foliage. Every man was stripped to his undershirt and bareheaded. Faces glistened with sweat, but the music of axes kept up its staccato time. Irving, pausing to drink, had scarcely a word for his admiring brother. He was a man starting on his life's work; he seldom spoke anyway, and almost as seldom smiled.

The wide front of the chopping narrowed as it moved up the long slope of the ridge until it came to a place where, instead of each axeman notching three and four trees in his row, it came down to six men working close together. Each notch, like a mouth opened wide to the east, was more than halfway through its tree, small growth giving out altogether. Irving stood back and watched. Henry, having left the smaller boys in the safe hands of his mother, came up and stood beside him. Just as the sun began to dip beneath the top of the ridge, the narrowed wedge came to a big birch just beyond two maples.

Harvey had brought his campaign to a head, and like a general of old, he chopped the last notch of the day. Then with a booming cry of "Timber!" he stepped back and said, "Lufkin, fall your chopping!"

Never in his life was Henry to forget the sight of his father, tall, straight, and smooth shaven among the bearded or stubble-faced men about him, laying his axe to the back of that last tree. It seemed as if he towered above the others, as did that giant of the forest above the maples down the slope. He chopped as easily as he seemed to do everything else, with swift sure strokes that threw chips almost in a shower. Almost in to the back of the front notch and a little above it, he drove his deep V. The top of the tree shuddered, there was a crack, and as every man—and the two boys—shouted "TIMBERRR!" the old birch went over. A bluejay screamed, and as the wide-spreading branches struck the maples, a breeze that had been playing in the young leaves sprang to a gust, and whoosh! Down the slope went the trees, toppling like a row of dominoes.

The land behind the apex tree rose a little more sharply, and the eight pairs of eyes saw the forest bend away from them with crashes echoing until the wave subsided against the windbreak that had been left unnotched. Not a tree was left—only a sea of brush through which now and then a tall sliver peeped from its broken stump.

George Bilings spoke almost for the first time that afternoon. "My God, what a drive! Not one tree missed! I never seen the likes before!"

"Never see Harve Collins plan a drive, did ye?" jibed Mark Ellis. "Think you're a woodsman! You've learned something today!" (From: Milton Teague Lufkin's Henry, A Man of Aroostook.*)*

The smooth fields are undoubtedly an incentive to extensive culture. The growth of the starch interest illustrates this. We do not have the permanent pasture so called. All our land is fit for the plow, but up to 1872 there had been no inducement to call for the great fields under plow.

Farm and farm could be found where the woods had been felled and burned. The clearing up was but partially completed, for the land had been seeded down and turned out to pasture. These pastures were full of old mortgages and log piles, and the bushes were sprouting all around them. The land itself was just as good as the rest that had come under the plow, but they had plowed all they cared to and the rest was waste. (From: Francis Barnes' "The Potato in Aroostook," *Agriculture of Maine,* 1886.)

But the eye of the world opened up on Aroostook on November 9, 1870, the day that the New Brunswick and Canada Railroad first lumbered into Houlton. With the rutted and mired roadways, the route to city markets proved to be a long haul but enter the age of rail and as Wilmont T. Ashby put it in 1910. "The shingle (making) tools were neglected and left to rot and rust in the swamps, and everybody was talking potatoes. A new era had dawned for Aroostook in an industry that changed the County from poverty to wealth."

While farmers continued to grow a variety of crops and husband a flock of animals, the entry of the railroad in Aroostook was coupled shortly thereafter by the visit of Albe Holmes of Medford, Massachusetts, whose experience with the production of potato starch in New Hampshire, opened the door for the "Garden of Maine" to specialize in that crop.

BOARD OF AGRICULTURE

Not till the advent of the railroad, and through connections with Boston were made, did the business of raising for market begin. In 1872 Kimball & Co., of Boston, established themselves as buyers at Houlton, and modern potato growing began...

The importance of the potato crop to the residents of the county is such as to put it foremost in the list of products. The enormous expansion of the potato business the past fourteen years is due wholly to the railroad facilities which have been given to us.

Before the cultivation of the potato began on its present scale, the ways were few by which a farmer could realize the indispensable ready money with which to meet the taxes and other cash items.

I am familiar with more than one instance where the man was paying interest on money and had been for years, who could not extricate himself from the burden; but the same man after a few years of potato raising raised the mortgage and has been a free man since.

—Francis Barnes, 1886
Agriculture in Aroostook

The *Maine Register* of 1873 lists "Alba Holmes, starch" among the manufacturers of Lyndon (Caribou). Eventually the expansion of his effort led to the building, at Caribou, of a plant then known as the largest starch factory in the world. The movement spread like wildfire. Toward the end of the decade, the *Maine Register* includes these listings (their spellings):

Ashland—C.W.Clayton, starch
Bridgewater—George Hebbard, starch factory
Caribou—Alba Holmes (Medford,Mass.), starch
Easton—Johnson & Phair (P.O. Presque Isle), starch
Fort Fairfield—Bedell & Gatchercole, starch factories
Frenchville—George W. Collins, starch factory
Houlton—R. M. Mansur & Sons, starch
Limestone—Alfred Lovering & Co., starch
Mapleton—Aroostook Starch Co., Johnson & Phair, agents
Mars Hill—George W. Collins, B. Howe, starch factories
Maysville—Johnson & Phair, starch
Monticello—Lovering & Crawford, starch
Sherman—Merrill, Piper & Co., starch
Van Buren—A. W. Holmes, starch
Washburn—Washburn Starch Co., Isaac Wilder
and this was but the beginning!

With the development of harvesters, migrant pickers were no longer needed, and the few farmers who harvested with a potato digger led to the decrease in school children needed, and school harvest recesses are now restricted to high school students only. The high cost of the huge harvesters has also resulted in a decrease of small farmers able

Arthur B. Gould, U.S. senator, the "Man From East Corinth" ventured north to Presque Isle in 1886. The founder of Gould Electric Company (now Maine Public Service Company) in 1909 began to lay the roots of the Aroostook Valley Railroad as an all electric rail line. Shown here are engineers stretching the trolley wire live with 1200 volts. Courtesy of the Presque Isle Historical Society

Prior to the mechanization of potato harvesting operations in Aroostook, a horse team draws the digger at left and a jigger wagon with loaded barrels may be seen at right. The potato barrels weighing more than one hundred pounds when filled had to be loaded on to the jigger wagon by hand. Later when trucks were used for hauling, a hydraulic hoist was invented to ease the burden of this lifting operation. Though the era of long lumber for pine masting was over, the farmer with need of potato barrels gave sawmill owners a new outlet and market. In a sense there was a symbiosis between the Aroostook farmer and the lumberer. This scene of the Jesse Baker farm in Fort Kent sits on the site of the present day Fort Kent Elementary School, the largest elementary school in Maine.
Courtesy of the Fort Kent Historical Society

When Lumber was king and 250 million board feet plied through Van Buren's sawmills at the turn of the century, the community went rip-roaring into the twentieth century. Development ensued at a rapid clip but competition was fierce as evidenced by the double set of power lines on Main Street. There were two banks on Main Street, generally one Republican (First National Bank) and one Democrat (Van Buren Trust). Two large hardware stores inched each other with Joseph Martin and Son being Republican and H. A. Gagnon's being Democrat. So its no wonder that one set of power lines was favored by Republicans and the other by Democrats. When the dust settled over a state supreme court case in a 1911 dispute as to which power company would serve the municipality, the Democrats won. Shortly thereafter Van Buren Light and Power District became the sole power supplier in town, one of the few such suppliers which did not merge into Arthur R. Gould's Power Company which became Maine Public Service with a power distribution network which spans the County.
Courtesy of Martine Pelletier, Van Buren, Maine

Eventually machines did replace the spiked hoe as the potato digging method. By the turn of the century when farms with fifteen acres in potatoes came to be replaced by the fifty-acre field, the horse-drawn Homer digger was employed to unearth the crop and render the picking operation more efficient. The bushel basket shown here was later replaced by an ash basket with a handle across the top to make lugging the basketful to a waiting barrel easier. These potato baskets were a specialty handmade with the craft skill of Native Americans.
Courtesy of ACHC

"Joseph E. Tarbell was born in Solon, Maine, December 20, 1837, son of Ira Tarbell, a soldier in the Revolutionary War. The father, with others, broke the trail which led to Smyrna and pushed ahead when his companies were discouraged. He took his family with him to the new home when his son was six years old, and there they continued to reside. As he grew up, Joseph E. Tarbell picked up limited formal education, but improved his mind by wide reading and much study. He worked with his father in taming the wilderness and in farming until the outbreak of the Civil War, when he displayed the patriotism which characterized his family by enlisting for service in the Union Army.

"On his return from war, Mr. Tarbell established the business now known as J. E. Tarbell and Sons. Its first headquarters were in the bedroom of the old home, and the goods for sale were brought there by team from Houlton. Groceries were the staple product. In 1913, a co-partnership was formed, and the old enterprise of J. E. Tarbell took the name of J. E. Tarbell and Sons....A store and warehouse today are located at Smyrna Mills, and a branch is found at Masardis ....Like their forebears, Mr. Tarbell's sons continue to be interested in farming, specializing in the growing and shipping of potatoes. The father, a Republican, held many offices of trust. He was a member of the Methodist church and zealous in its support. He died March 3, 1924, at the age of eighty-seven...." So states Harrie B. Coe's thumbnail sketch of Joseph E. Tarbell, whose business establishment figured prominently in turn of the century affairs in Smyrna, Aroostook County, Maine.

to compete, and much farm land is now owned by big businesses who also process the harvest.

Harvest crews work for twelve to sixteen hours a day, and accidents result. Although farmers try to get away from the one-crop gamble, and many are experimenting with broccoli, Aroostook without potatoes is hard to imagine.

The self-reliance of the early settlers has been evidenced throughout Aroostook history, and especially in its financial strategies. Early settlers bartered for necessities and luxuries, a strategy that cyclically returns, although the early settlers of Houlton had been well-to-do, and brought money with them. Many young men "went West" during the 1849 gold rush and returned to help finance homes and businesses. Jewett & Pritchard printed paper money to pay their bills in the 1870s depression following the Civil War. Until the first bank opened in Houlton in 1872, the Houlton Savings Bank, capital had come from the banks of southern Maine, perhaps one reason why the railroad did not reach Aroostook from Bangor until 1894. Another bank opened in Houlton in 1882, the First National Bank of Houlton. Arthur R. Gould operated a private bank until the Presque Isle National Bank opened in 1888, followed by Merchants Trust & Banking in 1890. By the turn of the century the larger towns had their own banks as the potato economy peaked in the early years of the twentieth century, when Aroostook was the Potato Empire of the World. Farmer cooperatives started at that time, as the Grange, then the Farm Bureau in 1930, and local cooperatives merged into Maine Potato Growers in 1932 in Presque Isle and continues today. Credit was available through Presque Isle Production Credit, and Farmers Home Credit.

Then the banks closed in March, 1933, and although most of them reopened in a few days, many banks closed permanently with loss to the depositors. Many towns solved the problem with printed scrip, used to pay municipal employees. The Northern National Bank opened in Presque Isle in late 1933, when the Presque Isle National Bank failed, and added branches throughout the County, until now there are several banks in each of the larger towns and cities, based on the economic upswing when Presque Isle Air Force Base closed in 1961 and many industries and the Northern Maine Vocational Institute moved onto the old base, and based on money brought into the area through Loring Air Force Base in Limestone, Potato Service in Presque Isle, McCain's potato processing plants in Easton and Washburn, and the universities at Presque Isle and Fort Kent, as well as continuing agricultural and lumbering activities through Great Northern Paper Company and International Paper. Now, of course, we have credit cards and instant cash, but people still barter, and share.

At mid-century, Aroostook's commercial isolation was entirely a thing of the past—as marketing potatoes spread throughout the United States. J. L. Budreau & Company, food distributors headquartered in Savannah, Georgia, were active in marketing a variety of food stocks from oranges in Florida to potatoes from Maine. Statistics show 1946, the post-war year with a high volume of 77,745,000 bushels. During the war a federal price support system encouraged potato production. Following 1947 when the price support system wound down, the acreage planted in Maine dropped drastically.

Despite original fecundity of the virgin soil, generations of use exacts its toll. Unless fertility is returned to the soil, farm productivity becomes a matter of diminishing returns. Shown here is a 1920s view of the County solution to the problem.
Courtesy of Jim Willette, Presque Isle, Maine

Central to many elements of the local business structure was the village blacksmith who served everybody from farmer to hosteler, and often filled the role of veterinarian.
Courtesy of Jean Sawyer

The Model A was on the market, but it cost money and one had to earn some before being able to move into the luxury and convenience of the future. Leon Rossignol of Van Buren made a living peddling door to door until he could afford to buy a farm.
Courtesy of the Madawaska Historical Society

Winter was no "Christmas Holiday" for the Aroostook farmer. That was generally the time when potatoes were brought to market, or to the starch factory. Starch factories provided the opportunity for the farmer to market "cull" or second-rate potatoes that could not be sold as table stock. The twenties brought the use of trucks in lieu of old horse-drawn jigger wagons. Note the transformer rack to adjust the power to the needs of the factory which sprouted an electrical ventilation system. The starch operator has its odorous components and power vents proved a boon in mitigating working conditions in the industry.
Courtesy of ACHC

Oaknoll Dairy Farm in Mapleton was owned by Everett Tarbell whose dairy herd of Jersey and Guernsey cattle helped supply the surrounding area, including Presque Isle, with dairy products. In this picture three sons of Everett prepare the cattle for a trip to the Northern Maine Fair. The bull at the right of the picture, King David, killed Everett Tarbell as he was led down Sleepy Hollow towards Presque Isle for the Northern Maine Fair Exhibition, in September 1917.
Courtesy of the Nancy Fields Estate

Ferry boats, unlike the wangan and the towboat, which served an up and down-river traffic, operated simply in a cross-river pattern. Set to draught lines anchored to either side of the river these flat-bottomed river craft served to assist land going vehicles across the river where bridges lacked. This turn of the century era photograph of the ferry crossing the St. John at Fort Kent, Maine, depicts the large two-man operated craft capable of transporting both horse team and vehicle. Smaller local ferries continued to be run on the St. John River well into the mid-century even after the construction of international highway bridges at Fort Kent, Van Buren, and Madawaska. Here, Emile Caron sits his farm tractor while Fred Z. Pelletier, who guided this ferry to Savage Island in this 1948 crossing, prepares to see Caron run his tractor to its work site at mid-river.
Courtesy of the Fort Kent Historical Society

With the municipal water systems in place and artesian well drilling outfits readily available, the Aroostook resident gives comparatively little thought to sources of water in terms of site selection for a home. Pioneer settlers were more limited in their option with the location of a natural spring being far more important than the view as to where one might locate his home. Back in 1905 James Watson's blacksmith shop was the work site where William Long built the first well drilling machine in use here. Shown here is Ellery Watson's 1927 drill outfit which was later loaded on a 1929 GMC truck to provide mobility to on-site projects. Through four generations Watson's Drilling has continued to serve the rural public now employing the latest technology in the artesian well drilling field.
Courtesy of Julia Watson

Silver's Stables was founded circa 1940 by Alex Silver at a location along the Houlton Road in Presque Isle. Originally established to provide Aroostook County farmers with work horses and cattle, Silver began handling automobiles during the late 1940s and acquired the Chrysler line in 1950. Since July 23, 1986, the business has been under the direction (ownership) of Darrell and Randy Norsworthy and does business as Norsworthy's Chrysler-Plymouth-Dodge. This view is circa 1947.
Courtesy of Paper Talks, *1987*

The first airplane load of potatoes leaves Presque Isle in 1946. Table and seed stock were freed from the problems of rail shipping and the need to keep the cars heated. Later, trucks took over transportation duties, and many farmers act as their own brokers and thus eliminate the middleman, allowing for more profits direct to the farmer.
Courtesy of the Presque Isle Historical Society

Racking potatoes is part of the grading and sizing operation which often takes place in mid-winter as stock is prepared to be shipped to market. The last decades have seen significant change in marketing practices from the day when field run sales in bulk and railroad car lots to the present practice of pricing potatoes by package sizing down to the peck or fifteen-pound level. Potatoes sold by the carload were accounted for in barrel measures. Table stock later came to be figured by the hundred-weight (cwt) but seed stock was sold by the 150-pound bag. Today potatoes are figured by the size of the container in which they are marketed.
Courtesy of Julie Boyd

A real labor shortage occasioned by World War II brought its unique solutions to the County as German war prisoners saw service in the potato fields or working in the lumbering camps around Houlton. Although not required to do so, many farmer's wives brought lunches out to the harvest crews, and shared with the POWs, with many lasting friendships resulting. The labor shortage also brought trainloads of men, too young or too old to be drafted, from Oklahoma, Kentucky, and other southern states.
Courtesy of ACHC

This sugar beet refinery was built in Easton in 1966 when both potato and dairy products declined, and agricultural diversification was seen as essential to the Aroostook economy. Operating as Maine Sugar Industries Inc., by Fred H. Vahlsing, Jr., also owner of Maine's largest potato processing plant, the sugar beet refinery was financed by the Area Development Administration, Maine Industrial Building Authority, Aroostook Development Corporation, and was built by Krupp International of Germany. Operation required pollution of the Prestile Stream which was permitted although the Prestile empties into the St. John at Centerville, New Brunswick, and caused some international concern. But the sugar beet harvests were not sufficient to operate the refinery profitably and Vahlsing defaulted on his payments in 1969, after which the refinery was repossessed by the state. With cash from Aroostook growers and a mortgage, Triple A Sugar Corporation was formed in 1976, but sugar prices dropped, and with disastrous weather conditions, only a fraction of the beets planted were actually harvested, so the plant shut down again. It was then "sold" to Nordic Sugar Company, but the contract was never completed, and in 1981 the factory was sold to Sugar Refinery Corporation of St. Hilaire, Quebec, who had it dismantled and transported to Quebec in 1982.
Courtesy of the Presque Isle Star Herald

Early contemporary sketch of Fort Kent Block House, shows the type of construction E. G. Dunn was involved in building at Fort Fairfield in 1839.
Courtesy of the Maine Historical Society

Old receipt of 1847 links major Aroostook lumber operators Shepard Cary and E. G. Dunn with the international interests at Aroostook Boom. Logs driven down the Aroostook River were sorted and rafted here for their final drive down the St. John River in New Brunswick. Note the use of shillings and pence in accounting sums and charges.
Courtesy of the George "Pete" Sawyer Estate; Ashland, Maine

160

Civil War veterans and residents of Fort Fairfield attend the unveiling of the cannon used during the Bloodless Aroostook War (1939) in 1921, after the cannon had traveled to Fort Kent several times under mysterious circumstances, and been reclaimed several times. Courtesy of the Fort Fairfield Public Library

AROOSTOOK: THE MILITARY IMPACT
by Guy F. DuBay

Though Aroostook has always been the land of promise, and peace ordinarily reigns through her meadows and glens, life's struggles that often led humanity to war have not left this land untouched. Indeed, the arrival of the first non-native settlers, the Acadians, may well be said to have resulted from war. Had George Washington and his compatriots not won the Revolution and the Loyalists from New York, New Jersey, and other American colonies not immigrated to New Brunswick, would the Acadians on the lower St. John River at Ste. Anne's Point (Fredericton, New Brunswick) ever have migrated upriver to Aroostook?

There are few Revolutionary War graves on Aroostook soil though it cannot be said that the Revolution did not impact on this county's history. The Acadians, who have tragic history of their own through the French and Indian wars of the colonial era, might well have remained among the Maliseet Indians at Ecoupahaq on the lower St. John had not the Loyalists in founding a new province crowded them out of that region. Thus began the migration into the hitherland, the highlands dubbed "Madoueskak" and "Waloostook" in the tongue of the native Americans whose ancient relics have been roused by pioneer plowshares. The foreign tongues which came to take over softened the tones and rolled their r's over the native nomenclature. In a brief time after the white man's presence, Waloostook became Aroostook.

The War of 1812 raged hot and strong on the Potomac and Great Lakes thousands of miles from Restiguam (Allagash), Ouagundy (St. John) and other headwaters of County rivers as yet untrammeled by the Euro-Americans. For fear of reprisals the settlers at Houlton saw their hunting arms confiscated by a nervous itinerant British soldiery from across the "border" in Woodstock, New Brunswick. Over in Madawaska, the French settlement quartered the 104th Regiment of Foot passing from Fredericton on the St. John to the St. Lawrence Valley and on to the battle scenes up the Ottawa to the Great Lakes. A few guineas might have been waylaid in the frontier settlement but the economic impact in the barely settled frontier region might be said to have been neglible except in the personal instance as we have it in the latter settlement by John Hafford of Fort Kent. As a veteran of that war, he would later be entitled to benefits which included, as per post-wartime legislation, a bounty of land. Nearly forty years after the fact, a letter addressed to John Harford (Hafford) at Fort Kent arrived in the mail from a former comrade in arms. Its contents bear out yet another impact of events and military posturing on the citizens of Aroostook.

A by-product of the American experience on the frontier at Houlton was to emphasize the need for direct communication between this region and the rest of the state. Thus the first highway link between Aroostook and

161

Bangor came to be called the Military Road since troops sent out to guard the frontier doubled as highway builders, that is, the federal government built the first road into the County. By 1827 that torturous route through forest wilderness of over one hundred miles at last linked the frontier region with those more settled parts of Maine.

Over in Europe the Napoleonic wars resulted in an embargo or blockade for British sources of Baltic pine masts, spars, and booms. A natural reaction to the situation for the British was to turn to colonial sources to replenish such vital needs of a growing British navy and merchant marine. Thus was born the ton timber trade in the British provinces of Quebec and New Brunswick to either side of Aroostook's forest country.

For some later County settlers such as Romain Michaud of Wallagrass this resurgent British interest in North America had a direct impact. Michaud figures among the so-called available youth impressed into the British navy. Once a British citizen, always a British citizen came the cry from Britain all the way to the colonial shores. From L'Islet in the British province of Quebec, Michaud saw himself consigned to serve on a British man-of-war. Following that experience and a brief hiatus back home, Michaud chose to seek opportunity in the resurgent forest economy. Thus in the prime of life we find him on the St. John River where marriage, family, and farming brought him upstream beyond Fort Kent to Soldier Pond on the Fish River.

The names Solider Pond and Eagle Lake are by-products of another military operation, dubbed informally as the Bloodless Aroostook War. The virgin pines of Aroostook still towered over vale and brook in these "hitherlands" when the Mistress of the Seas turned here to meet pressing masting needs. Generations of shipbuilding had denuded the coastal regions of much of its forests which originally gave Maine its pseudonym, "The Pine Tree State." Thus the post-war era after 1815 saw an American migration from the Kennebec Valley, Maine, into the upper St. John River Valley while Wilmot and Peters, a New Brunswick lumbering firm, reached upwards above Grand Falls in search of pumpkin pine which grew near the drivable rivers of the St. John, St. Francis, and Allagash regions of Aroostook.

From the American mindset which by virtue of the Treaty of Paris had ended the Revolutionary War, this territory fell in the American claim. The incursions of New Brunswickers such as Peter Bull and Alexander Cochran on the Aroostook River, much like those of Wilmot and Peters on the St. John were regarded by the Americans as "depredations" on their territory.

George W. Coffin, Massachusetts land agent in 1825, issued a land grant to Kennebec River immigrant, John Baker, to lands on the Meriumpticook which would later turn out to be set at Baker Brook in New Brunswick! The stage was set for a border conflict and the next dozen years saw a flurry of incidents which led to direct Aroostook involvement in military posturing narrated more specifically in this work in the chapter by Jere Green.

Speaking of those years, Francis Barnes of Houlton wrote in 1886: "The settlement grew slowly till the war time arose and the troops were quartered in the hamlet. Then came the first market of potatoes in 1832. The regiment of soldiers, with their families and attendants were all cash buyers and paid in gold. During the thirteen years of the garrison the settlement throve and made a good start."

The Treaty of Washington brought peace and eventual withdrawal of troops from the area but the wartime incursion brought increased knowledge of Aroostook geography as indicated by a comparison of pre-war maps with that of Maj. James Graham of the U.S. Topographical Engineers of the U.S. Army. Graham's map of 1843 indeed served as a reference work well into the twentieth century when an international commission held hearings on border considerations in the lumbering economy of 1909 to 1912. But this illustrates once more the by-product of military activity in Aroostook in that it might be said that Aroostook was "opened up" as a result of this increasing geographical definition of a hitherto wild region as yet sparsely settled with Acadians on the St. John, Yankees on the Meduxnekeag, Bluenoses on the Aroostook, and a few Scotch-Irish on the Allagash.

Though the upper regions of the Aroostook had been pioneered by Yankees at Masardis and Ashland, geography still required co-operation with downriver folk in New Brunswick and the broadening imperialistic activity of the British Navy still generated market potential for virgin pine from the headwaters of Aroostook's multiple watersheds.

E. G. Dunn of Ashland who came to Aroostook to do carpentry on the military barracks and blockhouse at Fort Fairfield settled into lumbering on the Aroostook to meet that need. Buying an Ashland pioneer's homesite, he turned to lumbering activity up on the Big Machias River to draw ton timber for Shepard Cary down to the Fredericton boom in New Brunswick. As noted in the impending work by Dr. Richard Judd, an internationalizing of the Aroostook economy was in progress.

The peace brought on by the Treaty of Washington also encouraged the homestead movement along the Maine-New Brunswick border, and the counties of Oxford, Somerset, and Franklin yielded a portion of their youth to Caribou, Presque Isle, and Mars Hill.

The next phase of military activity to impact the lives of Aroostook homesteaders and timber operators was the American Civil War. Abraham Lincoln's call to arms brought a patriotic response from Aroostook folk, and County villages were practically denuded of the vital energy of youth to the point that some homestead sites, cleared and pastured, reverted to bush and underbrush. Aroostook youths served in nearly every phase of the five-year war as thick volumes of the adjutant-general's reports show. Bull Run, Manassas, Gettysburg—each battle scene saw the flower of County youth, but Aroostook's own might be said to have been the Fifteenth Maine Regiment raised right here in Aroostook and commanded by Col. John McCluskey of Houlton. The Fifteenth Regiment saw service in Texas, Louisiana, and Florida campaigns where malaria and near-

*Robinson, on the Presque Isle side of the St. John (now known as the Prestile Stream), which empties into the St. John at Centerville, New Brunswick, was a stop for New Brunswick deputies taking prisoners back to Woodstock. Mars Hill Mountain is in the background.
Courtesy of Madeline Babar Estate*

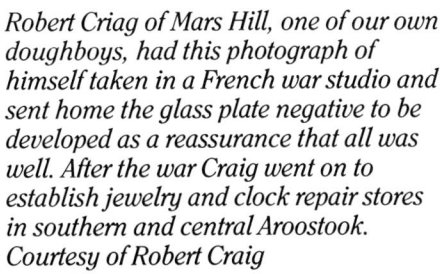

*Robert Criag of Mars Hill, one of our own doughboys, had this photograph of himself taken in a French war studio and sent home the glass plate negative to be developed as a reassurance that all was well. After the war Craig went on to establish jewelry and clock repair stores in southern and central Aroostook.
Courtesy of Robert Craig*

*The men of the famous old Company L which was a part of Houlton for so many years, were expert marksmen and distinguished themselves in many a competition. This picture is supposed to have been taken around 1902 while the outfit was at camp. Capt. Ralph Whitney is seated in the center. On the right, kneeling, are Frank Hussey and George T. Clark. Clark is reputed to have finished second in a national rifle competition. On the captain's left are, Billy Glen and Elson A. "Bill" Hosford. Standing left to right, are, Osgood Smith, Frank Dyer, Frank Chamberlain, Ben Batchelder and Harry Perry.
Courtesy of the Houlton Pioneer Times*

Aroostook youth saw service in World War I. Among the thousands of young men who served overseas were brothers Charles Tarbell, U.S. Army, and Karl Tarbell, U.S. Navy, sons of Everett and Anna (Smith) Tarbell, grandsons of Benjamin and Rebecca Kidder Tarbell, early Hodgdon settlers. Farm boys from Mapleton, they both saw service overseas. Returning from the Front and back to civilian life, the young seaman went on to Bates College and eventually became high school principal in Shelton, Connecticut. Courtesy of Nancy Tarbell Fields

tropical conditions contributed as much to the casualty list as did war wounds and fatalities. Among others, Maysville cemetery in Presque Isle contains the grave of George Pyle, a County boy who paid the ultimate price in the service of his country. This war, long after its passing, left a memory trail throughout the county as newspaper accounts of Grand Army of the Republic activity ran well into this century. A hunderd years after the fact, George Whitneck of Caribou would pen a commemorative series of County Boys in Blue recalling the war between the Blue and the Grey.

Recollections

"In 1859, when Oliver C. Smith was twenty-six years old, he came to Mars Hill from Readfield, Maine, and started to homestead on the West Ridge Road. When he and Isabel F. King were married in Readfield in 1861 they returned to Mars Hill to make their home and Oliver continued to clear land for farming.

"When the Civil War broke out he volunteered in the Infantry, Company E. of the 31st Maine Regiment. This regiment saw some of the hardest fighting of the war as they were in the Battle of the Wilderness and the Battle of Cold Harbour and at Spottsylvania. Some of the men from Mars Hill who were in the 31st Regiment with Oliver Smith were Henry O. Perry, Warren Preble, Wm. L. Merrill, Steward P. Townsend, Richard Murphy, John Ashenhaust and Albert Whitcomb from Easton. When the war was over the men were glad to return to their farms, and it was during the next years that a large number of folks settled in the county.

"Oliver C. Smith's homestead on the West Ridge Road is now being farmed by the fourth and fifth generation of Smiths."
Courtesy of ACHC

Though the British were said to have a penchant toward the Confederate cause, King Cotton of the South being a resource for the industrual resurgence of the cotton milling industry in England, the internationalization of the forest economy here never remained far off scene. When war brought on increased pressure to link the frontier by rail and in 1869 the former Civil War Brig. General and then Governor of Maine Joshua Chamberlain signed a deed granting well over a million acres of Aroostook forest land to the railway incorporated by the Civil War Era Frontier Defense Act. The European and North American Railway was structured to give Maine cities of Portland and Bangor quick access to Cunard Steam lines at Halifax and Sydney, Nova Scotia, to beat New York steam ship lines to London. Thus again Aroostook experienced an indirect by-product of military activity when ungranted wildland townships ended up in the hands of Bangor city railway men with the backing of the likes of former Vice President Hannibal Hamlin, who countersigned the railway bonds of the City of Bangor. The stumpage from such wildlands was expected to help capitalize the railroad from the Penobscot region to the New Brunswick border. Though the wartime resolutions spoke of extending the rail line "in defense of the Northeastern frontier" to the St. John River, and Aroostook folk early regarded the move to organize such a line under the European and North American Railway, the line never reached its speculatory objective in Aroostook. Heading northerly from Old Town on the Penobscot, the line veered at Winn, Maine, to strike the New Brunswick border at Vanceboro in Washington County. Aroostook was to wait yet another generation to witness a direct rail link to American market regions.

Civil War veterans returned to their homesteads to pursue careers as husbandmen and timber drivers. A generation of peace ensued in Aroostook if such distant military affairs as Custer's Last Stand on the Little Big Horn may be excluded. Yet Horace Greeley's call "Go West Young Man" did not fall on deaf ears in Aroostook County. Grounded in forestry by their youthful experiences, their pioneer spirit could be renewed by turning to the newly emerging logging regions of Wisconsin, Minnesota, and eventually North Dakota and Montana and the redwoods of Oregon and Washington. Some let the forest underbrush reclaim their lands which may be said to be the natural state of Aroostook Land. The depression in the Eastern lumber industry following the fall of the financial house of Jay Cooke of Philadelphia in 1873 and the default on the European and North American Railroad bonds in 1876 encouraged County migration out west. The Town of Presque Isle with a state valuation of $1,000,000 in 1870 fell down to $750,000 in 1877. Clearly for some the land of opportunity appeared to be in following the footsteps of the legendary Paul Bunyan, said by some to have been a native of Maine. In any case the Paul Bunyan song "Logging North Dakota" was heard clearly all the way east to Aroostook.

Coupled with the "Cleveland Hard Times" as Aroostook Republicans put it, the ensuing decades which witnessed a hiatus of military activity proved but an era of gradual and steady development of the agricultural and forest economies here as first Canadian and eventually American rail lines plunged their way into the hinterland.

The Bangor and Aroostook Railway, organized in 1891, arrived in Houlton in 1893 and reached the St. John River at Van Buren just about the time when "Remember The Maine" became a battle cry, and Teddy Roosevelt, who had enjoyed hunting and meditating in the Patten-Island Falls region, stormed up San Juan Hill in the brief conflict known as the Spanish-American War. Conscription once again brought County youth into service but fortunately the war was brief enough to limit American casualty lists.

With direct rail lines and peace, the most northerly portion of the state, formerly geographically linked to marketing routes through New Brunswick via the St. John River, at last could be Americanized. With the birth of the potato starch industry and the arrival of the first train links, the economy surged upward.

The gay nineties progressed to the age of invention of the new century where automobiles sputtered over rutty roadways and war and military activities seemed far removed from County residents' minds. Following George

Snowball over Aroostook—a Douglas C-54 of the vaunted Snowball fleet that helped whip the Axis powers is shown winging its way toward Paris across the Aroostook farmland in 1944. The rich farms of Aroostook with thousands of potato acres comprised a familiar picture to the men who flew the broad Atlantic. Courtesy of ACHC

Washington's advice against foreign entanglements, our country had passed up such European War theatres as the Crimean War and the Franco-Prussian War. At first it attempted to do the same with the conflict brought on by the Kaiser of Germany. Until the Lusitania was sunk, County boys had witnessed their Canadian neighbors head for the war front, though war hawks had advocated greater involvement in international affairs before this. 1917 brought on conscription and in Van Buren today, the American Legion Post bears the name Levasseur-Farrell in honor of two local youths who gave their lives on the European battlefield.

Here in Aroostook, for those not conscripted, we had a reversion to a wartime economy. Just as the Civil War had brought National Banks and Greenbacks into the economic picture, so also this war brought its own kind of currency as we see in the record of sugar rationing coupons such as those preserved by members of the Tarbell family of Presque Isle and Mapleton.

Some County boys such as Pvt. Edouard Michaud of Van Buren, though drafted, never made it to the war front; the Armistice was signed before he could pack his duffel bag to leave Camp Devens in Massachusetts. Michaud, as irony would have it, returned home safely where his diabetic condition was diagnosed. He died in 1922, the year Dr. Frederic Banting discovered insulin.

At. St. Mary's College in Van Buren, the American authorities set up a newfangled wireless radio station to convey to and from Europe vital military information at a time of news blackout. Western Union telegraph operator Margaret Walsh was hired to convey coded information back and forth between the continent and the overseas war front. Oral tradition has it that in early November 1918 one of the student aides at St. Mary's overheard radio room conversation regarding peace negotiations then in progress. As the news was being relayed to Washington, the student spread the rumors of peace around the campus. In short order the draft-age students of St. Mary's put together a joyful demonstration marching from the campus hilltop down to the village site where cheers and spirits (no doubt) rebounded through the public. Once satiated with revelry the students returned to St. Mary's only to learn that their response to rumor was premature, and that indeed the conflict was not yet ended but hard negotiations were as yet in progress.

A week or so later the armistice was signed but this time the celebration was conducted with due caution and some skepticism. But now even Margaret Walsh smiled although she knew that the armistice would end her job relaying vital military information. Peace was secured. An armistice had been signed that day, November 11, 1918, and Johnny would come marching home. A popular song of the day however ran: "How Can You keep Johnny on the farm after he's seen Gay Paree (Paris)?"

For the next generation Armistice Day was to be a holiday, in many ways like Memorial Day had been to the G.A.R. Even though the County furnished troops in two ensuing wars, the name Armistice Day stuck until the third or Viet-Nam conflict brought back a new generation of soldiers who did not know by experience the meaning of the word armistice. Thus as Aroostook County towns erected new monuments citing the casualties of three wars since Armistice Day was first proclaimed, that day through the efforts of multiple veterans' organizations came to be called Veterans' Day.

Those who fought in the trenches at Flanders and beyond the Maginot line turned home and began to give the old farm horse a rest. They bought up steel rimmed-wheeled tractors that would help to expand the ten to twenty-acre potato fields to fifty and even a hundred acres. The combustion driven tractor, linked by belts to threshers and even sawmills provided Aroostook farmers with a mobile source of power and energy not bound to rail or steam. Even in the woods where the Lomard log hauler had been the wonder of the age, the old steam haulers began to be replaced by combustion driven machines that in a sense were a by-product of wartime advances in military logistics and ordinance.

The twenties saw Aroostook folk work at putting outmoded practices behind them with spinning wheels and looms being remanded to the back sheds as ordering from Sears and Roebuck came into vogue. But the veterans of war and good times which followed (a return to normalcy they called it) were to face unprecedented challenge in a world economy that went into disarray. The veterans were then to be the older brothers and fathers of a new generation of soldiers that was to witness the era of Iwo-Jima, North Africa, and Normandy.

December 7, 1941, and a nation, now used to Fireside Chats on radio spoken by beloved President Roosevelt, was riveted to hear the message of a "Day of Infamy," the attack on Pearl Harbor, and the declaration of war by Japan. The military arsenal of the nation matched the progress of technology as the old single piloted bi-planes a la Red Baron gave way to the B-17s and the Flying Fortress of the day, the B-24. This technology provided Aroostook County the opportunity to be directly engaged in the ordinance activity of this World War.

As any pilot and navigator would tell you, the shortest distance between two points on a sphere is not a straight line but the grand arc or great circle. When Charles A. Lindberg flew from New York to Paris he didn't fly straight across the Atlantic but skirted northeasterly along the New England-Nova Scotia coast to Iceland and down to Ireland and Paris. Accordingly, Aroostook County being set in the extreme northeast is by aeronautical definition at the most proximate point to many places in Europe. As a result the flat open farm country just east of Quakajo Mountain in Presque Isle lay, as set in globular perspective, within the staging area of international flights to Europe. Thus the Army Corps found it expedient to develop here, in what was then Maine's newest city, Presque Isle, an airbase for military use. On Sept. 15, 1941, twenty-one trailers, being home to the advance guard of the Ninety-fourth Air Base Group trudged up to Presque Isle Fair Grounds. By the time that war was declared twelve hundred servicemen of the Air Corps serviced British-bound aircraft before setting them in the hands of trans-atlantic pilots.

Northeast Airlines, American Airlines, the Royal Canadian Air Force, and the U.S. Army Air Corps used the facilities intermittently. One hundred and thirteen years after fortifications had been erected on the frontier at Houlton, the Aroostook frontier once more harbored a military outpost. Thousands of B-17s, B-24s, and A-20 Mosquito Bombers made Presque Isle their last stop in the United States to set a record of more combat planes flown to Europe than from any other airport in the country. Anticipating the Normandy invasion, "Operation Snowball" airlifted 1,713,261 pounds of military cargo flown from the base, in April 1944. The drone of military conveyance flights became a familiar sound and in a world made smaller by aeronautics the communities of Aroostook experienced the wartime phenomenon of air-raid sirens and civil defense blackouts where all home lights were snuffed out and blackout curtains pulled to hide the presence of towns and villages from potential or alleged enemy reconnaissance flights. Local farmers and businessmen took on new jobs as air-raid wardens.

German spy activity was known to have reached American shores where here in Maine an avid shipbuilding industry was marshaled to put out such craft as the famed PT-109.

Wartime industry revived the timber trade from its Depression-era blues. The War-time Small Industries Act financed the refurbishing of the Van Buren-Madawaska Corporation sawmills at Keegan. Allagash River timber then contributed to the war effort as the inner wing structure of the U.S. Army Air Corps's fighter P-48 was made out

In 1943 over two thousand German prisoners of war from Houlton were put to work picking potatoes from Fort Fairfield to Sherman and Chapman. Another twenty-five hundred prisoners of war from Houlton were sent to work in the woods cutting pulp. The U.S. Army supplied one guard per fifteen prisoners. Those employing the prisoners paid the government the wages the men would have earned. These prisoners were well liked by those employing them, and they were well treated.

This picture of "Specks," the Germany spy, was taken in 1942 by Bill Clark. "Specks" was caught with a radio transmitter while working for Pete Clark cutting logs in the Pomkeag area. He had worked for about three months before he was caught. In this picture he stands in front of Pete Clark's lumber camp. Courtesy of Bill Clark

of wood, just like the chassis of post-World War I station wagons had wooden framework before synthetic fibers were used.

Those beyond the age of military draft found ample

The social impact of the military presence in Aroostook is evident in this picture of an airman who married a local girl, and returned to the County to raise their children. Gary Ellis and Agnes Lavaway of Presque Isle pose with their wedding party.
Courtesy of Roger Ellis

work in wartime industries with several County families emigrating to work sites such as Bath Iron Works on the Maine coast or Pratt and Whitney aircraft engine plants in Connecticut. These wartime pressures resulted in labor shortages here which were relieved in part by the use of German War prisoners in the construction of the international airfield at Houlton and others engaged in harvesting the potato crop. Young boys and women from Oklahoma, Arkansas, and Kentucky came north to help with the harvest, along with Indians from reservations across the Canadian border.

Wartime shortages resulted again in rationing and though such is beyond the memory of this wartime baby, among the heirlooms handed to me in this era are my own unused ration coupons.

To meet the wartime need Maine Public Service Company's 8200 Kilowatts generating capacity was boosted by the installation of interconnections with Bangor-Hydro Electric at Medway and Fraser Paper Company's steam plant at Madawaska.

For the County farmer the war brought on price supports aimed at bolstering production to meet heightened wartime needs. Peacetime readjustment called for the elimination of the price support system by December 31, 1948. The increased productive capacity developed during the war led to over-production as markets faltered. Supply and demand swung the economy to a buyer's market. Heightened development of transportation facilities with the railroad switching from steam to diesel engines, and then the arrival of big eighteen-wheel trucks, put the County farmer not in mere regional markets but stacked him up against national productive capacities. Truly the modern era had arrived.

With the formation of the U.S. Air Force in 1947 came a new mission which eventually put Aroostook on a nuclear war footing. Out of farm and forest lands of Limestone-

For thirty-one years—practically through our own generation—Loring Air Force Base has contributed to this country's nuclear punch from which our presidents drew power to negotiate with super powers of the world. Hollywood gave recognition to this role in the popular movie War Games *in which the Aroostook SAC Bomber base was identified as the first enemy strike in a computerized version of an enemy attack on the United States.*
Courtesy of the Marcoa Publishing Company

Caswell, the military developed facilities to respond to the Strategic Air Command mission which grew out of Cold War needs of the 1950s. By virtue of the great circle, here set over the North Pole, Limestone's new Loring Air Force Base became the closest SAC base on the North American continent to Moscow and other vital points in the Soviet Union. The turbo-prop driven B-36 rumbled regularly over Aroostook skies shaking our home windows each time to get enough power uplift from its extra four jet engines to get the heaviest aircraft in the U.S. military arsenal up toward its defense mission. Coupled with defensive Nike missile systems built on the perifery of the base, the impact of military personnel in the region was to boost Aroostook's pre-war population of 94,436 to a 1960 high of 106,064.

This writer recalls annual classroom visits by the school principal to ascertain the number of students whose fathers worked for the federal government since the local school districts qualified for federal impact monies and support. Not only were Air Force personnel housed in make-shift temporary housing rented by local residents but the need for a variety of skilled labor occasioned many residents to enter into the civil service field in a variety of job assignments from stock clerk to electrician.

So freely was the federal dollar flowing through the County economy that when the Van Buren-Madawaska Corporation sawmill, owned by New Brunswick industrialist K. C. Irving, burned in the early 1950s, the selectmen refused to grant Irving requested tax concessions in support of his plan to rebuild here. None realized at the time that the move in effect was as if one kicked capitalism in the teeth. Though some venture capital was later risked here in a variety of small plants such as those involved in the production of tennis rackets, cedar fencing, and tool and dye works, the basic underlying strength of the new economy lay in government support programs which saw subsidized housing, low income support programs, the Soil Bank potato production regulatory program, and state funds for education become the major sources of revenue for this community.

When the age of intercontinental ballistic missiles (ICBMs) altered Loring's basic mission, a move to shut the base was countered by needs it played in the basic economy

of the region. At this writing the U.S. Air Force has announced after thirty-one years the end of Loring's Nuclear Alert Status.

The military impact of the Viet-Nam conflict on Aroostook is akin to that of the rest of the nation. This was the subtle but little discussed aspect of removing the U.S. dollar off the silver standard. Just as Roosevelt had taken the country off the gold standard and Lincoln had placed the country on the greenback economy to cover war debts, Aroostook shared in the national debenture by paying for the change of the U.S. dollar from silver value to note value by experiencing the energy crisis of 1973 where many County homes reverted to wood burning for heating purposes. Our press accused the Arabs of inflationary escalation of oil prices yet an Aroostook County child with experience in the economy by virtue of picking potatoes may well be postured to say that the emperor has no clothes!

What seemed to be inflation as County banks merged into state-wide holding companies may well have been the direct result of military exigencies brought on by the Viet-Nam conflict. The simplest truths are the most elusive. As a twelve year old having earned a silver quarter for picking a barrel of potatoes, I had earned in fifteen minutes the admission price to the Saturday movie matinees. Following the Viet-Nam conflict when the Hunt brothers of Texas sought to corner the silver market of the world, regular tours were conducted by agents offering ten dollar Federal Reserve Notes for every silver dollar presented in hand. County residents joined in the national move selling pocket change, dimes for dollars, and yet we got miffed at the Arabs seeking fifty dollars for a five dollar barrel of oil.

My old silver quarter, if I had it, would still admit me to the theater or at least cover the cost of a VCR tape rental so there hasn't been inflation on that score. If the County student has to pay more for what he buys its because he has accepted payment for his work in devalued dollars that resulted from our country's need to pay Viet-Nam war financing.

Every war brings its profits. Every war brings its debts. The history of Aroostook County's war experience may well provide ample food for thought as to the relative values of humanity's war-like propensities.

THE Cottage Physician.

BEST KNOWN METHODS OF TREATMENT
IN ALL
Diseases, Accidents and Emergencies of the Home,

PREPARED BY
The Ablest Physicians in the Leading Schools of Medicine:

ALLOPATHY, + HOMŒOPATHY,
ETC., ETC.

BY
THOMAS FAULKNER, A.M., Ph.D., M.D.,
President of the Royal Medical Council, London.

J. H. CARMICHAEL, A.M., M.D.,
Of the American Institute of Homœopathy, Boston.

ASSISTED BY OTHER ABLE PHYSICIANS AND SURGEONS OF AMERICA AND EUROPE.

Complete Hand Book of Medical Knowledge for the Home.

NEARLY 200 ILLUSTRATIONS.

KING, RICHARDSON & CO.
SPRINGFIELD, MASS.
CINCINNATI.   SACRAMENTO.
CLARK PUBLISHING CO.
OMAHA.
1892.

PURELY VEGETABLE TREATMENT.
HOME MADE REMEDIES,
PREPARED FROM ROOTS, HERBS, BARKS, ETC.

As many of our friends may prefer the treatment of disease through the medium of herbs alone, we herein give, in addition to the herbal preparations in the previous parts, many other formulas; and amongst them will be found the principal forms used by the best eclectic physicians and botanical medicine practitioners of America and Europe.

Anti-dyspeptic Powder.—Cayenne and golden seal, of each two ounces, saleratus, half an ounce—mix in powder. Dose; half a teaspoonful in hot water, fifteen minutes after a meal, in indigestion, pain in the stomach, etc.

Anti-dyspeptic Pills.—Golden seal, powdered, three ounces; cayenne, five drams; inspissated oxgall, Q. S.—mix, divide into five grain pills. Dose, two to four, three times a day. They rectify acidity and wind in the stomach, and regulate the bowels.

Anti-spasmodic Tincture.—Lobelia seed, powdered, one pound; valerian and cayenne, of each four ounces; Holland gin, one gallon—infuse ten days, closely stopped, shake once a day, then strain for use. Dose: a teaspoonful two or three times a day, in fits of all kinds—hysteria, hypochondria, hydrophobia, etc.

Balmony, or Snake Head.—Is an excellent bitter tonic and laxative, and is useful in costiveness, indigestion, loss of appetite, jaundice, worms, etc., given in infusions and other forms.

Bayberry.—A native of the New England States. The bark of the root is the part used in medicine; it is an astringent stimulant, is an excellent medicine for canker, also for bowel complaints, and if given freely at the commencement, is said to be a certain cure. The powder is given in teaspoonful doses, in water, sweetened; or a strong infusion drunk freely. Taken every two or three hours.

Barberry.—The bark is the part used. It is a bitter tonic, improves the appetite, acts on the liver. Is taken in powder or infusion, similar to golden seal.

Bethroot, Wake Robin, True Love, or Jew's Harp.—The root is the part used. It is an astringent. Useful in all excessive discharges of the bowels, womb, or in bleedings internally of all kinds. The powdered root may be taken in infusion of one ounce to the pint for four doses.

---

416 MATERIA MEDICA.

Cloves (*Caryophyllus Aromaticus*). Stimulating and often used to relieve colic and expel wind. The oil of cloves is often used locally to relieve *toothache* and *earache*.

Cod-Liver Oil (*Oleum Morrhuæ*). Obtained from the livers of the common cod-fish. There are three varieties according to mode of extraction, known as *pale*, *light brown* and *dark brown*. The first named is the purest and most palatable; as a remedy for consumption and other constitutional diseases of an exhausting nature, cod-liver oil takes high rank. It is really more of a food than a remedy, its power of producing fat is well known. In scrofulous diseases generally, *hip joint diseases*, *white swelling of the knee*, *caries of the spine*, *lumbar and psoas abscesses*, *rickets*, etc., cod-liver oil will nearly always do good. It is also useful in *skin diseases*, some forms of *eye troubles* and *syphilis*. Young children who have grown very weak from diarrhœa in summer, and who seem unable to assimilate the food given them, can often be saved by rubbing cod-liver oil into their skin. Common dose of cod-liver oil is from one to two tablespoonfuls, three times daily.

Coltsfoot (*Tussilago Farfara*). Native of Europe, now naturalized in the United States. Useful in *chronic bronchitis* as a demulcent and expectorant. Given in infusion, one ounce of dried leaves to a pint of boiling water.

Compound Spirit of Ether (*Hoffmann's Anodyne*). Stimulant and anti-spasmodic, very useful in *hysterical paroxysms*.

Copperas. See Iron, Sulphate of.

Cranesbill (*Geranium Maculatum*) SPOTTED GERANIUM. See Illustration.

Creasote. Sometimes used internally to check vomiting. *Sea sickness* and *cholera infantum* frequently yield to its influence. Dose one or two drops. In an overdose it is a violent poison. When applied to the cavities of decayed teeth it will often relieve the pain.

Cubebs (*Cubeba Officinalis*). Chiefly used in inflammation of the urinary passages. It is also used in cases of *chronic bronchitis*, catarrh, and in certain throat troubles.

Dandelion (*Taraxacum Dens-leonis*). Has long been used for *dyspepsia* associated with congestion of the liver. Fluid extract is probably the best form of preparation.

Dogwood (*Cornus Florida*). See illustration.

Dover's Powder. This powder is composed of one grain opium, one grain ipecac., and eight grains sulphate of potash.

This copy of The Cottage Physician, *passed down from the last generation, has obviously been consulted many times as the covers have fallen off, and the pages are dog-eared, indicating that its advice was considered valuable by the generations before hospitals and medicare. Note the use of creasote [sic] for toothache pain.*
Courtesy of Eva Holmes

BLUE COHOSH.
PAPOOSE ROOT, SQUAW ROOT.

A perennial plant growing in all parts of the U. S. The root is the part used. It is antispasmodic, diuretic, diaphoretic, alterative, emmenagogue, anthelmintic, parturient and tonic. It is used in rheumatism, dropsy, epilepsy, hysterics, cramps, amenorrhœa, dysmenorrhœa, chorea, leucorrhœa, hiccough, to hasten delivery, and to relieve after-pains.

Dose.—Of the infusion, one to four fluid ounces three or four times a day.

The Curer, the Healer, is acknowledged with awe by the individual who is diseased, whose body/mind needs easing and curing. The earth supplies the plants that heal today as it has since the beginning of recorded time, and today those plants are supplemented with minerals and chemicals. Some use beams of light to cure with bloodless surgery. The caring is manifested in boarding homes and nursing homes as well as in the state-of-the-art hospitals throughout the County, and by some doctors who still make house calls,
But ultimately Nature heals...
"...a woodland walk
a quest of river-grapes.
a mocking thrush,
a wild rose, a rock-climbing columbine
salve my worst wounds."
—Ralph Waldo Emerson

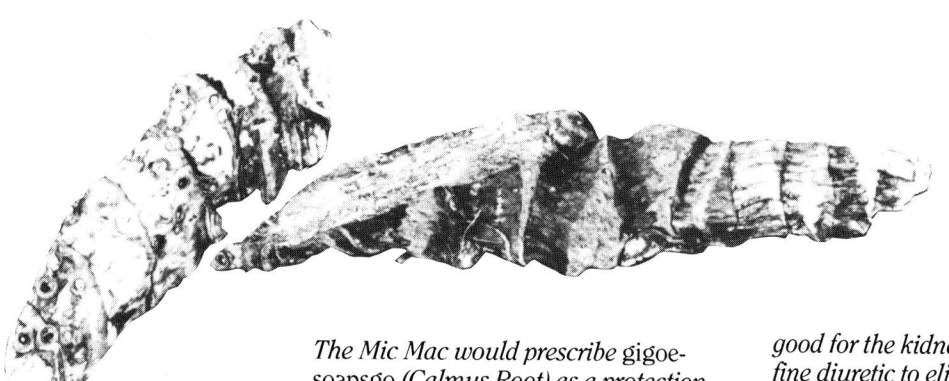

The Mic Mac would prescribe gigoe-soapsgo *(Calmus Root) as a protection against illness, including colds and flu. Another inhibitor of disease, that may have negated the sore throat, is* oipoisti-giitjitjit *(Labrador Leaves) which is also good for the kidneys, perhaps therefore a fine diuretic to eliminate harmful bodily humours. From Thomas Faulkner's* The Cottage Physician.
Photograph by Diana Higgins; courstesy of the author's collection, a gift of Gretta Moulton of Tobique.

ROOTS IN THE GARDEN
HISTORY OF MEDICINE IN AROOSTOOK COUNTY
by Richard Cohen

Presuppose a condition such as a sore throat which prevents vocal communication, that the only forms of exchange are either sign of the written word. The prescription for elimination of the disorder in Mic Mac remedies is to drink gaotago (spruce bark) tonic, or to chew upon the bark, whichever appeals. Wisdom would have dictated a deterrent, and Native Americans were aware of preventive medicine. Peculiarly, it has not been until possibly the past two decades that there has been concerted emphasis upon preventive medicine in the allopathic community, though there had been advocacy by individual physicians.

Reference to Native Americans and the conditions in the County prior to the arrival of trained physicians are a necessity. One must imagine not only the wilderness but the unseen hostility of disease confronted by the Negative Americans, and then the early settlers and their helplessness in combating many illnesses. Settlers arrived with their own remedies. They obviously also borrowed from the Indians. There was a corpus of cures written by Old World physicians, but pioneers seldom had access to those primitive prescriptions.

Aside from medicinal applications, however, contemplate the philosophy of health, of life, of death. The Native American says, "Death is not a failure." The dead have finished their responsibilities. The living still have their obligations to complete.

This recognition of life and of the body had its effects upon visitors to and settlers of this geographic area. Lord Edward Fitzgerald, writing to his mother in Ireland, though with a romanticized view, stated in September 1788:

Savages have all the real happiness of life, without any of those inconveniences, or ridiculous obstacles to it, which custom has introduced among us. They enjoy the love and company of their wives, relations, and friends, without any interference of interests or ambition to separate them. To bring things home to oneself, if we had been Indians, instead of its being my duty to be separated from all of you, it would, on the contrary, by my duty to be with you, to make you comfortable, and to hunt and fish for you . . . . Instead of being served and supported by servants, everything here is done by one's relations—by the people one loves; and the mutual obligations you must be under increase your love for each other.

Though Fitzgerald's simplicity may amuse the modern mind, consider what Native Americans judge to be protection against the ills of society and of disease: love. Sage and cedar are of use for purification of the Indian community while prayer and love are protection. Nothing is stronger than love which always overcomes.

Inevitably Native American practices and beliefs would influence the early settlers. Fitzgerald was writing as an officer stationed in New Brunswick, though it is certain that he traveled in what is now known as the County. Con-

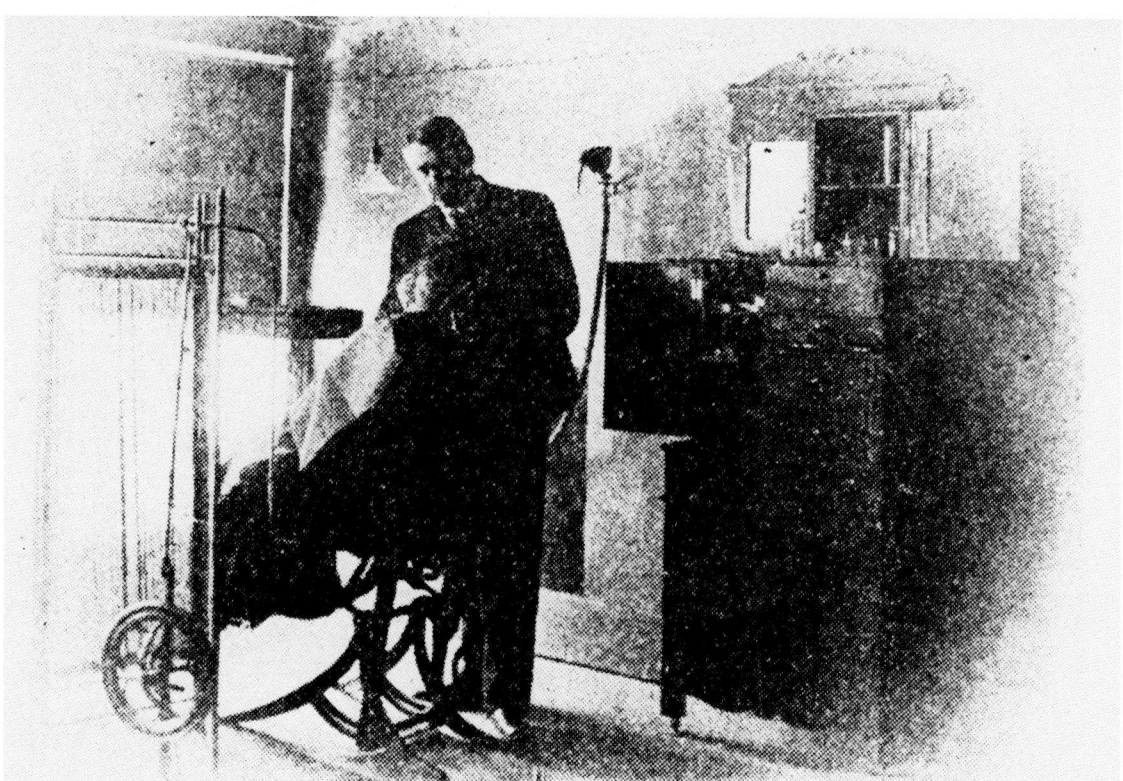

*Dr. M. L. Bonney began his practice of dentistry in Livermore Falls, Maine, in 1890. He went south looking for warmer weather, but had been so impressed with this area that he returned and set up a permanent practice in Caribou in 1904. Other dentists in the area included a Dr. Trundy who practiced in Washburn in the late 1800s, using a foot-operated drill. But dentists were a rare commodity for the early settlers.
Courtesy of ACHC*

sider his observations of the benefits of the simplicity of life which he extolled. Yet, that romantic innocence obviously had its perils. (He does, incidentally, show his exhilaration with winter and four-foot snows, for one can showshoe and keep warm by building encampments in the woods and further protect oneself by building mounds of snow about one.) Winter does, of course, bear its own perils of illness, given the lack of protective clothing, of centralized heat, of exposure to temperatures and weather changes which may affect bacterial growth. Thus, recognizing that one is susceptible to lung and other bodily afflictions, remedies relying upon nature were of inevitable use not only by the Indians but by the settlers.

For fever and ague mix a pound of the bark of yellow birch, a half pound of alder bark, of tag, two ounces of wort and a mixture of other ingredients, all made into a liquid. The patient then takes a dose of two tablespoons every two hours until the "shakes" come on. Now stop the dosage, wait, and continue the next day and for each day until the fever breaks. Certain cure.

Or, perhaps one has been taken with pleurisy. The medicinal potion includes lady slipper, red pepper, coriander seed, and ginger, all pulverized. Then take in liquid form a teaspoon every fifteen minutes until the pain diminishes, and administer this as much as the stomach will bear, until there is a thorough sweat of the entire body after which the patient wears a flannel band for several days about the abdomen. The cure occurs without resorting to the bleeding technique. Such healings were adapted from the Indians by the white settlers.

Diseases and cures may have been catalogued, but recovery was haphazard. It was necessary eventually to bring the methods of modern medicine to Aroostook, a science which over time has led to a lengthening of the life span and an appreciation of the happiness and change that wellness brings.

The doctors who came to Aroostook County during the nineteenth century were aware of the need for hospital facilities. Dr. Jefferson Cary, who died of stomach cancer August 25, 1912, bequeathed funds to the city of Caribou which would ensure the building of a modern facility. In 1876, after having been in business in Houlton, Cary attended Maine Medical School and after graduation came to practice medicine in Caribou. At the time, there was but one practicing physician in that city, a Dr. Thomas. One can assume that there were too many patients for the two. While Dr. Cary and Dr. Thomas were at work in Caribou, there were others in Presque Isle. As a matter of fact, Dr. George Freeman established a practice in 1855, joining a Dr. Dibblee who had been here since the 1840s. A number of other physicians began to move to the area, several of the trained physicians having come from medical school at the University of New Brunswick.

Quite early in the history of the area, it is obvious that there was a close connection between New Brunswick and Aroostook County that went beyond economics. Interdependence still remains. But with the coming of the twentieth century, Presque Isle did have the nucleus of a modern medical society which included general practitioners and surgeons.

Typical of the residences renovated for private hospitals is the York Street Hospital in Mars Hill. Opened in 1938 by Faye (Wilson) Johnson and her sister Ola (Saucier) Graves, both registered nurses, this hospital handled medical and surgical cases with Doctors Wallace Somerville, Robert Somerville, Sherman Boone, and Stephen Brown. Mars Hill supported another private hospital, the Brown Hospital on Main Street, bought by Janet Brown, registered nurse, who was assisted by her mother, Susan Brown, a practical nurse. Many Mars Hill doctors used this facility also, including Dr. Stephen Brown, Dr. Kincaid, Dr. T. Harvey, and others. Both hospitals closed in the mid-1950s.
Courtesy of Judy Saucier

Dr. Wallace Somerville and his homemade "ski-mobile" in the mid-twentieth century, used for making house calls and home deliveries before the roads were regularly cleared for emergency traffic. He came to Mars Hill from Bristol, New Brunswick, Canada, and practiced for forty-three years, using private hospitals and his home. A younger brother, Dr. Robert Somerville followed him to the County, and practiced in Presque Isle for many years, while another brother, Donald, stayed in Bristol and practiced dentistry. Homemade conveyances for doctors were not uncommon. Dr. Richard Savage of Fort Kent made his house calls with a side-car on skis attached to his motorcycle.
Courtesy of Joan (Somerville) Walsh

In Houlton the charitable Catholic hospital, Madigan Memorial, opened in 1914, staffed by the trained Sisters of Mercy. A bequest of Albert W. Madigan gave initial impetus to the creation of the facility which reached beyond the Catholic population to help any patient in need of modern services.

As the doctor's hospital grew, it was reorganized in 1938 and became the Aroostook General Hospital. After World War II, noting that physicians from Houlton, other towns, and Woodstock, New Brunswick, were working at both hospitals, it became apparent that a merger was in the best interest of the community to enable the most practical, economic, and modern medical services to be delivered. The consolidation occurred in 1976, and now Houlton Regional Hospital is an eighty-seven-bed facility.
Courtesy of Eugene Jackins

Marilyn Dean has written in her history of the Presque Isle hospital of Dr. Frank Kilburn who diagnosed a woman with a bowel obstruction as having an abdominal tumor. Dr. Sherman Boone who was a visting classmate, concurring in the diagnosis, operated on the patient on her kitchen table, perhaps similar to this room in the Salmon Brook Historical Museum. Because she survived the 1887 procedure, Dr. Boone established his practice in Presque Isle. Consider the plight of the patients as they waited for the physician. Consider the operations on kitchen tables, the home deliveries. Though home deliveries are becoming something of a vogue in the present, in earlier times there had to be a concern regarding, for example, pueperal fever or hemorrhaging. *Photo by Dennis Harris*

The question of hospital quarters was important to each of the large communities. Within several years of each other, Presque Isle, Caribou, Houlton, and Van Buren considered the problem. Already in Presque Isle, as in Houlton, there were hospitals in private homes. Dr. Cary bequeathed his seventy-five thousand dollars as mentioned. In 1905, the Daughters of Wisdom, in Van Buren, were asked to convert convent property for hospital use. The project was unsuccessful, though ten thousand dollars was set aside. Not until 1939 did Hotel Dieu come into being with the gift of a private home by Levite Thibodeau. Eventually, to meet the needs of the city, Van Buren Community Hospital was built when in 1954 the sisters found it necessary to close Hotel Dieu. The townspeople working together gathered funds, received a donation of land from Lillian Keegan, and with legislative approval for a hospital district, ensured the new structure. In Fort Kent came the erection of the Northern Maine Medical Center.

In Houlton, the earliest settled community in Aroostook (1807), Dr. Thomas S. Dickison who came from New Brunswick and who had trained in New York, began practice in the town in 1903, using his home for acute care while hiring trained nurses to aid him. As the need increased, Dr. Dickison built a large new home, and by 1911, he could manage sixteen beds with the help of ten more physicians.

Significance rests with dedication and the type of medicine which was practiced and how, and why the hospitals were established. Consider Dr. Charles Thomas, the first graduate physician in Caribou, settling in fall, 1873, practicing not only in Caribou but in Washburn, New Sweden, Stockholm, Limestone, Perham, Van Buren, and even up the St. John River.

One must imagine the conditions for the patients as well as for the physicians. There have been numerous movies and books linking the late twentieth-century population to that earlier difficult era. But if one has an association with Aroostook County for any length of time and considers the distances to be traveled, prolonged winters, it is not difficult to contemplate the physicians who walked, who rode their sleighs or horses and buggies, and who drove the first automobiles, neglecting the difficulty of unreliable machines and the hazard of poor roads.

Prior to the coming of the physicians, possibly the proposed cure could have been that for pain or cholic in the bowels in which the patient takes a mixture of cayenne pepper, cloves, unicorn, dogwood bark, and prickly ash berries which would be used the second day after making. There would be no danger, apparently, were the tablespoon dose taken ten minutes. However, should the mixture fail, the pain remain, then the advice was a physic. Chloroform and a kitchen table seem preferable, though the risk ratio may possibly have been close in either case.

What did occur in Aroostook communities was acknowledgment that private homes were inadequate and that the concerted effort of physicians and generous citizens and religious orders was necessary to ensure the establishment of modern hospital facilities.

The General Hospital in Presque Isle provided medical and surgical services since its incorporation in 1912. This building replaced a wooden home later used as a nurses' residence and opened in 1921. It was sold to the city and is now City Hall. The Arthur R. Gould Memorial Hospital was built in 1960, which was expanded in 1976, and again in 1988. Recently retired obstetrician George Higgins of Presque Isle delivered 6,353 babies in the hospitals of Presque Isle. The Rotary Club has been a staunch supporter of the hospital for many years. Courtesy of Marilyn Dean

The formal opening of Cary Hospital did not occur until Tuesday, May 12, 1925, National Hospital Day. Yet, by necessity of course, the building was available to patients as early as September, 1924, at a time when a state laboratory was also about to be installed at the hospital. The newspaper reports, contrary to patient-physician confidentiality, that the first patient operated on was Lewis Holmes who "submitted" to an appendectomy by Dr. Frank Blossom. What choice is there but to submit, should one realize the consequences of ignoring the physician's diagnosis and advice—peritonitis.

It became a rather regular reporting procedure to include news of operations and of hospital stays. More important, however, is the account of the implied meaning of modern facilities Roaring 20's fashion: laboratories, operating rooms, X-Ray, and beside general practitioners (now the family practitioner in medicine throughout the United States), the specialists, such as obstetricians and surgeons, nurses "daintily clad with white aprons and caps," and rooms with "a most beautiful and picturesque scenic view [that] can be obtained of the great Aroostook Valley, with its gentle sloping fertile fields." One may smile at a quaint description of sixty-three years past, but one must also consider the psychological effects of hospital stay and the tranquilizing impact of natural scenery which may enable a patient to adjust to the foreign and often frightening experience and environment of a health facility.

What has been noted about Cary Memorial Hospital may be applied to the other hospitals of the County; each

Before the paramedics and helicopters or air-lifts to Portland, Maine, and Boston, Massachusetts, hearses were also used as ambulances, as this first hearse bought by Dwight W. Dorsey in 1925, when he started the Dorsey Funeral Home in Fort Fairfield. The funeral home business is continued to the third generation, through Edward, and his son Stephen. The Dorsey ancestors were the third settlers on the area known as the Dorsey Road when its ownership was still in question. The grant to John Dorsey in 1840 was from the New Brunswick government.
Courtesy of David Dorsey

installed the latest equipment, and each established its own nursing school, enabling physicians and population the access to skilled and professional aid necessary for procedures and recovery.

Though the nursing schools ceased, the University of Maine System committed graduate nursing programs to Aroostook County at both the Presque Isle and Fort Kent campuses. Now there is a four-year baccalaureate study based at Fort Kent and cooperatively delivered by campuses of the System, and an R.N. program at Northern Maine Vocational Technical Institute.

As evolution occurred in nursing, it is evident that more dramatic changes came into being through the efforts of physicians and citizens. The modern facilities of the hospitals of the County in this latter part of the twentieth century include technology and procedures that range from ambulatory care, cardiac rehabilitation, and chemotherapy to CAT scans and ultra-sound, laser surgery, and patient education programs.

Significant health assistance also encompasses long term care. Aroostook County has nursing homes, Aroostook Home Care, and the Aroostook Area Agency on Aging. Each of these applies to the physical and mental well-being of people.

There still remain many mysteries associated with the human body and there are diseases, as we are agonizingly aware, for which cures have not been discovered as yet. But one must be in awe of what scientists, medical researchers, modern physicians, nurses, and technicians have accomplished. Their work does not occur in a vacuum. Moreover, consider the public scrutiny and awareness of the fallability of those in medicine, and yet, consider that despite what still remains unknown, without those who have come to Aroostook County to practice, and one can cover almost any specialty, medicine has given us longer, healthier, and more comfortable lives and has taken us beyond the kitchen tables.

Nor should one forget what present day Native Americans teach, that "nothing can harm you unless you allow it...that [people] have a responsibility to live as wholly and spiritually as they can...that we have a responsibility for ourselves."

This modern laboratory is located in the Aroostook Medical Center, established in 1982, consolidating Arthur H. Gould Memorial Hospital, Mars Hill Aroostook Health Center, and Community General Hospital of Fort Fairfield, known by the acronym TAMC. TAMC enables physicians to treat their patients in accord with the rapid advances occurring in medical science and technology.
Courtesy of The Aroostook Medical Center

The Northern Maine Sanitarium was built in Presque Isle in 1920 for the treatment and control of the dreaded TB, tuberculosis. With advances in pharmacology during World War II, specifically the development of sulfa drugs, tuberculosis was curable, and sanitariums were closed.
Courtesy of Blanche Beckwith

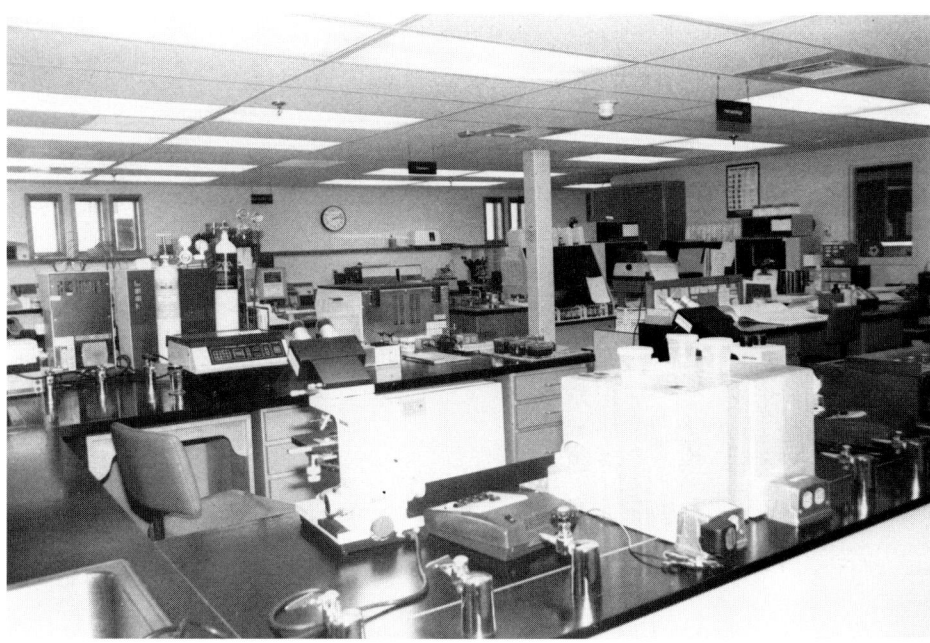

Psychological problems have long been with us, and Aroostook has not completely escaped. This residential treatment center for alcoholics, located in Limestone, Maine, is affiliated with TAMC, and allows sufferers to live-in and receive treatment in a home-like atmosphere. Photograph by Cathy Brewer Craig

The Presque Isle Nursing Home is an example of the current trend in long term care to meet changing needs of the elderly. The nursing home, with eighty-two intermediate care beds, is connected to an acute care facility, the Aroostook Medical Center, and to Leisure Gardens, twenty-seven individual apartments where aid in daily living may be purchased from the nursing home. These services may include: meals, housekeeping, laundry, or nursing services. For veterans of Aroostook County there will soon be nursing home quarters connected to Cary Medical Center in Caribou.

There are other long term care facilities in Eagle Lake, Van Buren, Limestone, Mars Hill, and Houlton.
Courtesy of Paul Cyr

> The three groups who settled the Aroostook came from very different political backgrounds. The Acadians had been a self-regulating group, generations removed from the French rulers of the seventeenth century, yet reliant on their traditional peasant ways, with rare visits from priests who came to convert the Indians, but who nonetheless provided a modicum of political structure to their lives, settling disagreements and disputes. The Massachusetts Academy Grant settlers of Houlton and Hodgdon were self-reliant, compassionate people who cared for each other, and had little need for regulatory structure. For the Loyalists from New Brunswick who settled and/or squatted on the Aroostook, Allagash, and St. John Rivers, before the Kennebecers came up from lower Maine later in the century, might usually made right, and law and justice were largely left to chance until the Aroostook War. But any garden needs a plan, and a structure for plants to take advantage of needed sun, so a developing area needs a structure, and structures did develop in the County.

The Aroostook County Court House was built in 1850, and enlarged in 1895. The jail, to the right, was built in 1858, and was completely modernized with an addition in 1987-1989.
Courtesy of Eugene Jackins

TRELLISES IN THE GARDEN OF MAINE: STRUCTURE IN A PIONEER LAND

by Anna Fields Mcgrath with John Lisnik and John Graves

The need for structure in relationships, and social conformity to the demands of that structure, are the social imperatives as a people gather together to live as a community, a nation, or a world; and certainly that was true here in this land we now call Aroostook.

Whether among aboriginal peoples, Acadians, Euro-Americans, or Yankee settlers of the rivers of Aroostook, the St. John, Aroostook, Allagash, or Meduxnekeag, when a group gathers, a leader emerges, with a group of individuals who assume responsibility for the welfare of the group, who promote the common good for the perpetuation of that group, and a structural order evolves.

As with the new United States, a government of the people, by the people, for the people, here in Aroostook there developed a government of rules, regulations, representatives of the people who make the decisions for the people, individuals, and groups. From the first political appointment in Aroostook, the appointment of Capt. Joseph Houlton as Register of Deeds for the Northern District of the County of Washington, by his excellency James Sullivan, governor and commander in chief of Massachusetts to a contemporary concern about acid rain, we are a people forming, and being formed by our governmental structure.

Aroostookans have always been independent, and perhaps Aldoux Huxley expressed our feelings when he said, "The free mind needs to know the past, to debate and discuss how the world came to be as it is, in order to know what to defend and what to change, and how to resist imposed orthodoxies."

For the lumbermen who came up the St. John and Aroostook rivers in the late eighteenth and early nineteenth centuries, to ravage the forests of their monster pines for the British navy, then for the new United States Navy, or clear the land for the farmers, law and order were largely dependent on the character and integrity of the lumberman in his relations with his crew. Later, when the lumber barons came in, the bull-boss, or foreman, maintained order on the job, and the cookie maintained order in the camp. Although the lumber barons hired professional, migrant loggers from New Brunswick or "outside" Aroostook, many of the loggers were farmers who lumbered in the winter for some real money.

INDEPENDENCE

FREEMAN! if you pant for glory,
If you sigh to live in story,
   If you burn with patriot zeal;
Seize this bright auspicious hour,
Chase those venal tools of power,
   Who subvert the public weal.

Black Hawk Inn, Houlton, Maine, was built by Samuel Wormwood in 1813, as the Aaron Putnam mansion, third of the frame houses in Aroostook, on the bank of the Meduxnekeag River. In consideration of the uncertain conditions of the boundary line between the United States and New Brunswick, Putnam had his home "bullet proofed," with a layer of bricks between the clapboards and the inner wall. Here the first court sessions of the northern district of Washington County were held, and a sundial was installed in the window sill. Two brick holding cells were built in the basement to hold prisoners until they could be conveyed to Machias, county seat of Washington County. Joseph Houlton was appointed justice of the peace in 1820, Samuel Cook in 1821, and Aaron Putnam in 1823.
Courtesy of the Aroostook Art and Historical Museum

> See, their glorious path pursuing,
> All Britannia's troops subduing,
>   Patiots whom no threats restrain.
> Lawless tyrants all confounding,
> Future times their praise resounding,
>   Shall their triumphs long maintain.
>   From the *Freeman's Journal,* 1774

All the idealism of the newly formed nation was clearly in the minds of the early settlers in New Salem Plantation (later Houlton), with songs of independence still ringing in their ears. The first settlers, the Houltons, Putnams, Taylors, and Pearces, had been the responsible leaders of New Salem, Massachusetts, and in this new land were able to govern themselves with few problems until the area became more thickly populated.

With the formation of Aroostook County on March 16, 1839, and with Houlton named as shiretown, seat of the government, Aroostook government commenced operation, and sheriffs were appointed, jurors chosen, judges named. Court was held in the new Houlton Academy for ten years.

Municipal police departments were formed in the early part of the twentieth century, Presque Isle's first chief of police was appointed in 1918, Ernest Lyons. Prior to this time sheriffs and constables kept the peace. The first constable to serve the settlers on the Presque Isle Stream was Ferdinand Armstrong. He received his appointment from the Parish of Kent in New Brunswick, in 1825, as the border was still in doubt.

Patterned after the English system of county government, early law enforcement was the responsibility of a county sheriff and his deputies. A county was designed to provide services to people in a particular geographic area. The headquarters of government was located in a county seat or shiretown. Houlton became the county seat of Aroostook. The jail and the courthouse were built there. The main duties of county government in the northeastern states, where town government grew strong, were to keep law and order, maintain a court system and jail and keep track of land transactions. In addition to a sheriff, important county officials were the county attorney, the register of deeds and the county treasurer. With little change, these officers are still important today. Another county office, which presides over such services as wills, name changes and adoption proceedings, is the judge of probate. Civil Emergency Preparedness is the part of county government responsible for disaster relief to its citizens. Today, the various officials of county government work together with town and state officials to provide the best service possible for County residents.

Environmental protection has become a major political issue in Aroostook. From the log drives of the eighteenth and nineteenth centuries that left water-logged bark on the bottom of the rivers killing fish eggs, to the discharge of pummy from starch factories in the late nineteenth and early twentieth centuries, and the discharge of sewerage into our rivers, a real crisis resulted in formation of the Sanitary Water Board in 1941. Air pollution was addressed in 1970, and we are now addressing hazardous waste. The Department of Environmental Protection is committed to protecting our beautiful home in Aroostook.

Women suffragettes parade for the right to vote in Houlton in 1875.
Courtesy of Frank Dunn

These three gentlemen represent over a half century of protection to Aroostook. Sheriffs Edgar Wheeler (present sheriff of Aroostook), Jasper Lycette, and Darrell Crandall. Being a sheriff has not been an enviable position, especially in 1873 in Presque Isle. Deputy Sheriff Granville Hayden and Thomas Hubbard followed the tracks of Big Jim Cullen who had stolen a pair of boots in Mapleton. They arrested Cullen and decided to spend the night in a woods camp, but while they slept Cullen freed himself, killed his captors and set fire to the building. The owner of the camp escaped to tell the story, and an enraged group of citizens tracked, found, and lynched Cullen. This is believed to be the only lynching in Maine history.
Courtesy of Edgar Wheeler

Sweden Street in Caribou served as the gathering place prior to the annual town meeting, circa 1905.
Courtesy of Paper Talks—The County, *1987*

181

The Houlton Municipal Police Department of 1913: First row: Leon Ingraham, Frank Hogan, Ralph Whitney (chief), Joe Anderson, and Mel Whitney. Second row: Robert Peabody and Del Atherton. Third row: Mike Rideout, George MacNair, John Cosboom, John McLaughlin, George Reed, George Slipp, Al Howard, and Kendall Jackins.
Courtesy of Frank Dunn

Troop F, Maine State Police, has its headquarters in Houlton, Maine. When the Maine State Police was formed in 1925 to assist the Sheriff's Department and local police with enforcement of criminal and motor vehicle laws, headquarters for the department was in Augusta, and three troopers were stationed in Aroostook County. The Fifth District Headquarters opened in Presque Isle in 1937, then moved to Houlton into new barracks in 1938. F Troop was formed in the 1940s, and men patrolled on motorcycles. Police cars were provided in the 1950s, and these troopers served the County in 1955. Troop F continues to serve this largely rural area with protection; many troopers live in those small towns which do not have organized law enforcement. Visible forms of law enforcement include criminal, narcotics, traffic, civil complaints, suspicious persons, and other problems, as Troop F members, many natives of Aroostook, serve "to make a difference."
Photograph courtesy of Jim Graves; information courtesy of Lt. Malcolm Hall

President William Howard Taft visited Presque Isle in 1917, and hopeful Jack Kennedy in 1959.
Courtesy of the Presque Isle Historical Society

International relations between the people of New Brunswick or Quebec Provinces and the people of Aroostook have varied with the policies of their respective governments, but many Aroostookans have close kinship and friendship ties with the "overhomers," and for many, across the border is scarcely more problematic than across the street. The Acadians, though escaping the British, have close ties across the river. The early settlers used the St. John to come to Aroostook, and many would have died without the supplies just across the border. During the War of 1812, the New Brunswickers protected the new settlers, against raids by Indians although requesting their rifles. And in the cold years after 1816 they shared food with starving settlers. Current problems with marketing potatoes is more of a reflection of government policies than competition with individuals. But a border patrol is required, and the first custom house was built in Houlton in 1923, followed at Fort Fairfield, Madawaska, Van Buren, Fort Kent and Bridgewater.
Courtesy of Eugene Jackins

This map of a proposed Dickey-Lincoln School Lakes project shows the proposed transmission route for electricity generated in northern Aroostook.

The project grew from a proposed Passamaquoddy Tidal Power Plant project study which began in 1958, following public and private studies which began in 1919, to attempt to harness electrical power from water sources for all of New England. In 1961 the tidal project was dropped as economically unfeasible, but in 1963 President Kennedy directed additional studies and the Dickey-Lincoln Project was funded in the 1965 Flood Control Act. It was a proposed multi-purpose project located on the upper reaches of the St. John River. Development would consist of two dams with assorted reservoirs and hydroelectric generating facilities, and transmission lines through western Maine to New Hampshire and Vermont, for the New England Power Pool Transmission System. Generation of the power would require Dickey Dam, on the St. John just above its confluence with the Allagash River, twenty-eight miles from Ft. Kent, and Lincoln Dam, eleven miles downstream from Dickey. The dams would result in damage to the Allagash Watershed, including elimination of the Forbus lousewort, an endangered species since 1973, as well as significantly harmful economic effects (after the initial boomtown). The projected social and aesthetic impact resulted in half of the money needed being deauthorized by Congress in December 1981, ending the work of the United States Corps of Engineers, and virtually eliminating further consideration of the project, which had been viewed as a "political football" for so many years, creating splits in political parties and even in families.
Courtesy of ACHC

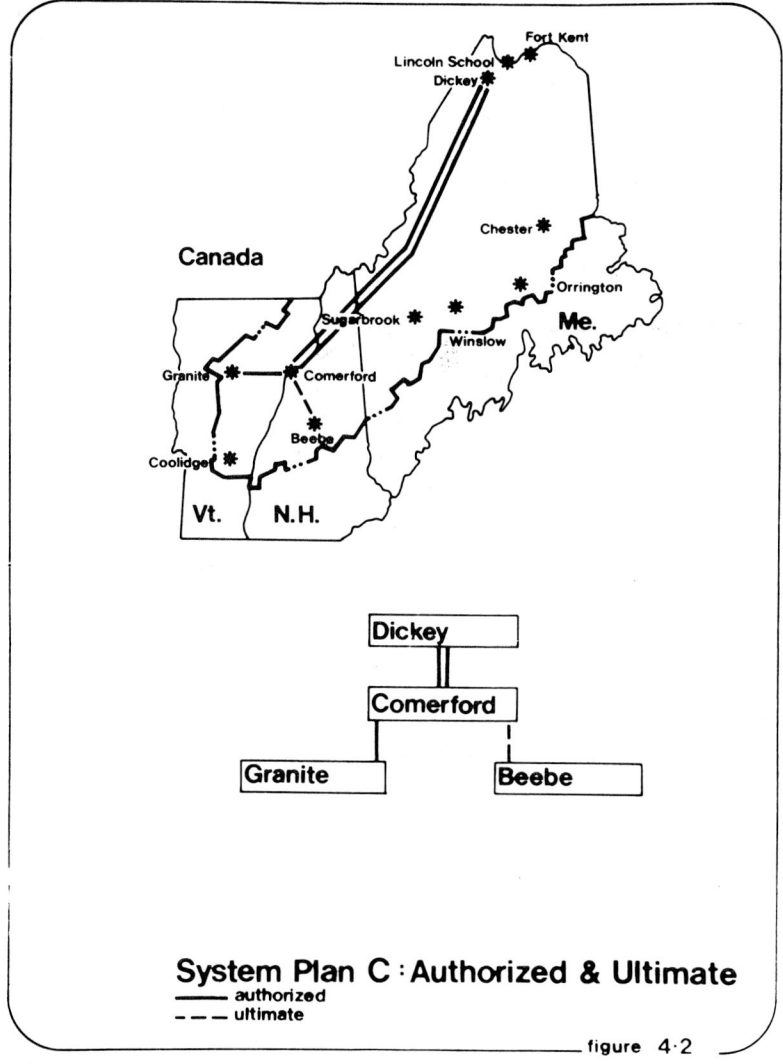

figure 4·2

The present speaker of the Maine House of Representatives is John L. Martin of Eagle Lake. He has helped to transform the position of speaker from a largely ceremonial one into that of a central figure in state government. His election to an unprecedented eighth term as presiding officer of the House stands in stark contrast to the historical custom of a speaker serving only one or two terms. During his tenure, he has been the catalyst to make this a truly independent and co-equal branch of government with the executive branch. Now, non-partisan attorneys and analysts have taken the place of lobbyists in drafting legislation and researching issues. He has been the preeminent spokesman for the causes of the working people, the elderly, the disadvantaged, and the ill in Maine for over two decades. He is currently the longest serving speaker in the United States, and regarded nationally as one of the most able parlimentarians in the country. He is believed to be the only speaker to have served under governors of three different political parties, Independent James B. Longley, Democrat Joseph E. Brennan, and Republican John R. McKernan, Jr. He has put his mark on virtually every major policy decision the legislature has made in the past fifteen years, including establishing the Bureau of Maine's Elderly and the permanent Committee on Aging. Martin considers all of Aroostook County to be his constituency, not just the area he represents, District No. 151.

Speakers of The House of Representatives from Aroostook, in chronological order of service, are:

B. Llewellyn Powers, 1895. Born in Pittsfield in 1836, he practiced law in Houlton, and had a distinguished career in state and local politics including the State House of Representatives, and in the United States Congress, and governor of the state. Republican

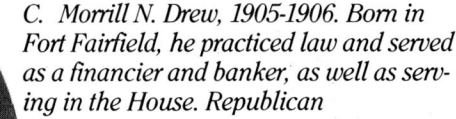

C. Morrill N. Drew, 1905-1906. Born in Fort Fairfield, he practiced law and served as a financier and banker, as well as serving in the House. Republican

D. Don A. Powers, 1907-1908. Born in Pittsfield in 1850, he practiced law in Houlton. As speaker he supported the temperance law in Maine. Republican

E. H. W. Trafton, 1915-1916. Born in Fort Fairfield in 1864, he practiced law in Houlton, served as a director of Fort Fairfield National Bank and as a trustee of Colby College. Republican

F. Charles Putnam Barnes, 1921-1922. Born in Houlton, practiced law, served as chief justice of the Maine Supreme Court. Republican

G. Nathaniel Tompkins, 1935-1936. Born in Bridgewater in 1879, he practiced law in Houlton, and he also served as president of the Senate, and on the supreme judicial court. Republican

I. Vinal G. Good, 1961-1962. Born in Houlton in 1906, he practiced law in Sebago and Portland. Republican

J. John L. Martin, 1973-   . Born in Eagle Lake, he has spent most of his life in politics. Democrat

George B. Barnes, 1945-1946. Born in ⟨…⟩way, Maine in 1904, he practiced law ⟨…⟩oulton, and served as county at-⟨…⟩ey. Republican

All photographs and biographies on this page courtesy of John Lisnik

Presidents of the Maine Senate from Aroostook

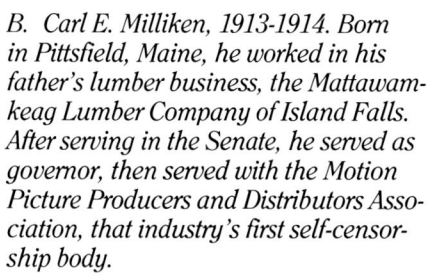

A. John Hodgdon, 1847. Born in Weare, New Hampshire, in 1800, he was bequeathed the land that is now Hodgdon, Maine. He moved there in 1843 and practiced law in Houlton. After serving as president of the Senate in 1847, he moved to Dubuque, Iowa, to practice law, and served as mayor. Democrat

B. Carl E. Milliken, 1913-1914. Born in Pittsfield, Maine, he worked in his father's lumber business, the Mattawamkeag Lumber Company of Island Falls. After serving in the Senate, he served as governor, then served with the Motion Picture Producers and Distributors Association, that industry's first self-censorship body.

C. Ira G. Hersey, 1915-1916. Born in Hodgdon in 1858, most of his life was spent in politics. After serving as Senate president, he was elected to Congress in 1917 and served for six consecutive terms. Republican

D. Frederick J. Burns, 1937-1938. Born in Washington, D.C., in 1900, he practiced law in Houlton and served as county attorney. Republican

E. Nathaniel Tompkins, 1941. Born in Bridgewater in 1880, he served in Maine politics, was speaker of the House as well as president of the Senate. Republican

F. John H. Reed, 1959. Born in Fort Fairfield, Reed continues to serve in politics, after serving as president of the Senate in 1959, he succeeded to the governorship on the death of then Governor Clinton Clauson.

Governors of Maine from Aroostook

A. Edwin C. Burleigh, 1889-1892. Born in Linneus in 1843, he farmed, taught school, and worked for the State Treasury Department, elected as state treasurer before being elected governor, then resumed management of the Kennebec Journal. He also served in the U.S. Congress and U.S. Senate. Republican

B. Llewellyn Powers 1897-1901. Born in Pittsfield, he practiced law in Houlton. After serving in the Maine Congress, including serving as speaker of the House, he was elected governor, opposing free silver. He later served in the fifty-seventh Congress. Republican

C. Carl E. Milliken, 1917-1921. Born in Pittsfield, he worked for his father in Island Falls. He served as governor during World War I and the First Maine Heavy Artillery was organized and named Milliken's Regiment in his honor. He was the first governor to live in the Blaine House. Republican

D. John H. Reed, 1959-1966. Born in Fort Fairfield, he joined the Navy, married and returned to the family business of growing and shipping potatoes. He was elected to the House and then to the Senate where he served as president. On the death of then Governor Clinton A. Clauson, he succeeded to the governorship, and then was reelected. He is remembered for working for higher education, establishing educational television in Maine, and working for a better highway system. He also served as ambassador to Sri Lanka, and now serves as a consultant to the Department of State in the Near East and Asian Bureau, and lives with his wife in the Washington area. Republican

All photographs and biographies on these pages courtesy of John Lisnik

Aroostook in the United States Congress

A. Shepard Cary House of Representatives, 1844-1845. Born in New Salem, Massachusetts, he moved with his parents to Houlton in 1822, engaged in extensive lumber operations and in agricultural and mercantile pursuits, served in the State Hosue of Representatives, and State Senate, then was elected to the twenty-eighth Congress. Democrat

B. Edwin Burleigh, House, 1877-1879, 1897-1911, Senate 1913-1916. After serving as speaker of the House, and governor of the state of Maine, he was elected to the fifty-fifth Congress, then to the Senate. Republican

C. Llewllyn Powers, House, 1908. Practiced law in Houlton before becoming speaker of the House and governor of Maine. Republican

D. Ira Hersey, House, 1917-1923. Born in Hodgdon, president of the Maine Senate. Then he served six consecutive terms in the U.S. Congress. Republican

All photographs and biographies on this page courtesy of John Lisnik

E. Arthur R. Gould, Senate 1926-1931. Born in East Corinth in 1857, he moved to Presque Isle in 1887, engaged in the lumber business, built power plants (Gould Electric Company, bought by Maine Public Service), an electric railroad connecting Presque Isle, Caribou and Washburn, the Aroostook Valley Railroad, which operated from 1910 to 1946. He served in the State Senate before his election to the United States Senate. Gouldville Elementary School, Gouldville Bridge, over the Presque Isle Stream, and the Arthur R. Gould Wing of the Aroostook Medical Center in Presque Isle, are named in his honor. Republican
Courtesy of the Aroostook Medical Center

F. Clifford G. McIntire, House, 1951-1965. Born in Perham, he was engaged in farming until he worked for the Farm Credit Administration, Springfield, Massachusetts, then as assistant general manager of Maine Potato Growers, Inc., at Presque Isle, before becoming a U.S. representative. Republican
Courtesy of Mrs. F. C. McIntire

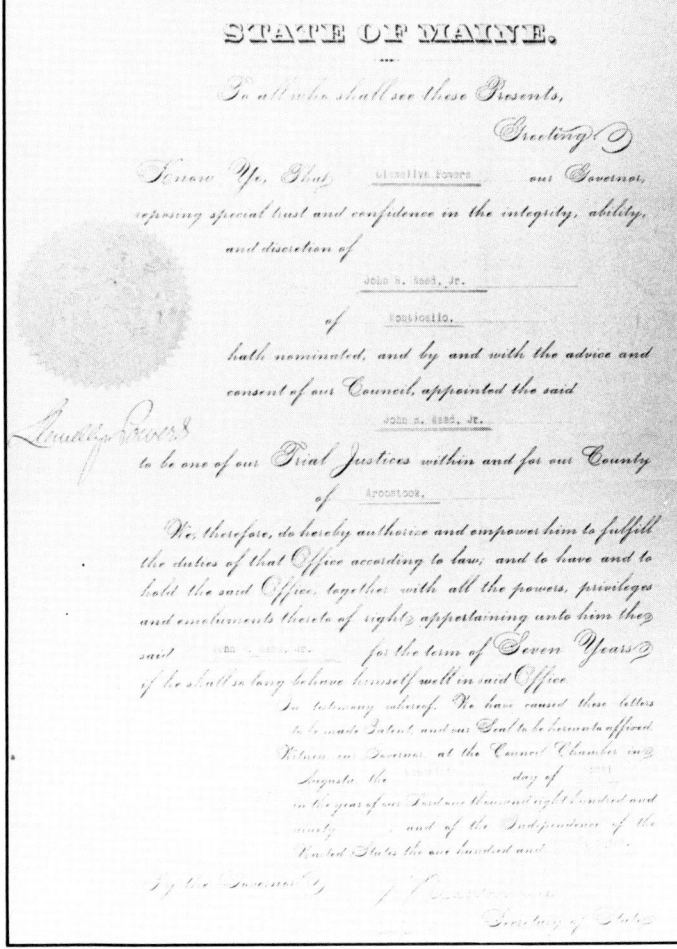

Governor Llewellyn Powers, from Houlton, appointed John R. Weed of Monticello as a county trial justice "in the year of our Lord 1899, and of the Independence of the United States, 123rd."
Courtesy of ACHC

Hose Company No. 1 at the turn of the century in Presque Isle at the corner of Church and Second streets, where the Police Department is now located. Hart Rand is the driver with Harry Pipes sitting next to him. Harry McKay is standing on the back in the middle and to his left is Gil Glidden. Standing on the ground far left is Sammy White and to the far right is Newell Smith.
Courtesy of the Presque Isle Fire Department

Presque Isle's first motorized fire truck was a 1917 American-LaFrance pumper which pumped three hundred gallons of water per minute and cost Presque Isle $7,150. Seated in front are driver Bird Macy and Ellery Jameson. This was a right hand drive truck. Standing on the running boards are, left to right: Leon Dorr, Frank Haines, and Harry Oak. On top, in the hose bed, left to right are: Bill McKay, Roy Reed, and Harold Hayden. The truck was equipped with hard rubber tires.
Courtesy of the Presque Isle Fire Department, circa 1920

*Main Street in Presque Isle is shown in 1921. In the aftermath of fires, the appearance of communities changed drastically. In an eight-day span in February of 1923, the town of Presque Isle suffered three major fires along Main Street. It was at this time that an ordinance was passed, like that of Houlton's, that structures within the business district be constructed of a fireproof material on the exterior. Also enacted at this time, as a result of the western side of Main Street being laid to ruins, was the widening of Main Street when reconstruction commenced.
Courtesy of the Presque Isle Historical Society*

ESSENCES OF THE GARDEN: NEIGHBORS CARING
THE HISTORY OF FIREFIGHTING IN AROOSTOOK
by D. A. Savage

The early settlers of Aroostook County found themselves always in danger of losing their lives and their possessions to fire. The use of fire at that time was a necessity for heating, cooking, and clearing of land, so the settlers learned to keep a proper perspective of fire.

During the growth of the County in the nineteenth century, structure fires were commonplace; the causes ranged from chimney fires to animals knocking lanterns over, natural causes such as lightning, to arson and improper disposal of stove ashes, and grass fires getting out of control. Fire protection was virtually unknown at that time. Drought conditions when combined with high winds contributed to the potential for major conflagrations, in light of the fact that all structures at this time were of wood construction, including the roofing material. *The Loyal Sunrise* of Presque Isle tells the story well:

Thursday, June 23, 1864, the wind rose to a hurricane, blowing at times from every point of the compass, kindling into terrific conflagrations, thousands of fires which were scattered through the forests and clearings, where for several weeks previous, there had fallen but little rain.

Our village was surrounded by fire in the woods, and enveloped by a dense cloud of smoke and dust all of the afternoon on Thursday, and also on Friday and Saturday. Yet fortunately, we were preserved from the calamity which was so eminent of being entirely consumed. In the terrific gale, whirling and eddying in every direction, a spark falling upon any of our buildings, would unquestionably have been fatal to the whole.

Not so fortunate, however, was the little village of Alva (Blaine), 15 miles south of our village, where almost the whole village burnt. Many structure fires were also reported in Glenwood Plantation, Ashland, Fort Kent, Eaton (Caribou) and Lyndon (Caribou). The day prior, Wilson's Mill on Rocky Brook in Mars Hill was completely destroyed by fire. On Sabbath morning, we were agreeably surprised to find a refreshing rain which continued through the day and night to dampen the severest drought since 1825. But three weeks later on Wednesday, July 20, 1864, the village of Washburn was burnt, including over thirty buildings.

Four years prior to this, the village of Presque Isle suffered its first conflagration as reported by the *Aroostook Pioneer*:

On Sunday, May 13, 1860, at about 2:00 P.M., after a long continued drought had caused fires to rage furiously in the woods surrounding the village, a strong wind sprung up which drove the flames across the Presque Isle Stream and nearly the whole northern part of the village was laid in ruins as nineteen buildings were destroyed at a loss of $25,000. The valuation of the village prior to the fire was $79,000 and the population was 723.

After suffering great losses to fire, men of each village

met to organive fire brigades, but complacency then, as today, left no officially formed protection.

As a direct result of a serious fire occurring August 3, 1879, in which twenty-one buildings were burned, on September 1, 1879, the town of Houlton voted to buy a steam fire engine, to cost not over three thousand dollars. On April 1, 1880, another fire cost the town a loss of seventeen buildings. The steam fire engine *Sockanosett* was purchased by public subscription in 1881. Two major fires within eight months had prompted the citizens of Houlton to take action.

On Thursday morning, May 1, 1884, around 2:00 A.M., Presque Isle suffered its second major conflagration—this time, nearly all of the business part of the village was destroyed. Many of the structures were three stories high and the strong winds which were blowing, coupled with the inadequate means of extinguishing fires, led to the great disaster.

Shortly thereafter, the village held a special town meeting to consider the securing of a suitable fire engine and hose, which was almost unanimously passed. On November 1, 1884, the Presque Isle Fire Association was organized, to be ready to "take charge of the engine when it comes." Three days later, a contract was awarded to J. G. Hilt, a local merchant, to build a hook and ladder truck for the sum of eighty dollars, thus inaugurating the beginning of continuous fire protection. The Presque Isle Village Fire Department was formally incorporated within the state of Maine on March 6, 1885. At the annual Town Meeting in 1917, by a vote of 330 to 308, the town assumed control of the Fire Department.

The most destructive fire in the history of Presque Isle, occurred between 4:00 and 5:00 o'clock on Monday afternoon, June 7, 1909. The blaze started in the home of Mrs. Jerry Turner on North Main Street and swept over an area of forty odd acres and consumed over one hundred residences and businesses. Due to a wind blowing at almost a gale force from the northwest, and owing to the long drought and dry roofs, in less than ten minutes after the alarm, the fire was beyond the control of the best facilities of any ordinary village fire department.

In its sweep across the village, the fire was quite freakish, missing some structures completely in its path. Fortunately, not long after the fire broke out, the wind shifted from the west, otherwise the entire village east of the stream would have probably been wiped out. Calls for aid were sent to Houlton, Caribou, and Fort Fairfield and they responded as quickly as special trains could be made up to transport the fire apparatus and men.

One death did occur from this fire when eight days later, Warren Chase died from internal injuries suffered while driving through Main Street during the fire, his horse having become unmanageable in the surrounding excitement, ran into an automobile.

While most communities organized fire departments/brigades after suffering conflagrations, some departments came into existence because of the efforts of an individual citizen. The Madawaska and St. Agatha Fire Departments are fine examples.

The Madawaska Fire Department was organized in the year 1928 under the direction of George R. Rice. Rice lived in Madawaska and was the Fire Chief in Edmundston in New Brunswick, Canada, which was Madawaska's Sister Community, and so became the fire chief of both communities. Also influencing the organization of fire protection for Madawaska was the construction of the mill, Fraser Paper Limited, at this time.

For St. Agatha, it was a different situation, with fire involved again. From writings in the Historical Society Newsletter *STE AGATHE*:

A man across the street from the Albert Michaud fire in August 1945 was fighting and praying to keep his property up. With a garden horse in hand, and a small stream of water coming out of it, his neck and back blistered, he could hardly stand the heat, and his heart was aching, afraid to lose the shelter he had worked all his life to build for his family. Mr. Dugal was making a promise, as he was thinking of all the people who are homeless on account of fires, and how many lives each year are lost by fires. Right then and there a fire department was born for the St. Agatha Community. It was through George Emile Dugal's sheer determination and concern for his fellow citizens that the St. Agatha Fire Department came into existence.

Prior to the Albert Michaud fire, the community had seen two other fire disasters. In 1931, the Town Hall along with eight other buildings, were lost to fire. Then in 1940, the good citizens were once again alerted to a fire at the Church. Their efforts to salvage their precious Church proved to be unsuccessful. The building was completely destroyed.

While these fires were raging, people were made aware of the necessity of a fire department. Nevertheless, the well-meaning ambitions of the concerned few died along with the fire until 1945, when Dugal decided to do something about it.

The destruction by fire of Fort Fairfield's Town Office on March 24, 1916, as well as two other structures on Main Street, resulted in the Fire Department, which was organized in the late eighteen hundreds, being housed in the new municipal building.

But fire, with all its destruction and havoc, has not deterred the hearty peoples of the last frontier east of the Mississippi. They still join together and come to the aid of their neighbors, as did those folks of 150 years ago.

On April 1st, 1923, a large portion of Main Street in Mars Hill was burnt to the ground and they, like Presque Isle, decided to widen their Main Street when reconstruction began. Thus the change as we see it today was not evident at the turn of the century. The lone chimneys are all that remained of the hotel, after the April Fool's Day fire of 1923, which is now the location of the Exxon Station in Mars Hill.
Courtesy of Elizabeth Gallup and the Mars Hill Fire Department

Records indicate that the Mars Hill Fire Department was organized in conjunction with the Water Company. In 1911, a water company was formed to build a gravity-flow system from Young Lake. Later that year on November 24, an organized fire department came into existence. The firefighters of the Mars Hill Volunteer Fire Department posed with their hand-drawn hose cart on May 5, 1915. Members of the department at that time were, left to right: (1) H. Adelman, (2) W. B. Burns, (3) G. L. Small, (4) H. W. Sylvester, (5) E. E. Sweet, (6) D. F. Cliff, (7) F. W. Shaw, (8) William Cullins, (9) Leon Blackden, (10) William Dickerson, (11) J. A. Pierce, (12) G. E. Pitcher, (13) H. G. Currie, (14) H. W. Robinson, (15) Amon Sennett, (16) Dale Blackden, (17) Harry Shaw, (18) George Donnelly, and (19) S. W. Green.
Courtesy of the Mars Hill Fire Department

Houlton's most destructive fire began at 12:40 P.M. on May 17, 1902. The fire started in the rear of Dyer's Market, which was housed in the Fogg Block on Main Street. Owing to the lack of water pressure and to the high wind velocity, the fire rapidly went out of control and spread burning embers to wooden buildings in its path. Over four hundred buildings were destroyed. Early in the fire, Chief Webber issued a call for outside help. Woodstock, New Brunswick, twelve miles away, was the first to respond. Fort Fairfield, Presque Isle, and Caribou responded in a like manner, although all, because of distance, could not get to the scene via rail before 6:00 P.M. when the fire had already been raging for five hours.

The Bangor and Aroostook Railroad organized a special train with help recruited from Bangor. This train was held in readiness at Old Town until 7:00 P.M. when word from Houlton was received that the fire was under control and that no further aid was needed.
Courtesy of the Houlton Fire Department

Houlton testing and displaying the pumping capacity of their steam fire engine in Market Square. The steam engine Sockanosett *was purchased by public subscription in 1881.*
Courtesy of the Houlton Fire Department

Ruins in 1910 of the Thibodeau Block or the Hotel LaFayette. In 1911, the Dunn Furniture Company of Houlton moved to this location on Main Street, where they remained until 1971.
Courtesy of the Houlton Fire Department

Bird Macy of Presque Isle stands with the reputed two fastest fire horses on the East Coast, Fred and Mage, in the early 1930s. The town took great pride in the pair of dapple grey horses and it is said that they were clocked at twenty-nine seconds in a quarter-mile run while hauling a long sled.
Courtesy of the Presque Isle Fire Department

Storms Over Aroostook
by Anna Fields Mcgrath

*The snows start as early as October and last into April in Aroostook, and with the frigid temperatures, it doesn't melt until spring, so can pile quite high. Aroostookans do anticipate the January thaw, when temperatures may soar into the high thirties or low forties for a couple of days. A "cold snap" can mean temperatures as low as forty degrees below zero, and if there is a wind, the wind-chill factor can make it seem much colder. Before the advent of the snow plow, roads were rolled to pack the snow for the horse-drawn vehicles. This snow roller was purchased for the town of Smyrna in 1919 for $175.
Courtesy of Jean Sawyer*

*Getting into Aroostook in the winter was never easy, and until 1928-1929 nearly impossible until Allie Cole decided he would plow the road to Houlton, since the State Highway Commission plowed only as far north as Lincoln. In 1931-1932 he got this REO and started plowing north to Presque Isle. It wasn't until 1945 that the state took the responsibility for plowing the roads into the County. Many people blessed Allie Cole!
Courtesy of Frank Dunn*

*The frozen rivers in Aroostook start to melt at the end of March and beginning of April, and the break-up often causes minor flooding along the Aroostook and St. John rivers. Washburn, Fort Kent, and Fort Fairfield seem especially vulnerable. The hurricane of 1957 flooded many areas, in some cases the water rose as high as thirty-four feet. This young calf was caught stranded when the water receded.
Courtesy of the Library, University of Maine at Presque Isle*

Det Utlofvade Landet (The Promised Land): Maine's Swedish Colony in Northern Aroostook was established in 1870 by a group of fifty-one Swedish immigrants under the leadership of William Widgery Thomas, Jr., of Portland. As the immigrant procession wended its way from the United States boundary and Fort Fairfield toward Caribou, Thomas stopped the wagon train on a hilltop and pointed out the distant forest ridges of Township 15, Range 3, in his fluent Swedish. The immigrants joyfully responded by shouting Det Utlofvade Landet. They had finally reached the promised land—Aroostook.

Thomas, (on white horse, center) poses with a group of people from New Sweden, Stockholm, and Westmanland at a re-enactment of "the coming of the Swedes" during a Fort Fairfield Centennial Pageant in August, 1916.
Courtesy of the New Sweden Historical Society

An act to promote immigration and to facilitate the settlement of the public lands.

Be it enacted by the Senate and House of Representatives in Legislature assembled, as follows:

SECT. 1. There shall be a board of immigration in this state....

SECT. 3. Said board may appoint some suitable person as agent, to proceed to Sweden or Norway for the purpose of obtaining a first colony of immigrants, and superintending their passage to this state and their settlement on the public lands....

(Excerpted from: 1870 Laws of Maine, Chapter 173. Approved March 23, 1870.)

One of the first log houses built in New Sweden in 1870, the Jepson house, is no longer extant. The log house was introduced to America in 1638 by the first New Sweden colony (in what is now Delaware, Pennsylvania, and New Jersey). As Maine's New Sweden colony prospered, these log houses were frequently replaced by more modern frame homes. However, many log homes and outbuildings still exist under the newer shingles and inside finish, while others were converted to various uses. The restored Lindsten Stuga, behind the present New Sweden Museum, is a fine example of the early Swedish immigrant log home.
Courtesy of the New Sweden Historical Society

From the fjords of Sweden and Norway, the Viking adventurers came to the coast of North America to trade with the Native People, but did not establish a lasting settlement. Perhaps it was some of their descendants who came to Aroostook County in 1870 to found New Sweden, Stockholm, and Westmanland, searching for a new life.

DET UTLOFVADE LANDET (THE PROMISED LAND) MAINE'S SWEDISH COLONY

by Richard Hede

The story of the founding of New Sweden records the conversion of virtually an entire township of virgin Maine forestland into a thirving community, under the leadership of one man, in a very short period. It has been said that New Sweden is the only successful agricultural colony founded in New England with foreigners from over the ocean since the Revolutionary War. The effects of this bold endeavor were almost immediately visible, and the ripple effects continue to this day.

The genesis of this unique happening began years before in response to the fact that while hundreds of thousands of immigrants a year were streaming west, Maine was losing population. In 1861 Governor Israel Washburn, Jr., presented the subject of Scandinavian immigration to the legislature. In 1864 some Maine gentlemen recruited and shipped several hundred Swedish laborers, but none ever reached Maine. Then Gov. Joshua Chamberlain of Civil War fame took up the cause, and in 1869 the legislature adopted "A resolve designed to promote the settlement of the public and other lands in the state."

A commission consisting of Parker P. Burleigh, William Small, and William Widgery Thomas, Jr., made a tour of observation and inquiry through Aroostook County in October 1869, and reported their findings to the legislature. Their plan was to send a commissioner of immigration to Sweden to recruit a colony of young Swedish farmers with their wives and children and a Swedish pastor to bind the colony together, lead the colony all in one group at one time into the township set aside in the northern forests, give each head of a family one hundred acres of woodland for a farm, and do whatever else was necessary to root the colony firmly in Maine. The plan, with Governor Chamberlain's support, was approved March 23, 1870, in a legislative act entitled "An act to promote immigration and to facilitate the settlement of the public lands." The act authorized a Board of Immigration consisting of the governor, land agent, and secretary of state. The board appointed Thomas as comissioner of immigration, based on his keen interest in the project and his intimate experience with Sweden as Lincoln's Civil War consul in Gothenberg. Thomas sailed for Sweden on April 30, 1870, and personally recruited a select group of fifty-one men, women, and children. All were certified to be of the highest character, all paid their own way, and in addition to being farmers, some were skilled as blacksmith, carpenter, basket-maker, wheelwright, baker, tailor, wooden shoemaker, and a lay minister.

On June 23, Midsummer's Eve (an ancient Swedish festival still celebrated here in Aroostook County as well as in old Sweden), the selected colonists from all over Sweden gathered in Gothenberg's Baptist Hall to become acquainted with one another and to bid farewell to their friends and relatives. After a rough passage over the North Sea, they went by rail across England, by steamship to

Halifax, Nova Scotia, Canada, across Nova Scotia and the Bay of Fundy to St. John, New Brunswick, up the St. John River by steamer to Fredericton, New Brunswick, in two horse drawn towboats (ploddingly, over six days) to Tobique Landing, and by horse-and-wagon train and walking across the Canadian-American border, to a "sumptous collation" at noon at the Fort Fairfield town hall. Continuing on to Caribou, they had another bountiful meal, and spent the night at Arnold's Hall, where one of the ladies happened to wait on Maine's land agent and exclaimed "Why, you speak very good English for a Swede!" The next day the colonists passed the last American clearing and went into the woods, picking their way along a newly cut woods road to their promised land. On July 23, the Swedes and their leader, Thomas, crossed the township line and christened the area New Sweden. The first religious service in New Sweden was held the next day, Sunday. It was the funeral of nine-month-old Hilma C. Clase, who had died on the tow boat en route.

Township 15, Range 3, boundaries were surveyed by J. Morris in 1859. In 1861, lots of 160 acres were surveyed by B. F. Cutter and offered to settlers essentially free under the settling laws, but there were no takers. Many lots in neighboring T14-R3 (Woodland) and T14-R4 (Perham) had been settled about 1861 but later abandoned as being too remote. In June of 1870, when it became clear that Thomas was being successful in recruiting Swedish immigrants, Parker P. Burleigh went to Aroostook, had T15-R3 and part of T14-R3 re-surveyed by Noah Barker into lots of one hundred acres each for the Swedes, and contracted with L. R. King and John S. Arnold of Caribou to begin clearing five acres on each of twenty-five lots. Construction was also begun on twenty-five log houses, but when the Swedes arrived on July 23, 1870, only six houses were built and only two completed. To assign farm lots to the settlers, the lots were divided into clusters of four and the settlers arranged themselves into groups of four families (generally friends from the same area in Sweden). Then each group drew a cluster by chance, and each family then drew a lot by chance. After two families swapped lots, all were satisfied.

Then the settlers went to work, clearing the forest and building houses and roads, with payment at one dollar per day to be drawn in tools and provisions. Within six days, two acres of land had been felled, piled, burnt, cleared, and sowed in turnips. This provided the first crop and by fall twenty acres were sown with winter wheat or rye. By the end of the year, 114 Swedes had settled in New Sweden, 180 acres of woods were felled, one hundred acres were cleared for a crop, twenty-six dwelling houses had been built, and a public building, the Capitol, was completed.

The settlement of New Sweden engendered widespread positive publicity, along with some negative letters and complaints. Expanded recruitment in Sweden continued apace. More immigrants flooded in, roads were extended in all directions, and new farms were taken up. Various businesses rapidly sprang up to serve the influx. A regularly ordained Lutheran minister arrived in 1871 and served as both pastor and schoolteacher. At times, the flow of immigrants was so great that the colony could not absorb them and Thomas was forced to divert them to various occupations in other parts of the state. Many of those who did settle in New Sweden also worked in lumber camps and other jobs during the winter. New Sweden became famous for its hand-shaved shingles, and these were the early currency used in bartering for goods in the stores. Most of the local businesses were operated by the Swedes themselves, but the neighboring American stores welcomed the Swedes in their own communities, and in time some of them opened branches in New Sweden. Some of the early newspaper advertisements were printed in Swedish. It is interesting to note that the first newspaper published in Lyndon (named changed to Caribou in 1877) was the *North Star*, W. T. Sleeper, editor, with the first issue dated January 3, 1872. The "Swensk Column," edited by E. Winberg, New Sweden, Maine, was printed in Swedish, and apparently ran from January 11, 1872, to January 29, 1873.

By the fall of 1873 the population had grown to six hundred, with as many more Swedes elsewhere in the state. The colony was firmly established, and at the end of 1873 Thomas took leave of New Sweden. He recommended that all special state aid cease and that his office be abolished. 133 men had declared their intentions of becoming American citizens, and in March, 1876, thirty of the first settlers were naturalized in Houlton. On April 6, 1876, New Sweden was legally organized into a plantation and on January 29, 1895, was incorporated as a town. With the influx of immigrants, the colony was soon overflowing into Woodland, Perham, Westmanland, Stockholm, Connor, T16-R4 (Madawaska Lake), and indeed throughout the state.

July 23 is celebrated every year in New Sweden as New Sweden Day, the anniversary of the arrival of the first settlers. An especially notable celebration was held at the Decennial in 1880, attended by Maine's Governor Daniel Davis, ex-Governor Joshua Chamberlain, Senator Hannibal Hamlin, the entire executive council, and over two dozen other dignitaries. In his oration of over two hours, Thomas recited the history of the enterprise and proudly enumerated the successes of the colony. On June 25, 1895, the Quarter Centennial Celebration was held in New Sweden. Maine's Swedish Colony had expanded to a total population of 1,452. There were 4 churches, 3 parsonages, 7 schoolhouses, 2 starch factories, 5 shingle and other lumber mills, 305 houses, 362 barns, plus the Capitol. Thomas and the other speakers were still proud of the colony. Some have credited the Swedish Colony with turning the tide from population loss to gain in the County and the state, bringing the railroad to Aroostook, developing the potato industry, bringing starch factories to Maine, and a multitude of other benefits.

As time went by, New Sweden developed several localized centers in addition to the south-central Capitol, each with its own rural school and sometimes its own post office, railroad station, chapel, potato houses, starch factories, saw and shingle mills, and stores. Among these were

The Capitol was the first public building in New Sweden. It was called Kapitolium by the first Swedish immigrants, and has always been the heart of the colony. Built largely by the Swedes that first fall, in 1870, it was originally owned by the state and thus Maine was said to be the only state with two capitols. The two-story building was used as a storehouse for provisions and tools, the headquarters of the commissioner of immigration, a schoolhouse, a church, a general meeting hall, and especially in early years, a temporary shelter and home for incoming immigrants. Later, a district school (the Capitol School, still standing) was built on the right side of the Capitol and a town hall on the left. The Capitol became a museum. In 1971, the year after New Sweden's big centennial celebration, lightning struck the town hall and it, together with the original Capitol building, burned to the ground. However, the citizens turned out to save virtually all of the museum artifacts as well as the large double front doors. A replica of the original Capitol now houses the New Sweden Museum. To the right of the Capitol in the photo is Benny Pearson's store, which also housed the post office and the telephone office. Telephone service began in 1905. To the left of the Capitol is shown an early bandstand, with stables in the rear.
Courtesy of the New Sweden Historical Society

This striking photograph was taken at New Sweden's great thirtieth Anniversary celebration when four thousand people from the colony and surrounding towns gathered with honored guests from throughout the state at Uppling's Grove in 1900. Identifiable near the front are: Captain N. P. Clase (front, far left), a seaman who spoke several languages including Chinese and English and thus was made an assistant to Thomas, who was in charge of the storehouse; Maine Governor Llewellyn Powers (prominent in front, left center); and Thomas (front, center) with his trademark forked beard. Many others are identifiable by their relatives and local residents.
Courtesy of the New Sweden Historical Society

This historic Swedish immigrant property on Station Road in New Sweden is presently being restored by a new non-profit preservation society, Maine's Swedish Colony, Inc. Noak Larsson, who came from old Sweden in 1871, likely in the 1880s, built the two-story log home (on left), the only one known in this area. His son, Lars Noak, built the blacksmith shop (lower right) in the early 1900s. It sat largely undisturbed since his death in 1940 until the current restoration project began. The George Ostlund family bought the Noak Larsson farm in 1910, built a typical Aroostook potato house (upper right) in 1928, and family members lived in the home until the end of 1988.
Courtesy of the New Sweden Historical Society

the areas known as the B&A (for Bangor and Aroostook Railroad) Jemtland Station, Jemtland, Rista, AVR (for Aroostook Valley Railroad), West Road, Nelson, Lebanon, Schoolland, and Madawaska. Businesses proliferated, including farm machinery and fertilizer stores, blacksmith shops, garages and car dealerships, creameries, and ski making (Henry Anderson even made skis for airplanes.)

Stockholm in 1881, like Westmanland in 1879, began as a small agricultural extension of New Sweden. But while Westmanland remained agricultural and sparsely settled with the population never going much over one hundred, Stockholm grew. The population was 66 in 1890, only 191 in 1900, then rose to a peak of about 1,300 in 1925, from which point it gradually declined to 319 in 1980.

The major impetus to growth in this area was the coming of the Bangor and Aroostook Railroad in 1899. The railroad station and the area north of the river was at first called Upsala. Edgar Perry and John P. Yerxa built a long lumber mill on the south side of the river, called Stockholm, in 1900. It was subsequently sold to M. P. and Carl E. Milliken (later governor of Maine). This mill operated until 1915. Company houses for mill workers were built and painted red, on a street which is still called Red Row. The first store was built by Lewis and John Anderson in 1900-1901, and a mill company store was built in 1902. Also, Allen Quimby, Sr., established the Standard Veneer Company in Stockholm in 1902, using birch logs to produce one-twentieth-inch single-ply veneer for chair-seat manufacturers in New York. In 1904, a starch factory was built. It was converted in 1909 to the Standard Box Company. A Winterville veneer mill was dismantled in 1910 and moved to Stockholm, where it was merged with the other two mills. The mill burned in February, 1912, but it was quickly rebuilt. Another plant was built in the early 1920s to make clothespins, pick-poles, peavy handles, whiffletrees, snowshoes, and perforated chair seats. It was later converted to a long lumber mill. At the peak of this development, 330 men and women were employed there. Stella King White in *Maine: Past and Present* (1929) reported that the mills used five million feet of birch annually, three to four million feet of softwood for box cleating, plus long lumber from the sawmill, all kinds of hardwood in the clothespin factory and shipped three hundred to five hundred carloads of finished product. Adding sizeable potato shipments, this kept the railroad busy, and Stockholm provided a large number of outstanding men for the railroad maintenance crews.

Stockholm had become a virtual boom town, and there was a great influx of French Canadians from the St. John Valley, as well as English speaking Americans and Canadians, and a few other nationalities. The good pay was an attraction, despite the long hours and the hazards of falling in boiling vats of water used for soaking logs. The Swedes for the most part remained farmers, although many worked in the mills to supplement their income. A variety of stores and businesses sprang up, including an inn, hotel, clothing store, grocery, hardware, and variety stores, meat market, liveries and garages, pool hall and barber shops, bowling alley, restaurant, hat shop, ice cream parlor, movie theater, dance hall, Odd Fellows Hall, and other enterprises. Baptist, Lutheran, and Catholic churches were built, and there were a number of other religious, musical, and cultural movements. A bandstand and ball park were built and well used. Hand in hand with the growth of Stockholm, camps, stores, and activities at nearby Madawaska Lake in T16-R4 proliferated. Then in 1926 the Veneer Company sold out to Atlas Plywood Corporation, which closed the mill in 1932 and moved it to Canada in 1935. During their tenure, Atlas Plywood posted a notice which (1) prohibited smoking, (2) required employees to be at work from 6:30 A.M. to 5:30 P.M., and (3) charged persons for taking anything from the mill. Sam Collins operated a lumber and shingle mill for some time, but when the mill burned, it was not rebuilt. Even farming began a steady decline after World War II, and Stockholm became a retirement and bedroom community, with most people working at the new Loring Air Force Base and other surrounding areas.

In recent years, both Stockholm and New Sweden have witnessed a new, slow growth in population and housing. Many who had moved away to make their mark in the world are now returning to their roots in "the promised land," either to work locally or for retirement. Maine's Swedish Colony, Inc., is the name of a new non-profit society dedicated to the restoration and preservation of historic buildings in the area, and making them accessible to the public. The Swedish cultural heritage introduced by that first band of immigrants in 1870 has continued strong, but has also blended with that of the more recent ethnic groups in the area with a fascinating exchange of one another's customs. The major traditional Swedish holidays were also carried over by the Swedish immigrants, namely Christmas, Easter, and Midsummer's eve, to which has been added New Sweden Day.

The most famous custom the Swedes brought to America is perhaps the smorgasbord, which means butter-and-bread table, but is now loosely interpreted as a rather sumptuous buffet. It may have originated as a rural Swedish potluck, with everyone bringing their contributions (many of them cold and/or preserved) to a large table, from which everyone could pick and choose. But there is a proper order to eating from the smorgasbord: first the herring tid-bits (pickled and preserved in a great variety, eaten with small, boiled potatoes, perhaps with chive, onion, and sour cream); then other cold fish and shellfish (salmon, sardines, eel, shrimp, lobster, etc.): then the cold meats (ham, roast beef or reindeer or moose, various sausages, tongue, liver pate, etc.); various other cold side dishes (stuffed eggs, pressed cucumber, fresh vegetables, fruit salad, relishes, pickles, etc.); then come various hot dishes (Swedish meatballs, herring au gratin, Swedish brown beans, sauteed mushrooms and kidneys, any of a variety of filled omelets, and the ultimate anchovy "Jansson's Temptation"); and of course the various cheeses, the butter and breads (such as Swedish rye bread called limpa, various hardtack/crisp breads—knackebrod—) and crackers. Then, believe it or

The widespread publicity about the Swedish Colony in northern Maine is credited with inducing Albe Holmes, a potato starch manufacturer of New Hampshire, to visit Aroostook in 1870. In 1872 he started the first starch factory in the County at Caribou (by 1895 there were forty-one in the County). At one time there were four starch factories in New Sweden itself, including the one pictured behind Youngren's store near the railroad station. A trestle across Gelotte's pond carried the waste from the factory to the outlet of the pond.
Courtesy of the New Sweden Historical Society

Axel Johnson and Carl Englund had a thriving Elgin automobile dealership going in the teens and twenties at Johnson's farm on Lebanon Road in Jemtland (the northern section of New Sweden). When Lebanon Road met the western branch of the Bangor and Aroostook railroad at Axel Siding in Stockholm, several potato houses were built. Further west on the railroad, Blackstone Siding in Westmanland became a major timber shipping point. John N. Johnson opened the first Ford dealership in the area at New Sweden Station in the early 1900s and operated it for many years. Concurrently, most people were still using horses, and a number of blacksmiths who did any necessary welding, machining, or woodworking plied their trade. Among these were Peter Nelson, Johnny Johanson, and Lars Noak.
Courtesy of the New Sweden Historical Society

not, the smorgasbord appetizer may be followed by the main course dishes, Swedish desserts, cookies and cakes, and the inevitable Swedish coffee.

The Swedish churches in New Sweden and Stockholm maintained the smorgasbord tradition through the years, and the Covenant church still offers an annual public smorgasbord. The New Sweden Historical Society generally has a somewhat simpler Midsummer supper every year. The Stockholm Historical Society again in 1988 presented an International Smorgasbord, which in addition to the traditional Swedish dishes, recognized the French and English heritage.

Christmas (called Jul and pronounced yule in Sweden and among Swedes around the world), begins with Lucia Day (December 13). That is when the Bride of Light (usually the eldest daughter) appears in a white gown and a crown of lighted candles early in the morning to serve hot coffee and Lucia saffron buns to her parents and others. The custom is spreading. Christmas Eve also has its special customs and foods: lutfisk (dried cod, soaked in lye or ashes to soften it, rinsed and soaked in fresh water, then cooked and usually served with a white sauce); julskinka (Christmas ham); risgrynsgrot (rice pudding); and Glogg (a hot, spiced alcoholic drink).

It has been pointed out that the "Viking Age" of a thousand years ago resulted in a strong infusion of Scandinavian blood (and blue eyes) into much of Europe, including Scotland, England, Ireland, and especially Normandy in France. Many descendants from those areas emigrated to New England, New Brunswick, and Nova Scotia (Acadia) during the early settlement of North America, from whence many have since moved to Northern Maine. Here they have met a new infusion from the descendants of the Vikings in Maine's Swedish Colony, and so long distant cousins have been reunited again. And from the Swedish Colony, succeeding generations have moved out over the width and breadth of America, but the "Colony" (the promised land), is still home.

In 1926 the Sons and Daughters of the Colony of New Sweden, the local historical society, dedicated an impressive granite monument on the exact spot where the original settlers first arrived; Thomas (standing in front of the monument) intoned "this is the happiest day of my life." Thomas was born August 26, 1839, and died April 27, 1927. But the colony he so successfully nurtured continues to evolve, and succeeding generations annually observe Midsummer and New Sweden Day at Thomas Park. The centerpiece of the park is the W. W. Thomas Memorial Shell, designed and built in 1937 by the citizens of New Sweden, headed by John J. Ringdahl, honoring the memory of the founder of New Sweden and the colony's life-long friend. Thomas also established a Memorial Fund to aid in the upkeep of Thomas Park and the historical facilities. The Shell is located in a natural amphitheater and is used for band concerts and religious and community observances.
Courtesy of the New Sweden Historical Society

The fortieth anniversary of the founding of New Sweden, held June 25, 1910, featured a very distinguished group of guests, including Thomas (shown at the rostrum); Adj. Gen. Elliot Dill (representing Bert M. Fernald, Governor of Maine); Joshua L. Chamberlain (governor in 1870 and a strong supporter of Swedish immigration, as well as the Civil War hero of Little Round Top); and others. There were proud narrations of the accomplishments of the Swedish colony and mutual congratulations at this joyful celebration. Thomas began his address, as he frequently did, with the Swedish phrase Mina Barn i Skogen (my children in the woods), and they affectionately referred to him as Father Thomas. The fiftieth anniversary in 1920 was also the centennial of Maine's statehood and the tri-centennial of the landing of the pilgrims. A procession was therefore conducted, headed by Thomas and the surviving original immigrants, with successive groups portraying the various historical periods. In December 1920, Thomas presented to the town of New Sweden a warranty deed for a public park and playground, aptly named Thomas Park.
Courtesy of the New Sweden Historical Society

Music has always played an important part in the life of the Swedish Colony, from Swedish folk songs to modern bands. A band was on hand at the tenth anniversary celebration in 1880. A band was organized in the northern section of the community, called Jemtland, in 1885, and this band played at the annual celebrations for many years. The New Sweden Band was organized by John Uppling and Andrew Nelson, and played under Alfred Strobeck from about 1909 to 1915. Walter Hedman then directed the band until his death in 1955, when Henry Anderson took over, and he was succeeded in turn by Ken Matthews and others. The band perhaps peaked around 1927, when it was using the uniforms from John Philip Sousa's All-American Band. It traveled widely throughout the County and neighboring New Brunswick, Canada, and it played for many years at the Potato Blossom Festival in Fort Fairfield. The photograph was taken in Caribou en route to one of the band's traveling performances.
Courtesy of the New Sweden Historical Society

The first store in Stockholm opened in 1901 after the coming of the railroad in 1899, and the construction of a dam and long lumber mill on Madawaska Stream in 1900. Cutting of railroad ties was a thriving business for the farmers, with extras bringing twenty cents each. The building also housed the first post office. It was later greatly enlarged, and now houses the Stockholm Historical Society Museum.
Courtesy of the Stockholm Historical Society

This view of Stockholm, from North Main Street (in front of the McGuire boarding house) looking south, was taken shortly after 1906. Clockwise, from the horse and buggy at the railroad crossing and early train stop (just to left of the road), may be seen John Anderson's store, house, and barn; houses on Red Row (left, rear); the long lumber mill on opposite river bank (mostly obscured by barn); boarding houses for mill workers; the Googins' house; the Rugan boarding house (by the river); the Company Store; the Baptist church; the veneer mill (on this side of river, both sides of road); the Anderson/Olson house (center, rear); (in front of it) the first store; the two-story grammar school (on rise, center, rear); the early farms (on top of Lind Hill, rear); houses on Lake Street; logs for the mill; houses on Station Street (to right, foreground). The town was mushrooming among the stumps and stones, and the streets were still pretty muddy. However, it was not much later that a local improvement group had wooden sidewalks built throughout the central village. Still later (1923-1924), a concrete bridge that is still in use finally replaced the old wooden bridges which periodically washed out.
Courtesy of the Stockholm Historical Society

Before 1900 Anshelm Carlstrom established a farm on the hill beyond Madawaska Lake in Township 16, Range 4. Soon thereafter he started a small business (shown here) on the shore of the lake where he built and rented boats as well as cabins. It is now operated as Rainbow Cove. At about the same time, John J. Sodergren, who had a farm in Stockholm bordering T16-R4, started a similar business on the shore of Madawaska Lake nearer Stockholm, now operating as Stan's with the famous ten cent coffee. The first settlers found fish so plentiful that there were reports of catches by the tubful. Deer were also plentiful. Moose, lynx, and bobcat were not uncommon, and there were even reports of a few caribou, cougar, and wolves. In the winter, the farmers cut ice from the lakes, ponds, and rivers to pack with sawdust in their ice-houses, so the ice would last until the next winter.
Courtesy of the Stockholm Historical Society

This bird's-eye view of Stockholm, 1938, was actually taken from the top of a high pole or tree above St. Theresa's Catholic Church, (bottom, right), high on Lind Hill, South Main Street. The Catholic Church celebrated its first Mass on December 24, 1928. The First Baptist Church (lower, right) was organized on November 3, 1904, and was built in 1905-1906. The Oscar Frederick (now renamed Trinity Evangelical) Lutheran Church (upper, center) was organized on November 2, 1906, and was built in 1907. The bandstand (on the corner in front of the Lutheran church) was used by the Stockholm band, formed in 1922. It has now been moved to the ballfield (left, center). The boxy two-story Odd Fellows Hall (upper, center), which was built in 1924, housed a movie theater/hall, bowling alley, barber shop/pool hall, and stores. Barely visible (at the top, right of center) is the State Forest Service fire tower, which remains a landmark. At the time of this photograph, the veneer, pin, and box mills were gone, but Sam Collins was operating a sawmill, with the dam intact and the mill pond used to float the logs in. Now only a portion of one of the old mill buildings remain, the dam and the water tower are gone, many farms are growing up with trees and bushes, and new houses are being built as the community has become primarily residential.
Courtesy of Stockholm Historical Society

This owner-built "envelope" house of Dennis Theriault in Presque Isle is constructed to allow air heated by the sun through south facing windows (supplemented with wood heat in the winter), to circulate between an outer insulated shell and the interior house construction, maintaining an envelope of warm air around the inner house in the winter, and a buffer against the heat of the sun in the summer.
Photograph by Rebecca Hayden-McGrath

Still the Land of Promise

Out of chaos grew Aroostook County. Eighty percent of the area remains forested and unsettled. The farms that spread over the countryside during the height of potato production from starch to seed stock, during the first half of the twentieth century, are now private homes. The population has remained relatively constant with the personnel at Loring Air Force Base and new industries. Much of the promise remains unfilled. But Aroostookans look to the future with hope and high spirits.

With advances in communication, from jets to satellites, and ITV (interactive television), the isolation characteristic of Aroostook in her early years is gone. The individuality too is diminishing as conformity required of government interaction increases, and dependency is displacing independency. But the call of the wilderness land still beckons, and people come from across the nation and from around the world to "homestead" again, far from the mainstream and congestion of contemporary civilizations. Military men return with their families for more of the good life, as they did from the Aroostook War, and Aroostookans who have left for more money, or more excitement, return.

Passive and active solar energy power this beautiful Willey house of the future in Caribou, Maine. It is earth bermed on the north, with plenty of south facing windows for solar gain in the winter, but cool in the summer.
Photograph by Timothy S. McGrath

THE COUNTY LOOKS TO THE FUTURE
by Richard Cohen

The future of Aroostook County, as with the rest of the nation, rests to a large extent on the development and the use of technology that if employed wisely, will enhance the likelihood of stemming the greenhouse effect which now affects weather patterns. Obviously, such weather changes must have an adverse effect upon forests and crop growth and harvesting, the vital parts of the economy of Aroostook. We must assume that scientists, government leaders, and other people, not only from the United States but throughout the world, will work cooperatively to combat what may possibly be the most damaging environmental danger now confronting everyone. Add to this the problem of acid rain, and its devastating effects upon water, soil, forest, and marine life.

These are not necessarily pictures of doom but of the need for awareness. The economy of Aroostook is tied to water, soil, and forest, and these must be protected both for the purposes of business and for the enjoyment and continued excellent lifestyle that the people of Aroostook County enjoy.

There is little doubt that technology will aid us, but we must also bear our own individual responsibility to see that a way of life thas has long been established will continue.

To sustain what Aroostook forebears pioneered, it is fascinating to contemplate some of the scientific work which is occurring that will affect us positively. For example, consider the field of genetic engineering. At first, such tinkering as some people view these projects, appears frightening. But strictly controlled studies have found that we need not be fearful, particularly when it comes to plant growth and hybrids and even to the development of compounds that may eliminate insect infestations and which may aid in the discovery of hardier varieties of crops. Controlled climate is another engrossing story given the will and the foresight of the people.

Aroostook County also appears to be an excellent site for the study of alternative energy resources. The cooperation which is now taking place between New Brunswick and the County in technological areas, enumerated below, can eventually take into consideration this significant aspect of our well-being. These studies are extremely important, not only because of the eventual problem regarding loss of fossil fuels but also because of the perils inherent for the environment should people shirk the responsibility of searching out fuels that do not adversely affect our surroundings.

New and cheaper fuels would benefit the County, not only in the home, but of course, in business. At issue are independence, cost, and survival in a safe and continuing magnificent environment of which Aroostook citizens are the benefactors.

Nor may one neglect the possibilities of laser, fiber-

The Alternate Energy Laboratory at Northern Maine Vocational Technical Institute in Presque Isle utilizes passive solar energy, is built with cord wood, and is earth bermed. The active solar collectors heat the conference rooms. The small building at the left is a solar heated aquifer with underground water as the storage medium.
Photograph by Timothy S. McGrath

optic, computer, and television technologies. Because of the developments in these areas, geographic distances become almost meaningless. Imagine library holdings throughout the country being available in Aroostook County through the use of laser disc techniques with encyclopedias on one disc and periodical articles available in hard copy in minutes with telecommunication reproduction. The university campuses such as those at Presque Isle or Fort Kent will grow as centers for the County for the gathering of information and for research that will be of benefit to farming and the businesses of Aroostook.

Moreover, as the County witnesses the introduction of fiber optics, there will be expanded learning capacity as a result of televised courses through interactive television. The University of Maine at Presque Isle campus is capable of sending TV signals to Loring Air Force Base and Houlton, but fiber optics will make it possible to extend educational opportunities to more remote, rural areas of the County.

There are also satellite dishes seen about Aroostook. These will not only continue to broadcast entertainment, but they will also bring information regarding technical advice and advances for farming, business practices, or the expansion of one's knowledge in the fields of the arts, literature, music, or human services.

It is true that information programs now exist through various television stations, but what one must envision is talking back to the television set, carrying on conversations and taking part in one's own education or family needs through the method known as interactive television or communication through computers and telephones.

Someone in Aroostook County could design a new food processing machine, push a button, and the design would occur almost instantaneously in a distant industrial center where the assembly occurs. Such is the meaning of new communications systems and electronic imaging.

Consider a significant partnership agreement signed between New Brunswick and the state of Maine that created the Maine Research and Productivity Center. The center, headed by Dr. William Forbes and guided through the legislature by Representative John Lisnik, is part of a scientific and economic pact that will solve problems beneficial to the County by using Electron Probe Imaging.

For example, the Analyzer can take a particle one hundredth of a micron in size and build a map showing the distribution of compounds and thus show how minerals, for instance, appear in rocks. These minerals may be of a value to society when scientists know how and where they are distributed so the element or compound can be more readily extracted and used.

Further, this technology, because of its sophisticated analytical capabilities will aid in such areas as food science and in business. Analysis within Aroostook County will assist in food processing applications that have world-wide significance.

Aroostook County is in an excellent position for taking advantage of the opportunities. There is inexpensive real estate; there is a reliable labor source (the work ethic still lives in Aroostook County); there are financial resources through County banks which are linked nationwide; there are communications systems such as satellite, mail service, and computer; there are good power resources (Aroostook is at the beginning of the power grid linking it to Canada). The state must be interdependent, as must Aroostook County. This does not mean an end to independence.

The industries of Aroostook are relatively clean and will remain so. In other words, high technology electronics is clean. And because of technology, geography will play less and less of a role.

Thus, when one states that Aroostook County is a geographically isolated area, the statement can no longer be taken as a truth. Technology has put the County close to metropolitan areas, close to other states, close to other countries; technology has made us interdependent; yet its application does not mean that the County has lost its unique character or its independence. Rather, technology has and will allow us to pursue the good, to benefit from an environment and a heritage bequeathed by pioneering forefathers to present generations and to those who will follow.

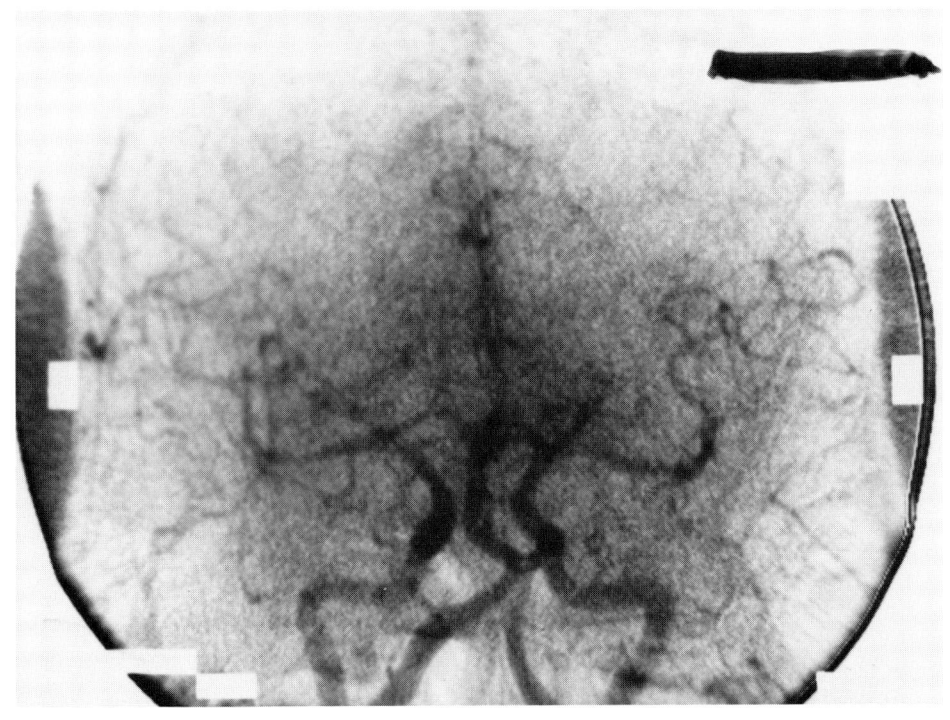

Laser photograph.
Photograph by Connie Tucker

An electron microprobe interfaced with an automated image analyser at the University of New Brunswick is shared with the University of Maine at Presque Isle through their cooperative Research and Productivity Centers.
Photograph by William Duncan

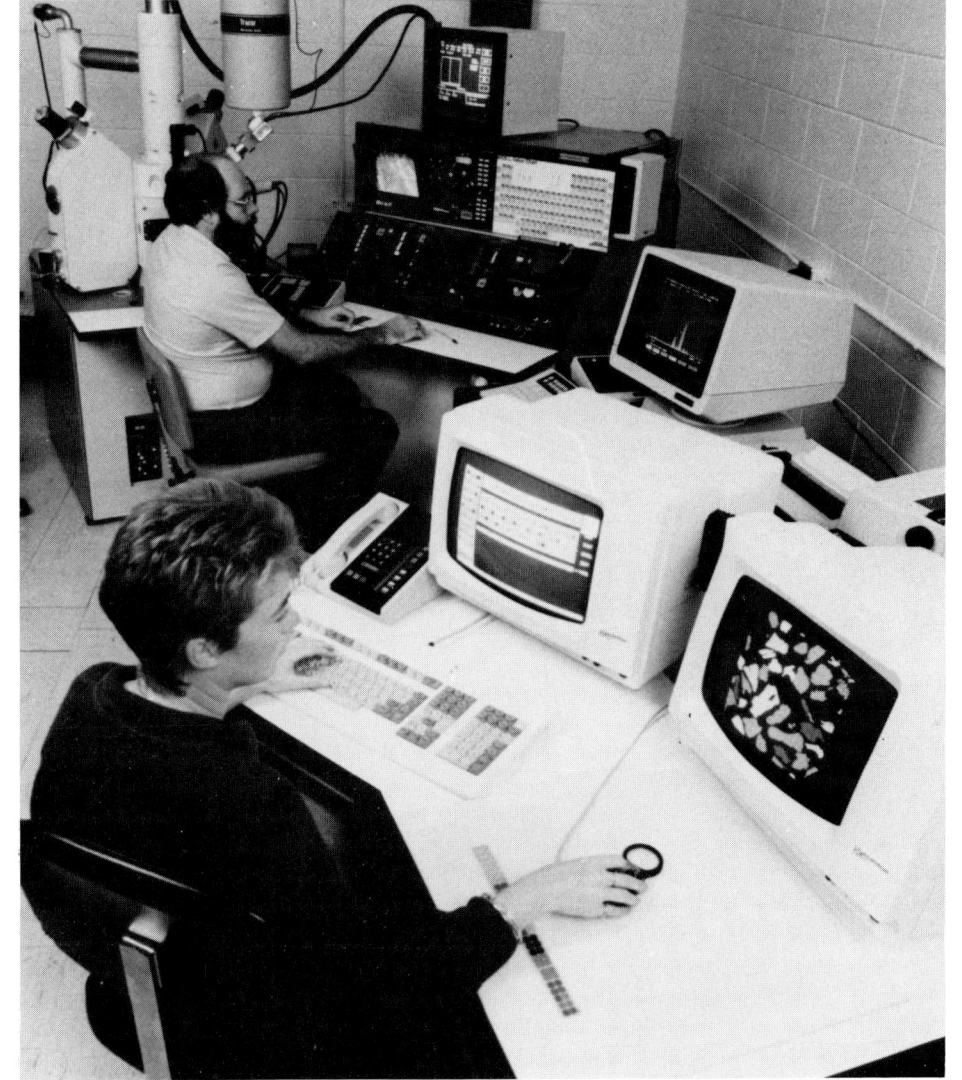

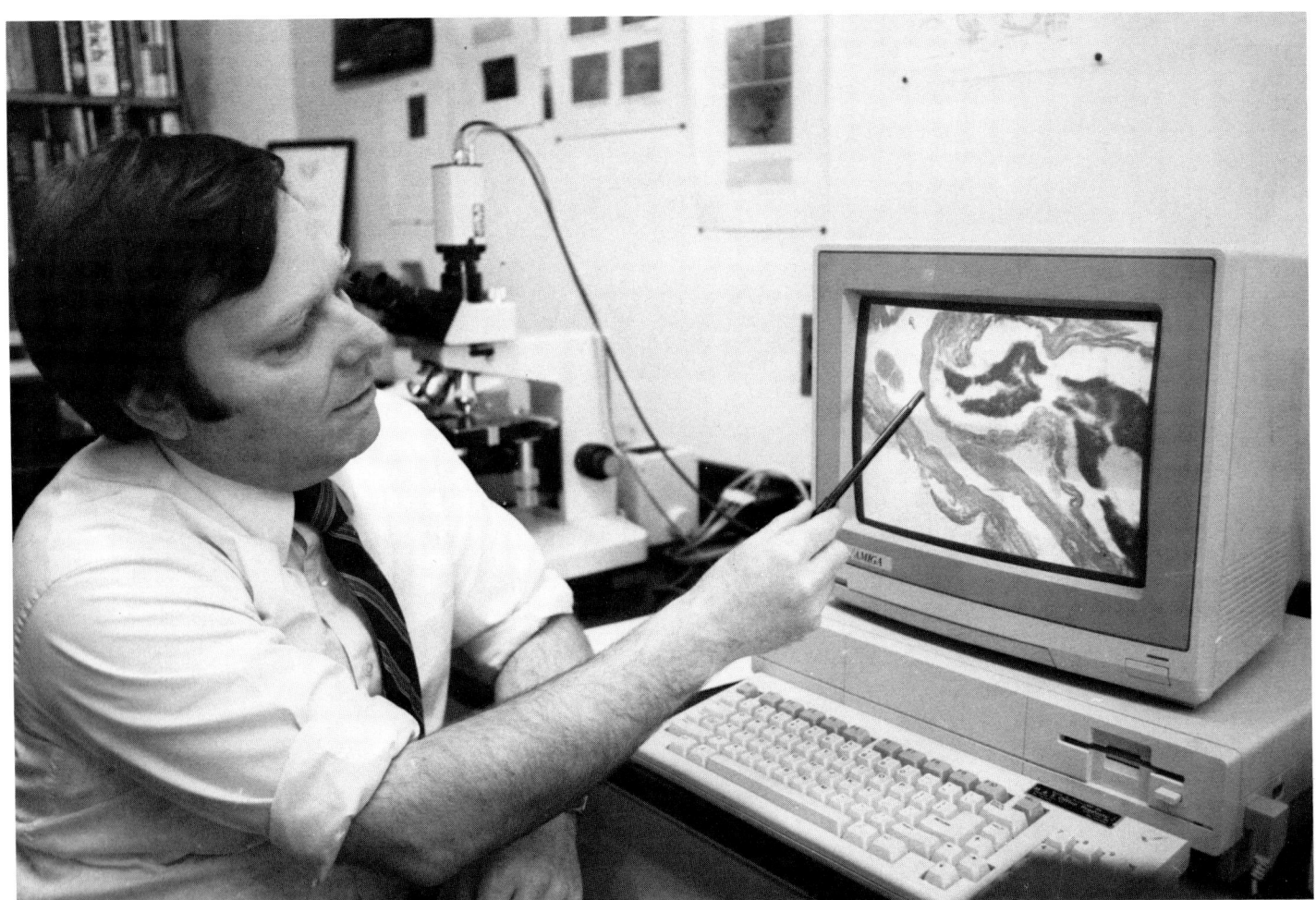

*Keeping our water pure is of continuing concern to Aroostookans, and investigations are underway to improve some types of sewage systems. One such system utilizes bacteria and fungi to break down organic waste, human or natural. The microorganisms are kept in check by excessive growth being eaten by worms and similar animals. An investigation to improve our understanding of this process, a study of the worms digestive physiology, is being conducted at the Universisty of Maine at Presque Isle by Dr. Stuart R. Gelder. The work involves determining the composition of the ingested food and monitoring the time it takes to pass through the gut. The investigation is being greatly assisted by the use of an image analyzer using a stereology computer program. Dr. Gelder has been assisted in this project by two undergraduate students, Jonathan L. Kimball and Bradford Potter. The ultimate aim of this study is to understand and enhance natural processes in the breakdown of organic waste products.
Photograph by William Duncan*

*Potato blossom in early summer.
Photograph by Larry Parks*

*This potato house for potato storage before shipping to market is built into the earth for protection from the cold. This one is on the Mapleton Road.
Photograph by Evelyn Kok*

*Harvesting potatoes by day, amongst the
colored fall foliage.
Photograph by Larry Parks*

*Harvesting potatoes into the night, to beat
the fall frosts.
Photograph by Larry Parks*

*Summer sky on the Aroostook.
Photograph by Connie Tucker*

Summer on the Aroostook River at midday.
Photograph by Clifton Boudman

Scene from At the Hop, *presented by the Pioneer Playhouse in 1988, directed by Joseph Zubrick, University of Maine at Presque Isle Theater Director.*
Photograph by Joseph Zubrick

Fossil-bearing limestone at a single isolated locality on the south shore of Square Lake was once part of a reef fringing a tropical, volcanic island.
Photograph by David Laing

Midsummer's Night celebration at the W. W. Thomas Memorial Shell in Thomas Park, New Sweden, dancing around the Maypole, under the American and Swedish flags.
Photograph by Kathryn Olmstead

Echo Lake at the foot of Quaquajo Mountain, Aroostook State Park. Only a brook when the first settlers arrived, traditional stories report that Indians sounding war whoops could hear their echo.
Photograph courtesy of Frank Appleby

The Saint John River, entrance into Aroostook for the Acadians and lumbermen, trade route for early settlers in Houlton, and communication route and camping grounds for Native People hunting and fishing.
Photograph by Joseph Donald Cyr

Selected Bibliography

Adney, Edwin Tappan, and Chapelle, Harold I. *The Bark Canoes and Skin Boats of North America.* Washington, D.C.: Smithsonian Institution, 1964.

Albert, Thomas. *History of Madawaska.* An English translation by S. Therese Doucette. Madawaska Maine: Madawaska Historical Society, 1985.

Ashby, W. T. *History of Aroostook.* Typescript. Presque Isle, Maine: UMPI, 1910 (?).

Banks, Ronald. *History of Maine.* Dubique, Iowa: Kendall/Hurt, 1976.

Barnes, Anna. *Pageant of Aroostook.* Lewiston, Maine: Lewiston Journal, 1916.

Bell, David G. *Early Loyalists: St. John.* Fredericton, New Brunswick: New Ireland Press, 1983.

Bennett, Dean. *Maine Dirigo "I Lead."* Camden, Maine: Down East Books, 1980.

Biggar, Henry Percival. *The Precursors of Jacques Cartier, 1497-1530.* Ottowa: Canadian Archives Publications, 1911.

Burrage, Henry S. *Maine in the Northeastern Boundary Controversy.* Portland, Maine: Marks Printing House, 1919.

Carlson, Shirlee. *The Proudwood People: 1886-1986.* S.1: Town Crier, 1986.

Chadwick, Henry., ed. *Atlas of the Christian Church.* New York: Facts on File, 1987.

Champlain, Samuel de. *The Works of Samuel de Champlain (1626).* Henry P. Biggar, ed., 6 vols., Toronto: The Champlain Society, 1922-1936.

Clifford, Harold B. *Maine and Her People.* Freeport, Maine: Bond-Wheelwright, 1976.

Coffin, George W. *Journal.* 1825 Typescript. Augusta, Maine: Maine Archives.

Cole, Galen. *Allie Cole, a Maine Pioneer.* Portland, Maine: Casco Printing Co., 1980.

Corbett, P. E. *The Settlement of Canadian-American Disputes.* New Haven: Yale University Press, 1937.

Cottage Physician. Springfield, Massachusetts: King-Richardson, 1897.

Cronon, William. *Changes in the Land: Indians, Colonists, and the Ecology of New England.* New York: Hill and Wang, 1983.

Day, Clarence. *Aroostook, the first 60 years.* Fort Fairfield: Fort Fairfield Review, n.d.

Day, Clarence. *The History of a Small Aroostook Town, the Story of Westfield.* Typescript. UMPI.

Deane, John G. *Report of John G. Deane and Edward Kavanaugh to Samuel Smith, Governor of Maine.* 1831. Typescript. UMPI.

DeGraaf, R. M., and Rudis, D. D. *New England Wildlife: habitat, natural history, and distribution.* Broomall, Pennsylvania: United States Department of Agriculture, Forest Service, North East Experimental Station, 1987.

Dickey-Lincoln School Project. (Maine) Final Environmental Impact Statement. Waltham, Maine: U.S. Army Engineering Division, 1980-1981.

Dietz, Lew. *The Allagash.* Thorndike, Maine: Thorndike Press, 1968.

Doane, Nancy. *Indian Doctor.* Typescript.

DuBay, Guy F., *Cheznous: The St. John Valley.* Augusta, Maine: Maine

State Museum, 1983.

Eckstorm, Fannie Hardy. *Old John Neptune and Other Maine Indian Shamans*. Portland, Maine: The Southworth-Anthoenson Press, 1945.

Elais, Norbert. *Quest for Excitement: Sport and Leisure in the Civilizing*. New York: Blackwell, 1986.

Elwell, Edward. *Aroostook: with some account of the Excursions Thither of the Editor of Maine, in the years 1858 and 1878, and of the colony of Swedes settled in the town of New Sweden*. Portland, Maine: Transcript Printing Co., 1879.

Flint, Laura A. *(Diaries.)* Fort Fairfield, Maine, 1868-

Gyles, John. *Memoirs of Odd Adventures, Strange Deliverances, etc., in the Captivity of John Gyles. esq. Commander of the Garrison and Saint George River in the district of Maine*. Auburn, New York: Derby and Miller, 1851.

Hamlin, Helen. *Pine, Potatoes and People*. New York: Norton, 1948.

Harris, Janet C., ed. *Play, Games and Sports in Cultural Contexts*. Champaigne: Human Kinetics Publishers, 1983.

Head, George. *Forest Scenes and Incidents in the Wilds of North America*. Toronto Coles, 1970. (Murray, 1829).

Hede, Richard. *Stockholm Centennial History,* Stockholm Historical Society, 1981.

Hill, Thos. *Hill's Album of biography and Art*. World's Fair Edition. Chicago: Danks & Co., 1892.

Historical Sketch and Roster of Commissioned Officers and Enlisted Men Called Into Service for the protection of the Northeastern Frontier, from February to May 1830. Augusta, Maine: Kennebec Journal, 1904.

Hitchcock, C. H. *Geology of the Wild Lands*. Maine Board of Agriculture, 1861.

Hussey, A. M. *Maine Geology: Field Trips of the Geological Society of Maine:* Maine: Geological Society of Maine, 1983.

Hutchison, Bruce. *The Struggle for the Border*. New York: Longmans, Green and Co., 1955.

Jackson, Charles T. *First Report of the Geology of the Public Lands Belonging to Maine and Massachusetts*. Augusta, Maine: Severence, 1838.

Jennings, Francis. *The Invasion of America: Indians, Colonialism, and the Cant of Conquest*. New York, London; W. W. Norton and Company, 1975.

Jones, Howard. *To the Webster-Ashburton Treaty, a Study in Anglo-American Relations, 1783-1843*. Chapel Hill, N.C.: The University of North Carolina Press, 1977.

Judd, Richard. *Aroostook: A Century of Logging* Orono, Maine: University of Maine Press, 1989.

Kidder, Frederick. *Military Operations in Eastern Maine and Nova Scotia During the Revolution*. Albany, New York: Joel Munsell, 1867.

Kendall, J. *History of the Town of Houlton (Maine) from 1804-1833 by an Old Pioneer*. Haverhill, Massachusetts: c.k. Morse & Son, 1884.

Kidney, Dorothy Boone. *A Home in the Wilderness*. So. Brunswick, Maine. A. S. Barnes, 1976.

Lacey, L. *Micmac Indian Medicine*. Antigonish, N.S. Formac, 1977.

Laing, D. *Earth Science: The Blue Planet*. Dubuque, Iowa: Wm. C. Brown, n.d.

Leland, Charles G. *The Algonquin Legends of New England*. Boston: Houghton, Mifflin, and Co., 1884.

Lescarbot, Marc. *The History of New France (1618)*. Toronto: The Champlain Society, 1907-1914.

Lufkin, Milton. *Henry, Man of Aroostook County, Maine*. Freeport, Maine: Bond Wheelsright, 1976.

McCarry, Charles. *Double Eagle*. New York: Little, Brown & Co., 1979.

MacLean, Janet R. *Recreation and Leisure: The Changing Scene*. New York: Wiley, 1985.

Maine, Past and Present. Boston: Maine Writers Res. Club, Heath 1929.

Maine Register. 1897, 1914.

Mann, John. *Travels in North America: Particularly in the province of Upper and Lower Canada, and New Brunswick, and in the states of Maine, Massachusets, and New York: Containing a Variety of Interesting Adventures and Disasters, which the Author encountered on his Journey among the Americans, Dutch, French, and Indians. Also, Several Remarkable Interpositions of Divinde Providence, in Preserving Him From Dangers, by Sea and Land, from 1816 to 1823*. 1824. Copyright William A. Spray: Fredericton, New Brunwsick, St. Annes Point Press, 1978.

Melvin, Charlotte Lenentine. "The Swedish People in Northern Maine." Master's thesis, University of Maine, 1950.

Melvin, Charlotte Lenentine. *Madawaska, a Chapter in Maine-New Brunswick Relations, 183-1843*. Madawaska, Maine: Madawaska Historical Society, 1975.

Moore, John B. *History and Digest of the International Arbitration to which the United States has been a Party*. 6 vol. Washington, D.C.: GPO, 1898.

Morrison, Kenneth. *The Embattled Northeast: The Elusive Ideal of Alliance in Abnaki-Euramerican Relations*. Barkeley, Los Angeles, London: University of California Press, 1984.

Nicolar, Joseph. *Life and Traditions of the Redman*. Fredericton, New Brunswick: Saint Anne's Point Press, 1979.

Kendall, J. *Old Pioneer. History of the Town of Houlton, Maine from 1804-1883*.

Osberg, P. H. *Bedrock Geologic Map of Maine*. Augusta, Maine: Maine Geological Survey, 1985.

Paper Talks magazine. "The County" ed. Hampden, Maine: G. Pierre Dumont, Sr., 1983-

Phair, Philip. *Journal*.

Pullen, Clarence. *In Fair Aroostook, Where Acadia and Scandinavia's Subtle Touch Turned a Wilderness Into a Land of Plenty*. Bangor and Aroostook Railroad, 1902.

Putnam, Cora M. *History of Houlton*. Portland, Maine: House of Falmouth, 1958.

Roy, D.C. *Ordovician and Silurian Stratigraphy of Northeastern Aroostook County, Maine*. New England: Geological Society of America Memoir, 1976.

Scott, Dr. Stanley., ed. *Northern Lights: Studies in Creativity. University of Maine at Presque Isle, 1983.*

Phair, Philip. *Journal*. Presque Isle, Maine: Turner Memorial Library.

Snow, Dean. *The Archaeology of New England, New World Archaeological Record Series*. New York, London, Toronto, Sydney, San Francisco: Academic Press, 1980.

Souvenir booklets: All Towns of Aroostook.

Speck, Frank G. *Penobscot Man: The Life History of a Forest Tribe in Maine*. New York: Octagon Books, 1970.

Sprague, John Francis. *The North Eastern Boundary Controversy and the Aroostook War*. Dover, Maine: The Observer Press, n.d.

Sullivan, James. *History of the District of Maine*. Augusta, Maine: Maine State Museum, 1970.

Steinhauer, Dale. "Stemming the Tide." Master's thesis, University of North Carolina, 1986.

Story of New Sweden, as told at the Quarter Centennial Celebration for the founding of the Swedish Colony in the Woods of Maine, June 25, 1895. Portland, Maine: Loring, Short & Harmon, 1896.

Thompson, W. B. *Surficial Geologic Map of Maine*. Augusta, Maine: Maine Geological Survey.

Thoreau, Henry David. *The Maine Woods*. New York: Crowell, 1961.

Trigger, Bruce G. *Handbook of North American Indians*. vol. 15. Washington, D.C.: Smithsonian Institution, 1978.

United States Senate. *Proposed Settlement of the Maine Indian Land Claims: Hearings Before the Select Committee on Indian Affairs, United States Senate, Ninety-sixth Congress, 2nd Session on S. 2829, July 1 & 2, 1980*. v. 1 & 2. Washington, D.C.: GPO.

Upton, L. F. S. *Micmacs and Colonists: Indian White Relations in the Maritimes 1713-1867*. Vancouver: University of British Columbia Press, 1979.

Wilson, Charles M. *Aroostook, our last frontier*. Brattleboro, Vermont: S. Daye Press, 1937.

Wiggin, Edward. *History of Aroostook*. Presque Isle, Maine: Star Herald Press, 1922.

Wright, Esther Clark. *Loyalists of New Brunswick*. Wolfville, Nova Socia: E. C. Wright, 1955.

York, Dena. *History of the Greater Ashland Area*. Madawaska, Maine: Saint John Valley Publishing, 1983.

York, Dena. *Mapleton, Maine*. Presque Isle, Maine: Northern Printers, 1980.

INDEX

A

Abenaki Confederation, 38
Abenaki Girl Scout Council, 137
Abenakis, 18-37, 137
Abruzzo, Ben, 99
Acadia Hotel, Fort Kent, 116
Acadian house, 42
Acadian mountain building, 16
Acadian Village, 134
Acadians, 22, 25, 40-43, 75, 76, 95, 103, 111, 123, 134, 138, 151, 162, 178, 184
ACHC Newsletter, 133
Act of Establishment, 70
Adams, John, Pres., 65
Adelman, H., 193
Alexander Baring Township, 67
Allagash, 58, 60, 130, 149
Allagash Falls, 149
Allagash Historical Society, 130
Allagash River, 4, 35, 39, 58, 59, 61, 67, 122, 139, 146, 149, 162, 178, 184
All-Aroostook Music Festivals, 116
All Saints Church, Masardis, 80
Allen, Charles, 72
Allen, G. Edward, Rev.,
Allen, John, 83, 89
Alley, Joshua, 110
Alternate Energy Laboratory, 206
Alton, Able, 82
Alva. See Blaine
Alva Corner, 86
Alwood, Glenna Walton, 82
American Airlines, 166
American Association of University Women in The County, 110
Amity, 62, 136, 139
ballooning, 96
Amours, Rene D', Sieur de Clignancourt, 22
Anderson, David, 82
Anderson, Henry, 202
Anderson, Joe, 182
Anderson, John, 135, 200
Anderson, Lewis, 200
Anderson, Maxie, 99
Anderson/Olson house, 203
Anderson store, John, 203
Anderson Toy Museum, 135
Andrews Building, 129
Androscoggin River, 24, 150, 162
Angier, Cleaves H., 141
Angier, J., 141
Annapolis, 22, 24
Annas, Phil, 116
Appalachian Mountains, 9
Appel, Karel, 97
Aroostook Agricultural and Horticultural Society, 96
Aroostook Area Agency on Aging, 175
Aroostook Band (Micmacs), 34
Aroostook County Court House, 179
Aroostook County Extension Homemakers Groups, 136
Aroostook County Historical Center, UMPI, 117, 131
Aroostook Development Corporation, 159
Aroostook Falls, 4, 150
Aroostook General Hospital, 173
Aroostook Historical and Art Museum of Houlton, 131
Aroostook Home Care, 175
Aroostook Ice Skating School, 101
Aroostook in the United States Congress, 188
Aroostook Lodge Building, 83
Aroostook Medical Center, 109, 176, 177
Aroostook River, 4, 20, 35, 44, 48, 49, 55, 71, 102, 147, 178, 179, 195, 211, 212, 216
Aroostook State Normal School, 98, 116, 126
Aroostook State Park, 5, 213
Aroostook State Teachers College, 116
Aroostook Telephone and Telegraph Company, 141
Aroostook Valley Beef Club, 137
Aroostook Valley Dairy Club, 137
Aroostook Valley Railroad, 189, 200
Aroostook War, 62, 67, 68, 71, 72, 73, 139, 145, 161, 162, 178, 204
Area Development Administration, Maine Industrial Building Authority, 159

Armstrong, Ferdinand, 180
Arnold Brook Lake, 5
Arnold, John S., 198
Arnold's Hall, 198
Arresaguntacooks, 29
Art Loan Program, 109
Asby, Wilmot T., 46, 154
Ashburton, Lord Alexander Baring, 30, 67, 72, 73
Ashland, 10, 35, 37, 54, 57, 80, 82, 86, 104, 105, 116, 129, 130, 132, 136, 139, 143, 145, 162, 191
Ashland Community High School, 136
Ashland Community Library, 129, 132
Ashland Lumber Company, 147
Ashland Municipal Cemetery, 132
Ashland Opera House, 104
Association Culturelle et Historique de Mont-Carmel, La— Museum and Cultural Center, 131
Association of Performing Arts, UMPI, 103
Astle and Paige, 131
Atherton, Del, 182
Atlas of the Christian Church, 82
Atlas Plywood Corporation, 200
Augusta, 70, 71, 182
Axel Siding, 201
Ayotte, Charles, 134

B

Bacon, James, 64
Baker Brook, 162
Baker, Jesse, 155
Baker, John, 64, 65, 162
Baker's Flag, John, 65
Baisley's (inn), 51
Ballad of Hiram Smith, 68
Bangor, 26, 44, 64, 66, 69, 70, 74, 82, 139, 140, 152, 156, 164, 193
Bangor & Aroostook Railroad, 56, 96, 133, 141, 152, 164, 193, 200
Bangor-Hydro Electric, 167
Banks, Mary L., 90
Banks, Thomas, 90
Baptist Church, 203
Baptist Park, 82
Baptists, 75, 82, 83, 84, 86, 87, 89, 92, 200
Barbershoppers, 116, 117
Barclay, Thomas, Col., 64
Baring, Alexander (Lord Ashburton), *See* Ashburton
Baring township, 67
Barker, Lucy Howard, 117
Barker, Nathaniel, Mrs., 117
Barker, Noah, 198
Barnes, Charles Putnam, 185
Barnes, Francis, 154, 162
Barnes, George B., 185
baseball, 96
Baskahegan-Grand Lake, 33
basketball, 96
Basques, 19, 20
Batchelder, Ben, 163
Bath Iron Works, 167
Bay of Fundy, 39
Bear, Ed, 37
Bear Hill Grange, 137
Bear, Newell, 31, 35
Bearce, Lew, 115
Bearce Store, 129
Beaubassin, 41
Beaulieu, Alma, 116
Beaulieu, Danna, 110
Beaulieu, Guy, 116
Beaupre, Addis, 134
Belanger, Phyllis, 110
Benedicta, 81, 139
Benjamin, Clarence, 117
Bernard, Eileen, 110
Bethany Baptist Church, PI, 89
Biard, Father, 21
Bible Point, 97
Bicentennial Committee of Fort Fairfield, 133
Bi-Centenniald Park, Presque Isle, 100

Bickford, Harold, Rev., 86, 137
Big Machias River, 147, 162
Big Rock, 100
Bilings, George, 154
Bingham Purchase, 69
Bingham Township, 69
Bingham, William, Sen., 29, 30, 72
Blackden, Leon, 193
Black Hawk Inn, 180
Black Hawk Putnam Building, 78, 81
Blackstone, Arthur, 55
Blackstone, Fred, 55
Blackstone, James K., 55
Blackstone, James K. (farm), 55
Blackstone Siding, 8, 201
Blaisdell Farm, 122
Blake, John, Rev., 80
Blake Library, UMFK, 130
Blaine, 45, 51, 52, 76, 83, 86, 87, 89, 141
Blaine House, 121, 187
Bloodless Aroostook War. *See* Aroostook War
Blossom, Frank, Dr., 174
B'nai B'rith, 90
Bolstridge, Eben, 52
Bonney, M. L., Dr., 172
Boone, Sherman, Dr., 173
Boston, Bishop of, 76
Bouchard, Phronie, 119, 121
Bouchette, Joseph, Col., 64
Boudman, Clifton, 103, 106
"Boundary March and Quickstep," 72
Boy Scouts, 137, 143
Braden, John R. (horse), 94
Brakhage, Stan, 97
Bray, Sullivan, the Reverend, 80
Breen, Ed, 106, 107
Brennan, Joseph E., Gov., 37, 185
Bridgewater, 75, 77, 82, 184, 185, 186
Bridgewater Academy, 69
Bridgewater Academy Grant, 49
Bridgewater Baptist, 75
Bridgewater Historical Society, 130
Bronsonia, 10
Brown, Barry "B-B", 116
Brown Hospital, 173
Brown, Janet, 173
Brown, Stephen, Dr., 173
Bubar, Joseph, 89
Buckmore, George W., 70
Budreau & Company, J. L., 156
Bull, Eunice, 52
Bull, Jasper, 117
Bull, Peter, 48, 52, 162
Bull, Peter, House, 48
Bull's Island, 52
Bunyan, Paul, 164
Burleigh, Albert C., 152
Burleigh, Edwin, Gov., 187, 188
Burleigh, Parker P., 197, 198
Burnett, Ryan, 110
Burns, Frederick L., 186
Burns, W. B., 193
Business and Professional Women's Club, Fort Kent, 129

C

Cabot, John, 20
Cain, Anthony, 81
Calais, 41, 67
Campbell, Archibald, Sir, 68
Campbell, Bill, 117
Campbell, Catherine, 86
Campbell, Thomas, 86
Campbelton, 59
Canadian Pacific Railroad, 152
canoeing, 100, 149
Cape Breton, 20, 22
Capitol (New Sweden public building), 92, 134, 198, 199
Caribou, 47, 54, 56, 81, 82, 83, 86, 87, 89, 93, 96, 97, 98, 99, 103, 105, 110, 116, 117, 125, 128, 133, 136, 153, 154, 163, 164, 172, 174, 177, 181, 192, 193, 196, 198, 201, 202, 205

Caribou Choral Society, 116, 117
Caribou Garden Club, 136
Caribou Historical Society, 128, 133
Caribou Praying Band, 86
Caribou Public Library, 128
Caribou Theater, 105
Carleton, Governor, 76
Carleton Map, Osgoode, 63
Carnegie, Andrew, 129, 130, 131
Caron, Emile, 158
Carpenter, Elbridge E., Rev., 80
Carter, Jimmy, Pres., 37
Carter, Ray H., 86
Cartier, Jacques, 20
Cary & Cunliffe, 149
Cary, Jefferson, Dr., 172, 174
Cary Medical Center, 177
Cary Memorial Hospital, 110, 174, 175
Cary Memorial Library, 128, 131
Cary, Shepard, 68, 146, 149, 160, 162, 188
Castine, 63, 64
Castle Hill, 53, 54, 130
Caswell, 167
Catholic Church, Fort Fairfield, 81
Catholic Church, Houlton, 81
Catholic Society, Presque Isle, 89
Caulkins, H. L., Rev., 84
Center for the Performing Arts, 103
Centerville, 50, 159, 163
Chadwick, John, 128
Chain of Friendship, 27
Chamberlain, Frank, 163
Chamberlain, Joshua, Gov., 164, 197, 198, 202
Champlain, Samuel de, 21, 38, 41, 63
Chapman, William, 82, 116, 130, 166
Chase, Ada May, 111
Chase, Frank, 116
Chase, George, 117
Chase, Lewis, 110
Chase, Warren, 192
Chaudiere River, 39, 64
Chipman, Ward, 63
Chiputneticook Lakes, 64
Christian Church, Crouseville, 86
Christian Science Society, 86, 92
Christie Complex, 130
Christie, Joshua, 52
Church of England. *See* Episcopal
Church of the Good Shepherd, Houlton, 80
Church of Jesus Christ of Latter Day Saints, Caribou, 93
Church of Pentecostal Power, Washburn, 86
Church of St. Benedict, 81
Church of St. David, 79
Church of Ste. Luce, Frenchville, 77
Churchill Dam, 146
Churchill, Nathaniel, Homestead, 102
Civil Emergency Preparedness, 180
Civil War, 82, 90, 145, 146, 156, 161, 162, 164
Cinema, The Caribou, 103
Cinema, The Houlton, 103
Cinema, The Presque Isle, 103
Clair, Alanna, 110
Clarence Town Coach, 135
Clark, Donald Ashby, 108
Clark, Pete, 166
Clase, Hilma C., 198
Clase, N. P., Capt., 198
Clauson, Clinton, Gov., 186, 187
Clef Club, 116
Clefford's Hill, 44
Cleveland, Edward L., 152
Cliff, D. F., 193
Clifford, H. B., 150
Clifford, Matt, 110
Clifford's Depot, 139
Clyde River, 39
Cochran, Alexander, 162
Cochran Lake, 128
Cochran's gristmill, 54
Coe, E. S., 146
Coe, Harrie B., 156
Coffin, George W., 51, 162
Colby College, 126
Cole, Allie, 195
Collins, 96
Collins Company, S. W., 133

Collins, Harve, 154
Collins, Sam, 200, 203
Community Concerts Association, 116, 117
Community General Hospital of Fort Fairfield, 176
Community Theater, Fort Kent, 105
Company L, 163
Company Store, 203
Comprehensive Training and Employment Act, 134
Congregation Beth Israel, 90
Congregational Church, Fort Fairfield, 75, 77
Congregational Church, Masardis, 80
Congregational Church, Presque Isle, 83
Congregationalist, 75, 77, 78, 80, 83, 92
Connecticut River, 62, 67
Connelly, Patrick, 65
Connor, 198
Connors family, 59
Consolidated School, 132
Constitution, U. S., 29
continental drift, 9, 11
Conway, 139
Cook, Samuel, 180
Cook's Brook, 60
Cook's Clearing, 60
Cosboom, John, 182
Cottage Physician, The, 170, 171
Cowperthwaite, Mr., 52
Craig, Daniel, 65
Craig, Robert, 163
Crandall, Darrell, 181
Creasy Ridge, Mapleton, 56
Crouseville, 48, 86, 102, 106
Crouseville Praying Band, 86
Cullen, Big Jim, 181
Cullins, William, 193
Cunliffe, Cora Dickey, 149
Cunliffe Pond, 149
Cunliffe, William, 149
Cunliffe's Depot, 59, 60, 149
Cunningham School, 37
Currie, H. G., 193
Cutter, B. F., 198
Cyr, Aimant, 45
Cyr, Bernice, 110
Cyr, Desse, 46
Cyr, Donald, 110
Cyr Hall, UMFK, 130
Cyr, Joseph Donald, 75, 131
Cyr, Laurent, Maison (house), 43
Cyr, Marguerite, 134
Cyr Plantation, 134
Cyr, Ron, 117
Cyr, Vital, 123

D

Daggett, Charles, 147
Dalton, 85
Dalton Historical Society, William, 130
Dana, Joel, 103
dancing, 115
Danville, J. B., Map, 39
Dashiell's Map of 1830, 67
Daughters of Wisdom of Sevres, 76, 174
Davidson, John, 65
Davis, Daniel, Gov., 198
Davis, Hunter, 114
Day, Holman, 149
Dead Man's Strip, 149
Dean, Marilyn, 173
Deane and Kavanagh, 52
Delano, Harold, 116
DeMonts Expedition, 38
Department of Environmental Protection, 180
Depot Stream, 149
Des Chutes, 64
deRozier Map of 1699, 29
Devon cattle, 102
Diamond, Annie, 59
Diamond, Elizabeth, 59
Diamond, Lucinda, 59
Diamond, Sarah, 59
Dibblee, Dr., 172
Dickerson, William, 193
Dickison, Thomas S., Dr., 174

Dickey Dam, 184
Dickey Hall, 149
Dickey-Lincoln School Lakes Map, 184
Dickey Village, 149
Dickey, William, Maj., 123, 146
Dietz, Lew, 149
Dill, Elliot, Adj. Gen., 202
Dochet Island, 63
dog teams, 140
Donnelly, George, 193
Dorr, Leon, 190
Dorsey, Dwight W., 175
Dorsey, E. J., 113
Dorsey, Edward, 175
Dorsey Funeral Home, 175
Dorsey, John, 175
Dorsey, Stephen, 175
Double Eagle II
Dow, Earl, 117
Dow, Wilmont S., 97
Downing, Colby, 117
Downing Company of Presque Isle, 105
Downing, Jack, 117
drama, 118
Drew, Morrill N., 185
Dubay, Ted, 117
Dudley, John W., 54
Dudley Winter Apple, 54
Dugal, George Emile, 192
Dummer, Governor, 25, 26
Dunlap, Governor, 70
Dunn, Elbridge G., 145, 147, 160, 162
Dunn Furniture Company, 194
Dunn, George B., 147
Dwinal, Rufus, 146
Dyer, Andrew, 110
Dyer, Frank, 163
Dyer's Market, 193

E

Eagle Lake, 76, 79, 105, 177, 185
Easton, 82, 85, 95, 125, 136, 159, 164
Eastport, 64
East Ridge, 86, 90
East Ridge Union Church, Mars Hill, 86, 90
Echo Lake, 5, 85, 100, 213
Eckstorm, F. H., 35
Ecouphaq, 161
Edmunston, 76, 116, 166
Edmunston pulp mills, 148
Educational Television (ETV), 116, 187
Eaton, General, 64
Eaton Grant, 64
Evangelical Missionary Society of Massachusetts, 78
Everett, Charles, 117
Exxon Station, Mars Hill, 193
electron microbe and automated image analyser, 207
Elgin automobile dealer, 201
Ellis, Gary, 167
Ellis, Mark, 154
Elwell. E., 44
Emanuel Episcopal Church, Ashland, 80
Emerson, Delmont, Mrs., 135
Emerson Hall, UMPI, 126
Emerson, Ralph Waldo, 170
"en colombage" (house), 43
Englund, Carl, 201
Episcopal, 80, 83, 85, 86
Erickson, Al, 117
Escovitz, Harry, 90
European and North American Railway, 164

F

Fact & Fiction Club, 128
Fairbanks. *See* Presque Isle
Fairbanks, Dennis, 51, 52, 53, 122
Fairbank's Mills, 51
Fairfield, John, Gov., 62, 70, 71, 72, 73, 133
Fall Foliage Plane Ride, 133
Farmers Home Credit, 156
Farnsworth Museum, 117

217

Farwell, Elliott, 117
Faulkner, Esther Orr, 67, 109
Felch, Alpheus, 68
Fenwick, Benedict, Bishop of Boston, 77, 81
Fernald, Bert M., Gov., 202
Fiddlehead fern, 55, 57
Fields, George, 65
Fifteenth Maine Regiment, 162
Fifty-second Regiment (British), 71
Finnemore, Kathy, 113
First Baptist Church, Caribou, 89
First Baptist Church, Houlton, 75
First Baptist Church, Presque Isle, 84
First Baptist Church, Stockholm, 203
First Brook, 97
First Church of Christ, Scientist, Houlton, 92
First Congregational Church, Houlton, 78
First Free Baptist Church, Blaine, 89
First Maine Heavy Artillery, 187
First Methodist Church, Presque Isle, 85
First Methodist-Episcopal Church, Hodgdon, 85
First National Bank, 155
First National Bank of Houlton, 156
First Swedish Evangelical Lutheran Church, New Sweden, 92
First Unitarian Church, Houlton, 81
Fish River, 79, 146, 149, 162
Fish River Railroad, 133
Fitzgerald, Edward, Lord, 171
Fitzherbert home, 52
Flint, A. S., 146
Flint, Laura, 115
Flood Control Act of 1965, 184
Flora, William, 135
Fogg Block, 193
football, 96
Forbes, William, Dr., 206
Ford, Richard H., 82
Forest Club, 128
Fort Fairfield, 35, 52, 81, 84, 87, 90, 100, 102, 105, 108, 115, 116, 125, 133, 134, 139, 141, 152, 161, 166, 175, 184, 185, 186, 187, 192, 193, 195, 196, 198, 202
Fort Fairfield Public Library, 129
Fort Fairfield Review, 142
Fort Fairfield Historical Society, 133
Fort Kent, 45, 72, 74, 103, 105, 110, 116, 123, 129, 133, 138, 139, 140, 141, 149, 155, 158, 160, 161, 162, 174, 184, 191, 195, 206
Fort Kent American Legion, 129
Fort Kent Block House, 62, 146, 160
Fort Kent Elementary School, 155
Fort Kent High School, 133
Fort Kent Historical Society, 133
Fort Kent Lions Club
Fort Kent Public Library, 129
Fort Kent Rotary Club, 129
Fort Kent Telephone Company, 141
Fort Road, 83
Forty-second Regiment (British), 71
4-H Clubs, 132, 137
Fox, Sam, 48
Francis Malcolm Institute, 136
Franco-Americans, 60. *See also* Acadians
Fraser Paper Limited (Fraser Companies Limited), 148, 167, 192
Fredericton, 24, 26, 41, 50, 64, 70, 71, 141, 149, 150, 161, 162, 198
Free Baptist Church, Presque Isle, 84
Free Baptists, 84
Free Christian Gospel Mission Church, New Sweden, 92
Free High School, 125
Free Will Baptist Parish, 86
Freeman, George, Dr., 172
Freeman's Journal, 180
French and Indian War, 26
French Canadians, 200
French missions, 24, 26
Frenchville, 76, 77
Friends of the Aroostook County Historical Society, UMPI, 118, 121, 133
Frisbie, Mary, 80
Frontier Defense Act, 164
Frost, Aubrey C., 129
Frost, Henry, 80
Frost Memorial Library, Robert A., Limestone, 129
Frost, Stella, 129
Frye, William, Sen., 131

G

Gagnon, H. A., 155
Gagnon, Henry, 117
Gamblin, Anthony, 110
games, 96, 101
Gardner, Ed, 115
Gardner, John, 59
Garfield, 129, 130
Garrison Hill, 66, 67
Gelder, Stuart, Dr., 208
Gelotte's pond, 201
Gem Opera House, Caribou, 105
General Hospital of Presque Isle, 174
General Meeting House, Fort Fairfield, 87
George III (England), 64
German prisoners of war, 159, 166, 167
Ginn's Pavilion, Fort Fairfield, 116
Giles, Anderson, 103, 107
Girl Scouts, 137
Glaciers, 6, 12, 13
Glasier, John, 146
Glenwood Plantation, 191
Glidden, Gil, 190
Good, Vinal G., 185
Gorman, John, 117
Gould, Arthur B., Sen., 155, 156, 189
Gould Electric Company, 155
Gould Memorial Hospital, Arthur H., 174, 176
Gouldville School basketball team of 1939, 37
Governor Dummer's War, 25, 26
Governors Agreement, 72
Governors of Maine from Aroostook, 187
Grand Army of the Republic, 164, 165
Grand Falls, 22, 60, 68, 71, 72, 150
Grand Isle, 134
Grand Lake, 27, 33, 38
Grant, Doug, 116
Grant, Job, 48
Grant, Mary Churchill, 48
Grant, Milton, Rev., 37
Grange, 156
Graves, Ola (Saucier), 173
Great Fire of 1902, 92
Great Ice Age, 13
Great Northern Paper Company, 156
Greeley, Ebenezer, 70
Green, Jere, 133
Green, Mildred, 48
Green, S. W., 193
Green River, 59
Grenville, Lord, 63
Griffith, Major, 49
Griffiths, Roberta, 121
Grotto of Our Lady of Lourdes, Van Buren, 79
Gustaf Adolph Evangelical Church, New Sweden, 92

H

Hafford, John, 161
Hagerty, Dr., 130
Haines, Frank, 190
Haines, Fred, 90
Haines, J. W., 44
Haines, Joseph Wingate, 102
Haines, Mary, 102
Hale, Eugene, 131
Hale's Map, 67
Half & Half Club, 131
Halifax, 26, 28, 64
Hall, J. B., 96
Hall, Joseph, 141
Hall's Stream decision, 67
Hallet, William, 66
Hamilton, A. L., 135
Hamlin, Hannibal, 164, 198
Hamlin, Jean, 121
Hamlin Plantation, 134
Hammond Hotel, Van Buren, 116
Hancock Barracks, 66, 67, 68, 76, 80, 81, 132, 139
Hansen Memorial Library, W. T. A., Mars Hill, 131
Hansen, Walter T. A., 131
Harding, Alpheus, the Reverend, 78
harness racing, 94
Harris, John, 64
Harrison, William H., Pres., 72

Harvey, John, Sir (Lt. Gov.), 70, 72
Harvey, King, 142
Harvey, T., Dr., 173
Haskell, William, 101, 117
Hatch, J. W., Rev., 87
Hatch, Mildred, 133
Hawes, Walter, 115
Hayden, Bob, 117
Hayden, Granville, 181
Hayden, Harold, 190
Haynesville, 139, 153
Haystack Historical Society, 130
Haystack Mountain, 6, 10, 14, 103, 130
Head, George, Sir, 50
Hedman, Walter, 202
Henderson, Flo, 59
Henderson, John, 59
Hersey, Ira G., 186, 188
Hewitt, Fred, 89
Higgins, Bessie, 110
Higgins, George, 174
Highlands, 62, 64, 67, 73
Hill, Warren, 116
Hillcrest Farm, 44
Hillside Gospel Mission, 124
Hilt, J. G., 192
hockey, 101
Hodgdon, 69, 82, 84, 123, 139, 178, 186
Hodgdon, John, 186
Hogan, Frank, 182
Holds, Walt, 117
Holland, Park, 30
Holmes, 97
Holmes, Albe, 154, 201
Holmes Jewelry Store, 131
Holmes, Lewis, 174
Holt, C. E., 129
Holub, John, 109
Holy Rosary Church, Caribou, 86
Holy Rosary Sisters of Rimouski, 76
Hone, John, 104
Hone's Opera House, 105
Hose Company No. 1 of Presque Isle, 190
Hosford, Elson A. "Bill," 163
Hospital Guild of Fort Kent, 110
Hotel Dieu, 174
Houlton, 30, 58, 60, 65, 67, 68, 69, 76, 80, 81, 82, 83, 84, 85, 86, 87, 89, 92, 95, 96, 99, 100, 102, 103, 109, 116, 118, 125, 127, 128, 129, 131, 132, 137, 138, 139, 140, 141, 142, 151, 152, 153, 156, 161, 162, 164, 166, 167, 172, 173, 174, 177, 178, 180, 181, 182, 184, 185, 186, 191, 192, 193, 195
Houlton Academy, 78, 126, 132, 180
Houlton Band (Maliseet), 33, 34, 35, 36, 37
Houlton Baptist, 75
Houlton Elks Band, 67
Houlton High School, 67
Houlton, Joseph, Capt., 179
Houlton Library and Literacy Association, 128
Houlton Municipal Police Department, 182
Houlton Petition, 69
Houlton Plantation, 52
Houlton Regional Hospital, 173
Houlton Savings Bank, 156
Houlton, Squire, 52
Houlton Women's Club, 128
Houlton Women's Group, 136
Howard, Al, 182
Howell, Arthur E., 136
Howell Wildlife Education Foundation, Arthur E., Amity, 136
Hubbard, Thomas, 181
Hudramics Club, UMPI, 103
Huff, Mark, 107
Hulling Machine Falls, 149
Hume, David, 53
Hunter, Pauline Colbrath, 131
Huot, Louis, Father, 79
Hussey Block, 131
Hussey, Frank, 137, 163
Hussey's Theater, Mars Hill, 105

I

ice ages, 12, 13

ice cutting, 57
Ile. St. Croix, 41
Ile. St. Jean, 41
Ile. Verte, 42, 43
Indian Point, 81
Ingraham, Leon, 182
Interactive Television (ITV), 127, 204
International Paper, 156
Irish, 58-61
Irvine, J. W., Rev., 87
Irving, Bertha, 113
Irving, K. C., 168
Island Falls, 54, 92, 97, 100, 134, 135, 164, 186

J

Jackins, Kendall, 182
Jackson, Charles T., 9, 49, 50, 52, 54
Jalbert, Willard, 58, 151
James School, 123
Jameson, Ellery, 190
Jamison, Hugh, 53
Jeffreys, Thomas, Map of 1755, 39
Jemtland Station, 200, 201, 202
Jenkins, James, 148
Jesuits, 27
Jewitt & Pitcher of Boston and St. John, 145, 156
Johanson Blacksmith Shop, Johnny, 134
Johanson, Johnny, 201
Johnson, Axel, 201
Johnson, Axel, (farm), 201
Johnson, Charles, 65
Johnson, Faye (Wilson), 173
Johnson, James, Rev., 129
Johnson, John, 50
Johnson, John N., 201
Johnson, Lewis, 65
Johnston, Raymond R., 105
Joseph, Francis, Map of 1798, 33
Joseph, Tomah, 18
Judd, Richard, Dr., 162
Jay, John, 63
Jay's Treaty, 36

K

Kamouraska territory, 41, 42
Kataadn, 69
Kavanagh, Edward, 72
Keegan, Lillian, 174
Keep, Marcus, Rev., 147
Kelley Commons Dining Hall, UMPI, 126
Kelly family, 59
Kelso, Sherwood, 116
Kendall, Deacon, 78
Kendall, Samuel, Jr., 128
Kennebec Journal, 187
Kennebec River, 24, 26, 64, 150, 162
Kennebecs, 18-37
Kennedy, John F., Pres., 183, 184
Kennedy, Erin, 110
Kent, Edward, Gov., 72, 73
Kesip, George, 117
Key Bank, 133
Kilburn, Frank, Dr., 173
Kimball, Alice, 116
Kimball, Dick, 121
Kimball, Jonathan, L., 208
Kincaid, Dr., 173
King George's War, 25
King, Isabel F., 164
King, L. R., 198
King Phillip's War, 23
King, William, Gov., 64
King William's War, 24
King's Arrow, 60
King's Grove
Kioxakick, 33
Kittinger, Joe, Col. (Ret.), 99
Kiwanis Child Health Care Clinic, 118
Kiwanis Club of Presque Isle
Knight, Wayne, 142
Knowlen, Rosewell, 52
Knowles, Benjamin Wesley, 55

Knowles, Caroline Rich, 55
Knox, Major General, 29
Kok, Evelyn, 121
Kok, Jan, Prof., 116, 118, 121
Krupp International, 159

L

Ladner, Dan, 117
Lafford, Harold, 37
Lake Champlain, 26, 27
Landeck, Beatrice, 118
Lander, James, 141
Landlais, Bernard, 127
LaPomkeag Stream, 21
Larsson, Noak, 199
Lavaway, Agnes, 167
Lawrence, Abbot, 72
Lebanon, 200
Leisure Gardens, 177
Lescarbot, Marc, 24, 39
Lescarbot, Marc, Map, 23, 38
Leonard, Amanda, 110
Lewie Boy and the Commanders, 115, 116
Levasseur-Farrell American Legion Post, 165
Levesque, Rene, 116
Lidstone Methodist Church, Ashland, 86
Lille, 76, 131
Lille Rectory, 131
Lincoln, Governor, 64
Lincoln, Joseph, 80
Limestone, 56, 100, 125, 129, 130, 167, 174, 177
Limestone Air Force Base. *See.* Loring Air Force Base
Limestone-Caswell Historical Society, 130
Limestone Women's Civic Club, 129
Limestone Women's Club, 130
Lindsten Stuga, 134, 196
Linneus, 69, 85, 139, 187
Lion's Club of Presque Isle
Lisnik, John, 206
Little Black River, 39, 59
Little Franciscan Sisters of Mary, 76
Littleton Methodist Campground, 82, 88
Livermore Falls, 172
Long, William, 158
Longley, James B., 185
Lombard, 150
Loring Air Force Base, 99, 124, 125, 127, 156, 168, 169, 200, 204
Lottery Lands, 29
Loyal Sunrise, 191
Luanes Opera House, Ashland, 105
Luce, A. E., Rev., 87
Lufkin, Henry family, 47
Lufkin, Milton Teague, 154
lumbering, 144-152
Lumberjack Roundup, 100
Lumberman's Warehouse, 130
Lutherans, 92, 200
Lyndon, 154
Lycette, Jasper, 181

M

McBraeirty family, 59
McBraeirty, Lillian, 60
McCarry, Charles, 99
McClintock, Jessica Hedrick, 113
McCrea, William, 65
Mcgrath, Anna, 131
McGregor, William 78
McGority, John, 81
McGuire boarding house, 203
Machias, 180
McIntire, Clifford G., 189
McIntire, Rufus, 70, 71
McIntire-Donworth House, 131
McKay, Bill, 190
McKay, Harry, 190
McKay, Kenneth, Rev., 86
McKernan, John R., Jr., 185
McKernon, John, Gov., 127
MacLaine, Shirley, 87
McLauflin, Ivan, 117

McLaughlin, John, 182
McMahon, Father, 76
McManus, H. B., Dr., 86
MacNair, George, 182
McNally, George, 115
McNally, John, 117
McNeal, Stephen, 66
McTighe, Mary, 45
McTighe, Pat, 45
Macy, Bird, 190, 193
Madawaska, 66, 69, 70, 71, 72, 105, 130, 152, 158, 164, 167, 168, 184, 200
"Madawaska crash," 111
Madawaska Fire Department, 192
Madawaska Historic Centre in St. David Village, 134
Madawaska Historical Society, 130, 134
Madawaska Lake, 200
Madawaska Lakeshore, 7
Madawaska Public Library, 130
Madawaska River, 28, 51, 70, 134
Madawaska territory, 41, 42, 64, 111, 123
Madawaska Training School, 123
Madigan, Albert W., 173
Madigan Memorial Hospital, 173
Magoon, Nelson, Rev., Mr., 86
Maine Baptist Convention, 86
Maine, Bishop of, 80
Maine Development Commission, 136
Maine Farm Bureau Federation, 136
Maine Indian Claims Settlement Act of 1980, 30, 35, 37
Maine Missionary Society, 86
Maine Potato Blossom Festival, 98, 100
Maine Potato Growers, 156, 189
Maine Public Service Commission, 155
Maine Register, 154
Maine State Bicentennial Commission, 134
Maine State legislature, 70
Maine State Police, Troop F, 182
Maine Sugar Industries, Inc., 159
Maison Martin, 41
Maliseet, 4, 18-37, 42, 95, 161
Mann, John, 50, 51
Manser, Phillip (home), 126
Maple Grove, 14, 44, 45, 46, 49, 51, 67, 76, 80, 83, 85, 86, 87, 100, 105, 131, 162, 163, 164, 173, 176, 177, 191, 193
Maple Sugar Camp, 57
Mapleton, 10, 45, 48, 55, 56, 57, 82, 110, 124, 130, 151, 158, 163, 181, 194, 209
Marcoux, Joseph, Father, 79
Marist Fathers, 76, 79
Maritimes, 41
Marks, Edward B., 118
Mars Hill Aroostook Health Center, 176
Mars Hill Methodist, 80
Mars Hill Mountain, 78, 80, 163
Mars Hill Public Library, 131
Marsan, C. T., Rev. Fr., 81
Martin, John, Speaker, 127, 185
Martin's Hall, Eagle Lake, 105
Masardis, 27, 52, 82, 129, 136, 139, 156, 162
Masonic Lodge of Mars Hill, 83
Masonic Temple, Houlton, 92
Massachusetts Academy Grant, 178
Mattanawcook. *See* Lincoln
Mattawamkeag, 35
Mattawamkeag Lumber Company, 186
Mattawamkeag Point, 44
Matthews, Ken, 202
Maureau, Paul, 80
Maysville, 56
Maysville Cemetery, 164
Meductic, 22, 30, 49
Meduxnekeag, 4, 51, 60, 151, 162, 180
Meduxnekeag River Canoe Race, 100
Medway, 167
Melvin, Charlotte Lenentine, 131
Merchants Trust & Banking, 156
Meridian Whist Society, Caribou, 96
Meriumpticook River, 162
Merrill, William L., 164
Merriman Hall, UMPI, 126
Messamoet, Chief, 21
Methodist Church, Caribou, 87
Methodist Church, Presque Isle, 87
Methodist Church, Spragueville, 85
Methodist Episcopal Church, Ashland, 86

219

Methodist Episcopal Church, Caribou, 87
Methodist Episcopal Church, Fort Fairfield, 85
Methodist Episcopal Church, Presque Isle, 80
Methodism, 80, 82, 85, 86, 87, 88
Michaud, Albert, 192
Michaud, April, 110
Michaud, Edouard, Pvt., 165
Michaud, Leon, 114, 115, 116
Michaud, Lew, 116
Michaud, Lou, 117
Michaud, Neil, 117
Michaud, Romain, 162
Micmacs, 18-37, 42, 95, 108, 171
Micmac quillwork, 108
Military Road, 66, 67, 68, 74, 96, 138, 139, 141, 162
Military Street Baptist Church, Houlton, 89
Military Square, 146
Miller, Maynard, 117
Millerites, 90
Milliken, Carl E., Gov., 135, 186, 200
Milliken, M. P., 200
Mills, John, 72
Miramichi Fire of 1825, 35
Mitchell, Edwin, 97
Mitchell, George, Sen., 37
Mitchell, Jonathan, Map of 1755, 62
Mohawks, 22
Moir, George, 59
Molunkus, 139
Mont-Carmel Church, Lille, 131
Monticello, 74, 77, 87, 92, 139
Mooers, Hadley V., 104
Mooers, L. C., 115
Moores, A. T., 54
Moores Arctic Plumb, 54
Mooseleuk Club, Presque Isle, 94
Moreau, Willie, 117
Morehouse, George, 64, 65, 66
Morenault building, 129, 134
Mormons, 93
Morris, J., 198
Moses Rose district, 84
Mosher, Jake, 115
Mount Desert Island, 29
Mt. Katahdin, 4, 73
Mowery, D. F., Rev., 83
Mraz, Ruth Reed, 108, 109
Mullen, Alice, 76
Mullen, Anthony, 81
Mullen, Mr., 60
Mullins, William, 59
Munford, William, 52
Munsungan Lake, 20, 21
Murchison, Amanda, 90
Murphy, Richard, 164
Murray and Gregory, 150
"Music Theater," 116
musical gatherings, 115
"Music on Ice," 101
Muskie, Edmund, Secretary of State, 37, 126
Myers, Jim, 143

N

Nashville, 129, 130
Nashwaak, 39
Native Americans, 139, 171, 175, 213
Nault, Jeffrey, 110
Neely, Bishop, 85
Nelson, Andrew, 202
Nelson, Peter, 201
New Brunswick and Canada Railroad, 154
New England Power Pool Transmission System, 184
New England Telephone and Telegraph Company, 141
New Hampshire School of the Air, 118
New Salem Academy Grant. See Houlton, 46
New Salem Plantation, 180
New Sweden, 92, 139, 174, 196, 197, 198, 199, 201, 203
New Sweden Band, 202
New Sweden Historical Society, 134
New Sweden Museum, 196
Newman, Larry, 99
newspapers, 139-140
Nichols, G. Howard, 56
Nichols, Jennifer, 110

Nickerson, Block, 131
Nickerson, Derek, 110
Nigger Brook, 59
Ninety-fourth Air Base Group, 166
Noak Blacksmith Shop, Lars, 134
Noak, Lars, 201
Non-Intercourse Acts of 1790, 29, 30, 32, 33
Nordica Club, Fort Fairfield, 116
North Aroostook Agricultural and Horticultural Society, 44, 141
North Lyndon. See Caribou
North Star, 198
Northeast Airlines, 143, 166
Northeastern Dissemination Center for the National Center on Deafness, 126
Northeastland Hotel, 90
Northland Hotel, Houlton, 109
Northern Aroostook Agricultural Society, 153
Northern Maine Chamber Society, 116, 117
Northern Maine Fair, 57, 96, 97, 110, 158
Northern Maine Lutheran Parish, 92
Northern Maine Medical Center, 110, 174
Northern Maine Sanitarium, 176
Northern Maine Vocational Technical Institute, 130, 156
Northern National Bank, 156
Normal Hall, UMPI, 126
Normal School, 37
Norridgewocks, 29
Norsworthy, Darrell, 158
Norsworthy, Randy, 158
Norsworthy's Chrysler-Plymouth-Dodge, 158
Norton Collection, Katherine and Leroy, 136
Norumbega, 21
Norumbega River, See Penobscot River
Notre Heritage Vivant—Living Heritage Historical Society, 134
Number Eleven, 85
Number Three, 139
Nylander Museum, 133, 136
Nylander, Olof O., 136

O

Oak, Harry, 190
Oak, Merle, 117
Oakfield, 87
Oaknoll Dairy Farm, 158
Odd Fellows Hall, 200, 203
Old Exchange Hotel, 129
Old Town, 165
O'Leary, Edward C., Bishop, 131
Olore, Joe, 118, 119
Olson, Nels, 92
O'Neill, Father, 130
Orient, 139
Ostlund, George, 199
Oswald, Richard, 62
Otis, John, 72
Owl, UMPI, 127
Oxbow, 97, 116, 129, 130
Oxbow, the, 50
Oxford, 90, 162
Oxford Presbyterian Church, 90

P

Pagan, Robert, 63
Page, George B., Store, 128
Paige House, Presque Isle, 103
Paleo-Indian Period, 29, 21
Palermo, Douglas, 99
Pangaea, 12
Papal Decree of 1537, 21
Paris, Governor, 65
Park, G. M., Rev., 84, 126
Park Hall, UMPI, 126
Park, G. M., Rev., 84
Parson field, 70
Passadumkeag, 30
Passamaquoddy, 18-37, 184
Passamaquoddy Song of the Drum, 22
Passamaquoddy Tidal Power Plant, 184
Passamaquoddy treaty of 1794, 30

Patten, 82, 139, 164
Paul's Arena, Maple Grove, 116
Peabody, Robert, 182
Pearce, family, 180
Pelletier, Fred Z., 158
Pemaquid, 24
Pennsylvanian Period, 11
Penobscot County, 68, 69, 70, 71, 73
Penobscot River, 4, 20, 21, 24, 26, 28, 32, 38, 44, 51, 64, 146, 164
Penobscot territory, 64, 164
Penobscots, 18-37
Pentecostal, 82, 86
People of the Beautiful River, 28
People of the Dawn, 35, 38
Perham, 55, 86, 135, 174, 198
Perrier, Edward G., 113, 142
Perry, Harry, 163
Perry, Henry O., 164
Perry, Edgar, 200
Person Store, Benny, 199
Phair, Thomas H., 129, 131, 147
Phillips, Butch, Tribal Chairman (Penobscot), 37
Philpot, John, 117
Pierce, J. A., 193
Pierce, James, 67
Piles, William, 65, 66
Pioneer Playhouse, UMPI, 103, 210
Piper, Clara, 133
Pipes, Harry, 190
Pitcher, G. E., 193
Piscataquis County, 65, 66, 73
plate tectonics, 13
Pleistocene Epoch, 12
Plymouth, 64
Pocaock (Pokiok) Stream, 49
Pocatierre, La, 42
Poland Springs, 116, 118
Polchies, Terrence, Houlton Band Chairman, 37
Pomkeag, 166
Port Royal, 39, 41
Portage, 37, 129, 130
Porter settlement, 85
Portland, 24, 152, 164, 175
Potato Blossom Festival, 202
potato industry, 36, 45, 56, 74, 98, 152, 153, 155, 156, 159, 164, 166, 187, 189, 202, 209, 210
Potato Service, Presque Isle, 156
Potter, Brad, 208
Powell's Drugstore, George, 131
Powers, Don A., 185
Powers, Llewellyn, Gov., 185, 187, 188, 189, 199
Preble Hall, UMPI, 126
Preble, Warren, 164
Preble, William Pitt, 72
Presbyterians, 86, 90, 92
Presidents of the Maine Senate, 186
Presque Isle, 5, 12, 35, 37, 44, 51, 52, 55, 56, 80, 82, 83, 84, 87, 90, 94, 96, 98, 100, 103, 104, 105, 106, 113, 115, 116, 118, 119, 124, 125, 131, 135, 136, 137, 139, 141, 152, 155, 162, 163, 164, 166, 172, 173, 174, 177, 180, 181, 189, 191, 193, 194, 206
Presque Isle Air Force Base, 99, 156
Presque Isle Barbershoppers, 116, 117
Presque Isle Fair Grounds, 166
Presque Isle Fire Association, 192
Presque Isle Historical and Genealogical Society, 135
Presque Isle House, 105
Presque Isle Indians (baseball), 37
Presque Isle Opera House, 103, 104
Presque Isle National Bank, 156
Presque Isle Nursing Home, 177
Presque Isle Production Credit, 156
Presque Isle Recorder Consort, 118, 121
Presque Isle Stream, 122, 180, 191
Pesque Isle River 35, 52
Presque Isle Village Fire Department, 192
Prestile Stream. See St. John River
Prince Edward Island, 41
Prince, J. D., 22
Pulcifer, Deanne, 110
Pullen Galley, UMPI, 113
Puritan Orthodox Congregationalist, 78
Puritans, 76
Putnam, Aaron, 68, 69, 78, 81
Putnam, Aaron (home), 180

Putnam, Cora, 76
Putnam, Samuel, 92
Pyle, George, 164

Q

Quakers, 87, 90
Queen Anne's War, 24
Queen Esther, Oxbow, 116
Quimby, Allen, Sr., 200
Quoggy Joe Mountain (also Quaqua Jo Mountain, Quakajo, Quaquajo), 5, 12, 14, 100, 103, 166, 213

R

Radio Stations, 142, 143
Rafford, Dana, 116
Rafford, Ray, 117
Rainbow Cove, 203
Ramo, Pee Wee, 116
Ramsdell, T. J., Rev., 89
Ramsey, John, 144
Red Paint People, 20
Reed, Cheryl, 121
Reed, George, 182
Reed, John H., Gov., 186, 187, 189
Reed, John, Gov. (family), 118
Reed, Pat, 80
Reed, Roy, 190
Reed, Ruth Ann, 121
Restigouche River, 21
Revolutionary War, 26, 27, 28, 41, 42, 63, 156
Rhythm Kings, 114, 116, 118
Rice, George R., 192
Richmond Corner, 86
Richardson, Elizabeth, 110
Ricker Classical Academy (later Institute), 126
Ricker, Joseph, Dr., 126
Ricker Plaza, 126
Rideout, Mike, 182
Ringdahl, John J., 202
Rista, 200
Riviere du Loup, 42
Riviere Ouelle, 42
Riviere St. Jean. *See* St. John River
Riverside Campground, 82, 88
Riverside Pavilion, Houlton, 116
Roach, James, Pres., 126
Roberts, Amos, 146
Roberts, Mike, 117
Robinson, 82, 163
Robinson, H. W., 193
Rocky Brook, 191
Roe, Nancy, 131
Rogers, Alphonso, the Reverend, 80
Rogers, Mary Elizabeth Barker, 54
Roman Catholicism, 24, 26, 27, 41, 42, 75, 76, 79, 81, 86, 89
Roosevelt, Franklin D., Pres., 165
Roosevelt, Theodore, Pres., 97, 135, 164
Roostook River Raft Race, 100
Roper, Harrison, 116
Rose Acres, 133
Rosie O'Grady Balloon of Peace, 99
Rossignol, Leon, 157
Rotary Club, 129, 174
Round Pond, 146, 149
Rousse's Point, 67
Royal Canadian Air Force, 166
Royal Proclamation of 1763, 26, 28
Royal Road, 68
Rubinoff (violinist), 82
Rudy's Theater, Caribou, 105
Rum Rapids, 102, 106

S

Sabins, George, 80
Saco River, 24
Sacred Heart Church, North Lyndon, 81
Saguenay River, 38
St. Agatha, 192
St. Agatha Fire Department, 192

St. Andrews, 63
St. Anne's Episcopal Mission, 83
St. Aquinas Catholic Church, Madawaska, 130
St. Basile, 43, 76, 77
St. Bruno, 79
St. Catherine's Mission Chapel, Washburn, 86
St. Croix Commission, 64, 65
St. Croix Monument, 64
St. Croix River, 21, 38, 62, 63, 64, 65, 72
St. David Village, 134
St. Francis (tribe), 39
St. Francis River, 39, 66, 67, 162
St. John, 141
St. John Lumber Company, 149
St. John River, 4, 19, 20, 22, 24, 26, 27, 28, 29, 33, 38, 39, 41, 43, 51,59, 60, 62, 63, 65, 66, 67, 72, 73, 75, 76, 97, 122, 134, 139, 146, 147, 148, 149, 150, 158, 159, 160, 161, 162, 163, 164, 174, 178, 179, 184, 195, 200, 214
St. John's Church, Houlton, 80
St. John's Episcopal Church, Presque Isle, 85
St. John's School, 126
St. Lawrence River, 13, 19, 22, 24, 26, 29, 35, 63, 67, 161
St. Mary's Catholic Church, 81
Saint Mary's College, 125
St. Mary's Convent, 125
St. Mary's, Presque Isle, 86
St. Peter, Laura, 110
St. Peters, Dorothy, 110
St. Theresa's Catholic Church, Stockholm, 203
Ste. Agathe Historical Society, 130
Ste-Anne-de-Pays-Bas, 41
Ste. Anne's Point, 161
Ste. Croix, 38
Ste. Marie, Church of, Eagle Lake, 79
Salem Academy, 78
Salmon Brook Historical Society, 135
Salvation Army, 82, 88
Salwak, Stanley, Dr., 126
Sanitary Water Board, 180
Saucier, Melissa, 110
Savage, Milnot J., the Reverend, 83
Savage, Reverend Mr., 78
Savage, Richard, Dr., 173
Savoy, Theater, Fort Kent, 105
Schoolhouse Rapids, 122
Scotch-Irish, 162
Scott, Stan, 97
Scott, Winfield, Maj. Gen., 72, 73
Sears and Roebuck Company, 148, 165
Second Advent Church, Crouseville, 86
Second Regiment of U.S. Infantry, 76
Seeley Store, 129
Senecott Range, 69
Sennett, Amon, 193
Sesquicentennial of the County, 133
Seven Island, 139
Seven Years' War, 25, 26
Seventh Day Adventists, 87, 90
Sewell, William, W., 97
Shaw, Cyrus, 90
Shaw, F. W., 193
Shaw, Harry, 193
Shaw, Ramsford W., 131
Sherman, 166
Sherman, Alice, 135
Sherman Elementary School, 125
Shin Pond, 114
Shire Town, 69
Sieur de Monts, 21, 63
Silurian Period, 12, 16
Silver, Alex, 158
Silver Slipper, Ashland, 116
Silver's Stables, 158
Silvia, Dean, 116
Sisson, James, 65
Sisters of Mercy, 173
Sixty-ninth Regiment (British), 71
skating, 97
skiing, 100, 136
Skillin, Emery, 117
Sleeper, W. T., 198
Sleepy Hollow, 158
Slipp, George, 182
Sluka, John, 117
Small, G. L., 193
Small, William, 197

Smith, Addison P., 92
Smith, Carl W., 45
Smith Food Distributors of Presque Isle, 45
Smith, Fred, 87
Smith, Hershel, 45
Smith, Hiram T., 68
Smith, Jamie, 110
Smith, Lucious Charles, 44, 45
Smith, Matthias, Capt., 44
Smith's Millinery Store, Laila, 131
Smith's Truck Stop, Blaine
Smith, Nellie, 87
Smith, Newell, 190
Smith, Oliver Carpenter, 44, 45, 164
Smith, Osgood, 163
Smith, Roy, 117
Smith, Thatcher, Deacon, 84
Smyrna, 111, 128, 139, 156
Smyrna Mills, 111, 156
Snell House, Houlton, 102
Snow, Fred, 51
Snow, Moses, 51
Snow, Warren, 51
Snowman, David, 132
Snowman School, 132
Snow's Hall, 76
snowmobiling, 97, 100
Sockanosett, 192, 194
Society of Friends, 87
Sodergren, John J., 203
Soil Bank, 168
Soldier Pond, 162
"Soldier's Song" 72
Soldiers Township. *See* Mars Hill, 46
Somerset County, 73, 162
Somerville, Donald, Dr., 173
Somerville, Robert, Dr., 173
Somerville, Wallace, Dr., 173
Sons and Daughters of the Colony of New Sweden, 202
South Hall, UMPI, 126
Sparks, Jared, 62
Spaulding, R. C., Rev., 75, 77
Spanish-American War, 164
Speakers from Aroostook, 185
Spear, Carol, 116
"Specks", 166
Spiritualist, 87
Sprague, Andrew, 85
Sprague, Elbridge, 85
Sprague, Herb, 117
Sprague, J. F., 71
Spragueville, 85, 87, 124
Spragueville Church, 87
Spruce Acres Refuge, 136
Squa Pan Mountain, 12, 14
Square Lake, 8
Standard Box Company, 200
Standard Veneer Company, 200
Star Herald, Presque Isle, 142
State Forest Service fire tower, 203
State Park, 100
State Register of Historic Places, 97
State Street Baptist Church, 84, 88
Steele, Thomas Sedgewick, 48, 49
Stetson and Cutler, 150
Stevens Clothing Store, Fred P., 152
Stevens, D. A., 152
Stevens, Fred P., 117
Stevens, Isadore, 116
Stevens, John C., 128
Stockholm, 92, 130, 174, 198, 200
Stockholm Historical Society and Museum, 130
Stratton, Frances Webb, 135
Strickland, Hastings, Maj., 70, 71, 146
Strobeck, Alfred, 202
Student Nurses Organization at UMFK, 127
Suffragettes, 181
sugar industry, 159
Sugar Mountain, 64
Sullivan, James, Gov., 179
Sweat, Joe, 116
Swedish Baptist Church, New Sweden, 92
Sweet, E. E., 193
swimming, 100
Sylvester, H. W., 193
System sterology computer program, 208

221

T

Tabor, S. W., Deacon, 86
Taconian mountain building, 16
Taft, William A., 183
TAMC, 176
Tante Blanc Museum, 134
Tarbell, Anna J. S., 84
Tarbell, Benjamin, 163
Tarbell, Charles, 156
Tarbell, Everett, 158
Tarbell, Frank, Dr., 111
Tarbell, Ira, 155
Tarbell, Joseph E., 156
Tarbell, Karl, 163
Tardy, Doris, 82
Tavaway, Fred, 117
Taylor family, 180
Telos Lake, 146
Temiscouata, 68
Terriault, Dennis, 116
Theaters, 103, 105
Theriault clothing store, Mrs. William, 129
Thibodeau Block, 194
Thibodeau, W. J., 60
Thirty-first Maine Regiment, Company E, 164
Thirty-sixth Regiment (British), 71
Thomas, Dr., 172
Thomas, Father, 79
Thomas Memorial Shell, W. W., 202
Thomas Park Memorial Fund, 202
Thomas, William Widgery, Jr., 196, 197, 198, 199, 202
Thompson, David P., 82
Thoreau, Henry David, 4, 18, 132
Thwaites, 21
Times, Aroostook, 88
Titcomb, Samuel, 64
Tobin, Michael, 81
Tobique, 66
Tobique River, 35, 81
Tompkins, Don, 82
Tompkins, Leitha, 82
Tompkins, Nathaniel, 185, 186
Townsend, Steward P., 164
Trafton, E. H. W., 185
Thrafton, Mark, the Reverend, 82
Triassic Period, 12
Trinity Evangelical Church, Stockholm, 203
Triple A Sugar Corporation, 159
Treaty of Ghent, 64, 65
Treaty of Paris of 1783, 28, 62, 63, 64, 162
Treaty of Washington, 162
Trundy, Dr., 172
Turner, Charles, Jr., 49
Turner, Daniel, 130
Turner, Jerry, Mrs., 192
Turner, Julian, 124
Turner Memorial Library, Mark and Emily, 131
Turner, Phillip, 45, 46
Tyler, John, Pres., 72

U

underground railroad, 87
Unger, Doc, 117
Union Cemetery, Fort Fairfield, 108
Unitarian Church, Houlton, 83
Unitarian Church, Presque Isle, 83
Unitarian/Universalist Church, Washburn, 83
United Baptist Church, Mars Hill, 86
United Baptist Church, Presque Isle, 83, 84, 89
U.S. Army Air Corps, 166
U.S. Topographical Engineers, U.S. Army, 162
Universalists, 80, 83
University of Maine Agricultural Extension Service, 137
University of Maine at Fort Kent, 103, 117, 127, 130, 149, 175
University of Maine, Orone, 127
University of Maine at Presque Isle, 103, 106, 107, 110, 113, 117, 119, 121, 126, 130, 133, 136, 175, 207, 208, 212
University of Maine hockey team, 101
University of Maine System, 175
University of Southern Maine, 127
Uppling, John, 202
Uppling's Grove, 198

V

Vahlsing, Fred H., Jr., 159
Vallee, Stanislas, Father, 79
Valley, Joel, 89
Van Buren, 76, 79, 100, 105, 116, 125, 134, 139, 147, 149, 150, 152, 157, 158, 164, 165, 166, 168, 174, 177, 184
Van Buren Community Hospital, 174
Van Buren, Martin, Pres., 70, 72
Van Buren Regatta, 100
Van Buren Trust, 155
Van Buren-Madawaska Corporation sawmill, 168
Vance, Dwight, 117
Venetian Garden, Edmundston, 116
Vickery, Myra, 98
Vienna, 84
Viet-Nam War, 165, 169
Violette Brook, 81
Voisine, Erica, 110

W

Wabanaki Conferacy, 29
Wabanakis, 18-37
WACM-TV, 116, 143
Waddell, Ivan W., Mrs., 116
Wade, 135
Walker family, 59
Wallagrass, 162
Walsh, Margaret, 165
War Cry, 84
War of 1812, 64, 161, 184
War-time Small Industries Act, 166
Watson's Drilling, Ellery, 158
Wawenocks, 29
Washburn, 48, 86, 87, 130, 135, 172, 174, 191, 195
Washington County, 66, 68, 69, 152, 164, 180
Washington, George, 27, 42, 63
Washburn, Israel, Gov., 130, 197
Washburn Memorial Library, 130
Watson's blacksmith shop, James, 158
Webb Museum of Vintage Fashions, John E. and Walter D., 135
Webber, Chief, 193
Webster-Ashburton Treaty of 1842, 54, 62, 67, 73, 139
Webster, Daniel, 62, 72, 73, 139
Webster Pond, 146
Wegener, Alfred, 12
Weinberg, Sylvia, 116, 119
West Branch Mattawamkeag, 97
West, Dr., 143
Westfield, 87, 97, 109, 124
Westmanland, 196, 198, 200
Weston, 49, 139
Wetherall, Samuel B., Rev., 78
Wheeler, Edgar, 181
Whidden, Cassius C., the Reverend, 85
Whidden, George F., 85
Whig, Bangor, 70
Whitaker, Collins, Mrs., 81
Whitcomb, Albert, 164
White Mountain Telephone Company, 141
White, S. L., 131
White, Sammy, 190
White, Stella King, 200
Whited Campground, 82
Whitely, Harry, Rev., 87
Whitneck, George, 164
Whitney, Mel, 182
Whitney, Ralph, Capt., 163, 182
Whittier, Mericos, 128, 133
Wieden, Clifford, O. T., 116, 126
Wieden Hall, UMPI, 126
Wiguidi River, 39
Wilcox, Gloria, 110
Wilder, Ben, 135
Wilder, Issac, 135
Wildlands, 4
Willard, John, 94
Willey house, 205
Wilmont and Peters, 162
Wilson, Guy, 141
Wilson's Mill, 90, 191
Winberg, E., 198
Winn, 164

Winslow, Alvin, 56
Winslow, Angeline, 56
Winslow, Francis, 55, 56
Winslow, Nellie, 57
Wiren, Andrew, Rev., 92
Witcher, Jay, 118, 119
Woiwode, Larry, 97
Women's Christian Temperance Union, 128
Wood, "Aunt Abbie," 86
Wood, Jenny, 110
Woodland, 132, 198
Woodland Historical Society, 132
Woodstock, 68, 70, 71, 72, 76, 161, 163, 173
Wording Hall, Ricker Classical Academy, 126
Works Progress Administration, 100, 136
World War II, 99, 126, 137, 159, 163
Wormwood, Samuel, 180

Y

York, Coleman, 80
York, Dena, 121
York, Street Hospital, 173

Z

Zubrick, Joseph, 212

Fall evening on the Aroostook River.
Photograph by Clifton Boudman

About the Authors

Clifton Boudman of Rum Rapids, Crouseville, senior professor of art at the University of Maine at Presque Isle, teaches sculpture and painting, and has a master of fine arts degree from the University of Maryland.

Iris Brewer of Blaine is director of adult education at the Presque Isle Learning Center, and has a master of education degree from the University of Southern Maine.

Shirlee Connors-carlson of Fort Kent is a freelance feature writer and has a degree from the University of Maine at Fort Kent.

Richard Cohen of Presque Isle is a professor of English at the University of Maine at Presque Isle and has a Ph.D. degree from the University of Massachusetts.

Joseph Donald Cyr of Lille is a private art teacher and instructor at the University of Maine at Presque Isle. He has a master of education degree from the University of Maine.

Guy F. Dubay of Van Buren has a master of education degree from the University of Maine and served as an educator on the Board of Maine Humanities Council.

John Graves of Presque Isle is an educator and principal in South Aroostook District No. 1, and has his master of education degree from the University of South Maine.

Jere Green of Caribou is an author and retired librarian with a master of library science degree from the State University of New York at Albany.

Richard Hede of Stockholm, retired physicist, is an author and historian.

Evelyn Kok of Presque Isle is a private art and music teacher.

David Laing of Presque Isle is a field naturalist and author with a master of science degree from Harvard.

John Lisnik of Presque Isle, legislator, educator, and director of Northern Maine RAISE, has his master of education degree from Notre Dame.

Maureen Murchison of Presque Isle, a student at the University of Maine at Presque Isle, Leadership Program Isle Alumni, is a freelance photographer.

Andrea Bear Nicholas of the Tobique Reservation, New Brunswick, is an educator and author with a master of education degree from the University of Maine.

Harald Prins of Hallowell is an anthropology professor at Colby College with a Ph.D. degree from the New School for Soc. Res.

D. A. Savage of Presque Isle is comptroller for the City of Presque Isle and a volunteer firefighter with a bachelor of arts degree from the Ricker College, Houlton.

Philip Turner of Caribou is a teacher, author, retired agriculturalist, and County Republican Chairman, with a Ph.D. from Michigan State University.

Dena Winslow York of Mapleton is a writing lab coordinator in School Administration District No. 42, and has a master of education degree from the University of Southern Maine.

Anna Fields Mcgrath of Presque Isle is acting library director at the University of Maine at Presque Isle and has a master of library science degree from the University of Rhode Island and a master of education from the University of Southern Maine.

Photographic Reproduction:

William Duncan is Coordinator of Publications, UM-Presque Isle, from which he has a bachelor's degree.

Connie Simon Tucker of Caribou is a freelance photographer with a master of art degree from Goddard College.

Diane Sadler Higgins of Presque Isle is a freelance photographer with a bachelor of art degree from the University of Maine at Presque Isle, and works at the Library Resources Center.